Praise ~~to~~

'Phenomenal'

Publishers Weekly (US), one of their Best Books of 2020

'This book is a first-rate analysis of Hendrix's "fretboard wizardry and showmanship" – but nothing became the guitarist's life like the leaving of it, aged 27. Philip Norman gives a forensic account of Hendrix's death, about which controversy still rages'

Roger Lewis, *Daily Mail*

'A good read that throws up interesting facts about the hugely exploitative nature of the 1960s music industry and its relationship to organised crime . . . *Wild Thing* reveals some of the man behind the well-encrusted mythology, and sends the reader back to those wonderful records that still radiate with supernatural light'

Jon Savage, *New Statesman*

'It's 50 years since Jimi Hendrix died and, as Norman puts it, became "president for eternity" of the infamous 27 Club. The guitar legend's excess all areas life story is familiar but new details emerge. Jimi's brother fills in the blanks on his wretched childhood in the US, and the racism of the UK, his adopted home, is sadly laid bare'

Sun

'Hendrix's short life is outlined in detail and with insight by Norman . . . From being rock music critic of *The Times* during the 1970s to writing acclaimed biographies (deemed by many to be definitive) of Elton John, the Rolling Stones, John Lennon and Eric Clapton, Norman has the historical perspective and authentic writing nous to dig deep and achieve results'

Tony Clayton-Lea, *Business Post Ireland*

Also by Philip Norman

Fiction
Slip on a Fat Lady
Plumridge
Wild Thing (short stories)
The Skaters' Waltz
Words of Love (a novella and stories)
Everyone's Gone to the Moon
The Avocado Fool

Biography and journalism
Shout! The True Story of the Beatles
The Stones
The Road Goes On For Ever
Tilt the Hourglass and Begin Again
Your Walrus Hurt the One You Love
Awful Moments
Pieces of Hate
Elton (reissued as Sir Elton)
The Life and Good Times of the Rolling Stones
Days in the Life: John Lennon Remembered.
The Age of Parody
Buddy: The Biography
John Lennon: The Life
Mick Jagger
Paul McCartney: The Biography
Slowhand: The Life and Music of Eric Clapton

Autobiography
Babycham Night: A Boyhood at the End of the Pier.

Plays and musicals
Words of Love
The Man That Got Away
This is Elvis: Viva Las Vegas
Laughter in the Rain: The Neil Sedaka Story

WILD THING

The Short, Spellbinding Life of Jimi Hendrix

PHILIP NORMAN

WEIDENFELD & NICOLSON

First published in Great Britain in 2020 by Weidenfeld & Nicolson
This paperback edition published in 2021 by Weidenfeld & Nicolson
an imprint of The Orion Publishing Group Ltd
Carmelite House, 50 Victoria Embankment
London EC4Y 0DZ

An Hachette UK Company

1 3 5 7 9 10 8 6 4 2

A CIP catalogue record for this book is
available from the British Library.

ISBN (Mass Market Paperback) 978 1 4746 1150 3
ISBN (eBook) 978 1 4746 1151 0

Typeset by Input Data Services Ltd, Somerset

Printed in Great Britain by Clays Ltd, Elcograf S.p.A.

www.weidenfeldandnicolson.co.uk
www.orionbooks.co.uk

CONTENTS

Prologue   1

1. 'He was hearing music but didn't
   have an instrument to bring it to
   earth'   11

2. 'Jimmy was a hippy before anyone
   knew what a hippy was'   29

3. 'I still have my guitar and amp and as
   long as I have that no fool can
   stop me living'   43

4. 'Everything's so-so in this big
   raggedy city of New York'   57

5. 'I've got just the person for you'   72

6. 'Quite honestly, Chas . . . he's
   almost too good'   89

7. 'Oh my God, I'm not God any
   more'   106

8. 'Go out and buy us a tin of lighter
   fuel'   124

9. 'Not on my network'   140

10. 'From rumor to legend'   155

11. 'He was a life-saver'   172

12. Electric Ladies   195

13 'I'm going to die before I'm
thirty'   211
14 'Nothing but a Band of Gypsies'   228
15 Miles and Miles   242
16 'Dad, my love . . .'   253
17 'Hey, man, lend me your comb'   268
18 'Just call me helium'   284
19 'Goodnight Sweet Black Prince'   303
20 'A tall black guardian angel in
a hat'   317
21 ''Scuse me while I kiss the pie'   329
    Epilogue   344
    Notes   359
    Acknowledgements   366
    Picture Credits   368
    Index   369

Jimi worked with light. He used light to bring walls down
Carlos Santana

PROLOGUE
'HE WAS A LOVELY FELLER'

All rock music's historic names began by doing cover versions of other people's songs, usually little more than pale facsimiles, to be discarded once the impersonators had a sound of their own. The great exception was Jimi Hendrix, who throughout his brief time at the top went on performing covers that were never straight copies and often radical reimaginings.. The Beatles' whimsical 'Sgt. Pepper's Lonely Hearts Club Band', for instance, he turned into a heavy metal broadside that Paul McCartney – no stranger to accolades – considered one of the greatest honours of his life.

Everybody whom Jimi covered felt the same: not pique at the deconstruction of their (often million-selling) handiwork but awe at the new dimensions to which he transported it. Indeed, the apogee of his genius, rather than original composition like 'Purple Haze' or 'Voodoo Child', is widely thought to be his treatment of Bob Dylan's 'All Along the Watchtower'.

The track had first appeared on Dylan's *John Wesley Harding* album in 1966 and, as usual, was a reflection of his reading rather than his life. The title came from a passage in the Old Testament's Book of Isaiah – one also containing the phrase 'Go set a watchman', which Harper Lee borrowed for an early draft of what became *To Kill a Mockingbird*. Dylan gave it a medieval setting filtered through the sensibility of some Victorian poet like Alfred Lord Tennyson, his great passion at the time.

The result seemed more a throwback to his folkie past than affirmation of his recent conversion to rock: a solitary voice, repetitive acoustic strumming, a harmonica pitched too high to pack its usual punch and no echo anywhere of his Victorian poetic muse, no Sad-eyed Lady of Shalott. Although generally greeted as as further consolidation of the Dylan miracle, it caught some flak from fellow musoes for being all portentousness without a pay-off. His former folk mentor, Dave Van Ronk, even criticised the syntax, calling it 'a mistake from the title on down. A watchtower is not a road or a wall and you can't go along it.'

Jimi's cover appeared on *Electric Ladyland*, his third album after being transplanted from New York to London and teamed with two white Britons, drummer Mitch Mitchell and bass-player Noel Redding as the Jimi Hendrix Experience. It is at once the quintessence of primal hard rock and a reminder that, whatever the medium, true genius demands not only matchless expertise and energy but discipline and understatement.

In Jimi's hands the rather aimless canter of the Dylan version is slowed down by an introductory chord sequence, simple enough in form yet with a wet, seething quality suggestive of some wild seashore with angry waves pounding the shingle, gulls screaming, bladderwrack glistening and dark clouds piling overhead. All the Tennysonian bleakness and melodrama that Dylan left out are there in a moment.

The lyric starts as a duologue between 'the Joker' – i.e. the traditional playing-card figure in stripey three-pointed hat – and 'the Thief', plotting escape from some unspecified confinement. Whereas Dylan's every syllable was soaked in irony and ambiguity, Jimi's mellow baritone plays it completely straight, with perhaps the slightest emphasis on 'There's too much confusion' and 'I can't get no relief', which happened to express what he was already feeling about his new life in Britain.

His voice carries the same utter conviction in the Thief's incoherently moralising riposte. Yet his guitar still holds back; not even B. B. King was ever so sparing with a riff.

At last, as 'the hour is getting late', a terse 'Hey!' announces a break which, for me, surpasses any other to have been recorded since guitars had electrical wires threaded through their bodies like keyhole surgery and metal pickups and volume knobs and tremolo levers dentist-drilled into their faces. Forget Eric Clapton in Cream's 'Crossroads' or Jimmy Page in Led Zeppelin's 'Stairway to Heaven' or James Burton in Ricky Nelson's 'My Babe' or Mark Knopfler in Dire Straits' 'Sultans of Swing' or Scotty Moore in Elvis's 'Heartbreak Hotel' or even Chuck Berry in 'Johnny B. Goode'; go, Jimi, go.

It comes in four distinct movements of which only the first is a conventional solo with notes selected as judiciously and 'bent' as elegantly as B. B. at his best. The second is played with a metal slide along the fretboard, which from Elmore James or Howlin' Wolf would be jagged and angry but with Jimi resembles a thrill-ride through some extraterrestrial cityscape, each gush of the slide like a glowing elevator, sibilantly ascending or descending. Down swoops one, then up goes another, and another still higher until it almost seems to be dancing in time.

Next, an extended passage with the wah-wah pedal (actually more of a 'thwacka-thwacka') replaces those soft machines with an almost human voice, as if the guitar is musing and chortling to itself over some private joke. Because there's no way of topping everything that's gone before, the finale is a suddenly melodious trio of treble chords in predictable order with grace notes played by the little finger much as a triple Michelin-starred chef might show his greatness in the simplest of dishes; a plain roast chicken, say, or heartbreakingly perfect poached eggs.

Back in the song, a watchtower finally materialises, albeit now less a security measure than an eyrie where 'princes kept the view'. Some Arthurian high drama seems promised in 'two riders were approaching', some apocalytic outcome prophesied with 'and the wind began to howl'.

But before any explanation of the two riders, just as Jimi's guitar begins howling louder than any 'hurricano' that ever tormented King Lear – everything starts to fade. This is the outro.

Whenever I hear it, I think the same : *don't go.*

'Arguably the greatest instrumentalist in the history of rock music,' says the Rock & Roll Hall of Fame's citation. But among the race of guitar superheroes raised up by the 1960s – Eric Clapton, Jeff Beck, Keith Richards, George Harrison, Jimmy Page, David Gilmour, Peter Green, Robbie Robertson, Duane Allman and Jerry Garcia – there has never been any argument. Each of them had only to hear Jimi once to metaphorically throw down his pick and raise his hands in surrender.

Half a century on, James Marshall Hendrix remains unique as an African American who broke out of the traditional 'black' genres, blues, R&B and soul, to play white, hard rock to an overwhelmingly white audience, almost single-handedly creating what became known as heavy metal. The likes of Billy Gibbons from ZZ Top, Slash from Guns N' Roses and Kirk Hammett from Metallica freely admit they could not have had careers without him. Yet he was about far more than a niche music which over the years has become increasingly cacophonous and self-parodic. Just as you can love Bob Marley without liking reggae, you need not like heavy metal to love Jimi.

He is an abiding symbol of genius tragically cut short: dead of a supposed barbiturates overdose aged only twenty-seven. Several other such first-rank talents have perished at the same age from drugs, drink or related hazards of the rock 'n' roll life – the '27 Club' whose (otherwise all-white) roll includes Brian Jones of the Rolling Stones, Jim Morrison of the Doors, Janis

Joplin and, more recently, Kurt Cobain from Nirvana and Amy Winehouse. Indeed, such early exits, invariably alone, despite phalanxes of minders and gofers, are widely regarded as the surest entrance-ticket to rock Valhalla. Jimi, whose demise had these dismal elements and more, is the 27 Club's President-for-eternity.

He was a young man of spectacular beauty with his mushroom-cloud Afro and a delicate face that, without its downturned moustache, could easily have adorned some female vocal group of the same era like the Supremes or the Ronettes. From the Sixties' fey male fashions, the braided Victorian military tunics, brocade waistcoats, ruffled blouses, chiffon scarves, ten-gallon hats and Apache headbands, he created a vagabond chic for rock stars that many still doggedly preserve into their dotage. Like Little Richard in the madcap days of Fifties rock 'n' roll, there was something not quite of this world about him; one critic at the time wrote that he 'took the blues out of the Mississippi Delta and sent it to Mars'.

Hitherto, a guitar maestro had needed no 'act' beyond one static pose of tortured creativity. But Jimi combined simultaneous singing and fretboard wizardry with showmanship that pushed boundaries as even Mick Jagger with the Stones or Jim Morrison never did. He would play his Fender Stratocaster behind his head or with his teeth or a serpentine tongue seemingly immune to electric shock, all never fluffing a note. Having milked it of every possible magic decibel, he would subject it to ritualistic sexual assault and torture, laying it flat and dry-humping it, then dousing it in petrol, setting it on fire and smashing its burning corpse to pieces. This voodoo-tinged porno-vandalism could not have been further from his true nature, which was humble and fundmentally insecure even though the queues of women outside his bedroom door made Jagger and Morrison look like virgins.

His epic promiscuity may seem unendearing in the early twenty-first century, when ancient rockers are regularly branded as 'sex offenders' for backstage bacchanalia five decades ago with female followers whose ages they seldom, if ever, bothered to check. But in the 'permissive' Sixties, it was considered quite normal, one of the more envied perks of the job. And Jimi was no predator; he didn't have to be. 'You couldn't call him a womaniser,' recalls his fellow musician and friend, Robert Wyatt. 'It was the women who were Hendrix-isers.'

Each year, he sells more albums than in any while he was alive, but that is only a part of his enduring presence. He has become inseparable from the iconography of the Sixties, the so-called 'decade that never dies'.

Any exhibition or coffee-table book by one of its many outstanding photographers, like Terence Donovan or Gered Mankowitz, is almost certain to include a shot of Jimi in the gold-braided hussar jacket which became his trademark. He is an icon in the exact sense of that over-used word. The youngest rock fan of any nation is likely to sport a T-shirt imprinted with his face, both shy and shameless under its curly aureole like some South American black Jesus or mass-produced Turin Shroud.

Although American to the core – African and Native – he will forever be identified with London during the most glamorous epoch in its history. For all his prodigious gift, he reached the age of 23 still unknown in his homeland thanks to the racism that confined all but the most celebrated black musicians to the 'Chitlin' Circuit' of segregated theatres and clubs.

In 1966, he was discovered in New York by the girlfriend of Rolling Stone Keith Richards and brought to London by the Animals' bass player Chas Chandler, as Chandler's first venture into management. It was the newly dubbed 'Style Capital of Europe' that finally unlocked his genius. British pop's entire social register, headed by the Beatles and the Stones, flocked to see him play live at clubs like the Scotch of St James and the Speakeasy, and to marvel.

Fashioned into the Jimi Hendrix Experience with his two white sidemen, Redding and Mitchell, he enjoyed immediate massive success with a string of hit singles and three albums instantly recognised as classics. As if in reprisal for the British Invasion of US pop charts in the Beatles' footsteps, he was a one-man American counterattack. At the same time, he settled happily into his adopted culture, embracing such British institutions as warm beer, fish and chips, A. A. Milne's Winnie-the-Pooh stories and *Coronation Street*.

From London, he first cut a swathe through Europe, then returned to America to steal the show with his burning guitar at the first great pop festival, at Monterey in 1967. The following year, when the country was torn apart by race riots and brutal official reprisals, he went on the road there as a black man leading two white ones – a blow for integration as courageous as any by the Civil Rights movement. In 1969, the enormous Woodstock festival was galvanised by his solo instrumental performance of 'The Star-Spangled Banner', implicitly protesting the havoc being wrought in Vietnam by the US military in which he'd once been proud to serve.

This blazing success came to a tragic end after only four years, just as new chapters of achievement were opening up, and in the same 'swinging' capital that had launched it. In September 1970, he met a lonely, squalid death in a west London hotel, so creating pop music's greatest unsolved mystery. Rumours of foul play have swirled around it ever since: that he was murdered by his sinister manager, Mike Jeffery, or by the Mafia or even a paranoid American government which viewed his music's disregard of racial barriers as a threat to national security.

*

I never met Jimi, despite being at the epicentre of Swinging London as a staff writer for the *Sunday Times*'s super-chic colour magazine, free to interview whomever I liked and with tables reserved for me at all the clubs where he appeared. I was too much occupied with getting myself to America to talk to more established black music stars like James Brown, Stevie Wonder and Diana Ross.

In late 1969, the *Sunday Times* Magazine ran my profile of Eric Clapton, whose worshippers had looked on him as 'God' before Jimi came along. When the news broke of Jimi's death a year later, the *New York Times* asked Clapton for an interview about his Nemesis-turned-dear friend. Clapton agreed, on condition that I was the interviewer. I turned down the assignment, being on the point of leaving for Detroit and LA to write about the Motown organisation and meet the eleven-year-old lead singer in their supposed 'black Beatles', the Jackson 5. I've always regretted not postponing my flight.

So why embark on a book about Jimi, especially in the exhausted aftermath of my Clapton biography when, as always at such times, I felt I never wanted to write another word about music or musicians? The answer is that, regardless of my feelings, the book seemed to go ahead and start assembling itself.

In 2018, my superlative research associate, Peter Trollope, alerted me to the fact that September 2020 would be the fiftieth anniversary of Jimi's death, still with no satisfactory explanation of it in prospect. During the 1980s, Peter had been a producer on a famous British TV documentary series named *World in Action* and had worked on an investigation into the case, which was never aired. All his unused files, including details of crucial witnesses never called at the inquest, could be at my disposal.

Then, out of the blue, I had an email from Sharon Lawrence,

a former reporter with the UPI wire service who became a close (platonic) friend of Jimi's following his triumphant return to America. Sharon had been a rich source for my biography of Elton John in the early 1990s, but we'd subsequently lost touch. Although herself the author of an intimate Jimi memoir, she generously agreed to act as a consultant for anything I might write.

Then I realised I still had a phone number for Ray Foulk who, with his brothers Ronnie and Bill, staged the 1970 Isle of Wight Pop Festival which Jimi co-headlined with the Doors just two weeks before his death (and only a year before Jim Morrison's). I recollected that the last time I'd seen Ray was at the launch party for his book on the brothers' three Isle of Wight festivals to which, as an island boy, I'd been of some small help. The party venue was the house in Brook Street, Mayfair, now enshrined as the former home of both Jimi and another great musical immigrant, two centuries earlier, George Frideric Handel.

Then, fortuitously, it came time for one of the twice-yearly get-togethers of old rock stars and the writers who chronicled them, held at a riverside pub in Barnes, west London, and known as 'the Scribblers, Pluckers, Thumpers and Squawkers Lunch'. There I sat next to Keith Altham, the *New Musical Express* journalist who had suggested to Jimi's first manager, Chas Chandler – jokingly, as Keith thought – that a good way to outdo the Who's instrument-smashing onstage might be to make a bonfire of his guitar. And at the next table sat Zoot Money, the veteran rhythm-and-bluesman who was the first person Jimi visited after arriving in London.

Then my milkman in north London, Ron Pluckrose, happened to let drop that in an earlier career as a painter and decorator he and his brother had done up a flat near Marble Arch that Jimi was renting from the Walker Brothers. 'He wanted it painted all black, even the lovely walnut wardrobe in the bedroom. The carpet was yellow and the bedsheets were orange, he had fan-mail scattered all over the bathroom floor and a cupboard full of gold discs that we nailed on the wall for him. He was a lovely feller . . .'

Then I listened again to his 'All Along the Watchtower', and gave in.

ONE

'HE WAS HEARING MUSIC BUT DIDN'T HAVE AN INSTRUMENT TO BRING IT TO EARTH'

Jimi's birthplace was a part of my childhood, albeit by proxy. When my Grandma Norman's sailor husband, William, was killed in the last year of the 1914–18 War (the ship he captained sunk by a German torpedo in the Irish Sea), she emigrated to Seattle to join her sister, Gwen, who had already settled there. With her she took my father, Clive, then four, his six-year-old brother, Phil, and two teenaged children by William's previous marriage, a boy named Calver and a girl, Iris. They crossed the Atlantic on an American liner whose breakfast menu, Grandma Norman loved to recall, offered 'as many prunes as you could eat for 10 cents'.

Her descriptions of Seattle circa 1918 made it sound still a wild-frontier kind of place. Not far outside the city limits were forests where bears raided picnic baskets just like Yogi and Boo-Boo in the Hanna-Barbera cartoon. ('We used to have to just sit in the car and watch them.') She and the children visited a Native American reservation – which tribe's she could not re-member, to my disappointment – and bought fringed buckskin jackets, embroidered with white and blue beads, which she still preserved alongside the mementoes of Grandpa Norman's naval career. Of the city itself, her chief memory was of hills so steep that the ubiquitous Model T Fords, known as 'Tin Lizzies', had to be thrown into reverse, the most powerful gear, to negotiate them.

During my years as a *Sunday Times* correspondent, I criss-crossed America, but visited Seattle only once, in 1973, while on tour with the soul diva Roberta Flack. Only then did the realisation dawn that 'Seattle, Washington' didn't mean up the road from the White House but the *State* of Washington in the far north-west, just below the Canadian border. I was there only one night, not long enough for any sightseeing beyond the city centre monorail, which by then had obliterated those hilly streets with their backward-whizzing Model T Fords. I remember the contrast between the American and Canadian news programmes on my hotel TV, the former always teetering on the edge of hysteria, the latter doggedly preserving a measured calm and dignity in keeping with their British heritage.

Bing Crosby, one of the twentieth century's greatest popular singers (along with Sinatra and Presley), was born in Seattle's satellite town of Tacoma. Otherwise, it is best known as one of North America's rainiest cities, as the original home of the Boeing aircraft corporation, as the setting for the *Frasier* TV series and the birthplaces of Microsoft founder Bill Gates and the Starbucks coffee house chain. To be sure, the few successful pop performers it has produced – the Ventures, Judy Collins, the all-female band Heart – might broadly be classified as flat whites.

It's generally thought that Seattle played little part in the history of black American music; that this incalculable gift to humankind was a product only of New Orleans or Memphis or Chicago or the cruel cottonfields of the Mississippi Delta.

But they are forgetting Jimi.

It was in Seattle's era of Tin Lizzies and enforced teddy bears' picnics that an all-black vaudeville show called the Great Dixieland Spectacle came through town. Even in the sentimental fantasy world of 'Dixieland', black could not be *too* black; the Spectacle's female dancers were selected for their lightness of skin, which had to match a white postcard held up to their faces. Among them was Jimi's paternal grandmother, Zenora Hendricks, whose paler pigmentation was partly down to her great-grandmother, a full-blooded Cherokee Native American.

Zenora's husband, Bertran, who worked in the company as a stagehand, was also light-skinned, though for a reason best kept dark: he was the illegitimate son of a former slave and the white merchant who had owned her. Such interracial relationships, known since the Civil War as 'miscegenation', remained a felony in most states, northern as well as southern.

Following the Great Dixieland Spectacle's Seattle engagement, Bertran and Zenora decided to come off the road, settle down there and have children. But after just one summer, they upped sticks and moved again across the Canadian border to Vancouver. It was then an overwhelmingly 'white' city with no openings for black dancers or stage -hands. Show business thus seemed done with a family which by now spelt its surname 'Hendrix'.

The youngest of their four children, James Allen – always to be known as Al – arrived in 1919, strong and healthy but with an extra finger on each hand. Back then, such infant deformities were widely believed to be marks of the Devil for which, not long previously, the luckless infant would have been quietly suffocated. However, infanticide had given way to do-it-yourself amputation: Zenora was advised to bind the superfluous digits with silk cords, starving them of blood until they simply dropped off. This they did, only to grow back in an undersized, shrivelled form, complete with miniature nails.

Al was short, muscular and aggressive, the total opposite of his tall, willowy, gentle future son. He showed an early talent for dancing and – in the single spotlight-gleam to fall on him until that future son became famous – was once photographed by a newspaper jitterbugging at a Duke Ellington concert. His build and pugnacious nature steered him inevitably to the boxing ring: he had a few fights as a welterweight, but never earned enough to make the punishment worthwhile. Unable to get a job on the Canadian railways as he wanted, and hungry for action, he soon lit out across the border to the American city where his parents had once briefly lived.

Seattle on the cusp of the 1940s had little of the overtly brutal racial discrimination to be found in the Jim Crow South. Its African American population lived mostly in the four-square-mile Central District, no monochrome ghetto but a polyglot community that also included Jews, Filipinos and Japanese. It was a smaller, wetter version of New York's Harlem, with its own newspapers and restaurants and a string of music clubs along Jackson Street including the famous Rocking Chair, where the young Ray Charles would later be discovered after finding his way there from Florida. Yet discrimination operated in subtler forms: the Central District's black residents inhabited its most run-down housing and, as throughout the rest of the nation, their employment opportunities were limited to the manual or menial.

In 1940, 21-year-old Al was working in an iron foundry when he met a stunningly pretty high school ninth grader named Lucille Jeter at a Fats Waller concert. They had much in common – Lucille similarly tracing her ancestry back to slaves and Cherokees – but most of all a mutual passion for dancing that soon had them bopping into bed.

In December 1941, Japan launched its surprise bombing attack on Pearl Harbor, thereby bringing America into the Second World War. Al, who by now was racking balls in a pool hall, realised he would soon be drafted and, with Lucille already pregnant, decided they should get married as soon as possible. The wedding took place in March 1942; three days later, Al joined the army, which immediately spirited him away, and his young bride returned to high school.

For a year afterwards, none of Al's army pay got through to Lucille, forcing her to quit school and seek work in the clubs and dives up and down Jackson Street, sometimes singing – for she had a good voice – sometimes waitressing until her pregnancy was far advanced. The once-innocent girl developed a taste for alcohol that quickly turned into a craving.

On 27 November 1942, she gave birth to a boy at Seattle's public Harborview Hospital. Al, by now stationed at Fort Rucker in Alabama, was refused special leave to see the baby and put into the stockade to prevent him from going AWOL. Immediately afterwards, his regiment shipped out for the Pacific; he was in Fiji before a photograph of his firstborn reached him.

He complained that Lucille barely wrote to him while he was away fighting for his country (although never in any serious danger-zone). In fairness, she had problems over and above that of becoming a teenage mother. Her father had died, bringing on a recurrence of the psychiatric problems that had always plagued her mother, and her family home had burned down, destroying everything in it. The war had brought about a huge increase in Seattle's black male population, to serve in the military bases created in expectation of a Japanese seaborne attack or to work in the shipyards on Pugin Sound. Without Al's army pay or much support from his parents, who disapproved of her nocturnal life on Jackson Street, Lucille was forced to turn to other men for financial aid and to pay its inevitable price.

Before long, 'Dear John' letters began to reach Al, signed 'A Friend' and informing him of his wife's infidelities and failures as a mother apparently so serious that another couple were seeking to adopt their son. The explosive Al made no attempt to discover the truth of the matter but, from the far Pacific, immediately started divorce proceedings.

By the time he returned to Seattle, the baby was aged three and had been turned over– permanently, it seemed – to a woman named Mrs Champ who lived in Berkeley, California, almost 800 miles to the south. Al immediately set out to reclaim him, never considering that to a three-year-old, being suddenly snatched from a doting foster mother and carried off by stranger would be inexplicable and frightening.

Nor did the long rail journey back to Seattle engender much empathy between long-lost father and bewildered son. 'I gave [him] his first spanking on that train,' Al would recall almost proudly in the autobiography which, at the time, he had no idea he'd ever need to write.

The tearful toddler's very name started the two of them off on the wrong foot. Without consulting Al, Lucille had decided on Johnny Allen but tried to keep it from him as long as possible: the single baby photo that reached him in Fiji was captioned only 'Baby Hendrix'.

She could not have picked anything more calculated to out-rage the jealous Al, for a longshoreman and aspiring pimp she had been involved with – and whom he half-suspected of being the baby's real father – was one John Page. After their return to Seattle, Al firmly re-registered Johnny Allen as James Marshall, his own official first name and the middle one of his deceased older brother, Leon.

Much to his annoyance, however, the otherwise mild and tractable little boy steadfastly refused to answer to either James or Jimmy. He insisted on being called Buster, after Buster Crabbe, the movie actor who played both Tarzan and Flash Gordon. In the end, Al gave up trying to make his new nomenclature stick, and Buster it was.

Far more serious was the discovery that he was left-handed, which many people still considered not far down the scale of

Satan-signatures from surplus fingers. That such a further stigma should be added to the midget digit on each of his own hands horrified Al, and he set about correcting it in the only way he knew how. If ever Buster were caught using the 'wrong' hand, he could expect an angry swipe around the head.

The naming question and John Page notwithstanding, Al and Lucille had decided to try to patch up their marriage. But the newly demobilised soldier had little taste for ordinary domesticity and the former Jackson Street habituée, not much more. Their home life soon became a continuous round of drunken parties that often ended in a screaming row between the two of them and Lucille's disappearance, sometimes for hours, sometimes days or weeks. And for the timid, anxious child of this blighted union, 'Buster' could hardly have been more inappropriate.

He has left behind an autobiography of sorts in a Netflix documentary called *Voodoo Child*, compiled from stage and TV footage and interviews from his last four crowded years. In it he is voiced by Bootsy Collins, formerly the virtuoso bass player with James Brown's stage band, who resembled him physically and speaks in the same caressingly soft tones.

Nowhere is there the slightest criticism of his father or his upbringing, although a great deal can be read between the lines.

'Dad was very strict and level-headed, but my mother liked dressing up and having a good time. She used to drink a lot and didn't take care of herself but she was a groovy mother . . . Mostly my dad took care of me. He taught me that I must respect my elders always. I couldn't speak unless I was spoken to first by grown-ups. So I've always been quiet. But I saw a lot of things. A fish wouldn't get in trouble if he kept his mouth shut.

'I remember when I was only four and I wet my pants . . . I stayed out in the rain for hours so I would get wet all over and my mom wouldn't know.'

17

In 1948, Lucille had a second son, uncontroversially named Leon after Al's brother. In both build and temperament, Leon was clearly no longshoreman's progeny but exactly like his father, and so received an indulgence Buster never had, or would. 'He was always a good kid, quiet, never talked back, calm,' Leon recalls. 'I was the one that rebelled against authority. "Bodacious" was our dad's word for me.' However, both boys knew that crossing Al meant a beating – a 'whoopin', as they called it – with his thick leather belt.

Lucille continued to have babies, but so frequent and lengthy had become her disappearances to unknown quarters that Al denied paternity of any of them. And, although both Buster and Leon had been born whole and healthy, something like a curse now seemed to descend. A third son, Joseph, who arrived a year after Leon, had a cleft palate, a club-foot, legs of unequal length and a double row of teeth. A daughter, Kathy, was born prematurely in 1950, weighing only one pound and blind. Needing care far beyond the power or pocket of her parents, she was immediately taken into a state institution.

As all this chaos and agony eddied around them, Buster became Leon's only stability and shield. Many was the time he would take the blame for some misdeed of his kid brother's and receive the whoopin' in his place. During their parents' drunken fights, they would hide in a cupboard, Buster with arms wrapped protectively around Leon. 'He absorbed the negativity day after day,' Leon recalls, 'and having no one to turn to for help, learned to lock his feelings deep inside.'

Al and Lucille divorced in 1951, with Al being awarded custody of Buster, Leon and the unfortunate Joe. But she continued to return to him spasmodically and children kept on coming, with Al denying paternity each time and the seeming curse relentless. A second daughter, Pamela, born in the year of the divorce, also had birth defects, less serious than her predecessors' but still requiring institutional care, as did another son, Al junior, born in 1953. By then, Joe's special needs had become too great a financial burden and he'd followed his three siblings into care, the difference this time being that Buster and Leon had to watch him being taken away.

Al struggled to support his two remaining charges on mostly manual work – heaving animal carcasses around a slaughter-house, sweeping up in a steel plant, pumping gas – which seldom brought in more than $90 a month, although he had hopes of becoming an electrician and was studying the trade under the G.I. Bill, which provided further education for demobbed vet-erans. The three lived with various relatives and friends or in cheap boarding houses and short-term apartments in the Cen-tral District's grim housing 'projects', generally moving on after only a few weeks; it was, Leon Hendrix recalls, 'like a constant camping trip'.

When Al was not working, he would usually be out drinking, chasing women or gambling – sometimes losing a whole week's pay on a single throw of the dice – while the boys were left on their own. If he was in funds, he would hire someone to cook and care for them, but mostly they were reliant on the charity of neighbours. 'The black ladies and Jewish ladies in the Central District kind of adopted us,' Leon says. 'Mrs Weinstein made us matzo ball soup, Mrs Jackson fried us chicken with mashed po-tatoes and Mrs Wilson, who had a little store there, washed our clothes for us and made us take a bath.'

Lucille would still periodically return to Al, creating the brief illusion of a reunited family. She tended to arrive during the night, and Buster and Leon would awaken to the smell of frying bacon or her speciality, brains and eggs. Despite her drinking, she was never other than sweet and loving to them both in equal measure and they missed her desperately.

Leon followed his brother everywhere, in an existence without supervision or boundaries. Once while they were playing on a railway line, his shoelace got caught in the rails just as a train was coming and Buster pushed him clear with only seconds to spare. 'He saved me from drowning, too, when I fell into the Green River. As I was struggling in the water, I remember, a dead pig floated by. Then he dove in and life-saved me to the bank.'

Al's continual moves around the city meant Buster continually had to change schools with no time to settle down at any one. His grades consequently were never more than mediocre, despite his sponge-like ability to soak up knowledge. 'I never saw him read a book,' Leon recalls, 'yet he could tell you about all the planets in the Universe.' He had a talent for drawing and spent hours on his medieval knights, racing cars, football players and caricatures (always taking care that Al didn't catch him using the 'wrong hand'). Unknowingly, he was following the same trajectory as naturally creative but undisciplined British boys like John Lennon, Keith Richards and Eric Clapton, although, unlike them, he had no sympathetic teacher to notice his ability and urge that he be sent to art school.

From an early age, he showed himself to be a natural athlete, able to run at extraordinary speed and so equally good at baseball and football – even then keeping a brotherly eye on Leon in the Little League games on the same field. His happiest childhood photos show him grinning from inside a cheek-hugging football helmet. But he was always painfully conscious of his shabby hand-me-down sports clothes and equipment and the crude haircuts, performed by Al, which earned him the school nickname of 'Slick Bean'.

Like most lonely children, he adored animals, and was always bringing home stray dogs that had followed him in the street and pleading with his father to be allowed to keep them. Al had no desire for an extra mouth to feed and, anyway, their temporary lodgings usually made it impossible, but finally one fortunate mutt he named 'Prince Buster' did get to stay. Wild creatures fascinated him, especially the deer he sometimes glimpsed in Washington's and British Columbia's expansive national parks and to which he felt an almost spiritual connection like a stirring of his Native American genes. The vivid dreams he had every night, always in brilliant colour, included a recurrent, mystifying set of numbers, one, nine and two sixes, which gave him 'strange feelings that I was here for something and I was going to get a chance to be heard'.

In their visibly neglected state, he and Leon inevitably came to the notice of Seattle's welfare authorities. Thanks to Al's dire warnings, they lived in terror of following their two brothers and two sisters into care, where they would undoubtedly be separated. 'We were always hiding and ducking from the welfare officers,' Leon recalls. 'While we were home alone, we'd keep the drapes drawn and the lights out and never answer when somebody knocked at the door.'

Although they never went hungry, there was no being finicky about their food like other boys their age. 'Horsemeat burgers we used to have, 'cause they only cost a nickel each. Buster had a job sweeping up a butcher's shop and one day the shopkeeper gave him a whole tongue to bring home.'

Life became its least stressful and most normal when the boys were sent across the Canadian border to stay with their grandmother, Zenora, in Vancouver. She was strict with Buster, spanking him for wetting his bed with no thought of the emotional state that caused it. But she also dressed him up in a little tasselled Mexican jacket, which he loved, and told him stories about her days in minstrel shows and his slave great-grandmother and Cherokee great-great-grandmother. Years later, one of the myths he would spin around himself was that Zenora had been the Cherokee and that he used to stay with her on an actual reservation.

'Before he ever played music, it was obviously inside him,' Leon says. 'He'd tell Grandma he had all these weird sounds in his head and she'd swab out his ears with baby-oil. He was hearing music, but he didn't have an instrument to bring it to earth.'

Around the age of twelve, he began strumming a broom-handle along with music he heard on the radio. 'He played air guitar before anyone knew that air guitar existed,' says his brother. 'I'm sure that if he'd gotten a piano before he did a guitar, he'd have been just as great on that.'

Al was by now working for himself as a landscape gardener, although the job equally consisted of clearing unwanted rubbish and selling it for whatever he could get. He would dragoon his sons into helping him and one day on a garbage pile, Buster found a beaten-up ukulele with a single string hanging loose. Al's first thought was that it might fetch a couple of dollars, but Buster begged to be allowed to keep it. He was intrigued to discover that if he twisted one of the end-pegs, the solitary string could be tautened to produce a musical note when he plucked it. So interesting was the result, Leon recalls, that he went around trying the same technique on everything he could think of, from rubber bands to pieces of string tied between two bedposts.

In 1955, he turned thirteen and so was no longer the concern of Seattle's welfare authorities. Eight-year-old Leon, however, was finally netted, taken, shrieking, from his father and brother and placed in foster care. But he proved impossible to tame, running away from a series of foster homes, or being thrown out of them, and finding his way back to Al and Buster's latest domicile.

Nineteen fifty-five also happened to be the year when Elvis Presley outraged America as the first white vocalist to perform with the uninhibitedness of black ones, and black R&B music, rebranded as rock 'n' roll, aroused its white teenage population to mass frenzy.

Racisim fought back with all the unrestrained weapons at its command. Presley was condemned and derided for propagating the 'jungle music', until then as strictly segregated as restrooms, lunch counters and drinking fountains, and thereby likely to corrupt and debase young white people as much as it did black ones.

Since there was no ignoring its commercial opportunities, however, R&B songs like Ivory Joe Hunter's 'Shake, Rattle and Roll', Roy Brown's 'Good Rocking Tonight' and Little Richard's 'Tutti Frutti', with their barely disguised sexual (and, in Richard's case, homosexual) jokery, were put out in watered-down cover versions by white performers like Pat Boone and Ricky Nelson, in which form a number entered the mainstream record charts. The long tradition of stealing from black musicians reached an unprecedented high.

Buster was fascinated by Presley: his Technicolor clothes, borrowed from country music, his supposedly 'obscene' body movements and the guitar that was so essential a part of the exploding package. Forgetting ballplayers and racing cars, he drew an elaborate portrait of Presley, surrounded by his song titles, like 'Blue Suede Shoes', 'Don't Be Cruel' and 'Parilized' (sic). 'The Pelvis's' trail of hysteria-rent concerts included one at Sick's baseball stadium in Seattle but, the $1.50 ticket price being way beyond Buster, he could only watch from the hill above the stadium, seeing little more of Presley than a hyperactive dot. 'He used to sing Elvis songs to me to make me go to sleep,' Leon recalls. 'My favourite was "Love Me Tender".'

Over the following months, Al Hendrix's fortunes took another of their frequent downswings. Having scraped together enough to take out a mortgage on a small house, he could not keep up the payments; the property was repossessed and he and Buster went to live in a boarding house kept by a Mrs McKay. There in a back room Buster found an old Kay acoustic guitar which had been bought for their landlady's paraplegic son and which she was willing to sell for $5.

He begged his father to buy it for him, but the cash-strapped Al bluntly refused to finance such a seeming total irrelevance. His pleas were supported by his mother's sister, Ernestine, a perceptive woman who had noticed the transformative effects of the one-string ukelele, and when his dad proved immovable, Aunt Ernestine gave him the money.

From that moment, Leon Hendrix recalls, he forgot all about sports and lived only for the guitar. 'He wasn't ever apart from it. There was a film out then named *Johnny Guitar*, where this guy played by Sterling Hayden went around everywhere, carrying his guitar on his back. My brother did the same. He'd play it in bed, fall asleep with it on his chest, then start playing it again as soon as he woke up. To keep me quiet while he was learning, he'd tie a pencil to my wrist to force me to draw or do my home-work. For me, it was as good as going to university.'

There was no question of his having a formal teacher or even someone who could show him how to tune the guitar; all he could do was go to a music store, surreptitiously stroke the strings of the instruments on display there until he could reproduce the sound from each one. After that, his only tutor was the radio in its two still-segregated spheres: the black stations that playing R&B and blues and the white ones playing watered-down rock 'n' roll. Like Chuck Berry, he had unusually long, slim fingers that reached around the fretboard with nonchalant ease, supple-mented by a thumb that covered about half its width from the other side. One of his earliest bits of showmanship was seem-ing to lose this masterful grip on his guitar-neck and making a pretend grab for it. He'd repeat the trick in every show to come, never realising the one thing his act didn't need was comedy.

From his parents' riotous parties, too, would come the sound of hardcore bluesmen like Muddy Waters, Elmore James and

Howlin' Wolf, whose jagged bottleneck-guitar technique was so often the precursor to real breaking bottles. 'I liked Muddy when he had only two guitars, harmonica and bass drum,' he was to recall. 'Things like "Rollin' and Tumblin'" . . . the real primitive guitar sound.'

One of the anti-rock brigade's main indictments was that Presley and the other guitar-flourishing white idols who came after him used their instruments merely as props and so were guilty of fraud as well as public indecency. In reality, several, like Buddy Holly, Eddie Cochran and Charlie Gracie, were brilliant players whose riffs could nonetheless be reproduced by the rawest amateur. So, while the young Eric Clapton in a faraway English village was learning from black blues and R&B musicians, Buster was learning from white pop ones – both of them coincidentally using Kay guitars.

He was left-handed as a guitarist, as in every other way, and thus in peril of swipes around the head from his father while he sat practising. So whenever Al appeared, Buster would flip the Kay around and play it upside-down (a trick that his fellow 'leftie' and exact contemporary, Paul McCartney, was also having to employ while using John Lennon's right-handed instrument). Then, instead of the whoopin', he'd receive a lecture about doing something useful with his life, which to Al, almost a craftsman now with lawn-rollers and secateurs, could only mean working 'with his hands'.

'Not that I cared but . . . well, he is my dad,' says the endlessly forgiving voice in the *Voodoo Child* documentary. 'I don't think my dad ever thought I was going to make it. I was the kid who didn't do the right thing.'

Whether black or white, the most exciting sounds came from electric guitars, of which the cheapest seemed astronomically expensive to Buster. But if a purpose-built model was out of reach, an acoustic one could be electrified by a metal pickup attached under the base of the fretboard with an exposed jack-lead that plugged into an amplifier. He saved enough for the pickup but, of course, had no amp: the only way to produce a similar effect was to wire it through his father's jealously guarded record player.

This worked as long as Leon held down a connection with one finger, which he loyally kept doing even though it gave him an electric shock. The unaccustomed power made the record-player's speaker crackle and buzz. 'Not only did we have an electric guitar going,' he recalls, 'but we had *distortion*.'

Rootless as they were, and having the kind of parents they did, the boys rarely saw the inside of a church. Buster was therefore deprived of a musical grounding that just about every notable African American performer received , not least the rock 'n' rollers (both black and white) now being denounced as agents of the devil. That he had never been in a gospel choir explained why, when he finally began singing, he would sound like no one else in blues, R&B or soul.

Yet it was to the church that he owed his first sight of a figure that would loom large in his future career. One day, Leon came home in great excitement to report having seen Little Richard downtown, getting out of a long black limousine. The piano-pounding Richard, who was not particularly little, had amassed a huge white following with his blend of primal shriek and mascara-ed camp (his biggest hits produced by Seattle-born producer Robert 'Bumps' Blackwell). Recently his fans in the US and Europe had been stunned by an announcement that he was quitting show business to enter church ministry.

It turned out that Richard had an aunt living in the Central District who worshipped at the Baptist Pentecostal church, and had come to preach there as a warm-up for his new career. 'Buster and I went to hear his sermon twice,' Leon recalls. 'We looked the best we could, in white shirts that were grey, odd socks, shoestrings that were broken and we had to tie together.

'The entire church hung on his every word as he pranced about the pulpit, hooting and hollering about the almighty power of the Lord. He explained that he had recently had a vivid dream in which a diamond-encrusted airplane he was flying in crashed to the ground . . . It was as clear as day to him that God was telling him he needed to become a preacher.' Buster, meanwhile, was receiving his first lesson in showmanship.

The boys at this time had not seen their mother for several months. Lucille was remarried, to a retired longshoreman named William Mitchell, thirty years her senior, and her years of drinking and self-neglect were starting to tell. In 1957, she was hospitalised twice with cirrhosis of the liver. Al seldom mentioned her and when he did, it was always disparagingly. Buster hated hearing her badmouthed, but always bit his tongue.

Early in 1958, they heard she was back in hospital again with hepatitis after being found lying in an alley beside a tavern. When they went to visit her in Harborview – Buster's birthplace – she hadn't been thought worthy of a room and was lying on a bed out in the corridor. 'They put her into a wheelchair,' Leon recalls, 'and she seemed to be all glowing white, like she was floating.'

That was the last time her sons ever saw her. A few days later, she died from a ruptured spleen aged only 32. To her eldest, it seemed like the fulfilment of a dream he'd had when he was very small, in which he'd had to stand and watch her being carried away by a camel train. 'It was a big caravan and you could see the shadows of the leaf patterns across her face. You know how the sun shines through a tree. Well, these were green and yellow shadows. And she was saying, "Well, I won't be seeing you too much any more."'

Lucille was buried at Greenwood Memorial Park, in a pauper's grave under her husband's surname, Mitchell. Al was supposed to drive Buster and Leon to the ceremony in his gardening truck, but he got drunk and lost his way so that they arrived six hours late. His way of comforting his grief-stricken sons was to give them a sip of whisky each, then finish the bottle.

Buster, as always, kept his feelings deep inside, although his Aunt Delores sometimes overheard him crying out on her front porch. Years later, in another, unimaginable life, he would write a song called 'Castles Made of Sand' about 'a young girl whose heart was a frown' who 'drew her wheelchair to the seashore' and 'to her legs smiled "You won't hurt me any more."'

'He was always sore at our dad,' Leon Hendrix says, 'for not taking better care of Mama.'

TWO

'JIMMY WAS A HIPPY BEFORE ANYONE KNEW WHAT A HIPPY WAS'

He was not the first future rock megastar for whom music, and in particular a guitar, providentially filled the void of becoming motherless as a teenager – a tragedy only a little less than for a newborn infant.

In Liverpool, two years earlier, fourteen-year-old Paul McCartney had lost his mother to breast cancer and found solace in joining a skiffle group formed by sixteen-year-old John Lennon (whose own mother was to be killed in a traffic accident a few weeks later). At the opposite end of England, in Ripley, Surrey, thirteen-year-old Eric Clapton's mother had not died but – perhaps even worse – had abandoned him to be brought up by his grandmother, then made him pretend she was his grown-up sister, thereby creating an emotional wound that only a Kay guitar and the grizzled voices and companionable pain of black American blues singers could assuage.

But for the down-at-heel fifteen-year-old in Seattle, still known as Buster Hendrix, there was another reason for the endless practice with the radio as his teacher. Against all the evidence to the contrary, he kept hoping it might be a way to make his father proud of him. The voice of his grown-up self in the *Voodoo Child* documentary articulates the thought he never dared express at the time. 'Oh, Daddy! One of these days, I'm gonna be big and famous. I'm gonna make it, man.'

Several of his friends by now owned all-electric guitars with flat bodies and spiky headstocks that made his once-treasured acoustic Kay feel as ancient as a Model T Ford and reduced it to silence if ever he tried to jam with them. Indeed, so long and hard had he practised that it was literally falling to pieces. Once again, his Aunt Ernestine came to his aid, telling her brother-in-law at every opportunity, 'You *have* to get that boy an electric guitar.'

Finally Al agreed to go with him to Myers Music store, but when confronted with its wall display of guitars, backed away muttering that they were all unaffordably expensive. This routine was repeated several times until, just when it seemed hopeless, he agreed to put a down payment on another, far superior Kay, a fifteen-dollar Supro Ozark whose gorgeously solid body had a 'champagne' (i.e., off-white) finish.

Ever unpredictable, Al also decided to buy a saxophone and teach himself to play it by ear, as his son had done with the guitar. But it soon became clear that he possessed none of the same innate musicality. 'He could only ever play one note,' Leon Hendrix recalls. We used hear it going on for half the night: "Da-a-ah . . . Da-a-ah . . . *Da-a-ah!*"'

For a left-handed player, the right-hand Supro Ozark had only one defect. Buster could restring it upside down, but the tongue-shaped black panel displaying its volume and tone knobs was immovable, so had to remain conspicuously above rather than below his strumming hand. There being no money to spare for a carrying-case, he had to use a dry-cleaning bag, consoling himself with the thought of Chuck Berry's Johnny B. Goode, who 'carried his guitar in a gunny [burlap] sack'.

In September 1959, shortly before his seventeenth birthday, he enrolled at Seattle's James A. Garfield High School, casting off the tearaway nickname that had always sat so uneasily with him and becoming known to one and all for the next five years as Jimmy Hendrix.

Although situated in the heart of the Central District, Garfield High was the city's most integrated as well as largest educational institution with a student body 50 per cent white as against 30 per cent African American and 20 per cent Asian. Jimmy was just a few years behind another black student from an identically slave-descended, deprived and motherless background, destined to vie with him as the school's most celebrated alumnus. This was Quincy Jones, who went on to win a music scholarship to Seattle University, play trumpet in the Lionel Hampton band and ultimately produce the biggest-selling album in history, Michael Jackson's *Thriller*.

Other adolescent males (not least those similarly motherless ones in Liverpool and Surrey) were discovering how possessing a guitar massively increased their appeal to the opposite sex. But Jimmy never had any need of such a six-stringed aphrodisiac, nor did either his colour or his poverty put any brake on his love life. 'He dated all the prettiest middle-class girls in high school,' Leon Hendrix says. 'He'd take me with him when he went to visit them out in the suburbs. I'd have to wait outside in the bushes while he climbed in through their windows.'

According to his own – not always reliable – account, Jimmy's first time onstage was at a National Guard armoury and it terrified him so much that he tried to hide behind the curtains. In fact, it was with some older boys in the basement of a synagogue, the Temple De Hirsch Sinai on Boylston Avenue, where regular dances were held. The appearance was merely an audition to see whether he was good enough to join the band permanently.

He played in their first set, but was fired in the intermission before their second one. His bandmates complained that his playing was so 'wild', it stopped people from dancing. The same problem was often to recur in the future, although the firings would never again come quite so quickly.

More successful was his audition with some high school friends calling themselves the Velvetones. They were a band in the old-fashioned sense with horns and saxes who did not simply play a set but performed a 'revue' with dance routines in the James Brown style. Their repertoire mixed R&B with white pop instrumentals like Duane Eddy's 'Rebel Rouser' and the theme from the *Peter Gunn* television series. They found plenty of work, including a weekly appearance at the popular Birdland club on 22nd Avenue. Jimmy's first featured spot was the four-note bass riff in Bill Doggett's 'Honky Tonk'.

Leon had just been collared by the welfare authorities yet again and returned to foster care and Al and Jimmy were sharing an apartment on First Hill, in those days one of the Central District's roughest quarters, with prostitutes working just along the street and a juvenile detention centre opposite. The apartment was filthy and vermin-infested and rendered even less attractive by Al's use of it as a store for his gardening equipment; not just heavy horticultural implements but also toxic chemical insecticides.

Nor was it a good rehearsal space for the Velvetones, since Al remained implacably hostile to Jimmy's guitar even after buying it for him, and continued clubbing him around the head for playing left-handed – an unspeakable embarrassment for a seventeen-year-old in front of his friends. He soon took to leaving it at the home of a bandmate and only practising there.

Before very long, he had moved on to another local band, the Rocking Kings, more successful and sophisticated than the Velvetones though performing in much the same 'revue' style. Onstage they wore matching red jackets, which each member was expected to buy for himself. 'The jackets cost five dollars and Jimmy worked for our dad gardening for five days at a dollar a day to get his,' Leon recalls. 'He wouldn't even buy a candy bar.'

He was on the point of switching from the Velvetones to the Rocking Kings when disaster struck: one night, he left the Supro Ozark backstage at the Birdland club and had it stolen. He was traumatised by its loss and, almost as much, by the whoopin' he could expect at home, despite Al's loathing of his music.

The guitar had not, of course, been insured, but thanks to his paltry pay from his father, a short-lived newspaper delivery job for the *Seattle Post-Intelligencer* and a magnanimous whip-round by his fellow Rocking Kings, he was able to replace it with a white Danelectro Silvertone, sold through the Sears Roebuck mail-order catalogue, whose $49.95 price tag included a small amplifier.

In recognition of his important new gig, he decided to follow the custom of many blues guitarists and give his instrument a woman's name. His mother's, Lucille, having already been taken by B. B. King, he chose Betty-Jean after his current girlfriend, Betty-Jean Morgan.

The Rocking Kings rocked far and wide throughout Washington and across the Canadian border, packed into one beaten-up Mercury sedan, playing military bases or ballrooms like the 2,000-capacity Spanish Castle in the town of Kent, where the audiences were predominantly white but blacks weren't discriminated against. Now Jimmy could learn from the guitarists in top regional bands such as the Fabulous Wailers from Tacoma, or visiting stars like Hank Ballard – African American despite his cowboy-ish name, and writer of a song called 'The Twist' that would soon spark an international dance craze.

As well as working with his own band, Jimmy was avid to sit in with such larger fry, who ordinarily might not welcome an unknown seventeen-year-old. So he would enquire respectfully whether they could use an extra amp and might care to borrow his. Then, when it materialised onstage, he'd already be plugged into it.

The Rocking Kings' star had always been their lead guitarist, Junior Heath, but Jimmy found other ways of attracting attention. 'It started when he found a pigeon feather and stuck it on his guitar,' Leon recalls. 'Then he painted it red, wrote "Betty-Jean" on the front and hung it with the little tassels you used to get on Seagram's Seven whisky bottles.

'Or he'd come onstage wearing a blouse. People used to ask me: "Where does Jimmy get his clothes from?" and I'd say, "His girlfriend." That was out with the other guys in the band, who were only about conformity. He was a hippy before anyone knew what a hippy was.'

The Rocking Kings disintegated after a catastrophic trip to Vancouver when their beaten-up Mercury finally gave out and their fee barely covered their bus fares back to Seattle. Their manager, Thomas James, formed a new band named Thomas and the Tomcats, keeping Jimmy on and giving him an expanded role including a share of the background vocals – much to his discomfort, as he thought his singing voice was too weak. Then, out of nowhere, came an opportunity that may come as news to the most hardcore Hendrix fans.

Ray Charles, although Georgia-born, had been discovered in Seattle, playing at the Rocking Chair club, and made his earliest recordings on the city's Down Beat label. In July 1959, he released 'What'd I Say', a song that lifted him out of the realm of 'race' music – out of any genre, in fact, save pure genius. Able to be stretched out almost indefinitely, it would come as a godsend to an unknown band called the Beatles as they played all-night sessions at strip joints in Hamburg's Reeperbahn district.

Grateful for the start Seattle had given him, Charles still made regular club appearances there. Early in 1960, he was in town again and looking for a back-up guitarist.

'Someone recommended Jimmy and he got the job,' Leon recalls. Even our dad was a little bit impressed by that.

I was home again and Jimmy back to babysitting me, so he took me with him every night. It was a club called the Penthouse where all the big jazz names like Wes Montgomery used to hang out. Jimmy got on real well with Ray; they played together for a few weeks and we'd have soul food afterwards.

The movie about Ray's life with Jamie Foxx has a scene where his manager says to him: 'You should never have left that kid back in Seattle.'

In October 1960, Jimmy dropped out of Garfield High School, giving up his former vague dreams of becoming either a painter or an actor. He would later claim to have been asked to leave for racist reasons; he'd been caught holding a white girl's hand in an art class whose female teacher had previously tried to grope him and was getting her own back for his unresponsiveness. But the truth was that he'd cut so many classes to play music, there was no hope of his graduating.

Apart from his father, who still nagged him incessantly to find an 'honest' job, working 'with his hands' – like, for example, landscape gardening – everybody he knew expected him to become a pro musician after that amazing interlude with Ray Charles. Instead, he ended up in the US Army, training as a parachutist in its 101st Airborne Division.

His military service would be the most thoroughly fictionalised chapter in the life story he would feed to journalists after he turned into Jimi and was expected to sound as wild offstage as he did on it. To them, he would pretend to have been a hardened juvenile delinquent, one of a gang who were always getting into 'rumbles' with 'bloody bastard cops' and being thrown into jail, The truth was that, throughout a near-feral childhood he had managed to avoid gangs along with every other snare of impoverished inner-city youth.

The first time he ever fell foul of Seattle's police department was in May 1961,when he was picked up for what has passed into legend as joyriding in stolen cars. However, the written confession he made at the police station was to petty larceny:

> A friend and I were playing around in an ally [sic] and we noticed a broken window in the back of a clothing store – we then got a clothes hanger which was lying on the ground and unbent it so we could stick it through the window and 'hook' some of the clothes, which we did. The clothes that did not fit us we gave to a Christmas fund at school.

After what he described as 'seven days in the cooler', but was more likely a few hours on remand in juvenile hall, a judge gave him the choice of two years detention or joining the army.

He unhesitatingly picked the latter, which at the time hardly seemed like punishment at all. He had long felt attracted to a life in one or other armed service, not from any bellicose spirit but because it seemed to offer all the security and stability his childhood had lacked. A couple of months earlier, he and a friend had tried to volunteer for the US Air Force but been turned away for not looking tough enough.

He knew the 101st Airborne Division as the crack outfit dropped behind German lines during the 1944 Normandy landings, and when he was younger had done many admiring sketches of its famous 'screaming eagle' badge. Despite its elite status, the 101st's Seattle recruiting office had no problem with the long, languid youth who looked as if he wouldn't hurt a fly. So, on 31May, he set out for basic training at Fort Ord in California, leaving his guitar, Betty-Jean, in the care of its human namesake.

He had never been away on his own before and was engulfed

by homesickness even for the indifferent homes Al provided, the more so as Leon was back with their father again. In these early days, he wrote repeatedly to Al, requesting money to pay for all the supplementary equipment he needed to buy but also sharing the most trivial events in his new life – such as losing a bus ticket – and always signing off 'Love James'.

Yet he was determined to get through these hellish weeks of ritual humiliation by bawling drill sergeants, and thus show himself every bit as much a soldier as Al used to be. 'I'll try my very best to make this AIRBORNE,' he wrote, 'for the sake of *our* name.'

The first terrifying step in parachute training was to climb to the top of a 34-foot tower, jump off and be carried to earth dangling from a harness. The three men ahead of him all chickened out, but Jimmy didn't hesitate.

He was to make twenty-five jumps from an aircraft, eventually becoming almost used to it. 'Physically, it was a falling over backwards,' says the voice in the *Voodoo Child* documentary, at times sounding almost like a song lyric. 'And it's almost like blanking and it's almost like crying and you want to laugh. It's so personal because once you get there it's so quiet. All you hear is the breeze – *sssshhhhhhh* – like that . . . And so you look up and there's that big, beautiful white mushroom above you.'

The America of 1961 was involved in no hostilities overseas: the Korean War had ended in the mid 1950s and its involvement in Vietnam was still only marginal. After basic training, Jimmy was posted to Fort Campbell on the Kentucky–Tennessee border with no prospect of serving overseas as Al had done.

The US Army was officially desegregated, although its white and black personnel tended to socialise separately. But outside Fort Campbell, conditions were very different from relatively tolerant Seattle. Jimmy was in the heart of the redneck South, where he could expect to be addressed as 'Boy', as if slavery had never ended, and young black men were beaten up – even killed – at the slightest provocation, or for no provocation whatsoever.

After all his dreams of airborne derring-do, he was made a supply clerk in a parts warehouse. The days became an automaton round of drill, fatigues and press-ups – or, as he termed it, 'pushing Tennessee around with my hands'. He followed orders, behaved himself and was duly promoted to Private First Class.

On arriving at Fort Campbell, he'd asked his father to get his guitar back from Betty-Jean Morgan and send it to him. 'It took our dad nine months to get that together,' Leon Hendrix recalls. 'That's how come Jimmy looked like he might be turning into a good soldier.'

But the six-stringed Betty-Jean's arrival brought an end to her owner's military keenness. 'He'd call home and go, "Listen to this song I just wrote" and play it to me down the line. I'd go away and do my thing and when I came back and picked up the phone again, he'd still be playing.'

The insularity of each unit in the 101st Airborne meant he didn't find a friend until well into his time at Fort Campbell. But what a friend that turned out to be.

One night, a fellow black recruit from a different barrack-block, Billy Cox by name, was returning from the base cinema when a sudden rain shower forced him to shelter in the doorway of its Number 1 Service Club. Through a half-open window he heard the sound of a guitar. 'I asked my buddy who was with me what he thought of the guy's playing and he said he thought it sounded like a bunch of mess,' Cox recalls. 'But he was only listening with a human ear and I thought I was listening with a spiritual ear. To me it sounded like a combination of John Lee Hooker and Beethoven.

'I walked in and introduced myself and told him I had played upright bass in the school symphony, but I wasn't that good. He said, "They have electric basses now, go check them out. By the way, my name is Jimmy Hendrix.'"

Born in West Virginia and raised in Pittsburgh, nineteen-year-old Cox came from a very different social sphere. His father was a major in the army and a minister and his family belonged to the 'black bourgeoisie' that was just beginning to attract notice. Though only a year older than Jimmy, he would become somewhat like the loving father and somewhat the protective older brother he'd never had.

'That was the most beautiful relationship between two guys that I ever saw,' Cox's wife, Brenda, recalls. 'Bill watched Jimmy's back in the army and wherever he went afterwards, he always knew Bill would be there for him.'

Jimmy would later claim that army routine had left him no time to further his career as a performer. In fact, the soldier's day at Fort Campbell ended at 4 p.m., leaving him pretty much free to do what he liked until 'bed-call'. Billy Cox proved to have a natural aptitude on bass guitar and the two of them formed a band called the Kasuals with buddies from their respective units, which the 101st Airborne made no attempt to shut down.

'The thing I noticed about Jimmy was that he never carried Betty-Jean in a case,' Cox recalls. 'But it wasn't because he couldn't afford one. He wanted to have that guitar ready and waiting at any time he felt like playing it.'

The nearest town to the base, Clarksville, Tennessee, sixteen miles away, had a number of bars and clubs catering to a largely military clientele. Here, the Kasuals found regular work at an establishment named the Pink Poodle. 'The guy who owned it had painted it pink because he thought that made people cooler and better behaved,' Cox says. 'Before that, he'd had a place where the walls were red, and there'd been nothing but shootings and fights.'

Their first gig at the Pink Poodle was backing a blues singer known as Crying Shame. 'And he had a sister named Damn Shame. We almost had to be hauled away because we laughed so much. But when he started, we stopped laughing, because this cat could sing his butt off. He was a great blues singer – one of many we learned from.'

'We shall overcome – long as we can run', ran the sour joke among black stand-up comedians. And Jimmy's abilities as a sprinter, allied to the physical fitness which army training had given him, proved to be a literal life-saver. Late one night, as he walked back alone from a Kasuals gig, a truck screeched to a halt beside him and a group of drunken white youths jumped out, screaming racial abuse. Jimmy took off across a cornfield, easily outdistanced his would-be attackers and then, rather like Cary Grant in Hitchcock's *North by Northwest*, lay doggo on top of Betty-Jean, until they gave up and drove away.

In July 1962, he was honourably discharged from the army after serving only two of the three years he'd signed on for. By then, the 'escalating' situation in Vietnam called for increasing numbers of American troops – albeit with the euphemism of 'military advisers' – and he might well have been among them had he stayed.

He would always claim to have been discharged on medical grounds after breaking an ankle and injuring his back in a parachute jump. In reality, he finagled his way out on spurious medical and psychiatric grounds, for he had come to hate military life and could think only of continuing his musical collaboration with Billy Cox, who was due to be discharged after serving a full term at around the same time.

To a succession of army doctors and psychiatrists he recited a long list of symptoms, most of which his barrack-mates had never noticed: 'dizziness, pain and pressure in the left chest, loss of weight, frequent trouble sleeping, personal problems.' He even claimed to be homosexual – something for which no tolerance yet existed in any armed service – and, almost as fancifully, to need glasses to correct faulty vision in both eyes.

Despite the flimsiness of his case, the 101st made little effort to keep him. His service file described him as 'one of the poorest [i.e. in performance] members of his platoon' who carried out his duties unsatisfactorily, needed constant supervision, possessed no esprit-de-corps and seemed 'an extreme introvert'.

Playing with the Kasuals until all hours often made him late for bed-check and he was always tired and nodding off to sleep while on duty. He was also suspected of 'smoking dope', though no firm evidence had been found. If the homosexuality also remained unproven, there was ample evidence of sexual ill health: one day, when he was meant to be in a fatigue detail, a sergeant had caught him masturbating in the showers.

'He seems unable to conform to military rules and regulations,' the army concluded, 'and his mind apparently cannot function while performing duties and thinking about his guitar.'

He left the army alone, for Billy Cox was not due to be released for another month. He would later concoct the bizarre fiction that he'd sold Betty-Jean, to a fellow serviceman, from whom he would have to buy it back later. 'He never sold his guitar,' scoffs Cox. 'I drove it out of Fort Campbell on the back seat of my car.'

His accumulated back pay amounted to several hundred dollars – more money than he'd ever possessed his life. His immediate intention had been to return to Seattle and marry Betty-Jean Morgan. Instead, he got diverted to a Clarksville jazz club, where he began buying drinks for everyone and very soon had spent all the money but $16.

He thought of sending his father an SOS but the idea of admitting failure to Al, and in particular having blown almost $400,

was too daunting. So he decided to stick around Clarksville, sub-
sisting on what he could earn with the Kasuals – and sneaking
back into the base for meals and even the occasional overnight
stay – until Billy got out, too.

THREE

'I STILL HAVE MY GUITAR AND AMP AND AS LONG AS I HAVE THAT NO FOOL CAN STOP ME LIVING'

The two friends celebrated their freedom from drills and inspections with a promotion, changing the name of their band from the Kasuals to the King Kasuals. Once his hair had grown back from its savage military crop, Jimmy had it straightened (an uncomfortable process involving a solution of corrosive potassium hydroxide) and styled into a conk, the thick wedge favoured by every R&B demigod from Little Richard to James Brown.

With no more bed-call curfew the King Kasuals could widen their radius to Tennessee, Indiana, even North Carolina. Their night's fee was seldom more than $10 between them, which unscrupulous club owners would seize any excuse to cut down or withhold altogether. One man used to slip their money into Billy's or Jimmy's pocket as they were playing; when they checked it later, there would be only a fraction of the agreed amount.

They still stuck to the standard R&B and blues repertoire, although Jimmy loved the new 'surfing' sound coming from California with the almost blindingly white Beach Boys, who had lately watered down Chuck Berry's 'Sweet Little Sixteen' into 'Surfin' USA'. Between gigs, he practised so relentlessly that his bandmates nicknamed him Marbles, meaning he must be losing them. 'He put twenty-five years on the guitar into about five years,' Billy Cox says.

In Indianapolis, they took part in a 'battle of the bands' with a local outfit named the Presidents. Inevitably the audience voted for the home-town boys, but the Presidents' guitarist, Alphonso Young, liked the King Kasuals so much that he volunteered to join them. Young could play a guitar with his teeth in the manner already made famous by the magnificent T-Bone Walker and, for the first time, Jimmy found someone stealing his limelight onstage.

But offstage, nothing could. During his army service he'd metamorphosed from a gawky kid into a young man of devastating good looks, made all the more irresistible to the opposite sex by his shy, thoughtful manner. There was seldom a gig that did not end in him spending the night with one – or more – of the most beautiful young women in the audience. Usually there was nowhere to take them but the bed which, for economic reasons, he shared with Alphonso Young. The unfortunate Alphonso, a devout Jehovah's Witness, would have to lie there and listen to Jimmy doing for real what he himself merely did to guitar strings.

It was a considerable step up for the King Kasuals when Billy Cox secured them a residency at a club named the Del Morocco in Nashville, Tennessee. Located in the district known as Printer's Alley – the city's two newspapers being quartered nearby – it was owned by a prominent Nashville character named 'Uncle' Teddy Acklen and had a celebrity clientele including the baseball superheroes Jackie Robinson and Roy Campanella. For $11 apiece per week, the King Kasuals played on their own or backed solo artistes like Carla Thomas, Nappy Brown and Ironing Board Sam. In 1962, Tennessee still retained prohibition but the police turned a blind eye to brown-bagging – customers bringing in their own liquor.

In this capital of country and western music, most black musicians felt like an embattled minority. However, Jimmy had always admired the dazzling dexterity of country 'pickers' like Chet Atkins and, back in Seattle, never missed the weekly live broadcasts from Nashville's chapel-like Ryman Auditorium, better known as the Grand Ol' Opry. Ordinarily, no greater barrier existed than between this white soul music and the black variety. Only Jimmy, genre-busting even then, was equally at ease playing rockabilly, the fusion of rock and 'hillbilly' that Elvis Presley had first unloosed at the Opry and elsewhere.

Printer's Alley's most glamorous R&B venue was Club Baron whose house band, the Imperials, featured the virtuoso guitarist Johnny Jones. Despite soon spotting a potential rival in the young ex-paratrooper, Jones went out of his way to befriend and encourage him and introduce him to the many guitar stars who passed through. So he got to meet Albert King, a huge, untidy heap of a man with the lightest of touches on the triangular instrument he called his 'flying V', and the dapper B. B. King (no relation) whose cherry-red Epiphone named Lucille, like Jimmy's much-missed mother, delivered a masterclass in less is more. But unlike other young pickers whom these real-life Rocking Kings tended to reduce to dumb adoration, he would boldly ask them for tips about technique.

As well as being a perfect foil to him on bass, Billy Cox was his equal in chutzpah. When the great Bobby 'Blue' Bland came to Club Baron, the pair were refused entry to watch him rehearse. So they sneaked to the utility cupboard, grabbed a bucket and a mop each and got in by pretending to be janitors.

One night, their audience at the Del Morocco included Larry Lee, a laconic student at Texas State University who lived off campus and was a keen, though as yet amateur, guitarist. 'That first time I saw Jimmy I thought he was the worst guitar-player I ever heard,' Lee recalled later. I was looking for a practice buddy, and thought, "That's him." I was just so happy *I* wasn't the worst guitar-player in Nashville.

'Alphonso Young, the other guitarist, he had a big, pretty guitar and Jimmy was just laying back, really doing nothing. When I came back a couple of weeks later, he had a different guitar [an Epiphone Wilshire on the instalment-plan for which Billy Cox stood guarantor] and man did he surprise me.

'I finally met him one night, when he broke a string. I told him I was a guitar player and I stayed right up the street. I brought him a new string and we were friends after that.'

Jimmy's hubris could land him in trouble, as when he challenged the Imperials' great Johnny Jones to a public 'duel', like some young gunslinger trying to take down Wyatt Earp, or Paul Newman as Fast Eddie chancing his arm against the pool *meister* Minnesota Fats in *The Hustler*. In his overconfidence, he used one too many well-known B. B. King tricks, and Jones blasted him off the stage. 'He came looking for a shoot-out,' Larry Lee would recall, 'but he was the one who got himself shot.'

Nashville brought him his first time in a recording studio and this, too, ended badly. After doing some session work for deejay and producer Hoss Allen, Billy Cox persuaded Allen to hire Jimmy as backup for Clarence Frogman Henry, who'd recently stormed the white singles market with 'You Always Hurt the One You Love'. But Allen thought his playing too loud and wiped all the tapes on which he'd played.

In December, impatient with the King Kasuals' lack of progress, he temporarily abandoned them and made his first north-westerly trip home since leaving the army. Not to Seattle – and undoubtedly sticky reunions with Betty-Jean Morgan and his father – but to visit his grandmother, Zenora, in Vancouver.

He stayed long enough to hook up with a local band, Bobby Taylor and the Vancouvers, with a regular spot at a club named

Dante's Inferno. They shared his musical open-mindedness, alternating R&B with some of the shiny new tracks now pouring from Detroit's Motown label like an automotive production line, and even the odd splash of 'surf'. Jimmy had to accept demotion to rhythm guitar as the Vancouvers already had a strong lead player, the part-Chinese Tommy Chong, who would find greater fame in the comedy duo Cheech and Chong. But it was worth it to be with Zenora , listening to her stories of Cherokees, slaves and minstrels – and not have to face Al or Betty-Jean.

For generations, racism in America was as nonsensical as it was brutal. When Hattie McDaniel became the first African American to win an Oscar, as best supporting actress for her performance as Mammy in *Gone With the Wind*, she was excluded from the film's premiere in Atlanta, Georgia, and had to sit apart from its white stars at the 1940 awards ceremony. No matter how internationally famous entertainers like Sammy Davis Jr., Harry Belafonte, Lena Horne and Nat King Cole might become, they were barred from staying at the Las Vegas hotels in whose cabaret rooms they appeared, even as their names soared up giant billboards outside.

Black music in all its forms – ragtime, jazz, blues, R&B – had evolved under the same apartheid as lunch-counters and washrooms, banished to a netherworld of so-called 'race' or 'speciality' records, radio stations and films in which even the great Louis Armstrong might pop up, demeaningly clad in a waiter's jacket. Yet the white people on whom it was supposedly such a corrupting and debasing influence, had always illicitly listened to and loved it. Jazz, in the end, involved too many whites and too much money to stay in that aural ghetto but the less easily homogenised blues and R&B still seemed literally beyond the pale.

Since the 1920s, there had existed a continent-wide network

of dedicated black music venues (though whites were never excluded with anything like the same ferocity as blacks from white ones). This was known with humorous self-deprecation as the Chitlin' Circuit – chitterlings, or pigs' intestines, being among the soul food dishes sold in such places. It included some large, often famous theatres like the Apollo in New York's Harlem, the Royal in Chicago or the Regal in Baltimore, but consisted largely of clubs, dance halls and juke-joints.

For artistes on the Chitlin' Circuit, the main problems arose from travelling the often immense distances by road to and from engagements. The majestic Duke Ellington avoided them all by chartering luxurious Pullman railroad coaches for himself and his orchestra, but others faced an ever-present risk of being pulled over by the police, often for the offence of driving too good a car or wearing too expensive clothes. When Little Richard arrived in uber-segregated Lubbock, Texas, to visit his friend Buddy Holly, he was arrested for 'vagrancy' despite having $2,000 in his wallet.

There was also the problem of eating when the roadside phantasmagoria of neon harboured so many NO COLORED signs. Here at least, the growth of colour-blind fast-food chains from the late 1950s can be accounted a positive social advance. 'Shall I tell you who saved us from starving to death?' Wilson Pickett, one of Jimmy's many Chitlin' Circuit employers, said to the present writer in 1973. 'It was Colonel Sanders!'

Jimmy did not properly join the circuit until early 1963, after he returned to Nashville to rejoin Billy Cox and try to reinvigorate the King Kasuals. They expanded to a six-piece with two horn players and, to be more of a 'revue', added an emcee who told jokes and did impressions.

But bad luck seemed to dog the band: they lost their residency at the Del Morocco but were unable to manage the next upward step to the elite Club Baron. The perk from one of their employers of a rent-free house backfired when its front door was shot up in an obviously racially motivated attack. Only then did they discover that the house's owner was currently on trial for killing a white man.

Then they lost Alphonso Young, from whom Jimmy had learned guitar fellatio. As a Jehovah's Witness, Young had been sorely tried by having to share beds with Jimmy and his ever-changing sexual partners. But the breaking point was the quantities of amphetamines, or 'Red Devils', he (like many others) was taking to help him stay awake through the long performing night. Fortunately, a replacement was to hand in Larry Lee, his faithful follower and provider of replacement guitar strings, who dropped out of Texas State without a qualm.

Their income as musicians being insufficient to sustain life, five of the six King Kasuals took part-time 'real' jobs. Only Jimmy refused to sacrifice hours that might be spent in playing or practising. 'He always used to say that when he was famous one day, he would have a thousand guitars,' Lee would recall. 'He didn't say "if", he said "when". At that time I figured that if he made it, he would do it on the guitar alone. I had no idea he would ever sing.'

His was a hand-to-mouth, often homeless existence, although not so very different from much of his childhood. In Nashville, he spent some weeks squatting in a building under construction, managing to conceal his nest and slip away each morning before the building crew arrived.

When the King Kasuals could keep going no longer, Jimmy, Billy Cox and Lee stayed together, hiring themselves out as a unit to bands with better prospects – and so joining the Chitlin' Circuit in earnest. As part of Bob Fisher and the Bonnevilles, they toured with Motown's first successful female vocal group, the Marvelettes, and the Impressions, whose leader Curtis Mayfield, like Jimmy, was destined to go solo with spectacular results and, also like him, die way too soon. When he began writing and recording his own songs, echoes of Mayfield's creamy-sweet guitar style constantly crept in. 'You can hear Curtis in 'Little Wing'',' Billy Cox says. 'And in "Castles Made Of Sand" and "Drifting".'

After a time, Cox and Larry Lee peeled off for the more settled lives of session musicians in Nashville, and Jimmy ex-soldiered on alone. During this year of his 21st birthday, he played for such Circuit veterans as Chuck Jackson, Carla Thomas, Slim Harpo, Tommy Tucker, Jerry Butler and Marion James. 'He always had good jobs,' his brother Leon recalls, 'because when he joined one band, a better one would always come along and steal him.

'Jimmy really didn't care if he was in a good band or not – he just wanted to play. All he'd asked them was "Where are we on, how do I get there and can you please get my guitar out of the pawnshop?"'

From the bottom of the bill, he studied and absorbed the stagecraft and showmanship of headliners like Sam Cooke, Jackie Wilson and Otis Redding – three more too-early departures. The first star's band in which he played was that of the 250lb Solomon Burke, who performed seated on a throne in a royal crown and ermine-trimmed robes and who, rather less regally, sold his own pork sandwiches and Solomon Burke Magic Popcorn out in the vestibule.

None of these jobs lasted for long. If he wasn't fired for stealing his employer's limelight onstage, it would be his chronic lateness for tour-bus departures. In an unpleasant echo of service life, some headliners fined their musicians for lapses in discipline; $10 for unpunctuality, $5 for dirty shoes and so on. Many a time, Jimmy's fines would almost wipe out a whole week's pay.

Curtis Mayfield expelled him for accidentally damaging an amplifier. On a tour with Bobby Womack, his behaviour was so exasperating that Womack's road manager brother threw his guitar out of the bus window while he was asleep. After a few days with the Solomon Burke revue, Burke bartered him on to Otis Redding in exchange for two horn players as if he was little more than a modern-day slave. A couple of weeks later, there were more problems about his too-flashy playing and Redding literally ditched him, driving off and leaving him at the side of the road.

Generally there would be another gig for him to step into and if ever he did find himself workless and broke, he knew he could return to the inexhaustibly kind-hearted, supportive Billy Cox in Nashville. 'Bill would always take him in, give him money and find him a job,' Brenda Cox recalls.

He knew he was on a treadmill from which many superb original talents – like Bobby Bland or the Mighty Hannibal, who taught James Brown his stage moves – would never escape. 'Bad pay, lousy living and gettin' burned' was how he would remember the Chitlin' Circuit. But through all those hard-sweating nights of playing formulaic chords behind vocalists he often despised, his optimism and self-belief remained undented.

'I still have my guitar and amp and as long as I have that, no fool can stop me living,' he wrote to his father. 'I'm going to keep hustling and scuffling until I get things to happening like they're supposed to for me.'

One night after some unmemorable show at some nameless joint, a booking agent approached him with a vague offer of work in New York. It was enough for him to make his way there in January 1964, sitting at the rear of the bus as black passengers in those days were made to do, a borrowed overcoat his only defence against the city's Arctic winter. But the promise of work proved an empty one and he was left stranded with only a few dollars in his pocket and no Billy Cox to come to his rescue.

Inevitably, he gravitated to the uptown quarter named Harlem by New York's first Dutch settlers but since the nineteenth century its black population's run-down home and world-renowned creative heart. For there on West 125th Street stood the (white-owned) Apollo Theater, the jewel in the Chitlin' Circuit's perspiring crown, where innumerable music legends of earlier generations had been given their first big break, from Billie Holliday, Pearl Bailey and Bo Jangles Robinson to Sammy Davis Jr., King Curtis and James Brown.

The Apollo held weekly amateur talent nights, where Ella Fitzgerald had famously been discovered and the audience was famously uninhibited in expressing its disapproval. A near-desperate Jimmy entered one contest devoted entirely to young musicians and was saved from destitution in the nick of time by winning the $25 first prize.

But winning an Apollo talent night was no passport to finding regular employment there. When Sam Cooke came in to play a one-nighter a few days later, Jimmy was just one of the crowd milling around 125th Street, roughly supervised by cops in their elegant double-breasted tunics.

Cooke had been the first R&B (or, more specifically, gospel) performer to enjoy major success in the white balladeer market with a succession of astutely chosen pop songs, backed up by the elegance and charm of a latter-day Nat King Cole. Thanks to his white manager, Allen Klein, he had recently signed to the RCA label for a $100,000 advance against royalties – then an unheard-of investment in any recording artiste, black or white.

Jimmy had known Cooke on the Chitlin' Circuit, but not well enough to get backstage at the Apollo to say 'hello'. Outside, however, he fell into conversation with a spectacular young woman in a tight pegged skirt and killer high heels, to whom that exotic region was almost a second home.

Lithofayne – 'Fayne' – Pridgon was only two years his senior, but already seemed to have lived many lifetimes longer. Born in Dirty Spoon, Georgia, she was the daughter of a professional 'hoofer' and, reputedly, the illegitimate great-granddaughter of the motor magnate, Henry Ford. At fifteen, she had begun an affair with Little Willie John, whose song 'Fever' sold a million for the white chanteuse Peggy Lee, and at sixteen she had been seduced by Sam Cooke. If that wasn't enough to get her onto the Apollo's VIP list, she was also Etta James's best friend.

Fayne offered to take Jimmy backstage to see Cooke, despite feeling 'he didn't cut much of a figure . . . He had processed hair and shiny black pants that showed where the knees bent,' she told *Gallery* magazine in 1983. 'But he had something about him, a warmth, that none of the other fast-rapping dudes had. He referred to Sam as what's-his-face and he thanked me for getting him to what's-his-face.'

Afterwards, Fayne took him home to be fed by her mother, when he 'ate and ate'; by evening they were in bed and the next day he moved into the room she shared with a friend at the inexpensive Hotel Seifer. 'It wasn't hard because he was carrying all his possessions around in his guitar case. He didn't have underwear. He wasn't into jeans. He had those shiny black pants, a very thin little jacket and high-topped boots.'

She recalled him above all her musician lovers as 'relentless in the sack. And he came to the bed with all the grace a Mississippi pulpwood driver attacks a plate of collard greens and cornbread after 10 hours in the hot sun. There would be encore after encore after encore . . . There were times when he almost busted me in two the way he did a guitar onstage.

'Jimmy loved fooling around with his guitar in bed and he always slept with it. Many times he fell back asleep with it on his chest. Any time I tried to remove it, he woke up and said, "No, no, no, leave my guitar alone." Funny thing was, he couldn't read a note of music and was terribly afraid someone would find out.'

Yet he also had more sensitivity and depth than either of his performer predecessors. 'Little Willie John and Sam Cooke . . .

they could sing the hell out of some love song . . . but they were all, as we used to say, from city to city and titty to titty.' Jimmy, by contrast, wrote her passionate, poetic love letters, which she still has.

He was also fiercely possessive and her naturally bold, flirtatious manner, which had first drawn them together, became unacceptable once they were a couple. When he began to get gigs in clubs and she went with him, she was forbidden to dance with other men except in uptempo numbers where there'd be no body contact. 'One night this cutie pie at a place in Harlem where Jimmy was playing kept leaping around tables to get me on the dance floor. Jimmy saw this and leapt off the stage with his guitar, dragging the cord and amplifier with him. He rapped the guy over the noggin with the guitar and told him to leave his old lady alone. The cord got wrapped around people's legs and they were falling all over the place. It was wild and terrible . . . but that's what life was like with Jimmy.'

After the fracas, none of the better Harlem clubs would employ him and he had to take whatever he could get, at one point backing a stripper named Pantera who worked with a snake. He even tried non-musical jobs, like delivering cars, but none ever lasted longer than a week. He spent the days holed up in Fayne's room at the Hotel Seifer, playing his guitar or tending to his conk, his only vanity. 'I can still see him as he used to open the door in his usual outfit, naked except for a greasy do-rag [headband] which held his process [hair] so tight in place that his eyes slanted.'

Fayne's contacts included Harlem's biggest drug dealer, 'Fat Jack' Taylor, who offered him a job as a pusher. Jimmy had known about marijuana since hanging out with Ray Charles, and amphetamines were the Chitlin' Circuit's lifeblood, but he wanted nothing to do with the hard stuff that was Fat Jack's principal stock-in-trade.

*

Finally, in early February, his luck seemed to change. Somehow or other, his name reached the Isley Brothers, at that time seemingly the only black vocal group not engineered by Motown in Detroit, who happened to need a new backing guitarist. The Isleys tracked him down and invited him to audition at their collective home in Teaneck, New Jersey.

The youngest, Ernie Isley, then aged eleven and not yet in the act, remembers the occasion well. 'When he arrived, he said he couldn't audition because his guitar was in the pawnshop. We got it out for him, but he said he couldn't play it because it had no strings, so we got him the strings.'

Older brother Ron continues: 'He said, "I liked something you all done called 'Twist and Shout'."' Even then, it seems, he knew how to pull off a dazzling cover version. 'Man, I never heard anything like it. We hired him after about thirty seconds.'

'Then he said he couldn't make rehearsals out in New Jersey because he didn't have a place to stay,' Ernie Isley recalls. 'He had all his worldly goods with him, so we said, "OK, there's a spare room at our mother's house that you can have."'

Even with all six strings present and correct, Ron decided his current guitar would not do for the Isley Brothers. 'We told him, "We gotta get you a new axe, man, what do you want?' He said, "Can I have a white Stratocaster?" We said, "Sure" and he was like "Oh, my GOD!" With that, he was the star of the band before the first rehearsal was over.'

He had been with the Isleys only a couple of days when the Beatles landed in New York, shattering America's immemorial resistance to British pop music. They had absorbed R&B from the crews of the transatlantic liners that docked in Liverpool, and were now exporting it back to its homeland with a pudding-basin haircut and a salty tang of Liverpudlian wit. Indeed, the Isleys' 'Twist and Shout' was practically their signature tune.

Two nights later, they appeared on CBS TV's *Ed Sullivan Show*, so riveting the nation's attention that crime in all of New York's five boroughs came to a temporary halt. Jimmy was already considered 'family' enough to be watching the programme with the Isleys. Afterwards, the oldest brother and bandleader, Kelly, called a meeting, warning the others that everything in music was now about to change.

'Kelly told us,"We don't know what the future holds, even for Elvis,"' Ron Isley recalls. '"But at least we've got Jimmy."'

FOUR

'EVERYTHING'S SO-SO IN THIS BIG RAGGEDY CITY OF NEW YORK'

His first recording session since the abortive one with Clarence Frogman Henry in Nashville was for the Isley Brothers' first single on their own T-Neck label. Entitled 'Testify', it lasted six minutes, a colossal length for those days, and flouted the convention of separate A- and B-sides by overflowing from one to the other.

It was essentially a comedy record, a parody of a revivalist meeting, with impersonations of other artistes like Ray Charles, Jackie Wilson and Stevie Wonder, and some Beatly ululations in good humoured payback for their appropriation of 'Twist and Shout'. The white Stratocaster took only one brief solo – but there, for a few soaring seconds, Jimmy turned into Jimi.

Back in New York, he began to get further work as a studio musician, playing on Bobby Freeman's 'C'mon and Swim', latest in a seemingly endless succession of dance crazes, and Don Covay and the Goodtimers' 'Mercy Mercy'. The latter became the first record he appeared on to make the Top 40, but Jimmy profited little from it. 'For that one,' his brother Leon remembers, 'he got ten dollars, a Denny's dinner and a carton of cigarettes.'

Meanwhile, the so-promising job with the Isley Brothers had come to an end, for in live shows even that amiable fraternity imposed the conformism he found so oppressive: 'white patent leather suits, patent leather shoes and patent leather hairdos, with fines if your shoelaces didn't match'. So, 'family' or not, he quit to join a tour of the South with Gorgeous George, a performer inspired by the white all-in wrestler of the same name who likewise wore a cape, as if about to go ten rounds with Primo Carnera, and a curly blond wig.

The Gorgeous George tour took him through Memphis, where the blues was said to have first cohered as a genre on Beale Street and Elvis Presley – who had learned so much there – still kept Graceland, his plantation-style mansion, though nowadays often away in Hollywood, making terrible movies.

The city's main point of interest for Jimmy was the Stax record label, home to some of his favourite soul acts, like Otis Redding, Sam and Dave, and Rufus Thomas, yet owned by a white brother and sister, Jim Stewart and Estelle Axton (hence the company's name). Deep in the Jim Crow South though it was, Stax carried this biraciality through to its employees and its house band, Booker T. and the M.G.'s, whose instrumental 'Green Onions', featuring a super-funky guitarist named Steve Cropper, had been a huge hit single in 1962.

Dropping by Stax on the off-chance of meeting Cropper, Jimmy was told he was in the studio and couldn't be disturbed, but nonetheless sat waiting in the front lobby, as it turned out, for the rest of the day. Then when Cropper finally appeared, the long-seasoned soul brother he'd visualised proved to be a towering white man only a year his senior with the look of a revivalist preacher.

The admiration was by no means one-sided, for Cropper loved the riffs that Jimmy had played, uncredited, on Don Covay's 'Mercy Mercy'. He took Jimmy to dinner, then back to the Stax studio for an extended duologue between themselves and their guitars.

In Atlanta, Georgia, Jimmy missed the Gorgeous George tour bus and was considering his not-very-plentiful options when another bus pulled in, carrying a personage he'd seen almost tearing apart the pulpit of Seattle's Baptist Pentecostal church five years earlier. Little Richard's vocation as a minister had soon waned and he was back to performing, albeit not quite at the same level as when he'd stood at the summit of the white pop market as a rock 'n' roll pioneer. Superstar in Britain and Europe though he might still be, America had him firmly re-anchored on the Chitlin' Circuit.

His band, the Upsetters, currently lacked a guitar player and Jimmy applied for the job, taking care to mention the Hendrix family's (very slight) acquaintanceship with his aunt, Mrs Penniman, in Seattle. According to Richard's autobiography, *The Quasar of Rock*, 'My manager [Seattle-born Bumps Blackwell] who knew Jimmy's folks ... rang Mr Hendrix to see if it was OK for him to join us. Al Hendrix told Bumps, "Jimmy just idolizes Richard. He would eat ten yards of shit to join his band."

'I will never forget Jimmy loading his belongings on the bus. His guitar was wrapped in a potato sack like Johnny B. Goode in the song and it only had five strings on it.' Evidently the ravishing white Fender Strat and its matching case had had to be left behind with the Isleys' white leather suits.

It is always said that he made the worst move of his life in signing up with black music's supreme extrovert and that Little Richard did more to stifle his nascent talent than all his other narcissistic and domineering frontmen put together. Not unnaturally, Richard himself claims to have nurtured Jimmy just as he did the Beatles and the Rolling Stones, directly or by example. 'He didn't mind looking freaky, like I don't mind it. 'Cos I was doing it before he was. I know that when he saw me, it gave him confidence and recompense and reward, oh my Lord.'

For once, the Quasar of Rock may not be indulging in his usual flights of fancy (as when recalling Al Hendrix being so well-acquainted with his son's musical tastes). 'Richard didn't hide Jimmy,' a former member of the Upsetters testifies. 'He used to allow him to do that playing-with-the-teeth thing and take solos. Richard taught Hendrix a lot of things and Hendrix copied a lot of things from Richard. That's where he got the charisma.'

But at the time, the best thing about the gig for Jimmy was his unprecedented monthly wage of $200. Little Richard classics like 'Tutti Frutti' and 'Good Golly Miss Molly' – which the singer now varied with interludes of preaching or striptease or sometimes both – had arrangments set in stone as well as rock, with no deviations permitted. Once again, too, the backing musicians had to observe a strict dress code of matching suits, the smallest departure from which meant a fine – and, in Jimmy's case, could also unleash a petulant roar from his boss of 'I am the only one allowed to be pretty!'

Richard had never made a secret of being bisexual, and Jimmy would claim to have received advances from him although self-evidently the last young man in the world likely to respond. 'After Jimmy was dead, I met Richard in Canada and he told me the two of them had had an affair,' Leon Hendrix says. 'I got so mad, I just went for him. I mean fisticuffs.'

In Los Angeles, the Upsetters were given a rare night off to bring in the New Year, 1965. Jimmy spent it watching the Ike and Tina Turner revue at the Californian Club. Later that evening, he got off with twenty-year-old Rosa Lee Brooks, a singer with an all-female vocal group who had more than a touch of Etta James. His chat-up line – one he often used, to invariable effect – was that she reminded him of his mother.

Rosa Lee owned a Chevrolet Impala, one of that era's coolest cars, and was soon driving Jimmy up and down LA's fabled Sunset Strip, still umbilically joined to his guitar. Half a century later, as a solo singer, she would recall, 'We owned that place. We soared like two eagles with our wings tip-to-tip.'

The West Coast music scene, still dominated by the Beach Boys' surfing sound, attracted him enormously despite its gold crew cut, Bermuda-shorted whiteness. Accompanying Rosa Lee to one of her gigs, he fell into conversation with Glen Campbell, then still years away from singing stardom with 'By the Time I Get to Phoenix' and 'Wichita Lineman' and an anonymous studio muscian and occasional stand-in Beach Boy. Jimmy already knew what many throughout Campbell's later career did not, that he was a guitar player at the level of Chet Atkins or Jerry Reed, and sought tips on technique from him as assiduously as from Albert or B. B .King.

Through Rosa Lee, he came into the orbit of a performer who did not resist musical apartheid so much as totally ignore it. This was Arthur Lee, who already played surf music and Byrds-style electric folk and would soon form the first biracial rock band, Love, and call himself 'the first black hippy'. He was also a noted eccentric, given to wearing only one shoe and dark glasses he couldn't see through. When Rosa Lee James recorded Lee's song 'My Diary' for the tiny Revis label, Jimmy was hired to play on the session, but only on the basis of his ability to mimic Curtis Mayfield.

From LA he wrote to his father that from now on he'd be using the stage name Maurice James. Maurice as Americans pronounce it, 'Mo-reece', has a classier sound than in Britain, where it suggests golf club secretaries and pub bores. The 'James' was not an inversion of his Christian name but a nod to the great blues slide guitarist Elmore James.

His affair with Rosa Lee caused further tension with Little Richard, who tended to make most women feel uncomfortable and, in this case, may have been feeling some competitive envy. She would later claim – uncontradicted by him – that he'd once asked to be allowed to watch while she and Jimmy made love.

After the next spat with Richard, he quit and walked straight into the Ike and Tina Turner revue, which he'd been watching with admiration on the night he met Rosa Lee. Ike Turner had made what is generally agreed to be the first-ever rock 'n' roll track, 'Rocket 88', and had lately brought his wife, the former Anna Mae Bullock, to the fore as a singer and stupendous dancer who for many years would keep secret the domestic violence she suffered at at his hands.

Tina's control-freak spouse had no more sympathy with Jimmy's stylistic adventures than any of his predecessors. 'I cut him loose because he had all these pedals on a board for fuzz and distortion,' Turner would recall. 'By the time he'd get through pushing the pedals, the solo spot would be over.'

In a couple of weeks, he was back with the Upsetters, where his disobedience to their dress code turned into open baiting of Little Richard. On the night of a big show at Huntington Beach, Rosa Lee curled his hair and he went onstage in a woman's blouse and black wide-brimmed hat of the kind Rudolph Valentino used to wear to dance the bolero in silent movies.

When the troupe moved on from LA, he promised Rosa Lee he'd soon return for more drives along Sunset and 'wingtip-touching'. Some time later, he sent her a letter asking for money to get his guitar out of hock – another reliable gambit with the opposite sex. She sent back $40, enclosing a photograph of herself, but never heard from him again.

Travelling through the South was an even more tense experience than usual for a black roadshow on the cusp of 1965 as the Civil Rights movement and the National Association for the Advancement of Colored People (NAACP) came into confrontation with those sworn to perpetuate segregation at any cost.

It was the time of the charismatic young demagogue known as Malcolm X, his call to black people to abandon pacifism and restraint for violent insurgency, and his assassination, at a meeting of his followers in New York'; the time when 3,000 peaceful demonstrators, marching from Selma, Alabama, with Dr Martin Luther King at their head, were brutally set upon by police with batons, tear gas and dogs, and when Sam Cooke, potentially the Civil Rights movement's most influential voice after Dr King, was shot dead during a trivial altercation with the (black) manageress of a Los Angeles motel. Little Richard, usually travelling between gigs by air, could stay above the fallout from these and other related horror stories, but for his band, the affronts and threats from roadside restaurants and washrooms were redoubled.

Jimmy's frustration was not only with his job but with black music as a whole. For the creative initiative was wholly with white pop, now termed 'rock', and suddenly dealing with all the big issues of the day, the Vietnam War, the inequality of society, even the segregation question itself.

In reaction to the Beatles and the 'British Invasion' that came afterwards, dozens of white American bands were springing up, especially on the West Coast he had just left, who performed in unmatching garments like Britain's Rolling Stones under names even more outlandish than 'Beatles', such as Jefferson Airplane and the Grateful Dead. Theirs was a genuinely new music, openly acknowledged to derive from a man-made – and still legal – hallucinogen named lysergic acid diethylamide (LSD), which seemed to affect the very guitars, furring and distorting them in all kinds of intriguing ways, and inspiring lyrics like the poetry Jimmy had always scribbled in secret, But for now, even LSD bore a WHITES ONLY sign.

Meanwhile, even the Chitlin' Circuit's biggest names carried on in the same old way, with fizzing horn sections, raunchily upbeat lyrics, formation dancing, wide smiles and pressed trousers. July 1965 brought Jimmy's first television appearance, backing a male vocal duo named Buddy and Stacey in Junior

Walker's 'Shotgun' for the *Night Train* show, transmitted from Nashville. The footage can still be seen on YouTube. Behind the dancing, smiling, well-pressed duo, dark-suited and bow-tied, ducking his head left and right in sync with his fellow sidemen, it's as if the shotgun is pointed at his head.

His unpunctuality and sartorial offences continued to worsen until finally, after an appearance at the Apollo, he missed the tour bus to Washington DC and Richard's road manager brother, Robert Penniman, fired him, making clear that this time it was for keeps. The Isley Brothers good-naturedly took him back for a month's residency at a New Jersey resort, after which he returned to New York, all his pay from Little Richard either spent or eaten up by fines, and thus no better off than when he'd first arrived there two years earlier.

He began looking for work as a studio musician, but could find it only with obscure artistes and tiny record companies. A diminutive soul singer with a Little Richard-sized voice known as Mr Wiggles hired him as – uncredited – back up for a series of singles on the Golden Triangle label. His contributions were never less than spectacular, especially to a talking blues entitled 'Homeboy', although one line that patently did not apply to Mr Wiggles did so even less to him: 'Went to New York, made it good . . .'

Once again, his former Harlem girlfriend, Fayne Pridgon, took him in, despite having since acquired a husband named TaharQa. When three became too much a crowd in Fayne's tiny apartment, Jimmy moved on to a series of cheap hotels around Times Square, which in the Manhattan of that era could come perilously close to dosshouses.

He continued to write regularly to his father, half the time building himself up and half putting himself down before Al could, if Al should ever reply. 'You may hear a record from me that sounds terrible,' he wrote in August 1965. ' Don't be ashamed, just wait until the money rolls in.' The letter was signed 'Maurice James' but he was now also using the names Jimmy James or Jimmy Jim.

In October, he joined another R&B band, Curtis Knight and the Squires, whose frontman he had first met the previous year. He felt some initial qualms since Knight combined running the Squires with pimping, but freelance session work had virtually dried up.

This time, the only travelling involved was to low-level gigs like George's 20 Club in Hackensack, New Jersey. He still had to wear a suit – this time, a sparkly tuxedo – but Knight let him play his guitar behind his head or with his teeth as much as he wished. And the quintet contained one other serious musician, a sax player named Lonnie Youngblood with whom he became close friends.

That October, Knight and the Squires were signed by a white record producer named Ed Chalpin who owned his own small independent label, PPX. Though technically Jimmy was just part of Knight's package deal with Chalpin, the producer was astute enough to offer him a separate three-year contract to 'play and produce' exclusively on PPX. For signing the contract, which he didn't bother to read – and which would cause him problems for the rest of his life – he received only one dollar, but was promised the first royalties of his career, 1 per cent of the retail price of every record sold.

Chalpin specialised in quickie cover versions of current hit singles, and one of the first assigned to Curtis Knight and the Squires was Bob Dylan's 'Like a Rolling Stone'. Jimmy had admired Dylan since the latter's days as a folk singer and pillar of the Civil Rights movement, though it was not a taste generally shared by hip young Harlem-ites. In his early days there, he'd once persuaded a club's deejay to play 'Blowin' in the Wind' and had been ridiculed for liking 'that hillbilly music'.

Now, Dylan stood accused of 'betraying' his folk audience and the Civil Rights cause by switching from acoustic to amplified guitar, to create his own languid, sneering brand of rock. But Jimmy loved 'electric' Dylan: when 'Like a Rolling Stone' came out as a single, he had already spent every cent in his pocket at the time on its parent album, *Highway 61 Revisited*.

Even Chalpin's cheapo product and a third-rate R&B band could not stop Jimmy's transformative way with covers shining forth. Dylan's sourly exuberant electric ode was meant to have been his final repudiation of the protest song. Now, retitled 'How Would You Feel?' it became just that, speaking directly to black Americans about the wrongs they suffered and their young men's obligation nonetheless to fight for the country in Vietnam. Spoken not sung, it was like rap twenty years too early.

But at other times, he could make no impression on Chalpin's raw material, as when he backed the Hollywood actress Jayne Mansfield in a breathy ballad entitled 'As the Clouds Drift By', totally drowned out by its string section. Actually, he was lucky even to be allowed near violins. Until recently – as his fellow Garfield High student, Quincy Jones, recalls – black arrangers had not been allowed to use strings, presumably because it implied a sophistication of which they were incapable.

Towards the end of the year, an old syndrome revived when he was poached from Curtis Knight by Joey Dee and the Starliters. They had shot to fame during the Twist craze as house band at New York's Peppermint Lounge, one of the Beatles' first ports of call on arriving in 1964. What had gone unnoticed amid all the Beatlemania and Twisting was that Italian-American Joey Dee headed the first biracial pop line-up (of three white musicians and three black) whose audience was predominantly white.

'He came to my house in New Jersey to audition,' Dee would remember. 'He takes his guitar out, it was in an old sack because he couldn't afford a case, I said "Play me something you like", and he plays some Curtis Mayfield.

'I tell him he's got the gig and to celebrate he lights up a big joint. I had my two boys, aged four and five, in the house and my wife says, "What the hell do you think you're doing?" and throws him straight out. As he goes through the door, I look out the window and say, "See you Friday."'

The Twist might now be history, but nostalgia for the age of the bouffant and the hula-hoop remained strong and the Starliters regularly played to crowds as large as 10,000. Though Joey was the star of the show with his oscillating midriff, he gave Jimmy plenty of room to play guitar behind his head or do the splits as the fancy took him.

A countrywide tour – during which Jimmy turned 23 – showed the true scale of Joey Dee's innovation. For the dates included several in places where a mixed-race band aroused even more detestation than an all-black one. To avoid trouble, they would stay in hotels up to fifty miles from the venue and take care never to leave the backstage areas during intermissions.

A bad case of late-blooming acne put no brake on Jimmy's sex life. In Buffalo, three women from India who had not even seen the show clamoured to sleep with him, saying he had 'the face of a Hindu god'. At another stop, a white woman volunteered to go to bed with all the Starliters at once. She later recalled Jimmy as the only one with the good manners to ask if he should take off his boots first.

One night, he had a dream in the lavish Technicolor of a Hollywood movie that 1966 would be when everything miraculously began to come right for him. It was in fact a very old dream, dating back to when a little boy still known as Buster would see the numbers one, nine and two sixes in his sleep, then awake with 'a strange feeling that I was here for something and that I was going to have a chance to be heard'. But until well into the year, there seemed to be no sign of it.

Much as he liked Joey Dee, and enjoyed troilistic romps with Indian ladies, he'd wearied of playing 'The Peppermint Twist' in the same way ('One-two-three kick, one-two-three jump!') night after night, so had quit before Christmas. January found him back in New York, his pay all spent and once again staring destitution in the face.

It was a particularly harsh winter, especially for someone with no overcoat nor even a lining to his jacket. He would huddle for warmth for hours in coffee shops, often unable to afford more than their 50-cent minimum for a glass of water, his long sprinter's legs carefully positioned to hide the holes in his ice-sodden shoes. Facing eviction from his hotel room for rent arrears, he still found the money for a postcard with a view of the Empire State Building to send to his father. 'Everything's so-so in this big raggedy city of New York,' he wrote. 'Everything's happening bad here.'

One day, in a coffee shop tormentingly named the Ham 'n' Eggs, his obvious predicament aroused the pity of a fellow customer who might have been thought even more pitiable. She was Diane Carpenter, a runaway from Minnesota whom the big raggedy city had forced into prostitution aged only sixteen. Despite the threatening presence of her pimp, Jimmy started to talk to her and was able to summon enough of his usual spirit to tell her she reminded him of his mother.

This having had its usual effect, he moved into the tiny room where Diane carried on her trade. Her neighbours in the building assumed that he was her pimp and, indeed, he sometimes had to act as her protector when one of her 'johns' turned nasty. Yet despite the poverty and squalor of their life together, his Technicolor dream kept its hold. If ever they passed a jewellery store, he would tell Diane he'd buy her everything in the window when he was famous. Like others before her, she noticed the 'when' rather than 'if'.

Diane was of the same concern to welfare authorities that Jimmy used to be, and at one point she was picked up by the police and put on a bus back to her parents' home in Minneapolis, When she found her way to him again, she became pregnant, thereby losing her former source of income, except from very peculiar 'johns'. Soon the two of them were reduced to shoplifting to survive.

After they'd been chased by a storekeeper with a baseball bat and only narrowly escaped, Diane went back to hustling again without telling Jimmy. His anger when he found out unlocked a strain of violence he'd never shown before, manifested in a way which had caused him so much pain and fear – and not just as a child. Momentarily turning into his father, he hit her with his belt.

As her pregnancy advanced, Diane decided to return to Minneapolis and have her baby there. The following February, she would give birth to a daughter, Tamika Laurice, whom she registered under Jimmy's stage surname of James although – for the present – making no claim on him for child support.

While still living with Diane, he had begun seeing his first white girlfriend, Carol Shiroky, a step up the social ladder in being a call girl rather than a streetwalker. This made her relatively affluent and in no time she'd been persuaded to buy him a new guitar, a Fender Jazzmaster whose customised carry-case put an end at last to that faithful old potato sack.

Unlike most white women in those days, Carol was heavily into black music, and knew many performers outside Jimmy's insular, predictable R&B set. Among them was a West Indian named Mike Quashie who had been on the cover of *Life* magazine for introducing limbo-dancing to America (when it was seized on by Chubby Checker as a successor to the Twist) and would be an even greater influence on the future Jimi Hendrix than Albert Lee.

Quashie, aka 'the Spider King', worked at a West Side club called the African Room, where he would go onstage in a bishop's mitre-shaped hat, a leather leotard and boots with eight-inch heels, and somehow manouevre his six-foot-two-inch frame under a limbo-pole only seven inches from the ground. A technical pioneer, too, for the garish lighting, smoke and pyrotechnics claimed by new 'psychedelic' rock bands as their own LSD-inspired milieu had been part of the Spider King's act for years.

Like Albert Lee, Quashie refused to recognise the concurrently emerging hippy culture as for whites only and swapped his bishop's mitre and leotard for Eastern kaftans, headbands and mystical amulets, urging Jimmy to do likewise. But for the present, if he wanted to eat, he had to stick to a jacket and tie.

The smash hit of the moment across singles charts of all pigmentation was Percy Sledge's piledrivingly honest 'When a Man Loves a Woman'. At the launch party thrown by Atlantic Records, a tuxedoed Jimmy with his new Jazzmaster backed Wilson Pickett in Pickett's own huge hit, 'Mustang Sally' – having already covered it many times with Curtis Knight and the Squires. But it wasn't long now before Pickett would be covering him.

In April 1966, *Time* magazine published a cover story, dubbing London 'the style capital of Europe' and describing the explosion of youthful creativity that had taken place among its Victorian monuments and red buses, not only in America-invading bands like the Beatles and Rolling Stones but in fashion, art and design. With *Time*'s story came a fresh wave of irresistible British singles including 'Wild Thing', originally released in the US by the Wild Ones, now covered by a quartet of seeming Neolithic cavemen named the Troggs. Carol Shiroky found Jimmy practising it in her apartment, and already taking it miles further.

By May, he was back with Curtis Knight and the Squires, but hated it so much that he soon quit again. His last appearance with them was to be at the Cheetah Club at 53rd and Broadway, a barn of a place, wallpapered in spotted fur and theoretically able to accommodate 2,000 people, but in their case never attracting anything like that number.

Here, where his Technicolor dream seemed furthest away, it would finally start coming true.

FIVE

'I'VE GOT JUST THE PERSON FOR YOU'

Any history of race relations in the twentieth century would have to include the sizeable contribution of young white British musicians during the 1960s by their devotion to and dissemination of black American music. In an era when travel to America was only for the rich and domestic radio the monopoly of the stuffy, puritanical BBC, it's a miracle they ever found it in the first place. Yet by 1965, they had built blues and R&B into a youth craze running alongside Beatlemania, but much cooler.

Even at its considerable commercial height, this had none of the barefaced exploitation its originators had always suffered in their homeland. If actual royalties seldom accrued to them, their songs were flatteringly reproduced in every detail by British bands, their authorship always scrupulously acknowledged. And whenever a genuine American bluesman – Big Bill Broonzy or Sonny Boy Williamson – found his way across the Atlantic, he was lionised by Mod-suited acolytes who could conceive of no greater honour than being allowed to back him onstage.

The Beatles' importation of what was essentially R&B with a Liverpool crack and a funny haircut initially brought little change in America's racial status quo. As the writer Charles Shaar Murray has noted, this black musical derivative was acceptable to most whites only 'if it had made a 6,000-mile round-trip first'.

But from their new position of power as successful 'invaders' of America, other British bands began to kick against its old racist idiocies. Chief among them were the Rolling Stones, who had started out as missionaries for the blues and retained that love even after their transition into commercial pop and rebranding as a menace to society.

When they appeared on a nationally aired TV pop show called *Shindig*, they insisted that one of the most hardcore of all bluesmen, Howlin' Wolf, should also be on the bill. From then on, their US tours regularly brought the likes of Muddy Waters, Ike and Tina Turner and B. B. King out of the Chitlin' Circuit to be guest artistes.

Almost as crucial to the Stones' evolution – though never shown remotely comparable gratitude – were the young women who took their three principal members to a higher social and cultural level than their modest provincial backgrounds had ever promised. With Mick Jagger, it was Marianne Faithfull, the daughter of an English academic and an Austrian baroness. With Brian Jones, the band's founder, and still their leader and star instrumentalist, it was Anita Pallenberg, a film actress of mixed Swedish and German-Swiss ancestry, fluent in four languages. With Keith Richards – his surname in those days shortened to the more stagey-sounding ' 'Richard' – it was Linda Keith.

Born in 1946, Linda came from a north London Jewish background both theatrical and musical. Her father, Alan Keith. combined stage and film roles with presenting the long-running BBC radio show *Your Hundred Best Tunes*; her uncle was the well-known character actor David Kossoff; her young cousin, Paul Kossoff, would grow up to be the guitarist in the 1970s rock band Free.

Unlike her studious brother, Brian, destined in later life to become a High Court judge, Linda had an incorrigibly rebellious streak; she was inattentive at school and uninterested in the preordained path of early marriage and childbearing. In her teens, that rebellion was expressed in rejecting all the classical and light orchestral music of her father's *Hundred Best Tunes* and developing what was seen as a thoroughly unsavoury and un-feminine passion for blues music.

She left Camden School for Girls at fifteen, without a single academic qualification but with rangy, long-legged looks that vaulted her more or less effortlessly into fashion modelling in the opening throes of Swinging London. Adding an appealing sardonic smile to the era's ever-shrinking miniskirts and ever-lengthening boots, she was photographed by David Bailey, appeared on the covers of fashion magazines and in catwalk shows for Ossie Clark, but never took her career seriously enough to reach the supermodel level of Twiggy, Jean Shrimpton or Penelope Tree.

She came into the Rolling Stones' orbit because her old schoolfriend Sheila Klein happened to be dating Andrew Loog Oldham, the Stones' teenaged manager and, by a long way, the most outrageous of any of them. 'Andrew was concerned because Keith didn't have a girlfriend and only seemed interested in his guitar,' she recalls. 'So I was set up with him.'

Thanks to a newspaper headline artfully planted by Oldham – WOULD YOU LET YOUR SISTER GO WITH A ROLL-ING STONE? – Linda's family expected to be living out a national nightmare. But Keith at this point gave no sign of the drug-sozzled, booze- and nicotine-pickled effigy he would even-tually become. 'He was very quiet and very shy. After our first date, he stayed the night at my parents' home, sleeping in the spare room, and the next morning when he left, he borrowed my mother's raincoat.'

In fact, it was Linda's own rebellious nature that drew her to drugs, a resort of old-school bluesmen from time immemorial, now being enthusiastically rediscovered by British pop musicians (though with the 'wicked' Stones far from the ringleaders they were portrayed). Like them, she progressed from marijuana to

the new 'mind-expanding' (but still legal) LSD. The Jagger/Rich-
ard song 'Ruby Tuesday' ('who can hang a name on you?') was a
tribute to her irrepressibly free spirit.

May 1966 found the Stones touring America for the fifth time,
ahead of their provocatively drug-themed single, 'Mother's Little
Helper'. Although Andrew Oldham had established the firm rule
'no wives or girlfriends on tour' (Bill Wyman and Charlie Watts
being already married), Linda was defiantly in New York at her
own expense, staying with an American friend named Roberta
Goldstein.

One night, bored with the city's 'in' night spots, they decided
to try a recently opened place called the Cheetah Club at Broadway and West 53rd Street, conveniently close to the apartment
where Roberta lived with her boyfriend, Mark Hoffman. The
three walked into what at first seemed a mausoleum with furry
wallpaper like a cheetah's spots and only about forty people
watching the house band onstage.

It was a moment comparable with Brian Epstein's first sight
of the grimy, undisciplined Beatles at Liverpool's Cavern club or
Andrew Oldham's of the blues-purist Stones at the Station Hotel
in Richmond, west London. For the house band were Curtis
Knight and the Squires with Jimmy James on lead guitar.

'His clothes were terrible,' Linda recalls. 'He had a kind of
frilly Cuban shirt, bell-bottom trousers that were too short,
cheap boots, hair that was obviously curled with rollers. But
his playing was sensational. I couldn't understand what he was
doing in a place like that, with a band like that.'

When he came offstage, Linda and Roberta told him how
they'd loved his performance and invited him to their table,
where they continued showering praise on him. That such a
thing should happen on the night of his tail-between-legs exit
from Curtis Knight and the Squires – or on any night – was
astonishing enough to Jimmy. That such compliments should

75

come from the beautiful consort of a world-famous British pop star was barely believable.

Nor did it stop there, for when they left the club he found himself invited back to Mark Hoffman's apartment, an exotic place with walls painted red and leopardskin upholstery. And when, soon afterwards, Roberta and Mark retired to bed, leaving Linda and Jimmy alone, he assumed it was a prelude to sex.

But Linda, despite her waywardness in other directions, had none of the promiscuity associated with the Stones nor, at this stage, any thought of being unfaithful to Keith. Jimmy's pique turned to fascination that she knew so much about music, the blues especially. They spent the rest of the night just playing records and talking.

One of the new albums Linda had with her was Bob Dylan's *Blonde On Blonde*. As a folkie, Dylan had sported an almost convict-like crop, but the album cover showed his pear-shaped face now topped by a bushy cloud rather like a piece of topiary untidily clipped by Jimmy's father, Al, on some landscape-gardening job. This Afro style, originally a mark of pride in African ethnicity, was becoming popular among fashionable young whites; indeed, Linda herself wore a modified version of it.

One of the first questions she'd asked Jimmy (aside from how someone of his ability came to be in a place like the Cheetah Club and a band like Curtis Knight and the Squires) was why he didn't sing as well as play. The answer was that he felt self-conscious because his voice totally lacked the soulful rasp of an Otis Redding or Wilson Pickett. 'I told him, "Listen to Dylan, That should be proof you don't need to sing in the way everyone else does."'

Blonde On Blonde's opening track, the laboriously titled 'Rainy Day Women numbers 12 & 35', found Dylan's voice as convivial as it had ever been or would be as he urged 'Ever'body must *git* stoned.' By now, 'stoned' automatically signified LSD

– something Jimmy was still itching to sample, despite his friend Lonnie Youngblood's exhortations to stay away from 'that white kids' drug'.

'I realised how naïve he was when I asked him if he'd like some acid,' Linda recalls. 'He said, "No thanks, but I'd like to try some of that LSD stuff."'

His first acid trip brought none of the horrors the drug could produce, and none of its mind-expanding visions either. All that happened was that when he looked into a mirror, he seemed to see Marilyn Monroe looking back at him. (And, alas, her fate and his would have something in common.)

At the end of that chaste night, Linda promised to use her connections with the Stones and other music industry figures to try to help him. However, he already had a plan of his own to escape the creative confinement of his skin colour.

America's folk music boom of the early Sixties had almost wholly sprung from the coffee houses of New York's Greenwich Village. Since its 'betrayal' by Dylan and the rise of folk-rock, pure folk had largely reverted to its former minority status. But the Village was still catacombed with bars and cafes offering a makeshift stage to guitar-playing troubadours. The fact that such troubadours had always been overwhelmingly white, and their guitars thoughtfully acoustic, was not going to stand in Jimmy's way.

The idea had come to him towards the end of his Cheetah Club residency, when Richie Havens played a one-nighter there. Havens was the nearest there had ever been to a black folk singer, combining a voice always seemingly on the verge of tears with a tortured guitar-action that did not strum so much as frantically scrub it. Brooklyn-born, he had first infiltrated Greenwich Village in the 1950s, and spent years around the coffee houses as a painter and poet before turning to music and being signed by Dylan's manager, Albert Grossman.

Havens encouraged Jimmy to try his luck in the Village and recommended he first try Café Wha? on MacDougal Street, where Dylan had often appeared and Mary Travers of Peter, Paul and Mary used to wait tables. He turned up there on a Monday night, when the café's drowsy name seemed only too well chosen, and persuaded its owner, Manny Roth, to give him an audition while the house band were on their break. 'The place was totally blown away,' a former employee recalls. 'All fifteen people.'

Roth immediately offered him regular work at its usual poet's rate of $6 for five sets during the opening hours from 10 a.m. through to 2 a.m. In his euphoria, Jimi repeated the same mistake as long ago at Seattle's Birdland club and left his guitar backstage overnight. When he returned for it the next morning, it had been stolen.

His main source of new instruments had always been women, so now, for the all-important launch in Greenwich Village, he turned to his influential new friend, Linda Keith. The result exceeded his wildest expectations. While the Rolling Stones were touring Middle America, they had reserved rooms at a midtown hotel, the Americana, where Keith Richard had left a number of guitars that weren't needed on the road. As Keith's girlfriend, Linda had access to his room, and was able to purloin a white Fender Stratocaster for Jimmy.

Though more than capable of filling the Café Wha? on his own, he began to look around for kindred spirits to back him. At Manny's Music Store on West 48th Street, an informal musicians' employment exchange, he quickly found two, both of them white – presaging things soon to come far across the sea – and considerably younger than himself. Randy Wolfe, was a fifteen-year-old guitarist and would-be songwriter from Los Angeles whom he nicknamed Randy California; and who would later be a founder member of Spirit; bass-player Jeff 'Skunk'

Baxter was a high-school student working part-time at Manny's (and in later life, a member of the Doobie Brothers and Steely Dan). This first band he'd ever fronted alone was called Jimmy James and the Blue Flames, a less-than-inspired choice when James Brown's superlative Famous Flames had been tearing up the Chitlin' Circuit for more than a decade.

Linda's pep talk with Bob Dylan as her unwitting ally had finally convinced Jimmy he had to sing as well as play. 'He was very glad I persuaded him because he'd already written a pile of songs that needed to be tried out on an audience,' she recalls. 'When his first album came out a few months later, I'd already heard most of it onstage at Café Wha?'

The Blue Flames also played current pop hits like the Troggs' 'Wild Thing', Wilson Pickett's 'In the Midnight Hour' and the McCoys' 'Hang On Sloopy', which Jimmy would stretch from a three-minute single to twenty minutes or more. Gaining in vocal confidence, he did his first Dylan cover, 'Like a Rolling Stone', a piquant choice while playing something so very like a Rolling Stone's white Fender Strat.

Despite his fears of being thought a presumptuous intruder in this living shrine to Bob Dylan, the Village's musical community gave only welcome and encouragement. One of his earliest converts there was John Hammond Jr., son of the legendary producer who'd signed Dylan to Columbia Records, ignoring fellow executives' mockery of the scrawny Minnesota youth they labelled 'Hammond's Folly'.

Hammond Jr., himself a talented guitarist, had been responsible for putting Dylan together with the young sidemen, afterwards known as the Band, who'd stoically shared the flak over his switch from folk to rock. They, too, were entranced by Jimmy when he sat in with Hammond, although their lead guitarist, Robbie Robertson, recognised the guitar-behind-head routine as a steal from T-Bone Walker. 'I told him, "I know where you got that from,"' Robertson recalls. 'He just grinned and said, "I know you know."'

He finally got to meet Dylan at a basement bar called the Kettle of Fish, just down the street from Café Wha? 'We were both stoned and we just hung around laughing – yeah, we just laughed,' he would recall. Dylan's studied scruffiness made the guileless Jimmy think 'he was starving down there', even though he had his own personal chronicler, the *New York Post* journalist Al Aronowitz, 'to put down whatever he saw around him'. The encounter was one of very few Dylan would ever admit to, from a past otherwise kept carefully scrubbed blank: 'I met Jimmy slightly before he became a star.'

At the opposite extreme, he found himself befriended by the Fugs, a collective of coffee-house poets who had formed a band in the conviction that they 'could do better than those dipshit musicians' and whose name was the only printable form of 'fuck'. By turns political, satirical and scatological, they would be described in an FBI surveillance report as 'the most vulgar thing the human mind could conceive'.

Early in Jimmy's residency at Café Wha?, the Fugs' guitarist, Pete Kearney, built him a crude kind of fuzzbox which distorted Keith Richard's guitar as no Rolling Stones' record yet had. Now he could add the sound of psychedelic West Coast bands like the Grateful Dead and Jefferson Airplane to a performance rolling up everything he'd ever learned from Little Richard, Albert Lee or Mike Quashie, the Spider King, and powered by the same acid-dazzled energy, whether his audience happened to be a crowd of ecstatic young females, each one hoping to catch his eye, or merely a handful of superannuated folkies, barely glancing up from their espressos, foreign newspapers and chess games.

Most of that summer of 1966 Jimmy spent hanging out with Linda Keith while she waited for Keith Richard to come back off the road with the Rolling Stones. By now he was renting a room at the rather grim Hotel Lenox on West 44th, but would often stay over at Linda's friend Mark Hoffman's scarlet and leopardskin apartment on 63rd that he called 'the Red House'.

One of Linda's first objectives was to stop him curling his hair in so dated and unbecoming a way. 'I made fun of him about it, but so did a lot of other people,' she recalls. 'He'd walk to a gig with his hair still in rollers, covered by a pink scarf. I've still got that scarf today.'

Her sardonic smile soon persuaded him to throw away the curling tongs and go for an Afro like Bob Dylan's on the *Blonde On Blonde* cover that needed no maintenance bar the occasional check for nesting birds. From then on, he became known around the Village as Dylan Black. In yet another identity change, he took to spelling his first name 'Jimi' – possibly at the example of blues guitarist Jihmhi Johnson – although the Café Wha? stuck to 'Jimmy' on its marquee.

His relationship with Linda continued to be platonic only, and punctuated by vigorous but never bitter arguments. She would have liked things to go further, but was put off by the sheer quantity of women with whom he was non-platonic. 'There were busloads of them. Six or seven just at the Hotel Lenox.'

Once a week, he went up to Harlem to visit Fayne Pridgon, who'd taken him in when he first arrived there – 'Auntie Fayne', he called her although she was only two years his senior and had never in any way resembled an aunt. He evidently still had a life in Harlem he kept completely separate from the one he led in the Village.

To supplement out his pittance from Café Wha? he made numerous appearances in other clubs for other pittances and would sometimes even go out busking, with Linda playing harmonica. These street performances brought back his bashfulness about singing, so he made her do so instead, changing the lyrics (as in Muddy Waters' 'I'm A Man') where necessary.

It was a summer of glorious sunshine and equally glorious white pop music that the newly renamed Jimi absorbed with delight and longed to replicate onstage: the Beatles' *Revolver* album, the Stones' *Aftermath*, the Beach Boys' 'Good Vibrations', the Mamas and the Papas' 'Monday Monday', the Lovin' Spoonful's 'Summer in the City', with the same taxi horns and construction drills he could hear through his open window. 'But at the Lenox or the apartment ' Linda says, 'he never played anything but the blues. He'd sometimes get depressed because he felt left behind by everything that was going on in music, and he could have very sudden, extreme mood swings. I've often thought that today he might have been diagnosed as bipolar. But if he had a dark side, as other people have said he did, I never saw it.'

Her friend Roberta's father co-owned a hotel in the Catskill mountains in upper New York state, a resort area whose largely Jewish clientele and consequently Middle European cuisine had earned it the nickname of the Borscht Belt. Unlike the Chitlin' Circuit, its entertainment consisted largely of sedate orchestras and some of the funniest comedians who ever drew breath.

When the city's heat became unbearable, Jimi and Linda accompanied Roberta and her boyfriend, Mark, on a trip to the Catskills – though there was, of course, no question of Jimi's staying at Mr Goldstein's hotel, the Concord. 'Nobody at the hotel liked the fact that we had him with us,' Linda recalls. 'But we were too stoned to care.'

In August, the Rolling Stones ended their tour and returned to New York, placing Linda in an uncomfortable quandary. With Keith Richard's reappearance, it was clearly advisable to minimise her involvement with Jimi, innocent though that had been. On the other hand, she was anxious to pitch him as a prospective signing to the Stones' manager, Andrew Loog Oldham.

It had been a stroke of marketing genius by nineteen-year-old

Oldham in 1963 to turn an inoffensive blues band into the antithesis of the cuddly, family-friendly Beatles – whom their manager, Brian Epstein, had metamorphosed the other way, from black leather-clad, disreputable rockers – and to persuade a London School of Economics student named Mick Jagger he could make his fortune by pretending to be the devil incarnate. Since then, Oldham had become Britain's first pop tycoon, setting up his own record label, Immediate, under the slogan 'Proud To Be Part of the Industry of Human Happiness'.

Linda persuaded Oldham to catch Jimi's act at Café Au Go Go but it proved not to be the same moment of epiphany he'd experienced with the Stones at the Station Hotel, Richmond. He felt that signing a guitarist of such obvious virtuosity might create problems not only with Keith but also the Stones' official lead player Brian Jones. And when Jimi kept speaking to Linda from the stage, Oldham caught a scent of intimacy that threatened danger. As he would write in his autobiography, *Stoned*, 'Keith was the kind of guy who might actually kill someone involved with his girlfriend.'

Linda tried again with Seymour Stein, founder of the Sire record label, who might have felt some mock-medieval affinity with an ex-member of Curtis Knight and the Squires. Stein also agreed to check out Jimi at Café Au Go Go but unfortunately it was on the night he first tried out another extreme sound effect, jamming the Stratocaster's strings against his amp to produce a protesting scream of feedback. Linda was horrified by this misuse of Keith's guitar and a furious argument broke out between her and Jimmy, during which Stein made a discreet exit .

The Stones were not the only British invaders in New York at that particular moment. The Animals also happened to be passing through on a world tour that still had a month to run.

The Animals were a product of the frantic search for musical talent in northern British cities that had followed the Beatles' discovery in Liverpool. They came from Newcastle upon Tyne, the principal port of England's north-east as Liverpool was of the north-west, whose populace, known as 'Geordies', had an accent and vernacular as unique as Liverpool's 'Scousers' and whose youth favoured R&B as hardcore as the coal mined throughout its hinterland.

In 1964, they had recorded 'The House of the Rising Sun', an ancient blues wail about a New Orleans brothel that had been a staple of folk singers from Woody Guthrie to Dave Van Ronk. Stripped down to a tolling electric guitar, a vocal equally steeped in Mississippi heat and River Tyne fog, and a manic organ solo, it had made them the first British band after the Beatles to achieve a US number one single. Hearing it by chance on a car radio was what prompted Bob Dylan (who'd already recorded it in its traditional form) to 'go electric'.

Unlike the Beatles, whose unity had always helped them deal with the pressures of sudden, dizzying fame, the Animals – to quote their vocalist, Eric Burdon – 'were designed like a fragmentation grenade'. Almost immediately, there was conflict between Burdon, who wanted to stay close to their R&B roots, and keyboard-player Alan Price, who was all for moving into mainstream pop like other former purists such as the Stones and Manfred Mann.

With all bands, money tends to become a sore point but with the Animals it was a gangrenous wound. 'The House of the Rising Sun' having long since been in the public domain, all the members felt entitled to an equal share in its royalties for a collective arrangement. Yet Price (who had since resigned to go solo) turned out to have been credited as sole arranger and so was collecting the lot.

In addition, there were growing suspicions about the honesty of their manager, a Newcastle club owner named Mike Jeffery.

After a string of hits following 'The House of the Rising Sun' and an average of 300 gigs per year, none of them was conscious of having become one penny wealthier. Drummer John Steel had also quit in disillusionment and, halfway through their 1966 world tour, Eric Burdon and bass player Chas Chandler agreed they, too, had had enough.

Chandler, a chubby giant with a slight resemblance to Paul McCartney, had no great hopes of a solo performing career. Instead, he was minded to emulate the Animals' record-producer, Mickie Most, himself a former pop singer, who had bottled the raw spirit of 'The House of the Rising Sun' in a single take. That same dual producer/manager role had since given Most a major stake in the British Invasion's second wave with acts like Herman's Hermits and Donovan.

One night, with the usual cameraderie of British bands, the Rolling Stones and Animals were out clubbing together with Linda Keith seated opposite Chandler. 'Chas was saying he wanted to move into management if he could find someone to manage,' she recalls. 'So I piped up, "I've got just the person for you."'

Determined that nothing should mess up this audition, Linda took Chandler to watch Jimi and the Blue Flames in an afternoon show at Café Wha? when almost nobody would be there to create a distraction over having an Animal in the audience.

Jimi had been forewarned, and went into instant overdrive with the latest in his repertoire of transformed cover versions. 'Hey Joe' was by the singer/songwriter Tim Rose – himself an occasional performer at the Wha? – and had the familiar blues theme of jilted lover taking revenge with a deadly weapon. But, unusually, it alternated the voice of the killer who'd 'shot his old lady down' with that of the friend who extracted his unremorseful admission to the deed. Jimi had first heard it on record by a country-rock band named the Leaves, so speeded up from Rose's original anguished version that it sounded positively cheerful.

His own replaced Rose's own jangly country picking with an almost somnambulistic rock beat, his voice – so unlike a traditional R&B singer's in its unruffled mellowness – switching back and forth between interrogation and confession in a conversational, almost offhand way that somehow heightened the brutality of the tale it told. Then, when the duologue seemed darkest, he raised Keith Richard's white Stratocaster horizontally to his face, to produce a lyric, rippling solo with fingers he could not possibly see and no plectrum but his teeth.

'This is ree-dic-lous,' Chandler marvelled to Linda in his broad Tyneside accent. 'Why hasna' anyone signed this guy up?'

That was soon remedied. Waiting for Jimi when he came offstage was an offer to become the first-ever management client of the world's best-known bass guitarist after Paul McCartney. Since Chandler, as he freely admitted, had no foothold in America's music industry, this would entail accompanying him back to England and staying for an indefinite period.

Fascinated though Jimi had been by the media furore over Swinging London, actually going there was a daunting prospect, the more so as Chandler's plans did not include the Blue Flames, so that if things didn't work out, he might find himself alone in a land of eccentrically accented strangers. What decided him was the thought of getting close to the spectacular guitarists he'd heard on British R&B records. 'He especially wanted to meet Eric Clapton,' Linda recalls. 'Eric was his idol.'

In any event, nothing could happen until Chandler finished the Animals' break-up tour, a month hence. The two having found an immediate rapport, it wasn't thought necesssary to solemnise their agreement with anything more than a handshake.

Chandler had been only just in time, for the word-of-mouth about Jimi now began to heat up. Mike Bloomfield, hitherto regarded as New York's best guitarist, also came to the Café Wha? to see him. '[He] knew who I was and on that day, in front of my eyes, he burned me to death,' Bloomfield was to recall. 'H-Bombs were going off, guided missiles were flying . . . I can't tell you the sounds he was getting.' So thoroughly unnerving was the experience that Bloomfield cancelled his next gig and Richie Havens had to fill in for him.

While waiting for Chandler, Jimi was invited to sit in with John Hammond Jr.'s band at the Wha?'s closest competitor, the unsteadily Frenchified Café Au Go Go. There, one night, Hammond brought his father, the revered Columbia Records producer whose string of discoveries before Dylan ranged from Billie Holliday to Aretha Franklin (and would reach a further peak in the next decade with Bruce Springsteen). But Hammond senior's eye for new talent seemed to grow a cataract and he discerned nothing special going on at the Au Go Go.

Linda Keith was not around to witness any of this. She had feared repercussions over the white Stratocaster she'd purloined for Jimi, which somehow had never found its way back to Keith Richard. Keith, however, had not seemed to miss the Strat, but had mistakenly accused Linda of being romantically involved with Jimi, and as a result the couple had broken up.

Not only that: in a fit of prudery few would have expected from a wild Rolling Stone, he'd told Linda's father she was heading 'down a dark road with a black junkie' and paid for Alan Keith to fly to New York and bring her home. 'I was lolling near the stage as usual when a man walked in who I thought looked like my dad – and it was,' she recalls. 'He was in such an agitated state, I realised I had to get him home rather than him getting me home.' She left the club with Alan immediately, leaving her friend Roberta to tell Jimi.

Back in London, the fact that she was still not yet 21 allowed her father to make her a ward of court and have her passport confiscated to prevent her from travelling abroad for the remaining months before she came of age.

She never did manage to explain to the 'black junkie' what had happened and he remained blissfully unaware of the whole drama. 'Roberta said that when she went backstage, Jimi was checking his hair in the mirror and asking, "Do I look all right?" as if he was about to meet my dad under completely normal circumstances.'

SIX

'QUITE HONESTLY, CHAS . . . HE'S ALMOST TOO GOOD'

Anyone familiar with the cult 1971 film *Get Carter*, starring Michael Caine as Jack Carter, the dapper London heavy at large amid the sooty grandeur of Newcastle upon Tyne, will easily picture Mike Jeffery. Carter favours the same dark blue suits that Jeffery did, enjoys the same connection to shadowy underworld figures, can turn on the same cold-eyed viciousness when necessary and meets the same violent premature death.

Little about the young Frank Michael Jeffery prophesied his future as the manager – some say, gross mismanager – of a superlative musical talent. He was born in Peckham, south London, in 1933, to parents who both worked at the local postal sorting-office, and received an ordinary state education, leaving school at the age of sixteen without any academic qualifications. His father hoped he might keep up the family tradition by becoming a postman, but his mind was on rounds of a rather different sort. He was fascinated by explosives and obsessed by guns.

After two years as a clerk with the Mobil oil company, the course of his life altered dramatically: he was conscripted into the army for two years, then opted to becoome a 'regular'. Having beeen taught to speak Russian, he was transferred to the Intelligence Corps and posted to the Italian port of Trieste, which in the 1950s was squeezed between Communist Yugoslavia and the capitalist West and thus a likely flashpoint for a Third World War.

In later life, to a girlfriend named Jenny Clarke, he described taking part in a covert operation during which he killed a Communist sentry. As proof, he showed her a photograph of the guard's family he'd taken from the body and kept in his wallet ever since – whether from remorse or as some kind of sick trophy can never be known.

After leaving the army, he enrolled as a mature student at Newcastle University, then got into jazz promotion and opened a jazz club called the Downbeat and a coffee bar named the Marimba with a music and dance club, the El Toro, above it. In 1961, the Marimba and the El Toro were destroyed by a mysterious fire while both were empty of customers. Although Jeffery was widely suspected of having the building 'torched', the insurance company paid up without a murmur and he used the insurance money to open a 'beat' music venue in Percy Street named Club A' Go Go.

A relaxation of Britain's gaming laws in the early sixties allowed casinos to proliferate throughout the country on condition they were part of members-only clubs. Suddenly, Newcastle was no longer associated with shipyards and flat caps but exotically named night spots like the Dolce Vita and Club A' Go Go. In 1963, Jeffery and his business partner, Ray Grehan, were heavily fined after undercover police discovered their roulette wheel was fixed.

In a tough city, the A' Go Go became famous for the ferocity of its doorman Tommy Findlay, a ruthless 'hard man' who kept order with the help of an axe – and would actually inspire one of the mobsters in *Get Carter*. The club's entrance staircase was painted scarlet, it was said, so that the bloodstains caused by Findlay wouldn't show.

Jeffery himself cultivated the air of a gangster, always wearing dark glasses – though he was genuinely short-sighted – and keeping a Colt 45 revolver in his desk drawer: a fact that emerged with his prosecution for not having a firearms licence.

Former associates recall him treating Club A' Go Go like his personal piggybank. When Ray Grehan checked the casino takings after one bonanza evening, there was no paper money. A croupier explained that Mike had already pocketed it all 'the way he does every night'. His then girlfriend, Jenny Clark, recalled: 'All the takings would be spent by the next day. Mike liked his Morgans and Aston Martins.' His conduct in the leisure business foreshadowed his career in pop management. 'Mike didn't believe in paying for anything,' a former employee remembers, 'and was permanently on the run from people wielding writs for debt.'

It wasn't long before Tyneside's lucrative *salons de jeux* attracted the interest of London's most feared criminals, the Kray Twins, Reggie and Ronnie, both of whom showed up at Club A' Go Go one evening to announce they were taking it over. As Jeffery would afterwards relate to his PA, Trixi Sullivan, he met the crisis with a combination of icy calm and audacity. 'The Krays went up to him and said, "'Ere, what are you wearing those pansy dark glasses for?" Mike lifted up his glasses and said, "Because I'm blind." The Krays were complete softies where women and people with disabilities were concerned. They said, "Oh, sorry mate", and never bothered him again.'

The Animals fell into Jeffery's lap as the north-east port of Newcastle's logical answer to the north-west port of Liverpool's Beatles and Mersey Sound. Like the Beatles at the Cavern, they became house band at Club A' Go Go; with Jeffery as their manager, they found a southern, then a national, then international audience when he brought them to London, to the producer Mickie Most and their one-take smash, 'The House of the Rising Sun'.

Intelligent enough to acknowledge his inexperience in pop management, Jeffery initially formed a partnership with the booking agent Don Arden, a terrifying figure, notorious for hanging business rivals out of high windows by their heels. In this area, he needed no tuition from the so-called 'Al Capone of Pop'. 'Mike's army training had made him very tough,' Trixi Sullivan recalls. 'I never actually saw him use physical violence on anyone, but he didn't have to. He knew how to frighten people to death without it.'

Where he differed most notably from the Beatles' Brian Epstein and the Stones' Andrew Loog Oldham was in seeking no publicity for himself. In his bespoke suits and dark glasses, he kept the anonymity he'd cultivated as an army intelligence operative. Utilising another old military skill, he made his company accounts incomprehensible to outside auditors by keeping them in Russian.

Although now manager of Britain's third biggest pop group, Jeffery still kept Club A' Go Go – and added to it. The Spanish island of Majorca had become a hugely popular destination for British holidaymakers who once would have ventured no further afield than Bognor or Margate. Jeffery acquired an interest in the island's first disco, Zhivago, and a clothes boutique. If ever his Majorcan business partners proved troublesome, Club A' Go Go's terrifying doorman, Dave Findlay, and his similar younger brother, Tommy, would be summoned from Newcastle to give assistance.

The Animals' only consolation for Jeffery's brutal work schedule was the thought of their earnings accumulating in an offshore company that would protect them from the crippling tax demands suffered by both the Beatles and the Stones. Jeffery, they believed, was paying the money into a company named Yameta, based in the Bahamian capital, Nassau, which put it beyond the reach of America's Internal Revenue Service.

In those days, the Bahamas allowed hundreds of such companies to operate in almost total secrecy, with no obligation to reveal their ownership or publish accounts, while back in the UK no awkward questions were ever raised about 'unpatriotic' tax avoidance.

The thought of this invulnerable collective nest egg in a sunshiny island paradise had sustained the naive Newcastle lads as they flogged around Britain, America and the world. However, in three years, the Bahamian fruit machine had not coughed out a single jackpot and the Animals had become convinced their dapper, self-effacing manager was robbing them blind.

Trixi Sullivan, who worked closely with Jeffery from the mid-1960s to the early '70s, rejects the widely held view of him as a predator ranking with the worst in the the business.

'I never knew Mike to screw any of his acts. In cases like this, you have to ask, 'Who did the money belong to in the first place?' The manager lays out the capital to get a band started in the first place, as Mike did with the Animals; he pays for the office, the clothes, the instruments, the transport, the roadies. And then they keep coming to him for money all the time . . . 'I need to pay the rent' . . . 'my girlfriend needs an abortion.' None of them ever remembers things like that.

'Say they earn £100,000 and there are four of them. 'Ah,' they think, 'that's £25,000 each.' They never take into account all the expenses that have to come out of it: the promoter's cut, the cost of the cars, hotels, the room-service tabs. Then the manager himself will probably be getting robbed all the way down the chain by the record companies, the accountants and bookkeepers. At the end, there's not going to be much of that hundred grand to share out.'

Chas Chandler was Jeffery's most vociferous critic in the Animals, having at one point gone to Nassau to ascertain the size of their nest egg only to discover that the bank supposedly holding it had gone out of business. Yet for his first foray into management, Chandler needed the backup of a professional organisation, and Jeffery's was the only one to hand. Besides, two other ex-Animals, Eric Burdon and Alan Price, were already following this same 'better the devil you know' philosophy in their solo careers.

Accordingly, Chandler went straight to Jeffery – who had a New York office – brought him to Café Wha? and suggested they co-manage Jimi. Jeffery agreed on the basis that Chandler should look after the recording side, in which he already had a head start, and himself the business side, which effectively made him senior partner.

'Mike was highly intelligent and very good at doing deals,' Trixi Sullivan says. 'But you could say he was stupid in that he never planned anything. Nobody did in the pop industry at that time. It was such a new business and no one believed it could last longer than a few months. "These pop musicians," people thought. "They're here today, gone tomorrow, you have to get the most out of them while you can." Mike was just making it up as he went along.'

Which, in the case of this particular 'here today, gone tomorrow' musician, was what pretty much what all his new white British sponsors would find themselves doing.

On Saturday, 24 September 1966 – so most accounts of Jimi's career agree – he landed at London-Heathrow airport on a Pan Am overnight flight from New York, accompanied by Chas Chandler and the Animals' road manager, Terry McVay. He had with him only a small overnight bag and $40, borrowed from a drummer friend from the Village named Charles Otis. In the last-minute rush and panic over getting himself a passport, he had not told his father and brother what had happened or where he was going.

Waiting in the arrivals hall were two members of Mike Jeffery's organisation: a roadie, who would not be needed, and the Animals' publicist, Tony Garland, who most definitely would. No UK work permit for Jimi had yet been obtained and Garland's job was to get him through Immigration and Customs without one. The smooth-tongued PR man succeeded in passing him off as an already established American star, here only to collect some royalties from a British promoter. Even so, the entry stamp in his new passport was first cancelled, then reinstated, and he was held up for two hours before being granted only a seven-day visitor's visa prohibiting any employment during that time.

Chandler and Jeffery had anticipated something of the sort and made plans accordingly. Since Jimi could not be launched with any kind of formal concert, he was to be covertly slipped into circulation via the clubs frequented by London's leading pop names and opinion-formers, playing solo or sitting in with their house bands for free. If ever challenged by the Immigration authorities, he could argue that jamming was not work but leisure.

Long-standing Hendrix mythology has Jimi playing in the most chic of these clubs on his very first night in London. However, it appears that Chandler did not succeed in getting him in anywhere for a further three days, by which time his temporary visitor's visa was nearing its end.

He had been booked into the Hyde Park Towers hotel in Inverness Terrace, Bayswater – as it happened, only a few streets away from the place where, after the incredible journey of the next four years, he would meet his bizarre, lonely death.

Like most Bayswater hotels, the Hyde Park Towers was a converted Victorian terrace house, devoid of either towers or park views and catering largely to Amerian and Australian tourist groups. As Jimi checked in, Chandler spotted a fellow guest he knew well and was particularly pleased to see at this moment – a

Welshman named Rod Harrod who managed the famous Scotch of St James club. 'Chas had this wild-looking character with him who he'd just brought from New York and said was a brilliant guitarist,' Harrod recalls. 'I'd never heard of him or seen him play, so I just said "I'll take your word for it, Chas."'

Also waiting at the Hyde Park Towers was Linda Keith, whose situation as a ward of court might prevent her travelling abroad but did not forbid her from associating with the alleged 'black junkie' on her home turf. She had by now broken up with Keith Richard and, hearing of Jimi's arrival, had reserved her own room at the Hyde Park Towers in hopes of starting the 'real' relationship they'd never had in New York. 'I only had time to speak to him briefly,' she recalls. 'Then Chas whisked him away.'

Before Jimi could go a step further, Chandler had an urgent matter to resolve. The white Fender Stratocaster he had never re-turned to Keith Richard was now missing – whether lost, stolen or lying unredeemed in some Manhattan pawnshop would never be known. After laying out for the flights and the hotel, Chand-ler could not afford to buy him a new instrument, so the only answer was to follow Linda's example and borrow one for him.

The musician friend most likely to oblige at such short notice was Zoot Money, whom Jimi might reasonably have expected to be some fellow refugee from the Chitlin' Circuit. However, Money – his real surname, though 'Zoot' had replaced 'George' – was a pioneer of the white British R&B movement, leading his equally pale-faced but soul-drenched Big Roll Band tirelessly in clubs up and down the country, albeit seldom into the record charts.

Chandler therefore drove Jimi to the house in Gunterstone Road, West Kensington, where Money lived with his Glasgwe-gian wife, Ronni, and assorted sub tenants. The basement was occupied by the Big Roll Band's guitarist, Andy Summers, who would find fame in the 1970s with the Police. Sharing one room on the top floor were two young women-about-town, Angie King, later the wife of the Animals' Eric Burdon, and Kathy Etchingham.

Twenty-year-old Kathy had run away from a chaotic home in Derby aged sixteen and been instantly absorbed into Swinging London, first as a server at a Golden Egg omelette bar, then as a deejay at the Cromwellian restaurant and discotheque, where her willowy beauty and natural elegance soon attracted notice. She smoked her first joint at Georgie Fame's house and had brief affairs with the Who's manic drummer, Keith Moon, and Rolling Stone Brian Jones.

When Jimi appeared on the front doorstep with Chas Chandler, Kathy was upstairs, asleep in bed after a late night behind her deejay's turntable. Ronni Money shouted to her with typical Glasgwegian unsubtlety to come and see this 'wild man from Borneo', but she replied she was too tired and would catch him later at the Scotch.

It was anything but a 'wild man' who sat quietly in the Moneys' living room (not instantly jamming with Zoot as Hendrix mythology has it). 'He was very shy and polite but, like any guitarist, getting a bit twitchy because he hadn't played for a while. I fetched him my rehearsal guitar, an Italian Wandre, which he was brilliant on even though it was right-handed and he was left-handed. I told him he could borrow it for the evening, but by then Chas had got on the phone and rounded up something else that suited him better.'

Zoot was surprised by his cavalier attitude to guitars – so different from the days when he would hug them to him like a security blanket. 'All the other players I knew obsessed about theirs, gave them human names or called them "my baby". But whenever I saw Jimi after that, he always seemed have a borrowed guitar, never caring what kind it was. I suppose he had to have that attitude to start smashing them up.'

Back at the Hyde Park Towers, while Jimi slept away his jet-lag, Chandler talked Rod Harrod into giving him a spot at the Scotch of St James club. 'He kept on and on at me,' says Harrod (who insists that Jimi arrived on Thursday, 22 September, not Saturday the 24th). 'I finally said, "OK, Chas, but I can't do it on the weekend – it'll have to be on Monday." His temporary visa ran out that week and Chas had no more appearances lined up for him so if it hadn't been for me, there probably would have been no Jimi Hendrix.'

'The Scotch' was located near London's oldest palace, St James's, where foreign ambassadors formally present their credentials to the Crown. 'Scotch' referred both to its plaid décor and the spirit that was its young clientele's beverage of choice, poured from inflight-style 'miniatures' and numbed by Coca-Cola.

Like all the innermost 'in' clubs it was subterranean, tiny and pitch-black, but harboured more alabaster pop-star faces per square metre of darkess than any of its main rivals, the Speak-easy, the Cromwellian, the Bag O'Nails or Blaises. On its opening night earlier that summer, Harrod had counted 'three Beatles, three Rolling Stones, two Who and two Kinks'.

But on the Monday night of Jimi's debut, few such luminaries were in evidence. Paul McCartney would later claim to have been there incognito, which, despite Harrod's scepticism, was more than possible. A couple of doors away was the Indica art gallery and bookshop, in which McCartney was deeply involved – and where, a few weeks earlier, John Lennon had first met an obscure Japanese performance artist named Yoko Ono.

The Scotch prided itself on having a different house band every week, and Jimi went onstage with the current one, an outfit from Carlisle called the VIPs, plugging his borrowed guitar into their amp. In observance of his visa, he was not being paid and had only time to play only four numbers before Chas Chandler decided not to push their luck any further and almost dragged him off the stage. However, as Rod Harrod recalls, he'd done enough to bring 'two guys falling over themselves and tripping over the chairs to get to Chas'.

The two guys were Kit Lambert and Chris Stamp, co-managers of the Who and the personification of Britain's tumbling class barriers. Oxford-educated Lambert's father was the classical composer and conductor Constant Lambert and his godmother the ballerina Margot Fonteyn. Stamp was the son of a Thames tugboat skipper and younger brother of the super-'in' screen actor Terence Stamp.

Lambert and Stamp had at first thought to manage Jimi but although Chandler and Jeffery had beaten them to that role, they had another, equally essential service to offer. The pair were in the process of setting up an independent record label named Track and proposed to make Jimi the first signing after their clients, the Who. Track was not due to begin operations until the following January; nonetheless, an agreement with Chandler was roughed out on one of the Scotch's burgundy-coloured napkins.

Alas for Chandler's hopes of a low-key entry into London clubland. When Linda Keith had arrived, she'd joined Chandler's party which also included Ronni Money and Kathy Etchingham, both strangers to her. 'After Jimi came offstage, I found myself being gradually edged out,' Linda recalls. 'Then he put his arm around Kathy and smiled across at me on my stool outside the charmed circle. I just said, "Fuck off, Jimi" and it started a huge fight. This woman who was with Kathy [Mrs Zoot Money] attacked me, punching me and pulling my hair, even getting a broken bottle from the bar and holding it against my throat.'

Terrified that the fracas would get into the papers and reveal Jimi to be working unlawfully, Chandler hustled him upstairs to the ground-floor lounge area and Linda was ejected from the club. 'He abandoned me at the very moment and at the only time I ever needed him.'

When Jimi left the club later with Kathy Etchingham, his British adventure almost came to a premature end. Unaware that motorists over here drove on the left, he did not see a black London taxi with its gold-lit 'For Hire' sign bearing down on him. 'I managed to grab his jacket and pull him out of its way just in time,' Kathy recalls.

The next morning, Linda returned to the Hyde Park Towers in a pale-blue Jaguar Keith Richard had bought himself despite being unable to drive. Letting herself into the room she had booked for that hoped-for night of passion with Jimi, she found him in bed with Kathy Etchingham. Kathy's later autobiography would depict the two of them cowering under the bedclothes while a mini-skirted tornado went through the room gathering up the things she'd left there (which in this account included Keith's white Stratocaster). Linda admits to 'absolute fury that he had abandoned me the night before to contend with some mad troll who looked as if she was going to hurt me.

The door slammed thunderously and shortly afterwards came the roar of a departing Jaguar. Jimi was free to begin the longest cohabitation with a woman in his short life.

Now that Chas Chandler had got him to London, the problem was where to position him in the British music market when he wasn't exactly rock nor pop nor soul nor R&B nor blues nor country nor folk nor jazz but a bit of everything.

Thinking that traditional blues might be the way to go, Chandler arranged for him to join a jam session at a club named Les Cousins, organised by the great British bluesman Alexis Korner for participants in the current American Folk and Blues Festival at the Royal Albert Hall. But while he proved he could play with the same passion and purity as any of those grizzled old masters, he looked far too young and hip to be in their company.

Chandler had many contacts throughout London's diverse and opinionated music trade press from whom to seek guidance. Perhaps the canniest was the *New Musical Express*'s features editor, Keith Altham. However, after seeing Jimi perform at the Scotch, even Altham confessed himself flummoxed. 'To me, it was like listening to some great jazz guitarist like Wes Montgomery. I said, "Quite honestly, Chas, I can see this stuff going straight over the heads of most rock fans because he's almost *too* good."'

The tag that Chandler chose for him inevitably mentioned his colour. Just as Greenwich Village had dubbed him 'the black Dylan', in London he would be 'the black Elvis'. There was a certain appopriateness in it, for Elvis Presley had originally shot to fame as a white man who could sing like a black one and Jimi would reverse the process.

When he outlined his previous history to the publicist Tony Garland for future press releases, Garland was astounded at all the big names he'd played with, from Little Richard to Ike and Tina Turner. Yet it didn't seem to have left him even with a pair of boots capable of keeping out the rain.

Meanwhile, further to Keith Altham's advice, Chandler was casting around for an opening for Jimi in jazz rather than pop or blues. His best hope, he decided, was Brian Auger, a gifted keyboard player, dedicated to using his band, the Brian Auger Trinity, to build a bridge between mutually hostile R&B and modern jazz.

Auger was summoned to Mike Jeffery's office, above a Chinese supermarket in Gerrard Street, Soho, and offered Jimi's services as both singer and lead guitarist. However, Auger was planning to work with a female vocalist, Julie Driscoll, and had no wish to replace his present guitarist, Vic Briggs. He was also leery of being involved in any way with Jeffery, whom he considered 'an out-and-out crook'. But out of friendship for Chas, he agreed that Jimi could sit in during the Trinity's imminent gig at Blaises club in Kensington.

There Jimi received the friendliest of welcomes from Vic Briggs, whom it had so recently been suggested he might oust from the band. As it happened, Briggs used one of the outsize Marshall amplifiers that had recently been developed in the UK, its cabinet housing twelve 6-inch speakers with a thunderous 100-watt output. For the former James Marshall Hendrix, added interest came from the fact that the monster – known as a 'stack', as if it were a hayrick or section of library books – had been invented by a former drum-shop owner named Jim Marshall. The good-natured Briggs said he was welcome to try it out.

Normally, even the loudest players did not turn the volume of a Marshall above 5 but Jimi switched it straight to its maximum, 10. 'I was afraid that in a club as small as that, it would blow all the windows out,' Briggs would recall.

When Jimi took the stage with Brian Auger, he said they would be playing something called 'Hey Joe', spelling out a chord sequence that to Auger seemed elementary. 'But as soon as he started playing, it was like "Oh, my God!" With most of our guitarists, you could still hear the people they'd learned from, like B. B. King, Freddie King, Albert Collins, Howlin' Wolf, but I'd never heard anyone play like that before.'

On 1 October, he achieved his greatest ambition – the main reason for letting himself be shipped to Britain – and met Eric Clapton. But it was not an encounter his hero would remember with any pleasure.

At the time, 21-year-old Clapton held the title of rock's greatest guitarist as securely as Wyatt Earp once had that of the Fastest Gun in the West. A few months earlier, while he was with Britain's foremost blues band, John Mayall's Bluesbreakers, an anonymous admirer had spray-painted CLAPTON IS GOD on the wall of a north London tube station. Even the Beatles had not been, and never would be, so literally deified.

Privately, Clapton was anything but god like. Born in an insular Surrey village, he had grown up motherless just as Jimi had – in this case, abandoned at the age of two by his teenage single mother, Pat, and turned over to his grandmother, who thereafter he had to pretend was his mother, and the cold, unpredictable Pat, his older sister. He had never lost the persona of a betrayed, wounded child that everyone around him felt obligated to protect from life's harsh realities, be it scoring drugs or taking a driving test.

Blues music had rescued Clapton from despair in leafy Surrey, he felt, as surely as it had any beaten and starved Mississippi slave. But had also been like a overseer's whip, driving him to replicate it in its purest possible form and to walk out of any band that failed to measure up to his exacting standards. Amid the adulation and wealth of a superstar, he pined to be just an ordinary sideman and, like Jimi, took centre stage to sing only with the greatest reluctance. Of all the blues masters, his greatest idol was Robert Johnson, in whom musical genius had combined with extraordinary physical beauty but who had died from drinking poisoned whisky aged only 27.

Clapton had lately left John Mayall's Bluesbreakers for a new band named Cream in an unusual trio format, already dubbed a 'supergroup' since its bass player, Jack Bruce, and drummer, Ginger Baker, both came from the highly respected Graham Bond Organisation. One of Cream's early gigs was at a London college, the Polytechnic in Great Titchfield Street. But such was the buzz about them that many people from the music business turned up, including Chas Chandler with Jimi.

Taking any opportunity to continue the infiltration process, Chandler had asked if Jimi could sit in with the superlative threesome for a number. Neither Clapton nor Jack Bruce had any objection; the volatile, red-headed Ginger Baker did, but was overruled.

By an unlucky coincidence, the number was Howlin' Wolf's 'Killing Floor', which Clapton had only just mastered after much difficulty. Now he saw it performed not only effortlessly but at breakneck speed by someone as beautiful as Robert Johnson whose idea of 'sitting in' was like nothing ever seen on a rock stage before – who first played his guitar behind his head as if trying to throw off a vampire bat, then with his teeth as if greedily fellating it, all while never fluffing a note.

'Halfway through the song, Eric stopped playing,' Chas Chandler would recall. 'Both his hands dropped down to his sides, then he walked offstage. I ran back to the dressing room and he was standing there, trying to light a cigarette with his hand shaking. He said, "You never told me he was *that* fuckin' good."'

Word of what had happened at the Polytechnic soon went around British rock's numerous other guitar heroes and brought them out en masse to see who had so summarily dethroned 'God'. This time the chosen club was not the Scotch of St James but the equally tiny Bag O'Nails in Kingly Street, just off Piccadilly. The vocalist Terry Reid from Peter Jay and the Jaywalkers later recalled standing at the entrance, counting the VIPs in with growing disbelief. 'Here's Mick Jagger . . . Keith Richards . . . Brian Jones . . . Paul McCartney walks in. Jeff Beck walks in. I thought, "What is this? A bloody convention?" Here comes Jimi, hair all over the place, pulls out this left-handed Stratocaster, beaten to death, looks like he's been chopping wood with it.

'And he gets up, all soft-spoken, and all of a sudden WHOO-RRAAWWR! He breaks into "Wild Thing" and it was all over. There were guiter players weeping. They had to mop the floor up. He keeps piling it on, solo after solo. I could see everyone's fillings falling out. When he finished, it was silence. Nobody knew what to do. Everyone was dumbstruck, completely in shock.'

SEVEN
'OH MY GOD, I'M NOT GOD ANY MORE'

With Jimi in possession of a three-month UK work permit, and so able to perform openly at last, the most urgent need was to find him a backing band. He himself talked vaguely about a Little Richard-style 'revue' with a horn section, but Chas Chandler was firmly against any such echo of the Chitlin' Circuit and decreed a straight rock format with two essential preconditions. Whatever sidemen Jimi acquired must be a) white and b) not so brilliant as to take attention away from their front man.

Noel Redding, a 21-year-old from Folkestone, Kent, had been playing guitar with the little-known Loving Kind when he travelled up to London in answer to a job ad in the *New Musical Express*. Rather than go totally solo after the Animals' split, Eric Burdon, had decided to form a new line-up under the same name. Redding, who had played with Burdon a couple of times previously, was hoping for a place in those New Animals.

He had just failed his audition at the Birdland club when the door opened to admit Chandler and what Burdon would later recall as 'a shadowy figure in a Western sombrero kind of hat [with] beads around it'. Burdon had heard about Jimi from Linda Keith, along with 'some wild rumours about this guy who'd been in prison and killed someone and played guitar with his teeth'. After the hat, what he noticed was the newcomer's pigeon-toed gait. 'You could tell that he'd had the wrong sized shoes on as a kid and his feet were all screwed up. It was like his toes made a triangle as he walked.

'He looked almost purple in the darkness of the club and he just grabbed a guitar and said, "Do you mind if I have a jam?" and these amazing sounds started to ricochet around the room.'

Meanwhile, Chandler's attention was fixed on the guitarist who had just failed to impress Burdon. Handling rhythm and lead as Jimi did, both roles would be equally redundant in any band he led. However, above Noel Redding's bespectacled, rather pinched little face was curly hair naturally forming an Afro as voluminous as Jimi's sculpted one. Tonsorially, if not musically, he was perfect.

By Redding's later account, he and Jimi went to the next-door pub, the Duke of York, and Jimi asked if he'd consider switching to bass. When he confessed that he'd never played one, Jimi offered to teach him and asked him to come back tomorrow to start learning on the instrument Chandler had used in the Animals. However, Kathy Etchingham disputes this. 'All Noel's stories had to do with pubs. I was at the audition and I know that Chas and Jimi agreed to hire him in the taxi afterwards.'

A somewhat greater problem was finding a drummer whom Jimi would not completely overwhelm. There was no shortage of applicants and in the end it came down to a dead heat between Aynsley Dunbar from a Liverpool group, the Mojos, and twenty-year-old John 'Mitch' Mitchell from Ealing, west London, until recently wielding the sticks in Georgie Fame's Blue Flames. Mitchell was a former child actor and member of the Ovaltineys, a troupe of shiny-cheeked tots who advertised the bedtime drink in dressing gowns and slippers. He had fallen in love with percussion as a schoolboy, working Saturdays in the drum shop of Jim Marshall before Marshall invented monumental amplifiers.

Dunbar was a talented player who would go on to work with Frank Zappa, David Bowie and Lou Reed while Mitchell, for all his diminutive build, was a powerhouse with a strong jazz bias. Unable to decide between them, Jimi tossed a coin and the ex-Ovaltiney won.

A pianist was also considered, but Chandler and Mike Jeffery decided to stick with a power trio line-up like Cream's, even though Jimi was still uncomfortable about doing vocals and neither of the other two showed great talent in that direction. Noel Redding would recall how, to begin with, the songs they played were 'virtually instrumentals with extremely minimal mumbling'. Jeffery would always claim credit for naming them the Jimi Hendrix Experience, a bit like the Brian Auger Trinity, but lending Jimi the aura of a theme park ride rather than a church.

Mitch Mitchell's arrival enhanced the band by more than just percussion. Since trying out Vic Briggs's mighty Marshall, Jimi had grown increasingly unhappy with the feeble 30-watt Burns amp provided by Chandler. Learning that Mitchell had once worked for the giant's inventor, Jim Marshall, the fortuitously named James Marshall 'accidentally' destroyed the Burns by kicking it down a flight of stairs, then personally ordered a brace of Jim Marshall's finest, for himself and Noel Redding. Marshall was impressed that his near-namesake wasn't looking for freebies but for special after-sales service.

As it happened, this quantum upgrade came in the nick of time. One of Jim's final 'secret' appearances had been at the Cromwellian on a night when Johnny Hallyday dropped in for dinner. Hallyday was France's only rock 'n' roll star, known as 'the French Elvis' and hugely famous there (though virtually unknown in the wider world). *Bouleversé* by what he saw and heard at the Cromwellian, he asked the Jimi Hendrix Experience to join him for four nights of concerts in his homeland, starting on 13 October.

A few days after the Hallyday invitation, a lowly young band named the Syn returned to London from a hard week of travelling around grim northern venues like Stoke-on-Trent, mostly in pouring rain. Their bass player was eighteen-year-old Chris Squire, later a mainstay of the globally successful Yes.

That Tuesday evening's booking at Soho's famous R&B club, the Marquee in Wardour Street, came as a welcome relief for the Syn. Top bands always played the Marquee on Tuesdays and they were opening for Cliff Bennett and the Rebel Rousers, who currently had a UK number 6 single with the Beatles' 'Got to Get You into My Life'. Supporting such a crowd-puller triggered a small percentage of the gate money on top of their fee, which for Chris Squire meant being able to go on eating until the weekend.

When he arrived at the Marquee, there was an unknown band rehearsing on its stage, something that ordinarily the club never allowed. 'The guitarist is a black guy and he's going "duh-duh-DUH" to the bass player who's playing "duh-duh-DOH" and I want to tell him "No, no, no, it goes like this." I went to the assistant manager, Jack Barry, and said, "Where are Cliff Bennett and the Rebel Rousers?" and he said, "No, these guys are the main act tonight." I went "*What?* They can't learn five notes together."

'In the dressing room I get talking to this guitarist, which is the first conversation with a black guy I've ever had – and odd as well because normally guitarists didn't talk to bass-players. He's looking at my bass and saying, "Oh yeah, I knew someone in Seattle who had a Rickenbacker bass," and all the time I'm thinking, "This guy has got this awful band that no one's going to come and see."'

A few doors from the Marquee was a café to which Squire and his bandmates went for a pre-performance meal, ordering the cheapest things on the menu. As they sat there, they watched the queue for the club extend past the window and continue all down Wardour Street.

'I went to the entrance, where Jack Barry was taking ten-shilling notes hand over fist, and said, "What's going on? Who are these blokes we're opening for?" Jack said, "I've no idea. I was just told by the front office that they're headlining."' The crowd was soon far beyond any Cliff Bennett and the Rebel Rousers could have drawn, meaning the Syn would get their gate percentage after all, so Squire could return to the café and order a dessert.

'Then when we go onstage, I look down at the first four rows and see all my biggest heroes . . . Pete Townshend . . . Keith Richard . . . Stevie Winwood . . . Eric Clapton, looking like "Oh my God, I'm not God any more."'

After the Syn's set, an anticipatory crowd in the wings blocked Squire's way back to the dressing room, leaving him no choice but to watch the mystery headliners sitting on the grand piano behind Mitch Mitchell's drums. A few seconds were enough to show that Noel Redding's unsteady bass-fingering mattered not a jot. 'Jimi just blew me away,' Squire would recall.

More than that, the shy eighteen-year-old realised later that some of the raw sex pumped out with 'Hey Joe', 'Killing Floor', 'Land of 1,000 Dances' and 'Wild Thing' seemed to have stuck to him. 'There were girls at the Marquee that night I never would have dared to talk to. But suddenly they were like "Oh hi, Chris . . . Weren't you on with Jimi? . . . Can I buy you a drink?"'

All this time after crossing the Atlantic, Jimi still had not let his father know where he was. His outward cheerful adaptability had masked a fear that the adventure might come to a premature end and he'd have only another story of failure to tell Al. But now there was so much that was positive to recount, he placed a phone call to Seattle from his room at the Hyde Park Towers in the presence of his new girlfriend, Kathy Etchingham.

Direct dialling from the UK to the US was then still in the future and connecting with one's 'party' involved going through a British and an American operator. Nervous of how all this might impact on his hotel bill, Jimi reversed the charges.

Al Hendrix's future autobiography, *My Son Jimi*, would recall an excited voice on the line, saying, 'Dad, looks like I'm on my way to the big time' as if to the most loving and supportive of parents, then chattering about the new spelling of his Christian name, his new bass player and drummer and recent reluctant plunge into doing vocals. 'All those other guys sing even though they ain't got no voice and they're just hollering and going on. You know I don't have no voice, but heck I'm gonna do it, too.'

Nor was he the only one with big news. Since they'd last spoken, Al had married a Japanese-American woman, Ayako Jinka, known as 'June' – a widow with five children – and had also moved house. Jimi, he maintained, had been delighted about the match and full of extravagant promises: 'I'm gonna buy you a home. I'm gonna buy you this and that. Whatever you need, just let me know.'

But in Kathy's recollecton, Al wouldn't believe Jimi was in England and he passed her the phone so that her accent would prove it. Once persuaded, all he said was, 'You tell my boy to write me. I ain't paying for no collect calls.'

'The phone went dead [and] Jimi's face just fell,' she would write in her own autobiography. 'In that moment, he looked like a hurt little boy.'

The Johnny Hallyday tour did not begin well. On its opening night, at the Cinema Novelty in Evreux, Normandy, Noel Redding and Mitch Mitchell's initial cohesion came completely unstuck and even Jimi seemed unnerved by his first exposure to France. One local paper called him a 'bad mixture of James Brown and Chuck Berry'.

Although the trio's playing grew progressively better at the second and third venues, Nancy and Villerupt, it was plain that all the audiences really cared about was their national treasure,

'John-ee', with his old-fashioned quiff, too-tight jeans and voice as rock 'n' roll as Gitanes and Pernod.

In fact, Jimi's most fervid French fan turned out to be 'John-ee' himself. A serious musician at heart, the French Elvis joined 'the black Elvis' onstage for 'Hey Joe' and was so moved by the song, he decided to record his own version with French lyrics by Gilles Thibault, who also co-wrote the words of 'Comme d'habitude', better known in its English translation as 'My Way'.

The tour finale on 18 October was at the famous Olympia theatre in Paris, where even the Beatles had struggled against France's historic prejudice against any popular music but its own. Added to the bill for that last night were the Brian Auger Trinity, whom Chas Chandler had so recently tried to turn into a vehicle for Jimi.

Two thousand peremptory Parisians started by roaring for 'John-ee' but ended by cheering wildly for 'Jim-ee', as Auger's lead guitarist, Vic Briggs, recalls. 'They may have had no idea who he was but it was obvious they'd never seen anything like him. The French were never big on finesse, but they loved a show of raw power and that's what Jimi gave them that night.'

Back in London a week later, the Jimi Hendrix Experience went into Kingsway Studios (later renamed De Lane Lea) to record 'Hey Joe' as their debut single with a female backing group, the Breakaways. It was Chas Chandler's debut as a producer and, with Noel Redding's bass-fingering still shaky, Chandler also returned to his former role in the Animals. The B-side was Jimi's own composition 'Stone Free', exulting in his sense of liberation, like 'Wild Thing' at Mach speed:

> *Stone free . . . to do what I please*
> *Stone free . . . to ride the breeze*

Rallying from his father's transatlantic apathy, he sent Al a post-card, saying he would have a record out 'in about two months' and clearly hoping to impress with his exotic travel news. 'We just left Paris and Nancy, France . . . I think things are getting a little better.'

The end of October brought Jimi his first mention in the British music press, when *Record Mirror* reported: 'Chas Chandler has signed and brought to this country a 20-year-old [sic] Negro called Jim [sic] Hendrix who – among other things – plays his guitar with his teeth and is being hailed in some quarters as "the next big thing".'

'Negro' was considered quite acceptable in 1966, and Jimi's first publicity with the Experience almost invariably referred to his colour, often in terms suggesting some untamed aboriginal or fairground sideshow. When touting him around, Chandler often used the 'wild man from Borneo' line that had originated with Zoot Money's wife, Ronni, on his very first day in London.

Distasteful as it seems now, it was a great deal milder than the racial slurs Jimi had been accustomed to in America; indeed, he rather liked it, thinking it made him sound interesting. Similarly demeaning tags that he wore without complaint, having no idea what they meant, were 'dervish' and 'Mau Mau', the name of the insurgency movement in British-ruled Kenya during the 1950s.

British racism was different from American in usually being without conscious malice, and he tended to ignore its grosser manifestations rather than seem a nuisance to his new white sponsors. One of the worst was BBC television's *Black and White Minstrel Show* in which white singers 'blacked up' to sing songs about Mammy and the Swanee River, rolling their eyes and waggling their hands in nauseating caricature.

'We were watching TV at Zoot Money's once when the *Black and White Minstrels* came on,' Eric Burdon recalls. 'I looked at Jimi for his reaction – and there was nothing. From that point on, I knew this guy was going to do whatever it took to get on.'

His Parisian coup was followed by a booking at a club named the Big Apple in Munich from 8–11 November, with one of the performances televised. West German teenagers proved far more quickly conquered than French ones and to whip up the frenzy of their female element, he used an extra-long guitar lead which allowed him to jump off the stage and walk among the screaming fräuleins while still playing.

One night, as he rejoined Redding and Mitchell, the crowd mobbed him and to protect his guitar, he threw it ahead of him onto the stage, cracking its neck. Impulsively, he picked it up and smashed it down again, much harder. At this, the audience went even crazier, dragging him off the stage again – and Chas Chandler told him to keep it in the act.

The Who were already breaking up their equipment as a climax to their set in what Pete Townshend grandiosely termed 'auto-destructive performance art'. But whereas Townshend always battered his guitar beyond any hope of repair, the cost-conscious Chandler would make sure Jimi inflicted no serious damage on his so that it could be abused and reused.

Jimi turned 24 that November, still registered at the Hyde Park Towers with Kathy Etchingham now sharing his room. What had started as a one-night stand had become a relationship that would continue for the next two and a half years.

Their respective fractured childhoods drew them together, even if Kathy's loveless and neglected early years in Derby had never reduced her to eating horsemeat burgers like Jimi and his brother Leon. He sometimes talked about his mother, a rare thing for him, admitting that she'd died of alcoholism but saying she'd been 'like a goddess in the sky and an angel'. Ten years after Lucille's sad end, he still often dreamed about her at nights and could even remember the smell of her perfume.

In lighter vein, he talked of hard times on the Chitlin' Circuit. Since when he'd got into the habit of always carrying dollar bill inside one boot 'for emergencies', usually caused by missing somebody or other's tour bus. He kept up the habit, though now with a British pound note, tucked into the lining of his silver-circled black ten-gallon hat. Inside the boot he taped a lock of Kathy's hair, an ancient voodoo trick supposedly ensuring she would never leave him.

Most of their time was spent in the high-priced darkness of the clubs where Jimi played and Kathy deejayed, or in bed, where he had instantly eclipsed her two previous rock-star lovers, Brian Jones and Keith Moon – but that was by no means all they did together. Although she hadn't been in London much longer than Jimi, she became his guide to the sights every visiting American seeks, like Buckingham Palace, Nelson's Column, the Houses of Parliament and, as they call it, 'the Tower of Big Ben'.

She took him to all Swinging London's hotspots like the Portobello Road open-air antiques market, and clothes shopping in Chelsea's King's Road, at boutiques where the division between cutting-edge and vintage – and male and female – scarcely existed any more. Such places furnished Jimi with a whole new stage wardrobe, much to the annoyance of Chas Chandler, who'd been pressuring him to wear something like the soft hued trouser-suits favoured by Kathy. With his love of flowered print blouses and floaty chiffon scarves, his taste was far more feminine than hers; one fellow musician described him as 'that guy who looks as if he's just walked into a girl's closet and put everything on'.

The male fashion fad of the moment was Victorian military tunics, either genuine from Portobello Market or replicas from a store named I Was Lord Kitchener's Valet. Though their usual colour was British Empire red, Jimi found one in dark blue with braid across its chest like external gold ribs and climbing each arm almost to the shoulder. It had evidently been the full dress of some mid-Victorian hussar regiment, though Jimi himself always believed its former owner to have served in the Royal Army Veterinary Corps.

With Chas Chandler handling most of Jimi's day-to-day routine, Kathy saw little of Mike Jeffery – and what she did see caused her no misgivings about Jeffery's management. 'I always liked Mike: he was very personable and entertaining and didn't seem to mind Jimi being with me at all. We'd sometimes go to the flat in Jermyn Street, where he lived with his then wife, Gillian. He'd talk a lot about his plans for Jimi, and he seemed to have real vision.

'Mike kept Jimi pretty well supplied with cash, although he was never that bothered about money. As long as he had enough to buy clothes and records, he was happy.'

Unknown though Jimi still was to the wider public, he attracted stares everywhere he went with Kathy, some for his clothes, others because, even in Swinging London, an interracial couple was still an unusual and far from welcome sight. The closest he had to a bodyguard was Chandler who, at six-foot-three, with a background in the River Tyne shipyards, was well qualified for the role. One day, as the three of them walked towards the 100 Club in Oxford Street, a couple of brawny men with Glaswegian accents began to taunt Jimi about his clothes and cast doubts on his heterosexuality. Chandler felled the larger and louder of the two with a single kick.

Jimi's record collection contained all the latest British rock and pop as well as blues and R&B and 'spoken word' albums by Bill Cosby, then America's most famous black comedian, whom he could mimic with uncanny precision. There were surprising choices, too, like *The Planets* by Gustav Holst, to which he was first attracted by his passion for science fiction.

Kathy's memoir also describes more innocent activities on their bed, such as playing Monopoly and Scrabble, or with the Scalextric racing-car layout Jimi bought himself in compensation for all the toys he'd never had as a child. One afternoon, they decided to visit the ice rink in nearby Queensway, where it took some time to find skates for Jimi's size 12 feet. The physical co-ordination of the former high school athlete had not disappeared: he was soon skating with ease and so enjoyed it that he returned for several more sessions. Jimi Hendrix, circling the ice in Afro, gold-ribbed hussar jacket and chiffon scarf, is a vision to linger on.

Despite his fixation on Kathy, Linda Keith had by no means vanished from Jimi's life after storming out of the Hyde Park Towers during his first few days in London. They often bumped into each other at gigs and parties, although Chas Chandler made every effort to keep Linda at arm's length. 'Chas was always very wary of me,' she recalls. 'I think he was afraid I'd ask him for money for steering him towards Jimi.'

It was Linda who first took him to Chelsea's coolest new boutique, Granny Takes A Trip, so named because the folds of the antique garments it sold to both sexes would likely soon reek of pot. As the shop's co-founder, John Pearse, recalls, Jimi always went straight for the women's section. 'He loved these highly coloured blouses with big puffy sleeves. He'd grab them by the armful, not even bothering to try them on.'

Linda would even visit him at the very hotel where Kathy had seemingly displaced her. Jimi said they were 'blood brothers' and once insisted they formalise it by cutting their wrists and mingling their blood. 'I remember how nervous he was while we were doing it in case Kathy suddenly walked in.'

That autumn, Little Richard visited Britain to perform to his still-faithful rock 'n' roll audience, and put up at the Rembrandt Hotel in Knightsbridge, just across the greensward from the Hyde Park Towers. Jimi had left Richard's revue in 1965 still owed $50 in salary, which would come in particularly handy at present. With Kathy in tow, he paid his old employer a surprise visit at the Rembrandt, naively hoping to collect.

Richard greeted them affably enough in a suite with a silent audience of stage wigs, even ordering a bottle of whisky from room service. But each time Jimi brought up the $50, he simply roared with laughter and answered, 'You missed the bus.'

Afterwards, as Jimi and Kathy walked down Knightsbridge, heading for the Cromwellian, a police car pulled up and two officers confronted him with a truculence he'd received from no other British 'bobby' in the past month, They had spotted his gold-braided hussar tunic and were outraged that such a figure should be wearing 'a uniform our soldiers died in'. Jimi's plea that it had belonged to a non-combatant army veterinarian cut no ice , so he slipped it off without argument, putting it on again as soon as they'd driven off .

Another time, his quick reflexes saved a potentially awkward situation over the tunic. While drinking in a Chelsea pub with Eric Burdon, he was approached by an army veteran from the nearby Royal Chelsea Hospital wearing the traditional 'Chelsea Pensioner's' scarlet frock coat and black peaked cap.

'"What regiment were you in?" this old guy asks Jimi,' Burdon recalls. '"The 101st Airborne," he says. "Ah . . . my lot fought next to yours at the Battle of Arnhem," the old guy says, and shakes Jimi's hand.'

A few weeks after Mike Jeffery took on Jimi, Patricia – 'Trixi' – Sullivan became his secretary/PA. The daughter of an East End dock worker, Trixi had proved formidably bright, winning a scholarship to one of London's most sought-after private girls' schools, Haberdashers' Aske's. She went after the job with Jeffery as a temporary measure, to make enough money to get her to America. Some of the duties involved were connected with the disco and boutique in Majorca that he still operated alongside his pop acts. Trixi was hired for being the only applicant who knew where Majorca was.

Her initiation into Jeffery's peculiar twilight world came quickly. 'Mike was away and was having his flat in Jermyn Street cleaned, so he asked me to go round there and keep an eye on the cleaners. "But don't look in the desk drawers," he told me, "or under any of the chairs."

'So I'm sitting at the desk and, of course, I open one of the drawers. Inside it there's a mousetrap that my hand just misses. Then the one of the cleaners comes in and says, "What do I do with this?" and it's a shotgun he's found under a chair. In fact, there's a gun under *every* chair.

'When I spoke to him next, I asked him, "What was all that about, Mike?" He just said, "You never know who's going to be visiting you."'

The job did get Trixi to America, although not in the way she'd planned. Soon after the shotgun episode, Jeffery asked her to courier £20,000 to his New York office. At the time, it was illegal to take more than £50 out of the country, but he continually flouted the law – or, rather, got other people to. On a previous occasion, Chandler had been found with £1,000 at Heathrow airport and had the lot confiscated.

'I put the money in a suitcase and covered it with packets of Tampax,' Trixi recalls. 'At JFK airport, they just waved me through.'

The Jimi she met in Jeffery's office was so shy as to be barely audible. 'You could tell what he'd gone through those years in America. He was all "Yes, Sir" and "No, Sir", hardly ever looking up and giving this little nervous giggle behind his hand. I was amazed at the difference in him when he went onstage.'

As they got to know each other, a common bond was

established, for Trixi, too, had grown up with a physically violent father against whom she'd retaliated in a way that Jimi never dared against Al. 'I saved up my pocket money and bought a little stiletto. The next time he tried to hit me, I just showed him the stiletto. He never tried it again.'

On 1 December, Jeffery took Jimi to the office of a London solicitor named John Hillman. There he was presented with a contract entitling his new management to 40 per cent of his future performance earnings, solemnised with a one-shilling (5p) postage stamp.

Jimi raised no objection to the terms – already having a long record of signing without reading pieces of paper put in front of him – but, at the crucial moment, he recollected a potential problem. In 1965, he had signed a three-year contract with the New York producer Ed Chalpin to record exclusively for Chalpin's cheapo PPX label. 'Don't use my name, man,' he told Jeffery in sudden alarm (although at the time he'd still been Jimmy, not Jimi). Jeffery told him to sign anyway and they would sort out Chalpin later.

The solicitor John Hillman was particularly relevant to the proceedings, having been the main instigator of Yameta, the Nassau-based company into which Jeffery had paid the earnings of his previous star act, the Animals, with the seemingly selfless motive of protecting them from US income tax. The same arrangement was now to be used for Jimi, more relevantly in his case since, after protracted negotiations with Britain's tax authorities, he was officially domiciled in New York.

The Hyde Park Towers was not an expensive hotel and had been talked into charging only single-room rate for Jimi's double occupancy with Kathy Etchingham. Even so, it had become too great a drain on Jeffery and Chandler (and, besides, was found to be suffering from dry rot) so they decided their charge must be moved to a flat. As Christmas approached, one became available that seemed almost to good to be true – a well-appointed duplex located at 34 Montagu Square, on the fringe of the West End, owned by Ringo Starr.

Having bought the property in the first flush of Beatle wealth, Ringo now let it out, mostly to musician friends, for a pepper-corn rent of £30 per week. Paul McCartney had worked on the *Rubber Soul* album there, previewing it in the living room to intellectual friends including the American beat writer William S. Burroughs, whose notorious third novel, *Naked Lunch*, had lately been prosecuted under America's anti-sodomy laws. John Lennon's mother-in-law was another sometime tenant.

With two good-sized bedrooms, one on the ground floor, the other in the basement, there was more than enough room for Jimi and Kathy, so Chas Chandler moved in, too, with his Swedish girlfriend, Lotte Null.

'Hey Joe' was released in the UK on 16 December. Kit Lambert and Chris Stamp's new Track label wasn't yet operational and, after rejections from the Beatles' record company, EMI, and the Rolling Stones', Decca, it was released by Polydor, who were to distribute Track's product in the UK.

Lambert and Stamp nonetheless took a hand in an impressive promotional campaign which introduced Jimi (sans guitar-fellatio) to two of Britain's three television channels. On 16 December, he appeared on commercial ITV's super-hip *Ready Steady Go!* programme along with the Troggs, the Merseys and the Four Tops; on the 29th, he was booked for BBC1's *Top of the Pops* – a minor miracle as the puritanical BBC routinely banned songs on themes far milder than shooting women in cold blood.

There was a press reception at the Bag O'Nails with Jimi, Redding and Mitchell playing live. Under the headline MR PHE-NOMENON!, *Record Mirror*'s Peter Jones, one of the first trade journalists to have spotted the Rolling Stones, seemed quite overcome by the 'guitarist – singer – composer – showman

– original – whirling like a dervish, swirling his guitar every which way'.

'What this man does to a guitar could get him arrested for assault,' wrote Keith Altham in *New Musical Express*. 'He kisses it, sits on it and treads on it. Quite apart from hitting it with his elbow and caressing the amplifier with it,' wrote another *Record Mirror* correspondent, Richard Green, noting how the two instruments Jimi had used continued to emit anguished noises on their own after he'd left the stage. 'Considering the number of indignities they had suffered during the preceding 45 minutes, I wouldn't have been surprised if they had got up and made a speech.'

Melody Maker's Nick Jones summed up what he'd seen and heard as 'flying music. Love and freedom. Body, soul, funk, feeling, feedback and freak.'

Three months earlier, Jimi had been a nobody in New York with nowhere else to go but Chitlin'-wards; now, in the words of one enraptured music journalist, he had hit Swinging London 'with the force of a 50 megaton H-Bomb'. Further still from home, he had seen Munich, Normandy and the Eiffel Tower, eaten in a real Parisian restaurant and afterwards competed with his new *meilleur ami* Johne-ee to blow the best smoke rings with their Gitanes. And to cap everything, he was living in a Beatle's flat.

The Jimi Hendrix Experience brought in the New Year of 1967 by playing a £50 gig at Stan's Hillside Club in Noel Redding's home town of Folkestone. Jimi's reputation had not yet reached the Kentish coast and Stan, the proprietor, was initially dubious about booking a group of unknowns (apart from Redding).

Afterwards, Redding took Jimi and Kathy to spend the night at the home of his mother, Margaret, where she and his grandmother were waiting up. The weather was bitterly cold and

Margaret Redding had a log fire crackling and spitting in the hearth – something Jimi had never seen outside movies. 'The first thing he asked,' Redding would recall, 'was "May I stand in front of your fire?"'

EIGHT
'GO OUT AND BUY US A TIN OF LIGHTER FUEL'

In 1967, pop music reached its public chiefly via the 45 revolutions-per-minute vinyl single, retailing in Britain at around six shillings (30p) and pressed by the hundred thousand – occasionally by the million – to meet orders taken far ahead of release. Thanks mainly to the Beatles, the 33rpm album, then better known as LP (for 'long-player') was catching up fast, and there was also the EP ('extended play') with four or five tracks as against the LP's dozen or so. But the true gauge of popularity remained the seven-inch, double-sided, paper-jacketed '45'.

These were heady times for British broadcasting hardly less than for music. Since 1964, so-called pirate radio stations had been operating in defiance of the BBC's historic monopoly from small ships or disused military installations far enough off the east coast to be exempt from government licensing or control. The pirates used American-style fast-talking deejays, commercial breaks, idents and jingles that delighted young Britons after the BBC's stuffy presentational style (even its record programmes had to be scripted) and delighted in playing everything the prudish 'Beeb' abhorred.

Britain's record industry was riddled with corruption, un-checked by the payola scandals that had convulsed America's in the late 1950s. Artistes' managements would routinely bulk-buy singles to push them into the charts while every record company kept a list of radio deejays who could be bribed to give a new release a few extra plays and television producers to book an act, then be generous with screen time.

Mike Jeffery had learned well from his apprenticeship with Don Arden and the Animals. Music journalists like Keith Altham were well aware that money had changed hands, both off- and onshore to plant 'Hey Joe' in the Top 30. Once Jimi was seen on *Top of the Pops* and *Ready Steady Go!*, it continued climbing of its own volition, peaking at number 6.

Having a Top 10 hit took the Jimi Hendrix Experience from the male-oriented sphere of rock to the female-oriented one of pop; from newsprint trades to glossy magazines like *Jackie* and *Honey* whose readers cared little about Jimi's virtuosity on the guitar, but expected pictures of him to add to the teeming pantheons of their bedroom walls.

For his first-ever photo shoot, Chas Chandler sent him to Gered Mankowitz, the son of the playwright Wolf Mankowitz, who had made a name by chronicling early Rolling Stones tours and whose studio was conveniently situated in Mason's Yard, only yards from the Scotch of St James. Mankowitz created what would be the most famous image of Jimi, in his gold-ribbed hussar tunic with a most unsoldierly flowered scarf spilling from its open collar. The shot came from a second session, made necessary when Mitch Mitchell also switched to an Afro and Chandler wanted the Experience shown with matching coiffures.

Much as the camera turned out to love Jimi, he did not return the affection. His innate shyness and modesty made it all but impossible for him to look straight into the lens and put on the glib smile that *Honey* and *Fabulous* readers expected. He liked it no better that Mankowitz was under orders to make him look as 'wild' as possible. He hated the sullen and defensive-looking portraits his managers picked out and always referred to them as 'horrors'.

But all Chandler's PR efforts could not fit him into the usual pop-celebrity mould. A 'Life Lines' questionnaire he filled in, to be circulated to the press, revealed both his exotic nonconformity and how many of those life lines he prefered to gloss over. He gave his age as 21 – evidently fearing that, to *Honey* and *Fabulous* readers, 24 might seem like getting on a bit – and in the box headed 'Family' mentioned only his father and brother Leon, not their four unfortunate younger siblings, so long in the care of Seattle's welfare authorities. As his 'Likes', he gave 'music, hair, mountains and fields'; as his 'Dislikes', 'marmalade and cold sheets'; as his 'Favourite Food', 'strawberry shortcake and spaghetti'; as his 'Favourite Musicians', 'Dylan, Muddy Waters and Mozart'; as his 'Professional Ambition', 'to be in a movie and caress the screen with my shining light'.

Only his 'Personal Ambition' was neither evasive nor flippant but heartbreaking to anyone who'd known a little boy named Buster: 'to see my mother and family again.'

London's adulation continued, undiminished. On 29 January, the Jimi Hendrix Experience supported the Who at the Saville Theatre in Shaftesbury Avenue, owned by the Beatles' manager, Brian Epstein, which presented straight plays through the week (Epstein having studied at the Royal Academy of Dramatic Art before stumbling on Liverpool's Cavern club) and Sunday concerts featuring his clients' particular favourites of the moment. The audience for this one included John Lennon, Paul McCartney and George Harrison, and all three members of Cream. Afterwards, their bass player, Jack Bruce, went home with a Jimi-like bass riff in his head that he would develop into one of the trio's greatest hits, 'Sunshine of Your Love'.

Such spots of metropolitan glamour were becoming rarer, however. For Mike Jeffery was turning the Experience into the same workhorses as the Animals, booking them for virtually continuous one-night club appearances all over the country, expecting the demand to dry up at any moment. Some of the bookings, made prior to 'Hey Joe', were for as little as £25. On their advance billing, Jimi appeared variously as 'Jimmy' or 'Jimmie' and was said to be 'like Dylan, Clapton and James Brown rolled into one'.

The three musicians had a single roadie, Gerry Stickells, an old friend of Redding's from Folkestone, who got the job mainly because he owned a Ford Thames van just about large enough to carry them and their two tons of Marshall amplifiers and other equipment.

The brawny Stickells proved both a sympathetic and resourceful aide. When, as often happened, Jimi blew out one of the Marshalls, the roadie would get it going again without having to halt the performance. When, as happened even more often, he broke a guitar string – usually the thinnest top E – Stickells would whip on a new one right there at the mic. An essential nightly duty was taping or nailing back together the long-suffering black Fender Strat after Jimi had battered the stage with it. The repair had to be carried out quickly because even after the most demanding gig, as Stickells would recall, 'he'd be looking for somebody to jam with'.

Kathy Etchingham was addicted to *Coronation Street*, then – and now – Britain's most-watched TV soap, the thrice-weekly saga of a Lancashire working-class community centred on its pub, the Rovers Return. The soap's northern idiom was at first too impenetrable for Jimi, but he soon became involved with its characters, especially the street's arch-gossips, Ena Sharples, Minnie Caldwell and Martha Longhurst, always to be found in the Rovers' back bar, sipping stout and eviscerating their neighbours like a coven of witches in hairnets.

Now, as he journeyed to Manchester's Twisted Wheel club, Sheffield's Mojo, Nottingham's Boathouse – and of course – Mike Jeffery's Club A Go Go in Newcastle, *Coronation Street* materialised everywhere in the rows of back-to-back houses, the rain shining on cobbled roads, the permanent taste of coal grit in the air. He discovered the north of England's friendliness, honesty and joie-de-vivre along with its insularity, touchiness and the suspicion of strangers, especially those in any eccentric dress, which caused Noel Redding and himself to be refused service in one pub because they were mistaken for circus clowns.

He learned the impossibility of getting anything to eat after 9 p.m. apart from takeaway fish and chips wrapped in newspaper, and grew familiar with such northern delicacies as black pudding, mushy peas and 'scratchings' – pork rinds coated in batter, born of the same economic necessity as Southern soul-food chitterlings. In truth, this was not the Chitlin' but the Scratchings Circuit.

Nowhere on the itinerary was more quintessentially northern than Ilkley, Yorkshire, where the Jimi Hendrix Experience appeared at the Troutbeck Hotel on the Sunday evening of 12 March. The hotel stood on the edge of Ilkley Moor, a wild, weatherblown tract immortalised by an ancient ballad named 'On Ilkla Moor Baht 'At', which British schoolchildren learn to sing in Yorkshire accents despite having no idea what it is about. Although the Troutbeck's regular clientele was largely middle-aged and conservative, it had turned its ballroom into a club called the Gyro, the very opposite of London's Stygian cellars, presenting live pop acts for a 10-shilling (50p) entrance fee.

When that night's attraction arrived, fresh from appearances at the Skyline Ballroom, Hull, and the International Club, Leeds, his Ilkley hosts wondered whether reports of his wildness might have been exaggerated. For Jimi sought neither drugs nor groupies but occupied the long wait for showtime with Redding and Mitchell by quietly playing cards or the board games they always carried with them: Monopoly, Scrabble and Risk.

At around 8.45, Ilkley's police station received a complaint about the number of cars parked in the lane outside the Troutbeck Hotel, which was the main access to Ilkley Moor. Dispatched to investigate, Sergeant Thomas Chapman found around a hundred vehicles clogging the lane and a ballroom designed to hold 250 people packed with at least 600, waiting for the show to start.

Sgt Chapman took the stage to announce that safety regulations were being breached and ordered the spectators to leave. Finding himself totally ignored, he withdrew to telephone the police station for backup, then returned to the ballroom where – as his official report would attest in classic British copper-speak: 'I found that the beat group booked for that night had gone onstage and commenced their performance.' However, no reinforcements were needed.

'I went on to the stage and spoke to the leader of the group, whom whom I now know to be a man called Hendrix. I told him the position and he stopped the music. He tried to persuade the persons to leave the hall but they would not do so and commenced shouting, stamping and chanting that they wanted their money back.'

On his own initiative, Sgt Chapman went to the back of the stage and rooted among the electrical plugs, trying to shut off the amps but succeeding only in killing all the lights.

There had never been any doubt about the follow-up to 'Hey Joe'. Back in December, Chas Chandler had overheard Jimi play a tolling, dissonant riff and told him, 'That's your next single.' He developed it into a rough version of 'Purple Haze' in a club dressing room the same afternoon.

What inspired this most famous, most exciting, most influential, most mysterious yet most personal of Jimi's original compositions has been debated ever since. Its most likely genesis seems to have been his passion for science fiction, still as strong now as in his childhood. One of his early London neighbours, the American producer Kim Fowley, noted with amazement that 'he had more sci-fi books than clothes.'

One of his favourite authors was Philip José Farmer, whose novel *Night of Light* is about a distant planet where sunspots create a purpleish haze that holds its inhabitants in permanent captivity. However, Jimi himself never cited Farmer as a source, sometimes claiming the song had come to him in one of his habitual Technicolor dreams, sometimes that it was about a voodoo spell put on him by a nameless woman in New York that made him take to his bed atypically alone. The augmented seventh, so suggestive of a drugged sleepwalk, would be known ever afterwards as 'the Jimi Hendrix Chord'.

But for now, 'Purple Haze' was just one among many tracks laid down by the Jimi Hendrix Experience for their new label, Track, to which they were committed to make four singles and two albums per year. The deal with Track Records did not include a recording budget, no money for 'Hey Joe' had yet come through from Polydor, so Chas Chandler had to fund the first album out of his own pocket. Far from affluent himself (thanks to the man who was now his management partner) he had to sell some of his treasured guitar collection to keep Jimi recording.

It didn't help that Chandler was unwilling to settle for anything but the very best. Having moved the Experience from Kingsway to CBS studios, he was unable to keep up the payments and pulled them out after a furious row with the management. It was starting to look as if Jimi might never complete a debut album when Polydor agreed to provide a line of credit at Olympic Studios in the Thames-side suburb of Barnes.

Olympic was London's leading independent recording facility, the place where the Rolling Stones made their albums and whence innumerable international hits had come, including the Troggs' original version of Jimi's showstopping 'Wild Thing'. The engineer assigned to its latest clients was 21-year-old, South

African-born Eddie Kramer, who had previously worked with talent as diverse as the Kinks, the Searchers and Sammy Davis Jr. 'The studio manager at Olympic was a lady with a very proper English voice,' he recalls. 'She told me, "We're giving the Jimi Hendrix Experience to you because you like all that kind of weird shit."'

Kramer wondered what to expect when Gerry Stickells staggered in with the two giant Marshalls, followed by 'a shy figure in a dirty raincoat'. But all such misgivings vanished directly Jimi picked up a guitar. 'When he played, it was a whole body of work . . . it was the guitar, the hands, the heart, the brain, all becoming one. It was so telling, so vibrant and so new.'

With Olympic for a home and the empathetic Kramer on board, the album was completed in only ten days at a cost of £1,500. The sessions had none of the trial and error that might have been expected from a band so new to recording. Jimi would arrive with the chords and tempos all worked out in advance. The value of Noel Redding and Mitch Mitchell was the speed at which they could learn what he showed them. 'We'd work from seven in the evening until midnight,' Chas Chandler recalled, 'and we'd end up with two masters.'

In contrast with Jimi's utter self-assurance instrumentally, he remained so insecure about his singing voice that a special booth had to be built to hide him from view while he did his vocals. Those many who saw him as a reincarnation of Robert Johnson, the blues *wunderkind* of the 1930s, would have shaken their heads knowingly at such moments. For Johnson was so humble that at his few recording sessions, he was too embarrassed to look the engineer in the eye, so stood in a corner facing the wall.

Like every other British studio in 1967, Olympic's recording capacity was only four-track, but its mixing consoles were the best in the country, perhaps the world. Although Chandler was nominally the producer, Eddie Kramer effectively took on that role, working with Jimi not so much co-operatively as competitively. 'He'd be in the studio, getting new sounds out of his amp, and I'd run up to the control room and start twiddling knobs, adding bits of reverb and compression. Then he'd be like, "What can I do to top that?" We kept upping the ante all the time.'

Olympic's technical resouces were given an unexpected boost after a young acoustical engineer named Roger Mayer saw Jimi in action at the Bag O'Nails club. Mayer had started out as a government-employed scientist, experimenting with underwater sound waves as aids to submarine warfare. That training he had turned to building and designing fuzzboxes for the relatively few British guitar stars then making use of them, notably Jeff Beck and Jimmy Page. Like everyone at 'the Bag', he was blown away by Jimi's virtuosity, but not so much that he couldn't see a way of significantly enhancing it.

While the two chatted afterwards, Mayer mentioned a new invention he had not yet unveiled to Beck or Page. This was a foot pedal named Octavia because, along with the usual fuzzing and disortion, it could raise or lower a guitar's pitch by a whole octave. At Jimi's suggestion, he brought a prototype to the Experience's next date, the famous Chislehurst Caves in Kent. Afterwards, Jimi tried it out with a small amp and was delighted by the sonic palette that opened up beneath his boot-toe.

'Octavio', as he preferred to call it, first joined him onstage at the Ricky Tick club, Hounslow, in a performance that ended with him poking his guitar neck through the stage's low ceiling. That same night, back at Olympic, he used Roger Mayer's miraculous pedal to overdub the guitar solos on 'Purple Haze' and another new composition, 'Fire'.

Chandler and Mike Jeffery decided not to keep 'Purple Haze' for the album but to release it as a single on 17 March, just after Jimi's return from Ilkley Moor. It reached number 3 in Britain and made the Top 20 in Australia, Germany, the Netherlands and Norway.

It was interpreted everywhere as an aural version of the LSD that had only recently become illegal, its refrain of "Scuse me while I kiss the sky' a seeming paean to the ultimate blissful acid trip, tinged by very Jimi politeness. And to be sure, no sound seemed more at home in London's new psychedelic clubs like Middle Earth and the UFO – barns rather than the traditional cellars where projectors sent amoeba shapes floating hypnotically across walls and ceilings or fast-flashing strobes created the effect of a blinding silent movie.

However, Chandler was always adamant that while writing and recording it, Jimi never took the smallest sparkle of acid. And he himself always said he hadn't intended a psychedelic anthem but 'a love song'. 'I dream a lot and I put my dreams into songs . . . If it must have a tag, I'd like it to be called Free Feeling.'

As 'Purple Haze' seeped into the British charts, the Jimi Hendrix Experience were on a national 'package' tour with the Walker Brothers, Cat Stevens and Engelbert Humperdinick – the first instance of the ill-assorted packaging that would always plague them.

Before the opening show, at the Astoria cinema, Finsbury Park, Chandler was discussing with the NME's Keith Altham how Jimi might go one better than the Who's equipment-massacres. Noticing that his five-song set list included one called 'Fire', Altham said, 'You could always get him to set his guitar on fire.'

'It was meant to be a joke,' Altham recalls now. 'But Chas immediately says to Gerry the roadie, "Go out and buy us a tin of lighter fuel."'

There was in fact a famous precedent during the rock 'n' roll fifties when Jerry Lee Lewis upstaged Chuck Berry, who was to perform straight after him, by immolating his grand piano. But whereas Lewis's piano went up with an instant 'Whoomp!',

Jimi's guitar needed several dousings of lighter fuel and three matches before bursting into anything like flame.

That finally accomplished, he whirled its smouldering corpse around his head, suffering superficial burns to the hand, then tossed it into the audience. In the uproar that followed, the tour promoter, former bandleader Tito Burns, picked it up and tried to hide it under his jacket as if to prevent its being used in evidence against him.

The stunt made headlines in the British trades, stealing the not-very-resonant thunder of the Walker Brothers and Engelbert Humperdinck as surely as Jerry Lee had once stolen Chuck's. But Jimi felt it had misfired and would not try it again until the following June, in a very different place, before a very different crowd.

Two couples could not have been more different than the ones sharing Ringo Starr's duplex flat in Montagu Square. For Chas Chandler and his girlfriend, Lotte, very seldom disagreed but Jimi and Kathy Etchingham very often did. And when this happened, their neighbours generally knew about it.

Kathy was far from the adoring, submissive 'dolly bird' usually to be found clinging to a rock star's arm; she was firm of opinion, fiery of temper and decisive of action. When she and Jimi were having one of their rows, she would tear open the wardrobe and fling his precious clothes at him, making ruffled shirts and flowery scarves fly around like a scene from a hippy *Great Gatsby*.

She would even commit the ultimate transgression of attacking his guitars – for only he was allowed to misuse them – once managing to put her foot through the back of a small acoustic. She regularly stormed out of the flat into Montagu Square with Jimi in hot pursuit. During one struggle on the pavement, he grabbed her by her pink wraparound skirt, which promptly unwrapped, leaving her in only her knickers and stockings.

Chas and Lotte were often away and thus spared some of the more spectacular blow-ups. But Chandler lived in fear of damage to their Beatle landlord's property. From time to time, he and Mike Jeffery would suggest to Jimi that Kathy might find alternative accommodation, but he would never hear of it.

A major cause of conflict between them was food. Like every male of that era, black or white, Jimi expected 'his' woman' to cook for him. And when they first got together, Kathy could hardly boil an egg. For a time, they virtually lived on the fish and chips to which the north had introduced him and sandwiches provided by the clubs where he appeared. But when he complained his diet was making him lose weight, she felt obliged to venture into Ringo's pristine kitchen.

As befitted someone whose childhood diet had included rattlesnake, Jimi was scarcely a picky eater. His only hates were tuna, marmalade and mashed potato, the latter too redolent of US army 'chow'. One evening when he criticised the particularly lumpy dollop Kathy served him, she picked up both their plates and smashed them onto the floor. Jimi retaliated by locking her in the bathroom, from which she escaped only because Lotte happened to be at home and heard her shouts and bangs on the floor. She then departed to spend the night with her ex-room-mate, Angie King, while the house-proud Jimi hurriedly found a broom and swept up the smashed china before Chas Chandler saw it.

When Kathy returned the next day, in lieu of an apology Jimi handed her a piece of paper with the lyrics of a song entitled 'The Wind Cries Mary'. Mary was her middle name which he normally used only to tease her; there was even a line about 'sweeping up the pieces of yesterday's life', which had come to him while he wielded the broom, thinking she'd gone for good.

Rock stars in those days could not admit to having regular

135

girlfriends for fear of discouraging their female public, so when Jimi did press interviews at Montagu Square, he would talk to the journalist upstairs while Kathy stayed downstairs, usually soaking in a bath.

Despite her firm-mindedness in other matters, she had resigned herself to Jimi being what her autobiography would, somewhat downplayingly, call 'a terrible flirt'. For a while, she tried to keep an eye on him by accompanying him to gigs, with Chandler and Lotte also along to remove any suspicion among the fans she might be romantically involved with him.

At one stop, the foursome found the hotel in which they'd been booked was called the Blackboy – 'boy' or 'boys' in English topography being a derivation of the French word '*bois*' for wood. But even with that explanation Jimi refused to cross its threshold. In Newcastle, to save money, they stayed with Chandler's parents, in deference to whose old-fashioned views Kathy and Lotte 'doubled up' in one room and Jimi and Chas in another. Afterwards, Chandler made Kathy swear never to reveal that he and Jimi had slept together.

She soon realised the impossibility of curtailing Jimi's 'flirtatiousness'. At a gig in Manchester, she was renewing her make-up in the ladies' when she heard loud noises coming from a nearby cubicle. Wrenching open the door, she found him with a woman he'd managed to get off with under her very nose. His story was that they were 'just talking' after the woman had 'asked for an autograph'. On toilet paper presumably.

Yet he was fiercely, even violently possessive where Kathy was concerned, especially after having too much to drink, especially if it were whisky – the sole negative trait he seemed to have inherited from his father.

He was still relatively abstemious – in contrast with both Redding and Mitchell – preferring the marijuana that still fearlessly perfumed every rock-star hang-out and home. Grass seemed

Al Hendrix with the little boy his mother named Johnny Allen and his father renamed James Marshall – but known throughout his childhood as Buster. Even in this happy 'Dad and his lad' pose, there's a perceptible unease about him . . .

Pioneer rock 'n' roller Little Richard was the biggest star to employ 'Jimmy' Hendrix as a back-up guitarist around America's segregated 'Chitlin' Circuit'. When Jimmy began attracting notice for his beauty and flamboyant clothes, Richard told him '*I* am the only one allowed to be pretty!'

Jimmy (second from left) with Curtis Knight and the Squires in
shirts themed for New York's Cheetah Club; (*below*) Café Wha?
in Greenwich Village, where he finally turned into Jimi.

Jimi in new threads from
Swinging London.

Jimi with new friends the Who, whose guitar-battering stage
act he would soon eclipse.

Hussar-jacketed Jimi in the studio with Chas Chandler, his record-producer as well as co-manager. Their initial camaraderie dwindled as he came to rely less on Chandler and more on his own creative instincts.

Above: Linda Keith, the fashion model girlfriend of Keith Richards, who discovered Jimi in New York and always remained his 'blood brother'.

Below: the Jimi Hendrix Experience with bass-player Noel Redding and drummer Mitch Mitchell in matching Afros.

Left: Jimi and his ritual guitar-burning at the 1967 Monterey Festival, stealing the show from Janis Joplin, Otis Redding and the Who. After that triumph, on a tour with teenybop band The Monkees, he found himself drowned out by 12-year-olds, screaming for their teeny heart-throb Davy Jones.

Jimi with Noel, Mitch and 'Flying V' guitar. He was always
closer to Noel although when it came to the Jimi Hendrix
Experience Mk 2, only Mitch made the cut.

only to heighten his sweetness and good humour and for the rest of his life he would always seem under his influence to a greater or lesser extent, his speech as furry as if it had its own Octavia pedal, although his singing remained as distinct and undistorted as ever.

Actually, 'The Wind Cries Mary' had been in Jimi's head for more than a year and he'd played versions of it as Jimmy James with the Blue Flames in New York. But it needed what Lorenz Hart, in another song, called 'the conversation with the flying plates' over Kathy's cooking to be fully realised.

Recorded back in January, during a spare twenty minutes at Kingsway studios, it was as clear and simple as 'Purple Haze' had been diffuse and mysterious, spoken rather than sung, with slow, lulling chords, steeped in the influence of Curtis Mayfield, that suggested wind dying away rather than calling names. It was released as the Jimi Hendrix Experience's third British single on 4 May 1967, while 'Purple Haze' was still in the charts, and by the end of the month had matched 'Hey Joe' by reaching number 6.

Only a week after 'The Wind Cries Mary' came the debut album that finally had come together so quickly and easily under Eddie Kramer at Olympic. Chas Chandler had worried about flooding the market with Jimi, but was reassured by the album's advance orders of 25,000.

Its title was *Are You Experienced*, without a question mark yet still suggesting Jimi's half-playful interrogation of some woman making a play for him. The cover showed him in a bejewelled cape, towering over Noel and Mitch amid darkness which, intentionally or not, minimised the difference between his skin colour and theirs.

All eleven tracks had been written by Jimi, and reviewers in the trades competed for superlatives to do them justice, *Melody*

Maker's anonymous critic marvelling at how 'they change speed mid-number, stop, start, fade, fizzle, simmer and burn in a cauldron of beautiful fire.'

The album's biographical notes supplied the customary highly selective, condensed and romanticised version of Jimi''s background and former career in America: 'Left school early and joined the Army Airborne but was invalided out with a broken ankle and an injured back. Started hitching round the Southern States, guitar pickin'. One night one of the Isley Brothers saw him play and offered him a place in their band . . .'

The music, however, contained several 'broken pieces of yesterday's life' that 'The Wind Cries Mary' had mentioned. 'Foxy Lady', with its salacious sighing refrain, seemed to be daydreaming of Fayne Pridgon, who'd taken him in when he first arrived in New York (though there were to be other claimants, principally Roger Daltrey's then girlfriend, later wife, Heather). Somnambulistic 'Red House' evoked the scarlet-and leopardskin apartment where he'd sat up all night arguing with Linda Keith, but, atypically, getting no further.

'I Don't Live Today' acknowledged the Cherokee in his ancestry and was dedicated to Native Americans and all minority groups. 'Third Stone From The Sun' returned to his love of sci-fi, its deep-space squeals and whistles, representing the height of Eddie Kramer's ingenuity with Olympic Studios' four tracks. 'May This Be Love' marked one of those rare moments when Chandler persuaded him to turn down his amp. 'Fire', so lately a soundtrack for onstage pyromania, derived from the cheery log blaze he'd so adored at Noel Redding's mother's house the previous Christmas.

And throughout ran the guitar that humbled all other guitars with its earthquake chords, gushing fretboard slides and finger-knotting arpeggios and triads; switching seamlessly from rhythm to lead and back to rhythm again; veering between blues, soul, funk, jazz and gothic rock in tempos from stampede to old-fashioned waltz; sounding sometimes like a sitar, sometimes a space station, but never a thing simply of wood and wires; telling a life story more plainly in its fuzz and distortion and backward-tracking than the restrained, reticent voice ever would or could.

Are You Experienced spent thirty-three weeks in the UK album charts, peaking at number 2. It has since been called, without dissension, the greatest debut album in rock history.

On 15 February, Jimi had signed a one-shilling (5p) contract making over his song-copyrights to Mike Jeffery's Bahamian-registered Yameta company in exchange for 50 per cent of the proceeds from record sales, broadcasting and sheet music. These might be the Swinging Sixties, but British people still gathered around family pianos to chorus the latest hit songs very much as they had in Victorian times.

NINE
'NOT ON MY NETWORK'

n mid-May 1967, Cream returned to London from New York, euphoric at having completed their second album, *Disraeli Gears*, in only four days with their inspirational new producer, Felix Pappalardi. But around the 'Scotch' and the 'Bag' and the 'Speak', no one wanted to talk about anything but *Are You Experienced*; as Eric Clapton observed, Jimi 'wasn't just flavour of the month but flavour of the year'.

Clapton harboured no resentment for his eclipse, which had been repeating itself more or less continuously since Jimi had 'sat in' with Cream at the London Polytechnic eleven months earlier. On the contrary, he remained consistently in the front rank of celebrity Hendrix-worshippers, almost relieved that someone else was taking over the 'God' tag that had so long oppressed him.

Lacking any strong identity of his own, Clapton modelled his appearance on whichever musician he happened to admire at the moment, constantly changing hairstyles and adding or subtracting moustaches and beards. Now his adulation of Jimi inspired tonsorial mimicry more extreme than ever before – an Afro so big and aerated, it seemed about to fly away with his rather foxy, wary white face.

For Jimi, blasting Clapton offstage at the Polytechnic had come to feel like the grossest bad manners. 'When I think back . . . it seems so pushy that I would have barged into someone else's show that way, especially as [Eric] was one of my heroes,' he admitted to *Melody Maker*. 'I knew I was being rude. But at the time, I had to get moving, so I did.'

A scrap of audio, recorded late one night at the Bag O'Nails, reveals how close they had become. 'It's so lovely now, I kissed the fairest soul brother of England, Eric Clapton – kissed him right on the lips,' Jimi's voice slurs. 'So now we're stoned completely out of our minds. Oh, beautiful!' Clapton refers to 'my darling Jimi here' with a warmth he showed to no other men and precious few women.

After the clubs closed, the two would often adjourn to the flat Clapton shared with the French fashion model Charlotte Martin, for long, pot-fuelled discussions about philosophy, religion and the nature of music – something on which Jimi, at least, was perfectly clear. 'Music is nothing but imagination,' he tells Clapton in audio. 'Sent out from somebody's soul, man . . . from somebody's real heart, that they can only express through notes.'

'He was so quiet and withdrawn, but he had such a surreal mind,' Clapton recalls. 'We'd start off talking about ordinary everyday things, but we'd end up talking about flying saucers and purple velvet moons. You couldn't keep him on the ground for any length of time.'

The Who were an even better instance of performers to whom Jimi posed an existential threat, yet who could not help admiring and eventually loving him. The exception was their manic drummer Keith Moon who – doubtless resenting Jimi's takeover of Kathy Etchingham, though it was no excuse – once alluded to him loudly in his presence as 'that savage'.

Pete Townshend would later admit having been 'absolutely destroyed' by someone who was not only a more daring showman on the guitar, but seemed to challenge Townshend's very right to play the material he did: 'Because [Jimi] took back black music. He came and stole it back . . . I went away and got very confused for a bit . . . I felt that I hadn't the emotional equipment, the physical equipment, the natural psychic genius of someone like Jimi. I realised that what I had was a bunch of gimmicks which he had come and taken away from me and attached them not only to the black R&B from whence they came but also added a whole new dimension. I felt stripped.'

One night, Townshend and Clapton were spotted standing together, watching Jimi surpass both of them at once and instinctively holding hands like awestruck toddlers at a firework-display.

One of his special friends was to be Eric Burdon, the diminutive Geordie who sang the blues with the relentlessness of a River Tyne foghorn, eyes smouldering as only coals from Newcastle could. Burdon's girlfriend and soon-to-be wife, Angie King, was Kathy Etchingham's former roommate at Zoot Money's house; like Jimi, he was a working-class boy now living in one of London's poshest districts, in his case Duke Street St James's, just round the corner from the Scotch.

'Jimi was a stranger in a strange land,' Burdon recalls. 'I tried my best to guide him in the right direction and introduce him to the right people and help him escape from occasions where he felt totally out of place. In fact, he always felt out of place if he didn't have his guitar with him. He'd even make breakfast with it hanging round his neck.'

Despite the major, if unwitting, part played by the Rolling Stones in Jimi's transmogrification, he was never to become a pet of theirs as he had of the Beatles. Keith Richard was the one British guitar star noticeably absent from the symphonies of Jimi-worship, thanks to lingering rancour over Linda Keith and a certain misappropriated white Stratocaster – although the two would eventually become close.

Mick Jagger was understandably wary of someone whose sexual charisma and audacity onstage were regularly pronounced superior to his. Indeed, one night Jimi had the gall to flirt openly with Marianne Faithfull, the once pure-as-driven-snow ex-convent girl with whom Jagger had just begun scandalously cohabiting. Forgetting good manners for once, he even asked her within earshot of Jagger what she was doing with 'that asshole'. She did not succumb, but ever afterwards called it 'one of the great regrets of my career'.

Brian Jones was quite another matter. An escapee from the genteel spa town of Cheltenham, Gloucestershire, Jones had started the Rolling Stones as a pure blues band, naming them after a Muddy Waters song. For as long as they played only cover versions, he had equalled Jagger in prominence, combining an instinctive mastery of any instrument he picked up with a mop of straw-blond hair and a subversive smile that created crowd-frenzy as effectively as any gyration of Mick's.

That dynamic changed when Andrew Oldham forced Jagger and Richard to forget their non-royalty-earning Chuck Berry homages and follow Lennon and McCartney into writing original songs. From then on, Jones found himself increasingly marginalised, even his role as lead guitarist downgraded by Richard's killer chord-riffs as the Stones moved from R&B into mainstream pop. If that wasn't enough, his stunning German-Italian girlfriend, Anita Pallenberg, had finally wearied of his paranoia, hysteria, hypochondria, sexual deviancy and domestic violence and left him for Richard. Well before Jimi wrote a song of that name, Brian Jones had been demoted to third Stone from the sun.

He'd first seen Jimi in action in Greenwich Village, as part of John Hammond Jr.'s band, and had openly wept for joy. That first espresso-flavoured epiphany never lost its force: in whatever dark London vault the Experience played, he would be visible as a dual glint of blond hair and tear-wet cheeks.

The Stones currently faced a concerted attack by the British Establishment which hardly suggested a 'Summer of Love' just

around the corner. Jagger and Richard were about to be convicted on minuscule drugs charges and led away in handcuffs
to separate grim Victorian prisons, while Jagger would see his
reputation as a sexual omnivore temporarily forge far ahead of
Jimi's. A baseless rumour would sweep the country – and still
linger half a century later – that when the police burst into Richard's Sussex cottage, the head Stone had been going one better
than Jimi with his guitar-strings by licking a Mars bar in Marianne Faithfull's vagina.

After a separate but carefully co-ordinated bust, Brian Jones
had been charged with possessing cocaine, cannabis and metha-
done. Pending his own trial, in an attempt to mitigate a similarly
vicious sentence, he was receiving psychiatric treatment, largely
nullified by acid trips which left him whimpering with fear at
the 'monsters' they summoned up. His former instrumental virtuosity was now all but gone: in the recording studio, he would
often be so out of it on acid or booze and barbiturates that he
could no longer play the simplest chord and the other Stones
would surreptitiously disconnect his guitar.

As the Summer of Love dawned, the only friend Jones felt he
had left was Jimi, and he clung to him and his consoling brilliance like a lifebelt.

Even at the zenith of the Swinging Sixties, Britain's national press
took little notice of 'Pop' musicians (as they were always punctuated) apart from the sacred Beatles and the repugnant Stones.
But by May 1967, Jimi had grown big enough to rate an interview
in the tabloid *Sunday Mirror* by Anne Nightingale whose introduction would not have given a moment's offence either to its
readers or subject:

You might think that Jimi Hendrix would appear men-
acingly swinging from tree-tops, brandishing a spear . . .

> For Jimi, who makes Mick Jagger look as respectable as [Conservative party leader] Edward Heath and as genial as [chat-show host] David Frost, could pass for a Hottentot on the rampage.

The interviewer's first impressions were quickly revised:

> Jimi offstage behaves with quiet, polite charm that's almost olde worlde. He stands up when you enter a room, lights your cigarettes and says 'Do go on' if he thinks he might be interrupting you.

Elsewhere in Europe, the media's language could be still more blatantly racist. The Swedish evening newspaper *Expressen* described him as 'a cross between a floor-mop and an Australian Bush Negro' and asked whether he regarded himself as black or white. 'I'm Cuban, man,' Jimi shot back. 'I'm from Mars.'

At the same time, the European press subjected his playing to analysis more serious and knowledgeable than it ever received in Britain. The Finnish jazz magazine *Rhytmi* compared him with the German avant-garde violinist Johannes Fritsch, whose Stradivarius was wont to suffer some of the same rough treatment as Jimi's Strat. Another Finnish journalist's review had an eerily clairvoyant ring: 'To compare him with Segovia fails because the Spanish maestro dates back to the previous century's upper-class salons while this Seattle youth is more a voice from the reality of today's worldwide information network that effectively spreads both terror and delight.'

Rock bands are intrinsically unnnatural and unstable constructs – the more successful, the more unstable. Four or five disparate characters, usually with nothing but music in common, are forced to live at such claustrophically close quarters under the pressure of non-stop performing and travelling, it's no wonder that few of them last long and most break up amid irreparable anger and bitterness.

If the band also happens to be a trio, the stresses increase expotentially for, as psychologists tell us, threes in any context virtually guarantee internecine strife. In 1967, the living proof were Cream, whose bass player and drummer frequently resorted to physical combat onstage, sometimes with actual homicide in view.

In Cream, the trouble stemmed mainly from the lion's share of attention always given to Eric Clapton. But although Jimi was self-evidently the star of his group and Noel Redding and Mitch Mitchell only sidemen in every sidelined sense of the word, he demanded no special treatment in terms of travel or acommodation, regarding the three of them as bushy-topped Musketeers, 'one for all and all for one'.

This was demonstrated by his solidarity with Redding and Mitchell when they began to chafe at the small wage they still received even now that Jimi Hendrix Experience gigs were pulling in £300 per night, and because no accounting ever came from Mike Jeffery that might support their claim for a better deal. With Jimi's support, Redding wrote to Jeffery, threatening to quit unless they were shown some figures.

Jeffery immediately called a meeting at which he announced Redding's and Mitchell's weekly pay would be raised to £45 and that in future their performance earnings (after their managers' percentage had been deducted off the top) would be split three ways, 50 per cent going to Jimi and 25 per cent each to the others. However, nothing was ever put in writing and Jeffery still managed to sidestep the question of exactly how much they would be splitting.

There were undeniable compensations of course. Bit-part players or not, Redding and Mitchell had each become immeasurably more famous than in either of their respective previous bands and instant members of British rock's innermost elite. And, as Chris Squire had already discovered, Jimi's erotic H-Bomb sprinkled its fallout generously on any musician around him. Especially on this Scandinavian tour where every young woman seemed to be a blonde-haired, blue-eyed, compliant goddess, Noel Redding would later recall 'overdosing on sex'.

In that pre-AIDS era when most young women took the new contraceptive pill, condoms had become all but extinct. 'The three of them were riddled with Clap [gonorrhea],' Trixi Sullivan recalls. 'As they often went with the same girl, they gave it to each other. I used to send them to the same doctor in Harley Street. When I phoned his surgery, I only had to clap my hands to say what the problem was – one clap for each of them who had it.'

Jimi was closer to Redding, a comparable jokester and his main guide to British culture, from beer to surreal radio comedy shows like *The Goons* and *Round The Horne*; he also adored Redding's kind, hospitable mother, Margaret. Sometimes onstage, he would introduce his Afro-ed but schoolmistressy-looking bassist as 'Bob Dylan's grandmother' or alter the refrain of 'Purple Haze' to ''Scuse me while I kiss this guy'.

Things did not go quite so smoothly with Mitch Mitchell, whose years as a child actor had left him with a theatrical drawl, unique among rock drummers, for which his bandmates nicknamed him 'Julie Andrews' or 'Queen Bee'. Early on, he had challenged Jimi's choice of material to the point where there was talk of replacing him with Aynsley Dunbar, the runner-up in their joint audition only by the flip of a coin. He was also, Kathy Etchingham recalls, 'an ugly drunk', notorious for picking fights in pubs with total strangers.

Most of the time, Jimi went through Jeffery's punitive work schedule with the professionalism he'd learned on the Chitlin' Circuit, somehow always managing to pull out a brilliant show, however stoned or sexually spent he happened to be. On a couple of nights, someone slipped him a tab of acid as he went onstage that reduced him to such fits of laughter, he couldn't play a note. He could also throw a tantrum that made him forget the first rule of performing: never turn on your audience.

From the Star Palace in Kiel, West Germany, the Experience ricocheted back to the centre of Britain's flower-growing industry, Spalding in Lincolnshire, co-headlining with Cream and Pink Floyd in a psychedelic extravaganza at the town's Tulip-bulb Auction Hall. But flowers in this case did not mean love and peace: when Jimi had trouble tuning his guitar (hardly surprisingly considering what it went through every night) the crowd began to jeer. 'Fuck you,' he retorted without a trace of olde-worlde charm. 'I'm gonna get my guitar in tune if it takes all fucking night.'

After a couple of lacklustre numbers, he poked the guitar through the speaker fabric of his Marshall, then toppled it over and walked offstage, leaving the way open for Eric Clapton to outplay him at last.

On 1 June, the release of the Beatles' album, *Sgt. Pepper's Lonely Hearts Club Band*, wiped out every other topic of conversation around the clubs, as well as in many other walks of life. Advance sales alone took it instantly to number 1 in the UK charts, where it remained for twenty-seven weeks – much of that time with *Are You Experienced* nestling immediately below it.

The *Sgt. Pepper* album would inspire many memorable cover versions: Joe Cocker's of 'With a Little Help from My Friends', Harry Nilsson's and Esther Ofarim's of 'She's Leaving Home', Elton John's of 'Lucy in the Sky With Diamonds', Fats Domino's of 'Lovely Rita'. But Paul McCartney's title track might have seemed immune to any reinterpretation, for Sergeant Pepper's lovelorn ensemble was the Beatles' alter-ego as a north-country brass band on acid and the song dripped with nostalgia for their childhood in 1950s Liverpool.

Three days after *Sgt. Pepper*'s release, the Jimi Hendrix Experience took part in a Sunday-night concert at what was in effect the Beatles' private West End theatre, the Saville, together with Procol Harum, the Chiffons and Denny Laine's Electric String Band. McCartney and George Harrison were both present, sitting in Brian Epstein's private box, and the audience included Eric Clapton, Jack Bruce and Stevie Winwood.

Half an hour before curtain-up, Jimi arrived backstage with a copy of *Sgt. Pepper* and informed Noel Redding and Mitch Mitchell that they'd be opening with the title track despite having never attempted it before. Accustomed as Redding and Mitchell were to such brinkmanship, they managed to pick it up from the record.

Even with his overloaded memory, Paul McCartney would never forget the curtains parting to reveal Jimi walking forward, singing 'It was twenty years ago today . . .' McCartney called it 'a shining moment' although for him it was an unheard-of overshadowing. Indeed, everything the Beatles and their brilliant producer George Martin had needed six months and £100,000 to create – and much more besides – seemed to erupt spontaneously from that willowy, black-hatted figure and his beaten-up Strat.

Having established Jimi in Britain and Europe, the next hurdle for Mike Jeffery was to sell him back to the homeland where he'd struggled in obscurity for so long. Jeffery's contacts and deal-making skills seemed to come good when America's Reprise label agreed to release a single comprising two of the Jimi Hendrix Experience's UK hits, 'Purple Haze' and 'The Wind Cries Mary' on 17 June.

Reprise had been founded by Frank Sinatra in 1960 to give creative freedom to himself and his 'Ratpack' cronies like Dean Martin and Sammy Davis Jr. As Beatle-phobic Sinatra's personal fiefdom, it had virtually excluded rock, but since the label's 1963 sale to Warner Brothers, the company's CEO, Mo Ostin, had wisely reversed this policy. Although Jeffery took the credit, what actually decided Ostin in Jimi's favour was a tip from Mick Jagger – magnanimously, given his attempted seduction of Marianne Faithfull – that he was 'the most exciting performer in London'.

It was not a straightforward signing: Warner/Reprise contracted with Yameta Ltd., the offshore company used by Jeffery, to supply master recordings by the Experience, of which Yameta retained the copyrights. The label paid a $40,000 advance, with a guaranteed promotional budget of $20,000, both impressive sums at the time. Jimi, Redding and Mitchell were not required to sign anything as they were already contracted to Yameta.

A promotional opportunity in itself worth a great deal more than $20,000 came with the announcement of a three-day music festival in Monterey, California, exactly coinciding with the single's release. Put together in just seven weeks by John Phillips of the Mamas and the Papas, record producer Lou Adler and the Beatles' erstwhile publicist Derek Taylor, its aim was to give rock the dignity of jazz, which had been holding such events for decades, plus an altruism not previously associated with rock people. All the participants were to appear gratis and the proceeds be given to charity.

Just as notably, the Monterey festival had no truck with the Chitlin' Circuit. Black artistes like Otis Redding, Lou Rawls, Hugh Masekela and Booker T. and the M.G.'s would perform alongside white acts like the Grateful Dead, Jefferson Airplane, the Mamas and the Papas, the Byrds, Buffalo Springfield and Simon and Garfunkel.

Even so, Jimi was not a natural choice until the organisers asked Paul McCartney to join its board of management and McCartney agreed on condition that the Experience were included. Brian Jones happened to answer the phone at Jimi's flat when John Phillips called to invite them.

So on 14 June, Jimi flew back to New York, accompanied by Jones and Eric Burdon, who was also to appear at Monterey with his New Animals. In London, Jimi might be idolised by Beatles but in Manhattan he was still an unknown African American, subject to the same old brutal slights. In the lobby of the Chelsea Hotel, where the trio stayed overnight, a female guest mistook him for a bellhop and on the street outside he couldn't get a cab to stop for him.

D. A. Pennebaker's classic colour documentary *Monterey Pop* forever enshrines that Friday, Saturday and Sunday at Monterey's County Fairgrounds as not only the first but overwhelmingly most successful of the decade's festivals with its balmy sunshine, its civilised seating, its benign cops (many wearing flowers more conspicuously than sidearms), its front rows of performers generously applauding their rivals onstage, and the peaceability and good humour of its 90,000 spectators. If the Summer of Love ever had any real meaning, it was here.

The programme's highlights are eternally watchable, the more so because of its several melancholy sequels. There is Otis Redding in his first real foray outside the Chitlin' Circuit, reinventing the old ballad 'Try a Little Tenderness' as a heart-stopping *cri de cœur* only six months before his charter plane plunged into a Wisconsin lake. There is Janis Joplin, backed by the hairy Big Brother and the Holding Company, wearing a sparkly trouser suit and matching kitten heels, almost tearing out her larynx in Willie Mae Thornton's 'Ball and Chain' with only a month more than Jimi left to live, her end destined to be similarly lonely and mysterious and at the same age.

The Jimi Hendrix Experience were not the only British act at Monterey with everything to prove. It would also be one of the Who's first live performances in America and they intended, in Pete Townshend's words, to 'leave a wound' on the country.

Both acts were scheduled to appear towards the end of Sunday night's programme, before the festival's grand finale with the Mamas and the Papas and Scott McKenzie singing the hippies' anthem, 'San Francisco'. Backstage there was a brief discussion, combined with a sampling of the free LSD handed out to all performers by the Grateful Dead's tame chemist, Owsley Stanley III. Neither band wanted to follow the other for fear of seeming like an anticlimax. In the end, they adopted Jimi's usual solution of flipping a coin and the Who got to go first.

It was a set with all the appearance of a show stopper, Keith Moon wearing a necklace allegedly made from human teeth and Roger Daltrey what was described as 'a psychedelic shawl' (actually a tablecloth bought at the Chelsea Antiques Market in London). 'This is where it all ends,' Townshend announced before the ritual mayhem of 'My Generation'. But even after he'd battered his guitar to shreds and Moon kicked over his drums amid eddying smoke and flickering ameoba-light, Monterey hadn't seen anything yet.

The Jimi Hendrix Experience did not follow immediately. There was a whole thunderous set from the Grateful Dead before Brian Jones in his Moroccan robes, with his haggard face, came onstage to introduce 'the most exciting guitarist I've ever heard'.

Above that twilit hippy sea, Jimi's outfit was deceptively low-key – Afro pinched in by patterned headband, yellow ruffle-fronted shirt, black, silver-frogged waistcoat, cherry-red flares. Almost conventional, too, his little opening speech about his absence overseas and the creative frustration that had driven him there: 'So groovy to be back here this way and get a chance to really play, I could sit up here all night and say "thank you, thank you thank you" but what I want to do is just grab you and . . .' There was not a female in the front rows, maybe not a male either, who did not feel that hugely amplified wet kiss.

It was the first time a young white American audience had

beheld the Jimi show and Pennebaker's cameras, passing among them, show virginal eyes in a mass deflowering like none since Elvis Presley had burst out of the South a decade earlier.

As 'Hey Joe' with its midway goumandising of guitar strings gave way to 'Purple Haze' and its half-apologetic tonguing of the sky – with the surprising addition of a back-somersault – Cass Elliot from the Mamas and the Papas turned to Pete Townshend, who was sitting glumly beside her in the VIP section. 'He's stealing your act,' she said.

'No, he's *doing* my act,' Townshend replied.

The climax – that word never better employed – was the display of ultimate guitar abuse Jimi had already tried out two months earlier at London's Finsbury Park Astoria, but now switched from 'Fire' to 'Wild Thing'.

With that priapic chant, he found new ways to ravish and torture the long-suffering Strat, rubbing it up and down the amplifier fabric in extended feedback-inducing frottage; lying it flat and bestriding it, first like a bucking bronco, then as if it were penetrating him; spraying it with what resembled urine more than lighter fuel; setting it ablaze first go instead of those fumbles in Finsbury Park; encouraging the flames with incantatory gestures; finally picking it up and smashing it down again and again, oblivious of its wails of protest and pain until it was past all hope of repair by Gerry Stickells, whirling the half-dismembered, smouldering corpse around his head and flinging it into the audience regardless of whom it might hit.

Other people's sets, including the Who's, ended amid cheers and whistles, but this one was followed by stunned silence. Meanwhile, Noel Redding recalled, Jimi was meekly listening to a tirade from Mike Jeffery for damaging a microphone stand belonging to the festival that Jeffery would have to replace.

Monterey Pop had been financed to the tune of $200,000 by ABC television for its Movie of the Week slot, but was never

seen there. When the documentary was edited, the festival's
co-organiser, Lou Adler, showed it to the network president,
Thomas W. Moore, an archetypal Southern conservative. The
sequence of Jimi – in Adler's words – 'fornicating with his amp'
brought the preview to an abrupt end. 'Not on my network,'
hissed Moore. 'Keep the money and get out.'

TEN
'FROM RUMOR TO LEGEND'

The *Los Angeles Times* spoke for Monterey's enraptured 90,000 in a review of unusual pithiness and prescience by its pop critic, Pete Johnson. 'The Jimi Hendrix Experience owned the future and the audience knew it in an instant,' Johnson wrote. 'When Jimi Hendrix left the stage, he graduated from rumor to legend.'

The press plaudits were far from unanimous. *Esquire* magazine's Robert Christgau, unable to get his head around the idea of a black man playing heavy rock, dismissed Jimi unpleasantly as 'a psychedelic Uncle Tom'. For jobbing journalist Jann Wenner, five months away from launching a new music paper called *Rolling Stone* and still freelancing for Britain's *Melody Maker*, he was 'not the great artist we were told'.

To be sure, wowing a few hippies in an obscure corner of California was not at all the same as 'cracking' America, as previous British exports like the Beatles and Chas Chandler's own Animals had done. Despite the excited word-of-mouth rippling through the counterculture, the Jimi Hendrix Experience's first two Warner/Reprise singles made no impact on the US charts: 'Hey Joe' did not reach the Hot 100 and 'Purple Haze'/'The Wind Cries Mary' stalled at number 65.

Unsure how Monterey would turn out, Mike Jeffery had not organised an American tour to follow it, so now had to hastily cobble one together on the spot. As a result, Jimi's triumphal return to his homeland was to end in long-drawn-out anticlimax.

Initially, the only offer of work came from Bill Graham, whose Fillmore auditorium in San Francisco had been the birthplace of West Coast psychedelic rock. Graham booked the Jimi Hendrix Experience for a week of twice-nightly shows opening for Jefferson Airplane, but quickly promoted them to headliners, paying them a $2,000 bonus. In his autobiography, *Bill Graham Presents*, Graham called Jimi 'the ultimate trickster and the ultimate technician . . . After Otis [Redding] . . . the first black man in the history of this country who caused the mass of white females in the audience to disregard his race and want his body.'

One night, the Fillmore's bill also included Janis Joplin, his Monterey colleague and future co-member of the 27 Club. The ladylike Janis was more than a match for any man in rock 'n' roll excess, and she and Jimi are said to have had sex in a backstage toilet (wrongly: it was at a nearby motel).

Afterwards came a few random Californian dates – a one-off performance in Santa Barbara, a free concert in San Francisco's Golden Gate Park – that didn't satisfy Jimi's need to play any more than it did Mike Jeffery's to exploit him. Zoot Money, who happened to be appearing at a club in San Diego, was astonished when Jimi turned up one night and asked to sit in with Money's band. 'He just played rhythm guitar. I kept trying to make him take a solo, but he never would, just nodded at my lead guitarist. He was perfectly happy playing rhythm.'

Another chance for national 'breakout' came with a booking at Los Angeles' Whisky A Go Go club on Sunset Boulevard, which had already been the making of the Doors and Buffalo Springfield and as such was haunted by talent scouts for national TV shows. Jimi's Monterey *tour de force* ensured a starry first-night audience including the Doors' Jim Morrison – another 27-Clubber, who would be around only a year longer than he

– and Mama Cass Elliot, who, though she made it past 27, would outlive him by only four years. Unfortunately, as Noel Redding would recall, the Experience were 'too drunk and stoned' to give of their best and Redding, for the first time, lost his temper with Jimi onstage for 'pulling a moody'.

Women had always flocked around groups of male musicians on the road, offering physical solace for wives and girlfriends left at home in exchange for reflected glamour, but in the America of 1967 it had turned into something like a vocation.

So-called groupies targeted famous rock bands with methodical precision, starting by sleeping with roadies and gradually working their way up to lead singers, accumulating famous names with the dedication of stamp- or butterfly-collectors. Their seemingly mindless calling actually demanded considerable intelligence, for the outwitting of their quarry's security, and physical courage, for climbing up hotel lift shafts or clinging to the roofs of escaping limos. In non-sexual matters they showed a morality that nowadays seems remarkable, the vast majority recounting their exploits only to one another without a thought of what might be earned by kissing and telling.

Normally groupies were white, but at a party in Laurel Canyon after the Whisky A Go Go gig, Jimi met a notable exception. This was a tall, stunning 23-year-old named Devon (originally Ida Mae) Wilson with an Afro rivalling his and a ghostly pallor hinting at already advanced heroin use.

Previously Devon's sphere of activity had been the Rolling Stones, pursuing that ultimate objective of all groupies, their equivalent to Mount Everest, Mick Jagger. She had, in fact, met Linda Keith when Linda was with Keith Richard, long before Jimi effectively put an end to the relationship. 'She was only interested in Mick, not at all in Keith, so the two of us became quite friendly,' Linda recalls. 'She was a very funny, interesting person who found all sorts of ways of making herself useful to people like the Stones. I liked her a lot, which isn't to say I trusted her.'

For Jimi, sleeping with Devon Wilson was just another one-night stand, made the more interesting by the revelation that she was bisexual. Little did he suspect that yet again he had knocked Mick Jagger clean off the board.

A couple of days later, a perfect way to enlarge Jimi's American following expotentially – perfect, that is, to anyone suffering from blindness and cloth ears – fell into Mike Jeffery's lap when the Jimi Hendrix Experience were offered a national tour supporting the Monkees.

These three Americans and one Englishman were the first totally prefabricated pop group, created for a television show as a blatant knock-off of the Beatles and selected for their cuteness rather than musical ability, of which they were said to possess none whatsoever. When they'd visited Britain a few months earlier, Jimi had described them to a music paper as 'dishwater'.

Chas Chandler protested that Jeffery risked throwing away all the credibility Jimi had built up at Monterey. But Jimi himself seemed to have no problem with it, Redding and Mitchell were game – and there was nothing else pending after a couple of New York City dates, one at a mini-festival in Central Park, sponsored by Rheingold beer. So on 8 July, they joined the Monkees' roadshow in Jacksonville Florida.

A few days previously, Jimi had mingled on equal terms with the titans of psychedelic rock; now he was opening for a quartet who mimed playing their instruments while session musicians provided accompaniment from behind a curtain. The audiences consisted largely of seven- to twelve-year-olds, screaming so dementedly for the confected group's English member, former child actor Davy Jones, that even mighty Marshalls became mute. 'Jimi would amble onto the stage, fire up the amps and break into "Purple Haze" and the kids would instantly drown him out with "We want Daaaavy",' their nominal drummer, Micky Dolenz, would remember. 'God, it was embarrassing.'

Contrary to public belief, the Monkees *did* have musical ability, especially guitarists Mike Nesmith and Peter Tork, who both seethed with frustration over their puppet masters' refusal to let them develop it. All four stood in the wings while Jimi was on, drinking in the act that was so far from their own choreographed antics. Dolenz thought it as instinctive and infallible as 'a royal wave from Queen Elizabeth'.

The Monkees could not have been more respectful, inviting Redding and Mitchell as well as Jimi to ride in their private plane from show to show. But the novel experience of flopping night after night soon wore him down. To make matters worse, two of the stops were in North Carolina, a state associated with some unpleasant white supremacist encounters during his time with the King Kasuals. Mixed with the infant shrieks came the first racist abuse he'd received since setting foot back in America.

Matters came to a head during the last of three shows in Forest Lawns, New York. The Monkees' manager hissed at Jimi to turn down his amps; he responded by turning them off, miming the rest of his set in parody of his headliners, then quitting the tour. A press release blamed his exit on the Daughters of the American Revolution, a far-right women's pressure group implacably opposed to all things hippy, which had supposedly made a formal complaint about his 'eroticism'. HENDRIX; DID HE QUIT OR WAS HE PUSHED? the *NME* wondered back in Britain.

The resulting gaps in the diary could be filled only by New York clubs, the very minor and informal kind that booked acts at short notice. Jimi thus found himself playing three nights at Café Au Go Go in Greenwich Village, where the great producer John Hammond had passed on him two years earlier. Back in the Village, his first act was to track down his old bandmate Charles

Otis, and pay back the $40 Otis had lent him to go to London.

He also reconnected with Curtis Knight whose City Squires had been a lifeline during his days of near-destitution in Manhattan. Knight harboured no resentment over his defection and the two jammed amiably together at the Studio 76 club. Afterwards, Jimi wanted to take Knight to dinner, but found he had no money on him. Knight suggested he should borrow some from Ed Chalpin, for whose cheapo PPX record label they both used to work and who conveniently lived nearby.

The impromptu reunion with Chalpin should by rights have been anything but friendly. For the three-year contract to 'record and produce' Jimi had signed with PPX in 1965 without bothering to read it was one of the things he'd left behind in New York and never thought about since. Although solemnised by only a single dollar bill, this negated the whole slew of British contracts involving Chandler, Jeffery, the Track label and the Yameta company – and it still had a year left to run. Jeffery had been aware of it when he signed Jimi to Track and Warner/Reprise, but made no move to deal with the problem.

Chalpin had monitored Jimi's success in Britain and Europe and even now was considering legal action against his new management as well as how best to profit from PPX's Hendrix material. Nevertheless, he greeted his surprise visitor without a trace of animosity, not only lending Jimi the money for dinner, plus a little extra, but accompanying him and Curtis Knight to the restaurant where they lingered until the small hours, reminiscing about old times.

So infectious was the bonhomie that – with no one around to say, 'Are you crazy?' – Jimi went straight from the dinner table into the PPX studio and recorded several more tracks for Chalpin with only the vague caveat 'You can't use my name, man.'

A return to his former uptown haunts proved less pleasant. In Harlem, no one knew or cared what he'd been doing in Europe.

And the Jimi wardrobe, newly augmented in California's hippy souks, looked downright weird on 125th Street where the *de rigueur* male look was supercool: pencil slacks rather than flappy flares, not headbands but undersized trilbies known as 'stingy brims'. An outsize witch's hat, of which he'd been particularly proud, attracted mocking shouts of 'trick or treat'.

Fayne Prigdon, his one-time mistress-cum-mentor – the prototype Foxy Lady – still lived in Harlem and she, at least, was gratifyingly impressed by his 'wild and nappy hairdo' and air of affluence. 'He was raving about all the money he was getting and I must have looked unconvinced,' Fayne recalled. 'So he peeled off $200 and handed it to me: "You can have it, it's yours." . . . It came to me that the skinny kid in shiny black pants I'd known way back when was now a media shooting star.'

For him, Fayne's bed still hung out a Welcome mat. And there, for all his rock-star flash, she found lingering the insecurity of the skinny kid who'd needed constant reassurance he was the best lover she'd ever had. 'When I felt devilish, I'd say no, he wasn't the greatest thing since sliced bread. And he stopped in the middle of a stroke and the wham-bam was over. Something like that just devastated him.'

The ramshackle tour wound up in another swing westwards, stopping off at the Ambassador Theater in Washington DC and the Fifth Dimension Club in Ann Arbor, Michigan, and ending back in California with another potentially great moment that again dribbled away into bathos. On 18 August, the Jimi Hendrix Experience appeared at the famous Hollywood Bowl as support to a headline act almost as laughably dissimilar as the Monkees: their late Monterey colleagues the Mamas and the Papas. The Bowl that night overflowed with hippies as conservative in their way as the Daughters of the American Revolution, wanting honeyed four-part harmonies not guitar-dismemberment. 'We died the death,' Noel Redding would recall.

Flying back to London – and straight into a BBC-TV appearance at Lime Grove studios – brought the Experience their first brush with authority when Mitch Mitchell was arrested for possession of a tear-gas pistol. Airport officials were unmoved by his protest that it was only a souvenir, purchased 'round the corner from the White House'.

Jimi and Kathy Etchingham were still living together, although no longer at Ringo Starr's Montagu Square flat. Chas Chandler broke the news that they'd have to move on because the lease had been found to prohibit 'blacks' – something perfectly normal in that era – and Ringo was getting complaints from neighbours about the noise. The real reason was that John Lennon, shortly to leave his wife and small son for Yoko Ono, needed a hideout from the inevitable media storm.

So, still in a foursome with Chandler and his now fiancée, Lotte, Jimi and Kathy had transferred to a fourth-floor flat in the even posher quarter of Upper Berkeley Street, Mayfair. They'd accumulated so few domestic effects apart from clothes and records that no removal van was needed; they carried their own stuff the few blocks' distance on foot. Jimi was still sufficiently unknown to be able to lug armfuls of albums through London's West End in broad daylight without attracting notice.

The ménage continued to work well even though Chandler once again exercised a manager's prerogative by claiming the larger of the two bedrooms. Unlike in Ringo's sacred domain, they could change the décor to suit their own tastes. Pets were not forbidden and, knowing Jimi's love of dogs and how much he'd longed to have one as a child, Kathy bought him a basset hound puppy with the pedigree name Ethel Floon that he called 'Queen of Ears'.

One of the first journalists to visit him in Upper Berkeley Street was Keith Altham, for an interview about his song 'Burning of the Midnight Lamp', just out as the Jimi Hendrix Experience's fourth British single. When Jimi proudly showed off his newly personalised bedroom, Altham picked up on the lamp theme to describe 'a kind of Aladdin's cave, hung with lace shawls, tapestries and great coloured balls of cloth pinned to the ceiling. The colour red predominates . . . Suspended from the lampshade in the middle of the ceiling are two little gilt figures of cherubs . . . one with a broken arm.'

'Burning of the Midnight Lamp' co-opted the most unlikely of instruments into the service of hard rock. During its recording at Olympic Studios, Jimi began picking out notes on a harpsichord left behind after some previous classical session. The sedate little riff that he vamped ended up running through the otherwise raucous track like a maiden aunt in bed with a tattooed biker. Altham's interview was meant to translate the lyrics for *NME* readers but they seem clear enough: the lamp symbolises the loneliness Jimi could feel even at peak rush hour in his bed. As he calls it 'more than enough to make a man throw himself away', it's hard not to feel a chill of foreboding.

The single did not do as well as its three predecessors, reaching only number 19 in the UK charts. And *Are You Experienced*, which Warner/Reprise had released in the US after Jimi's departure – with a few minor changes from the British version, like the inclusion of 'Hey Joe' and spelling 'Foxy' with an 'ey' – received a cool initial reception. The *New York Times* called the album 'a nightmare show of lust and misery' and palpably shuddered at the cover image of Jimi, Redding and Mitchell 'sneering out from beneath their bouffant [sic] hairdos like surreal hermaphrodites'.

The *Times*, in fact, could hardly have provided more of a come-on and FM rock radio across America finished the job. *Are You Experienced* quickly rose to number 5 in *Billboard*'s Hot 100, spent twenty-seven weeks in the Top 40 and became one of the Reprise label's most successful albums, outselling any by its founder, Frank Sinatra.

There was barely time to celebrate on the ceaseless treadmill of live shows, in venues ranging from grandiose to grotty. This random selection from the last months of 1967 suggests the era of galley slaves or Victorian boy chimney-sweeps:

Sept 2, ZDF TV Berlin; Sept 25, Royal Festival Hall, London, 'Guitar-In' with Bert Jansch, Paco Peña and Sebastian Jorgensen; Oct 9, L'Olympia, Paris; Oct 17, Play-house Theatre, London, BBC *Rhythm 'n' Blues Show*; Oct 22, Hastings Pier Ballroom, Sussex, supported by the Orange Seaweed; Nov 8 Mancheser University Students Union; Nov 14–Dec 5, UK package tour with Pink Floyd, the Move, Amen Corner and the Nice; Dec 22, Kensington Olympia, London, All-Night Christmas Dream Party with Eric Burdon and the Animals, the Move and Soft Machine; Dec 31, New Year's Eve party at Speakeasy club (Jimi plays 30-minute version of 'Auld Lang Syne'); January 2, Rail-way Hotel, West Hampstead, jam with John Mayall and Al Sykes.)

It was was for the most part a life of exhaustion and mono-tony, of dreary car rides, bleary plane rides, bad food and hotels that almost always recoiled at the sight of Jimi even if few in the UK and Europe actually tried to keep him out. Here, musicians of any colour in funny clothes and Afros were pariahs. Arriv-ing at one grand establishment, in Switzerland, the Experience were surprised when doormen and concierges rushed forward *en masse* to help them with their gear. The reason was that a member of the British Royal Family was due at any moment and the unsightly weirdos had to be got out of sight as quickly as possible.

As with most other bands on the road, drugs were a fuel as much as a recreation. Along with pot and cocaine, just-outlawed acid had become as essential a part of the baggage as travel-sickness pills. (Since Monterey, Jimi insisted on only the best 'Owsley'.) For coming down from the high of performing, there was a newly marketed sedative named Mandrax; for shaking off the Mandrax-coma and cranking oneself up to perform again, there was amyl nitrite in glass phials that had to be 'popped' under the nose and whose vapour rush turned the user white, red, then white again in quick succession like a stick of seaside rock.

Getting high, Noel Redding would later write, became 'a game of Russian roulette. Only instead of holding a gun to your head, you boasted "I can take more than you." . . . Jimi seemed to have higher tolerances than me . . . if I took two tabs [of acid] he would take four.'

Unable to endure the boredom of travelling and waiting around backstage, Kathy no longer accompanied Jimi on tours and turned a resolutely blind eye to what he was assuredly getting up to. 'I gave him his freedom to mess around with anyone he wanted to while he was away,' she recalls. 'I realised I would much rather stay at home in the warm and go out with Angie [Burdon] in the evenings.'

She might have felt differently had she known that Linda Keith, whom she thought to have replaced in Jimi's life, was still very much part of it. Despite Chas Chandler's attempts to keep Linda at arm's length, the two had stayed in touch and Jimi had never ceased to regard her as a 'blood brother' after the ritual they had enacted. 'He thought of me as a security blanket because when we first met, I'd been the one who took care of business.'

During the recent rash of European touring, he'd phoned Linda once from Sweden and twice from Paris, the second time sounding so 'depressed and insecure' that she flew to join him there – and that which hadn't happened at her friend Roberta's apartment in New York the night she discovered him, nor at the Hyde Park Towers on his arrival in London, did so at long last.

The one good-looking young woman definitely never in his sights was Mike Jeffery's PA, Trixi Sullivan, though when she went on one German tour, a rumour got back to Jeffery that they'd spent a night together. 'All that had happened was that after a show I'd been smoking pot with the guys in Jimi's room and I passed out on the floor.

'Mike was like, "What's this I hear about you sleeping with Jimi?" But I didn't. At least, I don't think I did.'

The deal wth Track Records in the UK committed the Jimi Hendrix Experience to two albums per year, which meant that a follow-up to *Are You Experienced* had to be ready for release in December 1967. The recording sessions with Eddie Kramer at Olympic had to be fitted in around the Monterey festival and incessant touring, and were still going on in late October.

The album, to be entitled *Axis: Bold as Love*, had many of the same elements as its predecessor. This time, there were two sc-fi spoofs, 'EXP' and 'Up From the Skies', both featuring Jimi in the role of visiting alien with which he so much identified. 'Wait Until Tomorrow' had a *crime passionnel* theme similar to 'Hey Joe' while 'Little Wing' used the lulling tempo of 'The Wind Cries Mary' to anthropomorphise Monterey and its altruistic glow as a young girl 'with a thousand smiles she gives to me free'.

Elsewhere, Jimi allowed more glimpses of his real self than he ever had before. 'Spanish Castle Magic' commemorated the enormous Spanish Castle ballroom in Washington state where the teenage Jimmy used to hang around in hopes of sitting in with some top Seattle combo. But there were no nostalgic snapshots in his almost conversational – almost rapping – vocal and the guitar took off on such drawn-out flights of improvisation, it was nearing the frontier of bebop by the time Mitchell's drums called it back into line.

'Castles Made of Sand' referred directly to his dreadful childhood and its greatest and still unassuaged tragedy. 'The little Indian brave playing war games with his friends and dreaming of growing up to be a warrior chief, that was all about Jimi,' his brother Leon says. 'And the young girl whose heart was a frown and who draws her wheelchair to the edge of the shore before she dies, was our Mama. The last time the two of us ever saw her, she was sitting in a wheelchair.'

Underlining the Experience's democratic spirit, there was a song by Noel Redding, entitled 'She's So Fine', boasting some of the most laboured psychedelic lyrics ever written ('her hair glistens like robins on a deck') and with a lead vocal amply justifying Redding's Jimi-bestowed nickname of 'Bob Dylan's grandmother'. Jimi, however, liked the track for the open G it allowed him him to play, and contributed backup vocals and a breakneck solo.

The sessions also marked the only known appearance on record of Mike Jeffery, lending his shiny black loafers to a chorus of stomping feet alongside Graham Nash of the Hollies and Gary Leeds of the Walker Brothers. By a delicious coincidence it ended the track called 'If 6 Was 9'; how much more perfect for someone so adept at juggling figures?

Previously in the studio Jimi had always followed Chas Chandler's guidance but with *Axis: Bold as Love* he became increasingly assertive about what he recorded and how he recorded it. In reaction to Chandler's 'fuck it, that'll do' approach, he turned into a niggling perfectionist, demanding retake after retake which his monumentally patient engineer, Eddie Kramer, always allowed. 'Chas was always worried because the studio cost £30 an hour,'

Kathy Etchingham recalls. 'So to keep him quiet, Jimi took over paying for the sessions himself.'

He showed more interest than Chandler ever had in the control console and loved to see what effects resulted from twiddling its knobs and sliding its levers. Other engineers would have regarded this as an intrusion, but Kramer uncomplainingly shifted along and made room for him. He proved to have a natural feel for 'the desk' and, for the first time, contemplated the possibility of someday becoming a producer himself.

Whereas *Are You Experienced* had cost only a few hundred pounds, *Axis* cost £10,000. Almost a third of it was spent on a cover reflecting the current craze for all things Indian – a painting of Jimi as Vishnu, the four-armed Hindu deity, flanked by Redding and Mitchell in indistinct profile. He accepted the cover made commercial sense, but said he would rather it had shown the other kind of Indianness in his family tree.

The album almost failed to make its pre-Christmas release date when Jimi left the only master recording of side one in the back of a London taxi and all enquiries failed to trace it. However, Kramer, Chandler and he managed a remix in a single night.

It reached number 5 in the UK charts (where the Beatles' *Sgt. Pepper* still occupied the top spot) powered by reviews like Nick Jones's in *Melody Maker*: 'Amaze your ears, boggle your minds, flip your lids, do what you want but please get into Hendrix like never before . . .' For Jones, it was 'the culmination of all Jimi's blues, all his soul, all his urging, all his crying, all his shouting, all his grooving, all his everything'.

His triumph was marred somewhat by the consequences of that too-pally evening with Ed Chalpin in New York six months previously. Subsequently, Chalpin had filed suit against Jimi, his management and Track Records for breach of the contract he'd signed with the PPX label in 1965. At the same time, Chalpin

had realised the commercial value of the tracks Jimi had recorded for PPX with Curtis Knight and the Squires, albeit only as a
guitarist.

Soon afterwards, Chalpin released an album entitled *Got That
Feeling; Jimi Hendrix Plays, Curtis Knight Sings*, its mostly old material spiced up by the tracks Jimi had so obligingly recorded
after their reunion dinner. Reviewers damned its low quality but people still bought it and Warner/Reprise put a stop on
the royalties from *Are You Experienced* because of the Chalpin
lawsuit.

In a year-end interview with *Melody Maker*, whose readers had
just voted him 'World's Best Pop Musician', Jimi admitted to
feeling worn out, both physically and creatively. 'I'd like to take
a six-month break and go to a school of music,' he said. 'I'm tired
of trying to write stuff and finding I can't.' But everyone knew
that Jeffery wouldn't be sending him to any school of music and
in the same interview he hinted at a desire to work with a larger
band, but keeping Mitchell and Redding as its core.

Thus far, the Jimi Hendrix Experience had not been among the
many travelling rock bands whom drunkenness, drugs – or
sheer boredom – had driven to wreck their hotel rooms. Jimi enjoyed staying in hotels, which he still considered a great luxury,
and would convert the bleakest accommodation into a twilit den
by draping scarves over the lamps. Holed up thus with his guitar
and sci-fi books and women, he became known to Redding and
Mitchell as 'the Bat'.

On 3 January 1968, the Experience arrived in Gothenburg,
Sweden, for their second Scandinavian tour in three months.
Having checked in at the Hotel Opalen, they visited a night-
spot named Klubb Karl, where they attracted the usual bevy of
admirers and media people. No drugs were available, only alcohol served in Sweden's bumper measures. Jimi, that infrequent

tippler, drank whisky, which brought out the worst in him as it used to in his father.

When Klubb Karl closed, a small group continued partying in Mitch Mitchell's room at the Hotel Opalen, among them a Swedish journalist who, it emerged, was gay. According to Noel Redding, Jimi reacted in a manner astounding to the bandmates who'd travelled with him for the past eighteen months; he first made a move on Redding, then suggested they both take part in a gay foursome. When Redding declined, the atmosphere became tense, the journalist left in a hurry and Jimi started 'going crazy'.

Redding wrestled him to the floor and tried to pacify him but after doing it for the third time gave up and retired to his own quarters. Hotel staff, responding to complaints about noise, found the room wrecked, a window broken and Jimi lying on the bed with the hand that he'd clearly just put through it bleeding all over the covers.

Charged with criminal damage, he was forced to surrender his passport and remain in Gothenberg for the two weeks until his appearance in court, reporting to the police every day. (The English-language court order would one day be sold by a London auction house for £8,400.) He was fined 3,500 kronor, around £2,500. The 'move' on Noel Redding, if it really happened, can only be put down to the malign effect that whisky always had on him. By the time the Experience moved on to Stockholm, pot had restored his equilibrium and any doubts on his bandmates' part about his heterosexuality had vanished, never to recur.

Not many women ever said 'No' to Jimi Hendrix but one of this rare breed was a Swedish student named Eva Sundquist, whom he'd met on a previous trip to Stockholm while riding a tram to that night's performance at the Konserthuset. Eva was no groupie but a highly respectable young woman, the daughter of Swedish opera star Erik Sundquist. She had no idea whom she'd been talking to until she passed a record shop later and saw

Jimi's face on an album cover. In forthright Swedish fashion, she left a single rose and a note for him at the Konserthuset and soon found herself in his dressing room. But that was as far as it went; as Eva briskly informed him, she was still a virgin and, for the present, had no wish to be otherwise.

Rather than moving on to the next in line in his usual amnesiac way, Jimi had stayed in touch with her and sent her advance notice of his return to Stockholm. Eva attended the first of his two shows with her mother but the second on her own. And when she and Jimi got together later at the Hotel Carlton, she proved to have had a change of heart.

ELEVEN
'HE WAS A LIFE-SAVER'

Nineteen sixty-eight was a time in America when a black face, no matter how inoffensive, could get one beaten with a club by a crash-helmeted cop, savaged by an Alsatian or swept away by a water cannon. But to Mike Jeffery such things weighed little against the need to monetise Jimi to the maximum for so long as the opportunity lasted.

Back then, it was unheard of for a rock tour – even over perfectly tranquil terrain – to take almost a full year. This one theoretically consisted of three separate instalments, but the breaks between them lasted only long enough to soak up a few stray performance fees back in Britain and Europe before a return to a United States which, each time, seemed more traumatically disunited.

The first instalment began in February when the Jimi Hendrix Experience and Eric Burdon's new Animals flew to New York to begin separate tours, Burdon's nowhere near the length of Jimi's. With them went two newly signed Jeffery bands, Soft Machine and Eire Apparent, to act as support to each as the need arose. 'The British are coming!' trumpeted their advance publicity as if the Beatles hadn't got there first four years earlier, though Jimi was highly amused to find himself so classified.

Four bands coming off the same flight at JFK Aiport might have been expected to provoke an orgy of strip-searches by US Customs. As it was, only the Experience's new roadie, Neville

Chesters, found himself beckoned to one side. 'And I was the only one who'd taken the trouble to look normal,' Chesters recalls. 'I was even wearing a white suit.'

Their flamboyant American publicist, Michael Goldstein, had staged a press conference on the roof of the Pan Am airline building on Park Avenue, to which they were to have been wafted from JFK by helicopter. Thick fog had grounded the chopper, however, and by the time they had struggled into midtown by road, most of the press had left. 'Even the canapés were gone,' Noel Redding recalled.

One photographer who did stick around was a rangy young woman with high cheekbones and rather unkempt blonde hair, celebrated for gaining access of the most intensive kind to super-studs like Mick Jagger, Jim Morrison and Warren Beatty. Her name was Linda Eastman and in a year from now she would marry Paul McCartney. Jimi was among her last conquests as a freelance.

This first formal return to his homeland – Monterey and its aftermath having been more in the nature of a hit-and-run – would veer between adulation on a near-Beatle level and the racial snubs and slights he remembered of old.

In America even more than Britain he was a fashion icon whose Afro, gaudy waistcoats, chain belts, paisley shawls and chiffon blouses thousands of young white males faithfully copied at love-ins, sit-ins, teach-ins and other forms of protest against conscription into the Vietnam War. *Eye*, a new magazine for affluent hippies, painstakingly listed all the ornaments he wore on the chain round his neck – 'an Oriental green jade medallion, a gold three-leaf clover, an elephant-hair ring, a Sagittarian symbol surmounted by a surfer's cross' – and noted 'even his guitar strap is a work of art.'

He would grow accustomed to looking down in mid-performance and seeing white fans crawling onstage to try to kiss his boots. Yet still when he needed a cab, he'd ask a colleague to flag one down, assuming that no driver would want him as a fare.

Neville Chesters was one of the most experienced roadies in the business, having previously worked for Cream and twice for the Who, including at Monterey. Gerry Stickells, who'd been with the Experience from the beginning, continued on the payroll.

In New York, Chesters' first job was to go to Manny's Music Store and buy yet another Stratocaster. 'It amazed me that he didn't want to go and pick out one for himself, but was quite happy to leave it to me. When I saw what he did to his guitars, I understood why.'

As yet, few tours carried guitar 'techs' to care for their star players' instruments. Chesters filled that role along with many others, carrying around a repair kit in a US Army metal ammunition box. 'Jimi by that point was getting a bit more sensible: he'd play three-quarters of "Wild Thing" on a good Strat, then switch to a rubbish one to smash to pieces. And I discovered a cheaper make called Danelectro that were made of hardboard, so much easier to break.' (Long ago, when playing with the Rocking Kings, how Jimi had prized his Danelectro Silvertone.)

With the lack of geographical logic that had characterised his previous American visit, the tour went straight from East to West Coast, first playing Bill Graham's Fillmore and Winterland venues in San Francisco, then making an extended stop in Los Angeles, where something like Hendrixmania had broken out along Sunset Strip. A new club named Thee Experience had just opened for business and the Whisky A Go Go added a new item to its menu: 'Jimi's Favorite Super-Sausage on a Wah-Wah Bun'.

In LA, the Jimi Hendrix Experience passed into the care of a

British publicist at the opposite extreme from the excitable Michael Goldstein. Les Perrin was a chain-smoking elf of a man who'd represented everyone from Frank Sinatra to the Rolling Stones and whose dedication to his clients was expressed in a letterhead inviting journalists to 'call me at any time – day or night'.

On the evening of the band's concert at the Anaheim Convention Center, there was heavy rain, so Perrin asked a young journalist named Sharon Lawrence, a film industry reporter for United Press International, to drive him the twenty-odd miles there. Sharon was fond of Perrin so she agreed, even though her father was seriously ill in hospital with cancer.

Having read about Jimi in the British music press, she had pictured someone 'wild and terrifying' but instead found herself shaking hands with 'a shy, polite human being . . . dressed with such subtle elegance' in a deep-purple silk crepe shirt, velvet pants and a black cut-velvet jacket in which 'he looked as if he should be invited to pose for the cover of *Vogue*'.

She mentioned having seen him at the Hollywood Bowl the previous year, when he'd opened for the Mamas and the Papas. Jimi seemed more interested in the fact that she'd taken along her mother, a connoisseur of fine fabrics who'd said of his clothes, 'That boy has beautiful taste.' In the course of their conversation, she mentioned that her father was in hospital and the gravity of his illness.

When she returned home later, she learned he had died. After a terrible night at the hospital, she was at her parents' house with her mother, Margaret, when there was a ring at the front door. 'It was Jimi. Les Perrin had told him about Daddy and he'd gotten the address and come right over.

'I'd been trying to take my mom's mind off things by suggesting we get some new cushions and stuff for the house and Jimi picked up on it and spent a couple of hours talking to her about furnishings. "I'm going to buy you something you'll really like," he said. "I don't know what it is yet, but when I'll see it, I'll know."

'He was a lifesaver.'

On 12 February, the tour took Jimi to Seattle, his first return to his home town since leaving to join the army rather than face prison eight years previously.

Despite far from happy memories of the place, he had not intentionally cut himself off from it and during his years of struggle had kept in regular touch with his father and brother. After his move to Britain, however, his phone calls, letters and postcards had all but ceased and Seattle's insular media had brought no news of the startling change in his fortunes. Al and Leon Hendrix were both totally unaware of it until October 1967, when they overheard the *Are You Experienced* album being played by their next-door neighbour.

Since then, Jimi's growing fame in America had made even his father sit up and take notice. The name Hendrix on Al's garden-landscaping business brought such an influx of new clients that he could give up the sideline of clearing and salvaging household junk to which Jimi owed his very first guitar.

Leon Hendrix, now twenty, was shedding no such lustre on the family name. Prevented from playing guitar by Al's refusal to have 'two idiots in the family', Leon had taken to drinking, gambling and dealing pot while still in high school and had served six months in juvenile hall for burgling a department store.

His talent for drawing, fostered by Jimi when they were children, resulted in a trial as draughtsman at the Boeing aircraft factory, but he soon became bored and drifted back to his old ways. For him, as he writes in his memoir, *A Brother's Story*, Jimi's celebrity merely provided the entrée to a higher class of criminal, including a gang of would-be jewel thieves.

The entire Hendrix family were waiting at Seattle airport when Jimi's plane landed after its 1,100-mile flight from Santa Barbara, California. At first sight he barely recognised his father, for Al had shaved off the moustache he'd worn since his sons were babies. It was also the first time Jimi ever saw him wearing a tie.

After Al and Leon, the most welcome member of the delegation to Jimi was his mother's sister, Aunt Ernestine, who'd recognised his talent before anyone else and bought him his first proper guitar – the five-dollar Kay acoustic he used to sleep with like a lover instead of battering like an abused wife. During his seven-year absence, the family had increased greatly in size. Al's second wife, Akayo ('June') Jinka was a divorcee with a son and four daughters, the youngest a six-year-old named Janie whom he had adopted. There was immediate tension when Al expected Jimi to call June 'Mom', not realising that to him only one person could ever bear that name.

Noel Redding, Mitch Mitchell, Mike Jeffery and Chas Chandler were included in the family reunion at the Seward Park house where Al and June had set up home together. The Englishmen were totally confused when Jimi's relations instantly reverted to his childhood name of 'Buster'. They went out of their way to be charming, all but Jeffery who – Leon thought – 'looked like an undercover cop in his sharp suit and dark glasses' and was 'cold and distant' as if he resented anyone getting between Jimi and himself.

All the relations agreed that, despite his wild clothes and seeming wealth, fame had hardly changed Buster. That it had not changed his deference to his father was plain from the beginning. Al still drank the same Seagram's Seven whisky from whose bottles Buster used to steal the gold tassels to decorate his guitar in the Rocking Kings. Now, star or not, he asked Al's permission to help himself to a refill.

Before the sold-out show at Seattle's Center Arena, Aunt Ernestine helped Jimi curl his hair. Leon hadn't yet tried acid, so his brother slipped him a tab, saying they'd take it together later so that he could look after him as of old. Leon couldn't wait, however, and had his first trip during the show, 'witnessing first-hand what the rest of the world was losing its mind over'.

Front-row seats had been reserved for the family, and Al's new stepdaughters, Donna, Marsha and Linda held up a proprietorial banner reading WELCOME HOME JIMI LOVE YOUR SISTERS. At several of the louder moments, Al was seen to grimace and stick his fingers in his ears.

Afterwards, the party continued in a luxurious suite at the Olympic Hotel, with Jimi showing a somewhat more than brotherly interest in his new grown-up stepsister, Linda. As the night wore on (some of it occupied by a game of Monopoly) he asked his brother to order food for everyone from room service. When Leon proposed *filets mignons*, Al was horrified by such extravagance and said snacks from a vending machine would be quite enough. For the first time ever, Jimi contradicted him without fear of a whoopin' with his belt

A couple of weeks previously, he had contacted Pat O'Day a local radio deejay and promoter whom he considered one of his earliest benefactors. For O'Day had run the dances at the Spanish Castle ballroom where he'd hung around so many nights, hoping to sit in with Hank Ballard or the Fabulous Wailers from Tacoma.

'Jimi asked me if he could arrange for him to visit his old high school while he was in town,' O'Day recalled. '"They kicked me out," he said, "so I'd like to go to one of their assemblies and play some music."' In fact, James A. Garfield High School never 'kicked him out'; he had left voluntarily in 1960 when chronic absenteeism to play music made it impossible for him to graduate.

High-school assemblies customarily take place before classes at 8 a.m. When Jimi rendezvoused with Pat O'Day, he had come straight from the family beano at the Olympic Hotel without showering or changing clothes and badly hungover. Then his roadies suffered a temporary fit of amnesia over where they had parked the equipment truck, so no music could be played. Instead, it was decided that O'Day should simply introduce him to the students, then conduct a brief Q&A session.

Whatever pleasant anticipation he had felt disappeared as he once more trod those familiar locker-lined, strip-lit corridors. 'He absolutely froze,' Pat O'Day recalls. 'Here's a guy who can get up in front of thousands of people and play and sing, and he walked into his old high-school gym and was struck with fear.'

In Jimi's day the school's white and black populations had been about equal in number but now the latter were far in the majority The racial tension building up in the country could be felt even in stable Seattle and the musical idols of Garfield's black students, like James Brown and Aretha Franklin, stressed and celebrated their ethnicity rather than downplaying it. There was thus only a muted welcome for the rumpled, hesitant figure in the tall black Stetson, despite the presence of the school orchestra, poised to provide accompaniment, and O'Day's fulsome introduction of 'a man who may soon surpass the Beatles in popularity'.

When Jimi went to the microphone, he was able only to mumble – untruthfully – that he'd written 'Purple Haze' for Garfield, whose colours were purple and white, and to quote a line from the school song about 'fight, fight, fight', written in more innocent times when fighting happened only on the sports field. As some of his audience began to boo and heckle, Pat O'Day hastily called for questions.

A male student asked how long ago he'd left the school. 'Oh, about 2,000 years,' Jimi replied half under his breath. Then a purple and white pom-pommed cheerleader asked how he went about writing a song, and the memory of assembly procedure finally loosened his tongue:

'Right now, I'm gonna say goodbye to you and go out the door and get into my limousine and go to the airport. And when I get out the door, the assembly will be over and the bell will ring. And when I hear that bell ring, I'll write a song. Thank you very much.'

With that, he fled. The whole visit had lasted less than five minutes.

A hard gig of a different kind presented itself two weeks later in Chicago when a serious-looking young woman handed Jimi a visiting-card introducing herself and her two female companions as 'The Plaster Casters'.

The most bizarre groupie activity ever recorded had begun in an art class at the University of Illinois when nineteen-year-old Cynthia Albritton was assigned to make a plaster cast of anything that caught her fancy. She had immediately thought of a rock star's penis, and decided to make Jimi's the first in a projected series.

He proved a willing subject, as did Noel Redding, and the event took place right away in their respective hotel rooms, albeit more in the spirit of a lab experiment than an orgy. Jimi had to insert what the three young women jocularly termed his 'rig' into a metal canister like a cocktail shaker lined with a dental mould-making substance called Alginate and keep it at full attention as liquid plaster was poured around it and then allowed to set.

With no external assistance, he was able to maintain the required silhouette (begging the question of how his support band, Soft Machine, might have fared). His good humour persisted even when, as Cynthia would recall, 'his pubes got stuck in the mould [and] I had to very gingerly pull them out without hurting him.'

The cast was later exhibited in an art gallery along with contributions from other travelling musicians who had received the Plaster Casters' treatment. But there was no doubt about the star of the show, captioned in one press photo 'the Penis de Milo'.

The Jimi Hendrix Experience's on-road maintenance team on this perversely routed transcontinental marathon remained as modest as ever; just Chas Chandler and the two roadies, Neville Chesters and Gerry Stickells, with Mike Jeffery joining them from time to time at the more prestigious and accessible venues, sometimes accompanied by his PA, Trixi Sullivan. Their retinue, in fact, was smaller than that of their support band, the jazz-rock Soft Machine, which had a portable psychedelic light show known as Mark Boyle's Sense Laboratory.

'We knew our management only regarded us as cannon fodder,' Soft Machine's drummer Robert Wyatt recalls. 'But Jimi never treated us like that. We'd expected him to be like something from outer space, but he was modest and polite and, although he was only a couple of years older than me, I remember a film crew once came into the communal dressing room and all plonked themselves in front of Jimi with their backs turned to the rest of us. But Jimi made a point of introducing us before he did the interview.'

If a journey between shows involved crossing several states, the Experience travelled by air on domestic flights in economy class; otherwise it was usually by rented station wagon with the equipment in a U-Haul trailer behind and Chesters at the wheel. 'In nine months,' he recalls, 'I drove 19,000 miles.'

After each appearance, the band's share of the gate would be collected in cash by Chandler or Chesters. There was no security to protect either the money or the musicians, apart from the police at the different venues whose attitude was seldom helpful or friendly. Mitch Mitchell carried around a double set of bolts which he attached to the door of each hotel room he occupied, but this was merely to strengthen it against the groupie-onslaught when he needed sleep.

Equally little care was taken over their drugs, purchased in advance from the Beatles' song-celebrated 'Doctor Robert', but constantly topped by the local dealers who flocked round Jimi almost as thickly as women. Noel Redding carried the collective stash quite openly in a blue Pan Am flight bag, one compartment of which was labelled 'leapers', another 'sleepers' and another 'creepers'. In Vancouver, the guitarist with their current support band, Eire Apparent, was caught with marijuana and deported, but Redding's Pan Am bag seemed to bear a charmed life.

The badges on Jimi's hat included one saying 'Make Love Not War' and from the start of the tour he had repeatedly made mention of the Vietnam conflict, which by now had brought many college campuses to a state of open insurrection. Even an insulated travelling rock star could not escape the TV footage of helicopters attacking straw villages and Napalm-scorched children that the government still made no attempt to censor. But as an ex-GI, his sympathies were as much with the young soldiers fighting a clearly unwinnable war, especially the black ones he might so easily have joined, who were allowed to die for their country yet not granted equality in it.

The war was currently headline news thanks to Communist North Vietnam's Tet offensive, which had raised American casualties to an all-time high. However, Jimi was incapable of the bitter eloquence with which other rock stars denounced it, especially with a brain and tongue furred by pot as they invariably were onstage. 'Instead of all that action happening over there,' went a typical rambling aside, 'why doesn't everyone just come on home and instead of M16 machine-guns, hand grenades and tanks . . . why don't they come back with feedback guitars on their backs? That's better than guns.'

In the rare interludes between playing almost nightly gigs, the Experience returned to New York to work on their next album, *Electric Ladyland*, at the Record Plant studios. For Jimi, these trips always meant jamming in old club haunts with old friends like John Hammond Jr. and B. B. King and new ones like Al Kooper, Johnny Winter and the Paul Butterfield Blues Band.

One night at the Scene club, a session that was being taped included the Doors' Jim Morrison, his closest rival in onstage outrage and offstage sexual athleticism who had recently become the first rock star to be charged with 'public obscenity'. It might have been a brilliant duet had not Morrison been helplessly drunk and ruined the recording by shouting 'I want to suck your cock' at Jimi until Janis Joplin subdued him by breaking a bottle over his head.

'Jimi always stayed amazingly placid,' Neville Chesters recalls, 'and he never seemed to hold grudges. The only time you might see him riled was after having too much to drink, which he very seldom did. Or when he thought someone was after a woman he'd decided he liked even though nobody could ever compete with him. Once he'd picked out his dozen, that was it.'

While playing Cleveland, Ohio, he went out shopping for cars with Noel Redding, despite not having a driving licence, British or American. Nonetheless, he bought himself a top-of-the-range sports car, a Chevy Corvette Stingray in 'Le Mans' metallic blue. Like many rock people, he was a hopeless driver and on his very first outing, drove the Stingray the wrong way up a one-way street, was stopped by a policeman and ticketed for that and non-possession of a licence. Since, for all sorts of reasons – mainly chemical – Jimi could not continue the tour in it, the car was then shipped back to New York.

On 5 April, during their 350-mile road journey from Virginia

Beach to Newark, New Jersey, the road company stopped at a restaurant where a group of white men were noisily opening bottles of wine. Their waitress then told them that Dr Martin Luther King, had been assassinated in Memphis, Tennessee. The noisy men were drinking the health of his killer.

Dr King's murder would unleash the worst social unrest in America since the Civil War with race-riots in 125 cities across the nation, tanks and tear gas on the streets and machine guns mounted on the steps of Washington DC's Capitol building lest the rioters should attempt to storm it.

In Newark, things were already so bad that one of the two Jimi Hendrix Experience/Soft Machine shows at the city's Symphony Hall had been cancelled and barely a quarter of the other's 2,000 ticket-holders dared venture out of their homes. On the streets, for once, it was safer to have a black face that a white one: the Experience's limo driver would venture into the downtown area only with Jimi sitting in front beside him and the others crouching out of sight in the back.

During Soft Machine's set, their light-show operator, Mark Boyle, found himself wondering if Dr King's assassination had been the start of a concerted campaign to kill off every black figure of any power and influence and it might be Jimi's turn next, perhaps this very night.

When Jimi came on, the Experience's usual routine was abandoned: he simply said, 'This next number is for a friend of mine' and went into a long improvised blues which Redding and Mitchell picked up in their usual way and which to Boyle – a poet as well as a lighting wizard – had 'an appalling beauty . . . Everybody knew what this was about . . . this was a lament for Martin Luther King . . . and within minutes the whole audience were weeping and even the much-maligned redneck stagehands came on to the side of the stage and were standing there, too, with tears running down their faces. When Jimi came to an end, there was no applause, the audience were still sobbing and he just walked quietly off the stage.' Afterwards, he sent $5,000 to the fund established in Dr King's memory.

The tour proceeded as a combination of pomp and the chaos and ignominy so typical of Mike Jeffery. On 18 May, in New York, Jimi met with the Reprise label's top brass for the ceremonial insuring of his hands for $1 million, a larger sum than even the greatest classical pianist had merited.

Afterwards, accompanied by Jeffery and Trixi Sullivan, the Experience flew to Miami for the first of its two 1968 pop festivals, headlining over the Mothers of Invention, Chuck Berry and John Lee Hooker, with Eddie Kramer on hand to make the first live recording of Jimi. 'At the Everglades Hotel, Mike came up to me and told me the festival hadn't paid us,' Trixi recalls. 'So we were going to have to sneak out without settling our check.'

After a scatter of European shows which hardly seemed worth crossing and recrossing the Atlantic for – like the opening of Mike Jeffery's new Majorcan club, Sgt. Pepper's – the second American instalment began early in June, at a moment almost as inopportune as the first. Senator Robert Kennedy had just been shot down in a Los Angeles hotel following a speech that seemed to guarantee him the Democratic nomination in the coming presidential election. Only two months after Dr King's assassination – and only five years after that of Kennedy's president brother – the nation's shock and incredulity were expressed in an oft-replicated headline: NOT AGAIN.

That instalment was just a brief foray back to New York, but the third, starting on 31 July, was even longer than the first and, moreover, made its wildly zig-zagging way through the heart of what F. Scott Fitzgerald called 'the undissolved Confederacy' – Louisiana, Virginia, Texas and Utah, the Mormon state where black people were still widely believed to bear 'the curse of Cain'.

John F. Kennedy's posthumous Civil Rights Act of 1964 had supposedly banned racial discrimination but in the South it was still everywhere, now without the candour of signboards. And the self-preservational instincts of the Chitlin' Circuit remained strong in Jimi. En route to Shreveport, Louisiana, when the musicians stopped at a plainly redneck hang-out – signalled by cropped hair, short-sleeved white shirts with cigarette packs outlined in their breast pockets and eyes set much too close together – he refused to go inside until almost frog-marched by a hungry Redding and Mitchell. He was not refused service, but found himself the only black customer and the atmosphere was so tense that the party bolted their food and left as quickly as possible.

'We British were all so stupidly innocent,' Neville Chesters admits. 'We'd never thought of Jimi as black. To us, he was just an American guitarist – and a mate. We were amazed when stuff like that happened.'

There could be moments of sheer farce, as when a local driver, hired to relieve Chesters at the wheel, turned out to be a prominent member of the white supremacist Ku Klux Klan. Jimi always took care to ride up front next to the Klansman, figuring that around here there could be no better protection.

Most inflammatory to racist sensibilities was the sight of him in the admiring company of white women – an area where his usual caution could desert him. This produced an ugly incident when he arrived for a show with a blonde personage known only as 'Poopsie' clinging to his arm. A policeman in the security cordon shouted, 'That nigger has no right to have his hands on that girl' and drew his gun. Two other cops, called to the fracas, also drew their firearms but, thankfully, no trigger was pulled; instead, the entire police contingent walked out in protest.

Far from sharing his white colleagues' outrage, Jimi thought it wonderful to have been protected by Southern cops in the first place and had the last laugh on them by spending that night with Poopsie.

'I was called "white trash", just for being with him,' Trixi Sullivan recalls. 'We were getting out of a limo to go into a department store when this woman popped up and screamed it in my face. And she followed me all around the store, still screaming it.'

When finally the tour turned north again, the overt hatred diminished. 'But in a way,' says Robert Wyatt, 'we almost preferred that because at least you knew where you were. It was preferable to what you got in the north – the big false smiles with the hatred behind them.'

One trouble spot, at least, was fortuitously avoided. The show in Chicago on 10 August came two weeks ahead of the Democratic party convention when Mayor Richard Daley's blue-helmeted police ran amok through anti-war demonstrators, indiscriminately beating up delegates, TV crews and any black people or hippies who got in their way. What they might have done had Jimi, that mixture of both, happened to cross their path is awful to contemplate.

In September, he returned to Seattle, this time to play the city's Center Coliseum. But it was not as pleasant a homecoming as before. Since their last meeting, the gang to which his brother Leon belonged had been caught burgling a drugs company for pep pills known as 'Crossover Speed'. Leon had somehow ended up taking the rap for the whole gang and was currently on bail awaiting sentence.

Notwithstanding Jimi's gifts of a new Chevrolet Malibu *and* a new truck for the landscaping business, his father's new paternal pride already seemed to be waning. Al had been deeply put out by his refusal to address his new stepmother, June, as 'Mom' – something which, Jimi told the UPI reporter Sharon

Lawrence, 'would have stuck in my throat'. Even with a son of 25 who'd become an international star, it seemed to Al that some old-fashioned discipline needed restoring.

During Jimi's stay, Al invited a crowd of his friends and neighbours to his home for a party which he took it for granted both his sons would attend. Instead, Jimi and Leon went off with their own friends for the night. When they showed up at dawn, an enraged Al threatened them both quite seriously with a whoopin' from his belt.

Jimi's next tour stop was Vancouver, where his grandmother, Zenora and Aunt Pearl still lived. Seeing a chance to placate his father, he suggested a family trip there in Al's new Chevy Malibu with Leon, June and his adopted sister, Janie. 'Mike Jeffery was really pissed that he wanted us all along,' Leon recalls.

En route they stopped at a restaurant where no one would take their order until Jimi signed autographs for some children who'd recognised him. A waitress then told them it was not normally the manager's policy to serve non-whites but he would make an exception in this case.

A couple of hours later, Jimi was reunited with the hardy little woman who traced her ancestry to both Cherokee reservations and slave plantations via the vaudeville stage, and was the first person he'd ever told about the music he could hear inside his head. 'Grandma Nora' was in the front row for his show at Vancouver's Pacific Coliseum and had 'Foxy Lady' dedicated to her; quite rightly since she'd been the first one he ever knew. Afterwards, a reporter asked what she'd thought of her grandson's performance. 'Oh my gracious,' she replied, 'I don't see how he could stand all that noise.'

'Our grandma lived to 104,' Leon Hendrix recalls, 'and when the time came, she was perfectly happy to go. She said, "I've been a slave and I've seen Jimi Hendrix. I'm done."'

*

Before Jimi left Aunt Pearl's 'early Thanksgiving dinner', he invited Leon to meet him in Los Angeles where he was to return to the Hollywood Bowl on 14 September. He had already made cash gifts of $5,000 each to Pearl and Zenora and now slipped his brother the same amount for a plane ticket and some new clothes. Leon needed no persuasion despite still being on bail awaiting sentence for the drug company break-in.

The twenty-year-old spent the next month in LA, sharing Jimi's rock-star lifestyle, occupying a suite at the luxurious Beverly Hills Hotel, driving around in his personal chauffeured limo, shopping on Rodeo Drive, hanging out in the VIP section at the Whisky A Go Go and mingling at parties that practically snowed cocaine with the likes of Mick Jagger, Ringo Starr and Jerry Garcia.

In proposing the visit, Jimi had said he needed 'someone to help keep the women away', but this hardly seemed a serious concern. He was currently dividing his attention between two semi-regular girlfriends, one black, one Puerto Rican: Devon Wilson and a former cocktail waitress at the 'Whisky' named Carmen Borrero. Even so, no matter what hour of the night he and Leon returned to the hotel, there would be a line of females waiting as patiently as for the start of a sale.

'I once burst into Jimi's room without knocking and he was in bed with two blondes,' Leon recalls. 'I said, "Hey, man, come on . . . there's a party, let's go." But I went to that party alone.'

As a rule, Jimi chopped and changed bedfellows with a dexterity and tact that aroused no ill-feeling towards him or even among themselves. It was only when he drank alcohol – especially whisky – that his deep-seated insecurity came to the surface, almost always in this area where he seemed most secure.

One night, for example, he got the idea that Carmen was two-timing him with Eric Burdon and threw a bottle at her head, hitting her in the eye. The emergency room that treated her said she could easily have lost it. Burdon never quite got over the sight of Jimi 'beating up his girlriend in Bel Air'.

Rock stars' younger brothers live with the knowledge that most people are interested in them only as a means of access to their enchanted siblings. However, Leon had no complaints about the many beautiful women who used him as a stepping stone to their ultimate objective. 'Make sure Jimi knows you got the best pussy you ever had last night,' he would often be urged

While Jimi was around, Mike Jeffery was cordiality itself to Leon. But, he recalls, Jeffery regarded the brothers' closeness as a threat and seized every chance to separate them. When the tour departed for one of its various out-of-town gigs, he would try to exclude Leon or feed him false information in case he thought of going under his own steam. 'Like one time, Mike told me my brother was in San Diego and I found out he was actually in Hawaii.'

Jimi's sold-out Hollywood Bowl concert took place on a night of such tropical heat that people in the front rows splashed around in the floodlit pool below the stage, oblivious to the dangerous proximity of hugely powerful electrical equipment.

Among the audience was Buddy Miles, the drummer for Mike Bloomfield's Electric Flag, a fellow African American among whites who had played incognito on both *Axis: Bold as Love* and the album that would become *Electric Ladyland*. During the show, Jimi appreciatively dedicated a song to Miles and invited him onstage to play, but even on a night like this, racism couldn't quite let go: he was stopped by security guards, roughed up and hustled away.

Jimi's set included the most unexpected of all his cover versions, 'The Star-Spangled Banner', played as a solo with deafening, squealing feedback. But this first time, his reinterpretation of the world's most sacred national anthem went almost unnoticed and was judged on its musical qualities alone. Nat Freedland in the

Free Press complained mildly about 'a lengthy, discordant treatment' of what 'just isn't a freak-out tune, let's face it'.

Rather than go on paying the huge tab at the Beverly Hills Hotel, Jeffery rented a large house in Benedict Canyon that had previously been used by the Rolling Stones for himself, Jimi, Mitchell, Redding and Trixi Sullivan. Though intended to give a measure of privacy, it became as overrun with hopeful females as every other Hendrix habitat. 'There was a huge television in the wall that no one knew how to switch on,' Trixi recalls. 'As we were puzzling over it, one of these girls turned to me and said, "Are you a retired groupie?"'

A room was also found for Robert Wyatt, the young drummer in Soft Machine. 'Jimi, Noel and Mitch were all incredibly kind to me,' he recalls. 'I was only on $200 a week and couldn't afford to go to all the places they did, but they'd take me along, saying they needed to be mob-handed, to save me feeling embarrassed about being paid for.

'They even gave me a little room at the recording studio to work on a song I'd written called "Slow Walkin' Talk", a mixture of Mose Allison and Georgie Fame. Jimi dropped by one day, listened to it and then said, "Would you like me to put a bass-line on that?"'

Now that he was to be in the same place for some time, Jimi sent for the metallic blue Corvette Stingray he'd impulse-bought in Cleveland, which had been awaiting his pleasure in New York. Still without a licence and disdaining any kind of lessons, he took it out alone, hurtling at Le Mans speed around the steep and twisty canyon roads.

On one particularly treacherous hairpin bend, he sailed off the edge, landing in a gulch some twenty feet below. Though the car was written off, he sustained little more than a scratched face – and immediately ordered an identical Stingray. It was the kind of escape that makes people think one must have nine lives.

Wherever rock comes to rest, it generates crowds and squalor, and the house soon became a seeming rendezvous for every drug dealer, hustler and shady character on the West Coast. Although Jimi was their willing magnet, he hated their mindless chatter and disrespect for the place's furnishings and fabrics, and frequently longed to turn back into 'the Bat', alone with a scarf-shaded lamp and his guitar. 'Sometimes,' Leon recalls, 'he'd yell and curse and tell them all to get the hell out.'

His main respite from rock 'n' roll riff-raff was Sharon Lawrence, the young news agency reporter to whose mother he had brought such comfort after her father's death. Plain spoken, sensible and humorous, Sharon was always differentiated from the groupies who surrounded him – in her pungent phrase – 'like chirping sparrows intent on capturing the same juicy worm.'

She recalls how thrilled he was to be living in a mansion in the Hollywood Hills, however seedy the company. 'He often used to look around the place and say, "If only all this could last." I knew he was smart enough to know nothing ever lasts. I just never dreamed how short a time he'd have.

'Jimi was an unformed character, but highly intelligent – and about so much more than music and sex and going to a party. When he was really happy, his face would light up and he'd be in the mood for talking. If I got tired of the crowd in that house and said I was going home to read a magazine, he'd say, "Can I read it after you?"'

Sharon was a link with the normality he felt he was missing as a galley-slave rock star – indeed, felt he'd always missed. For example, he loved hearing about her job with United Press International and the speed with which it and other wire services in that pre-internet era sent breaking news around the world. 'I arranged for him to have a tour of the office, see the teleprinters and meet the guys who operated them. He was fascinated.'

He soon told her the real story of his early life, confident that it would never go out on UPI's wire. She therefore understood his tolerance of Leon's often brash behaviour. 'Leon did embarrass him, but he was still the same protective older brother as when they were growing up in Seattle, and didn't want him to turn into the lost soul he himself could so easily have become. They'd have long talks when Jimi really tried to make Leon forget about being a wild boy and think seriously about the future.'

After all that Leon had seen this past month, the only future he thought seriously about was to work with Jimi in the music business. Jimi seemed equally keen to renew their childhood bond and suggested he had reached a point in his career where it could happen. For, he said, he was weary of playing 'Hey Joe' and 'Purple Haze' – 'S.O.S.', he called it, the Same Old Shit – night after night, month in, month out. He wanted to go to New York and start his own record label, like Frank Sinatra with Reprise and the Beatles with Apple. 'He told me,"I want to write symphonies with string sections, violins and horns,"' Leon recalls. '"I want to *compose*."'

For now, he convinced Leon to return to Seattle and face punishment for the drug company break-in, a pretty much assured spell of incarceration. But when the truant arrived home, it was to find a draft-notice from the army, which automatically overrode his sentence. His brother had likewise been spared detention seven years earlier by volunteering for the 101st Airborne.

The advance single from *Electric Ladyland*, released in September 1968, was Jimi's cover of Bob Dylan's 'All Along the Watchtower'. It sounds different from anything else by the Jimi Hendrix Experience, past or to come, because two supernumerary musicians were involved: guitarist Dave Mason from Traffic and Brian Jones of the Rolling Stones.

Mason can be heard on twelve-string guitar and Jones on Vibraslap, a percussion instrument played by striking a wooden ball on a wire against a box of loose metal 'teeth'. It was they who between them created the initial atmosphere of a wild Tennysonian beach with lowering skies, crashing waves, screaming gulls and slithery bladderwrack.

But there the quasi-medievalism ended. Jimi's 'All Along the Watchtower' seemed to belong wholly to that slaughtering, rioting, divided American year, a reflection of a splintered society in 'too much confusion' that 'couldn't get no relief', the wail of his guitar like police sirens in the burning nights. Impartially relevant to all sides of the conflict, it became the first – and only – Jimi Hendrix Experience single to reach the *Billboard* Top 20.

Dylan would later claim to have been 'overwhelmed' by Jimi's interpretation, particularly its 'spaces' – meaning the economy and understatement as well as the splendour, savagery and abandon he brought to it. 'I took license from his version actually, and continue to do so to this day.'

But at the time, no response came from Dylan. Unassuming as ever, Jimi reminded anyone who commented on this seeming gracelessness that 'Bob Dylan is a very busy person.'

TWELVE
ELECTRIC LADIES

That nightmarish American Odyssey of '68 put an end to Jimi's relationship with Chas Chandler and was the beginning of the end for the Jimi Hendrix Experience.

When Chandler first brought him to London, there had been genuine cameraderie between them. But wherever rock strikes it rich, cameraderie is always the first casualty. As many other managers have found, the more successful their artiste, the less secure their position tends to become and the greater the debt their artiste owes them, the more easily forgotten.

It seemed a very long time ago that Jimi had followed Chandler's instructions in the recording studio without question. Now he made every creative decision for himself, aided by engineers who revered and adored him. He'd even begun to impinge on Chandler's territory by acquiring a 'discovery' of his own. Eire Apparent, his erstwhile support band, so impressed him that he produced their debut album, *Sunrise*, as well as playing on several of its tracks.

Finding himself virtually redundant in the studio, Chandler spent most of his time on the road with the Experience, hating every minute. The colossal pressures of this last tour had begun to affect his health, most visibly in a bout of alopecia, a stress-related skin complaint which caused his hair to fall out by the handful. 'What had made him leave the Animals in the first place was to get away from touring,' Trixi Sullivan recalls. 'And

Jimi didn't like having him around on the road either because Chas was still trying to tell him what to do.'

As the journey finally began tailing off, Chandler returned to London, where he was supposedly in charge of Mike Jeffery's office. 'But he hadn't any interest in running an office. He preferred being in the pub down the street.'

When Trixi next came over from New York, she found a scene of devastation: the phones had been cut off for non-payment of bills, the furniture (which Jeffery always preferred to hire rather than buy) had been repossessed and, as a result of other long-outstanding debts, bailiffs were in the process of distraining everything that was left.

As she watched, one of them picked up a filing cabinet and dumped its contents – crucial paperwork relating to Jeffery's artistes, including Jimi – into a heap on the floor before removing it. The bailiffs had no objection to her rescuing the documents, which are still in her possession as her employer never asked for them back.

Jeffery had long been seeking a pretext to cut Chandler loose and this was it: he told Jimi the management partnership was no longer working and he must choose between them. Despite all that Jimi owed to Chandler, it did not seem to cause him any great heart-searching. 'One day, Chas came in with a face like thunder,' Trixi recalls. 'There was a huge shouting-match between Mike and him, then he went storming off and Mike said to me, "That's it. He's out."'

Chandler sold his interest in Jimi for £300,000, equivalent to around £3 million today. His two years in the entrepreneurial superleague proved to have been no one-off fluke. He went on to discover and manage the Wolverhampton band Slade who had a run of hit singles in the early 1970s, to buy the famous IBC recording studios in London, set up various record labels and management companies and co-found a 10,000-seat sports and performance arena in his native Newcastle.

Yet walking away from Jimi Hendrix would always be considered on a par with Sam Phillips selling Elvis Presley's contract to RCA Records for $50,000 or Andrew Oldham handing the Rolling Stones to Allen Klein for a bargain-basement $1 million. And to Chandler's dying day (in 1996, aged only 57) he never quite got over Jimi's rejection.

The demise of the Jimi Hendrix Experience happened more slowly, with several temporary reprieves along the way.

Noel Redding and Mitch Mitchell were shocked and upset to lose Chandler, whom they both had liked and trusted, without any prior consultation with them. Their morale was already at rock-bottom, exhausted by the the pitiless travelling and the monotony of playing what Redding would recall as 'sloppy repeats of old hits as we stared at the audience with dead eyes'.

Redding in particular had grown increasingly bitter over the little exposure he received as a songwriter and vocalist within the Experience. As a protest, he had put together his own band, Fat Mattress, which he proposed to front while continuing to back Jimi. To complicate matters still further, Chas Chandler was currently trying to get Fat Mattress a record deal And at some shows, they would open for the Experience, putting Redding onstage for twice as long as Jimi. He himself offered no objection (though covertly mocking them as 'Thin Pillow') and Jeffery, indifferent to the music side as always, just let it happen.

Redding and Mitchell fulminated behind Jimi's back about his unpredictability onstage: the 'moodies' when he could barely be bothered to hit a chord, the drugged trances when he was barely capable of it and his habit of buying musical instruments for his hangers-on, then charging them to the band's account. Yet he could always disarm them with a sweetly apologetic handwritten letter – or a performance touching new levels of brilliance.

He was less sensitive to their feelings at the Record Plant studios in New York, where the most important sessions for *Electric Ladyland* had somehow been slotted in between the incessant shuttling back and forth across the continent and the Atlantic.

Despite its industrial-sounding name (inspired by Andy Warhol's Factory) and state-of-the art facilities, the Record Plant had a homely ambience and prided itself on being welcoming to musicians. Its co-founder, Gary Kellgren, was a gifted engineer who'd previously worked with the Velvet Underground and Frank Zappa, and a pioneer of psychedelic audio effects like 'phasing' and 'flanging'.

Kellgren worshipped Jimi, and happily made him his 'copilot' behind the Record Plant's brand-new Scully twelve-track console. With Chas Chandler gone, all restraints of time and expense disappeared: takes were unlimited and mixing and re-mixing one track could go on for days. To make him feel even more at home (and further swell the eventual $70,000 tab), Eddie Kramer, his former engineer at Olympic in London, was flown over to lend a hand.

For most of the time, Jimi's ease and self-assurance in the studio seemed absolute. But there was one area where all his hit singles and albums had created no confidence whatsoever. When time came to do the vocal for 'All Along the Watchtower', –Robert Johnson-esque humility returned and he insisted on retiring behind a three-sided screen.

Only two blocks from the Record Plant was New York's best-known musicians' hang-out, the Scene. Usually Jimi would come to the studio straight from the club, bringing along a crowd of friends for one of the impromptu jams he so adored, disrupting the scheduled session and pushing Redding and Mitchell even further to the sidelines. One night, when he appeared with Stevie Winwood from Traffic and Jack Casady from Jefferson Airplane, Redding complained that it was 'not a session but a party' and walked out, It was a somewhat empty gesture since Jimi had taught him to play bass in the first place, and could switch over to it without missing a beat. And, 'party' or not, the jam initiated a quintessential Hendrix track, titled 'Voodoo Chile' in that first spontaneous version but 'Voodoo Child' in the formal one laid down the following day.

Electric Ladyland was finally released as a double album in the autumn of 1968. 'Electric Ladies' was Jimi's politer term for groupies and the cover – devised by Track Records' Chris Stamp for a world still largely untouched by feminism – showed twenty-one naked women with the implicit suggestion that they were but a section of his permanent seraglio.

Jimi was meant to have been shown in their midst, but failed to turn up for the photo shoot. In fact, he hated the image, thinking it vulgar and tasteless; his own conception, discarded by Stamp, had been a photograph by Linda Eastman (soon to become McCartney) and his own earnest liner-notes. Nonetheless, the album billed itself as 'produced *and directed* by Jimi Hendrix'. Inside the gatefold was a double-width portrait of himself, flanked by minuscule ones of Redding and Mitchell which did nothing for their sagging self-esteem.

Despite a near-overload of premium Jimi, it puzzled contemporary reviewers who expected double albums to have a recognisable theme. *Melody Maker* spoke for many in calling its sixteen tracks 'mixed-up and muddled', though acknowledging 'All Along the Watchower' to be a masterpiece. Decades would pass before critic Robert Christgau's recognition of 'an aural Utopia that accommodates both ingrained conflict and sweet, vague spiritual yearnings, held together by a master musician'. Put more simply, psychedelia and the blues became one.

Because of those 'electric ladies' on its cover, many stores in the US refused to stock it or would display it only clothed in plain brown paper. It still reached number 1 in Billboard's Hot 100 and stayed on the chart for the rest of the year. In Britain, although the nudity caused less panic, it stalled at number 6. Some British critics jibbed at the double-disc format, to which Jimi replied he would have liked it to be triple.

The old rapport between Noel, Mitch and himself could still revive, especially with pot smoke in the air. On 6 January 1969 – with the bizarre miscasting that still dogged them – the Jimi Hendrix Experience were booked to appear on a peak-time BBC television show named *A Happening For Lulu*. Its eponymous star was tiny, bluesy-voiced Glasgwegian who'd had her first hit single with the Isley Brothers' 'Shout' but had since moved so far into the middle of the road that she would be joint winner of that year's Eurovision Song Contest.

The programme went out live in black and white in front of a studio audience, and was choreographed as carefully as only the BBC knew how. Jimi was to perform 'Voodoo Child', Lulu was to join him in 'Hey Joe', then they were to close the show by duetting the theme song from her new film, *To Sir With Love* (a sly reminder that her screen co-star was the African American Sidney Poitier).

In the dressing room beforehand, the trio took the opportunity to smoke a joint together. While it was being rolled, a lump of grass fell into the washbasin and disappeared down the plughole. Redding would later recall how a BBC maintenance man was summoned to retrieve what they said was a valuable ring and was so concerned that he offered to dismantle the entire fitment.

Amid that shared smoke was born the notion of an alternative *Happening For Lulu*. The previous October, Jimi had sat next to George Harrison at the Los Angeles Forum, watching one of the last performances by Cream, a power trio that had self-destructed far more quickly than the Experience. 'Jimi must have had the actual idea,' Trixi Sullivan says 'but the three of them were in it together.'

Their spot opened with 'Voodoo Child' as arranged, Jimi a monochrome vision of puffy silk shirtsleeves and transfigured face, playing the intro that was his closest yet to a heavy metal concerto. Things began to come unstuck when Lulu, seated in the audience, began to announce the next segment and a shriek of feedback silenced her. 'Hey Joe' began but before she could join him, Jimi brought it to a halt. 'We'd like to stop playing this rubbish,' he said, 'and dedicate a song to the Cream [sic] regardless of what kind of group they may be in. We dedicate this to Eric Clapton, Ginger Baker and Jack Bruce.'

The three then launched into an instrumental version of Cream's 'Sunshine of Your Love', the song Jimi had inspired Jack Bruce to write. When the floor manager gesticulated frantically at him to get back on script, his only reponse was an upraised finger. The 'tribute' continued all through the time allotted to his duet with Lulu and was still going as the end-credits rolled.

After so many months of slogging around America, the Experience were desperately in need of an extended break. Instead, Mike Jeffery flung them straight into a two-week European tour, kicking off in West Germany. On 12 January, when they appeared at the Rheinhalle in Düsseldorf, Jimi was introduced to Baron Reiner von der Osten-Sacken, a flamboyant young aristocrat sporting sidewhiskers and a top hat. Of more immediate interest, however, was one of the party the baron had brought to the show, 23-year-old Monika Dannemann.

Blonde and athletic-looking, Monika had been mildly famous in her homeland as an ice skater at national championship level before an injury forced her to give up competitive skating for teaching. She and Jimi fell into conversation – in which, it can be safely speculated, he mentioned his own exploits on the

Queensway Ice Rink in London – and ended up spending the night together.

It appeared to be a Hendrix one-night stand like a thousand others for, although Monika followed him to his next gig, in Cologne, he almost immediately moved on to the German super-model Uschi Obermaier, with whom he was photographed being extravagantly affectionate outside Berlin's Hotel Kempinski.

On 18 February, the Experience were to headline at London's Royal Albert Hall, a 'first' in a venue that previously witnessed some of Cream's greatest moments. The show was to be filmed for an American television documentary (never aired in Jimi's lifetime) and also recorded for a live album Jeffery hoped to put out before their end-of-year studio one aimed at the Christmas market.

Despite the multi-media importance of the Albert Hall gig, Jeffery was busy elsewhere and left its organisation to Trixi Sullivan. During the rehearsals, Jimi was so plagued by technical problems that he asked Chas Chandler to come in and rescue things. With shaming generosity, Chandler agreed.

Then on the night, as film cameras waited to turn over and tape-spools to spin, Jimi arrived at the Albert Hall coked out of his head. 'I literally had to kick him onto the stage,' Trixi recalls. 'But he was incapable of playing and the other two guys couldn't do anything about it.

'Finally I went out there and said to the audience, "You may have noticed that Jimi isn't quite up to it at the moment. I'd like you all to come back next week and we're going to do this concert again."'

The split with Chas Chandler meant that Jimi and Kathy Etchingham's two years of flat-sharing with Chandler and his girlfriend, Lotta, had to come to an end. But finding alternative accommodation in central London was no easy task: landlords had by now become even more wary of renting to rock stars thanks to a crackdown by Scotland Yard's Drugs Squad in the person of its self-appointed witchfinder general, Detective Sergeant Norman ('Nobby') Pilcher.

In October 1968, Pilcher had busted John Lennon and Yoko Ono at the foursome's previous domicile, Ringo Starr's flat in Montague Square, deploying seven officers and two police dogs and alerting the media in advance. Before moving in, mindful of Jimi's tenancy, Lennon had had the flat swept clean of drugs, and he maintained that Pilcher's squad had planted the cannabis he was accused of possessing. That minor conviction – his first and only one – would haunt him after he moved to New York in the 1970s and had to spend years fighting against deportation as a 'subversive'.

The open season on pop's first division also inevitably hit Jimi's friend and devout admirer, Rolling Stone Brian Jones, who was raided at his Chelsea flat by officers climbing up its garbage chute and charged with possession of a lump of cannabis hidden in a ball of brown wool. Next on 'Pilcher's List' came Eric Clapton, with whom Jimi had got high in public so many times – though Clapton managed to escape by the back door of his King's Road eyrie in the nick of time, leaving his flatmates to face the music.

It soon become clear that Pilcher had become addicted to the publicity he received as a collector of rock-star 'scalps' and had indeed been wont to plant evidence, just as Lennon and Jones and many other of his victims unavailingly claimed. In 1972, he would be convicted of conspiracy and perverting the course of justice and sentenced to four years imprisonment.

Yet Jimi never seems to have featured on Pilcher's list, even though his next address was hardly inconspicuous. Before his return from America at the end of 1968, Kathy found an apartment for rent on the top floor of 23 Brook Street, Mayfair, one of a pair of perfectly preserved eighteenth-century houses a short walk from Claridge's hotel and Oxford Street.

The adjoining number 25 was a site of historical interest, having once been home to George Frideric Handel, the German-born composer who, like Jimi, had to come to London for his genius to be properly appreciated. The owner of number 23, who operated a restaurant on its ground floor, didn't care who rented the upstairs so long as its £30-per-week rent was paid regularly.

Although the house was in the heart of the West End, its 200-year-old walls muffled almost all noise from outside. There were no other flats in the building and no other residential properties nearby, so Jimi could play his guitar with the amp turned up as high as he liked.

'It was a real retreat,' Kathy would recall, sitting in their old bedroom fifty years later. 'We could get away from everyone and all the madness. It was a proper home where you got up in the morning and had a cup of tea. People did visit us, a lot of other stars, but we never had it packed out. Jimi didn't really like that. If we wanted to be in a crowd, we went to the Speakeasy or the Bag O'Nails.'

For someone looking the way he did, living in the wealthiest part of Mayfair brought occasional brushes with the police, though they were mild compared with those on his American tours. Returning home one night, he and Kathy found access to Upper Brook Street sealed off for the arrival at Claridge's of newly elected President Richard Nixon. Both of them were interrogated, and suspicious looks cast at Jimi's guitar case, but eventually they were allowed through the cordon..

The couple's relationship had stabilised since the rows and plate-throwing at Ringo's flat. Part of the reason was that Jimi now openly acknowledged his involvement with Kathy to journalists instead of making her hide away in the bath. '[She] is my past girlfriend, my present girlfriend and probably my future girlfriend,' he told the *NME*. 'My mother, my sister and all that bit. My Yoko Ono from Chester.'

She had become his muse in a gentler way than when a fiery exit after his complaints about her cooking had inspired 'The Wind Cries Mary'. The Experience's second single from *Electric Ladyland*, 'Gypsy Eyes', was a reference to the Romany strain in her family and a declaration of commitment: 'I found her/I ain't gonna let go.'

Number 23 Brook Street brought out all Jimi's love of domesticity – and army-style orderliness. He enjoyed helping Kathy choose cushions and fabrics to brighten the flat's slanting wood floors and panelled walls and, unusually for any man in that era, took an equal share of the housework. 'He was very good about tidying up and making the bed,' she recalls, 'and he was always going round with the Hoover.'

It fascinated him that Handel had lived in the next-door house, not as a fellow transient musician like himself but for thirty-six years, dying there in 1759. He bought albums of Handel's *Water Music* and *Messiah*, and played them often, especially the latter with its exalting 'Hallelujah Chorus'. The building had no reputation for being haunted, but Jimi was convinced he once saw Handel's ghost, describing how 'an old guy in a nightshirt and a grey pigtail just walked through the wall while I was standing there.'

Although Jimi now had money, it did not stay with him long. If he earned £10,000, he regarded the whole amount as available to spend on clothes or records or lavish cash gifts to family members, friends or even total strangers (like the two girls to whom he gave $3,000 to go shopping just to get rid of them) with never a thought of all the deductions that had to come out of it. At the same time, he remained blissfully unconscious of the cost to him of accountants, lawyers and litigation – like that involving his old PPX label-boss, Ed Chalpin, in New York – and of bottomless tabs that so many other people made use of at clubs like the Speakeasy.

Credit cards were still almost unknown in Britain, and most of his day-to-day expenses were paid out in cash. 'Gerry Stickells the roadie usually carried it and Jimi would just say, "Pay them, Gerry", then forget about it,' Trixi Sullivan recalls. An account had been opened for him at Martins Bank in Edgware Road, but he used it only for withdrawals, once sending Kathy there to collect £3,000, equal to around £30,000 today.

He was totally unaware of – and uninterested in – whatever Mike Jeffery might be doing with his earnings through the offshore Yameta company, the more so since Jeffery had transferred operations to New York. And his infrequent moments of financial anxiety were quickly dealt with by Jeffery. When Kathy discovered that the rent on 23 Brook Street had fallen into arrears, it wasn't long before Trixi appeared with a briefcase full of US dollars.

For some time past, Jimi had been following Noel Redding's example and keeping a diary. Despite his natural verbal gifts, this was little more than an itinerary, couched in an invariable tone of sunny optimism: 'The weather in New Orleans is beautiful' . . . 'We played out there at Red Rocks and I had a lot of fun . . .' 'This tour's a merry-go-round. Tomorrow, it's Muncie, Indiana . . .'

However, at 23 Brook Street, he tape-recorded a spoken version of a song he'd previewed at the Royal Albert Hall, revealing a darker, more troubled side of himself than anyone around him could have imagined. In it he likened his existence as a rock star to 'a room full of mirrors' without windows or a door – a labyrinth of images of himself stretching to infinity from which no escape was possible.

It ended on a note of despair verging on the suicidal: 'What has the world to offer me except pats on the back? . . . Somebody help me. Somebody please help me.'

Jimi's relationship with Kathy had lasted this long mainly because of her remarkable tolerance of the sexual Olympiad which he conducted on the road in America and Europe, which their domestic idyll at 23 Brook Street barely reduced.

Most of these 'electric ladies' remained unknown to Kathy, but there was one she found it increasingly difficult not to notice. This was Devon Wilson, the ravishing light-skinned African American whom Jimi had met first in Los Angeles. From mere groupie, Devon rapidly progressed to being his drug-scorer, then to an unofficial but crucial member of his American entourage.

Often, she and Jimi seemed more like brother and sister: they would tell each other of their sexual adventures with other people, Devon's as likely to have been with women as with men. Despite her deadly drug habit, she was bright and funny, seemed to know everyone and found numerous ways of making herself useful, from controlling the traffic through Jimi's dressing room to arranging, as well as participating in, the threesomes he so enjoyed.

She even followed Jimi to London and insinuated herself into 23 Brook Street without Kathy having any idea who she was. 'She was just another visitor. I remember her sitting on the end of our bed while we were in it, or on it, and serving us tea.'

Nor was this the only one of Jimi's overseas bedfellows refusing to stay in a neat, discreet geographical compartment. In April 1969, Monika Dannemann, the German ice skater he'd met in Düsseldorf three months earlier, came to London on the off-chance of running into him again. She did so easily enough at the Speakeasy and they spent another night together, unbeknown to Kathy.

Kathy's tolerance might have been less elastic had she known that a woman she thought she'd dismissed from Jimi's life during his first few hours in London still remained very much a part of it.

Despite the passage of three years and all those unnumbered females though his bed, he'd never got over Linda Keith, who had first discovered him in New York and whom he'd called his 'blood brother'. Their paths had widely diverged since then but, Linda recalls, 'There was aways a sense between us that one day we'd solve all the problems we both had and finally get together.'

Their meetings were irregular and nowadays completely chaste. 'Once, a limo turned up outside my parents' house in north London and Jimi was sitting in the back. We just went for a walk, then sat on a public bench and talked.'

When Jimi and Linda first met, her boyfriend had been the second most important Rolling Stone, Keith Richard. Now it was the doomed one, Brian Jones.

Brian's escalating drug-use had obliterated his former instrumental brilliance – its last time on show the Vibraslap in Jimi's 'All Along the Watchtower' – while his two drug convictions barred the Stones from touring America, their most profitable market. Yet, with a compassion of which few suspected them, his bandmates could not bring themselves to fire him.

Linda had known Brian for years as a friend, but now their common dependency on drugs drew them together in an infinitely less healthy way. One evening in a club, they made a spur-of-the-moment decision to drive together to Marbella in Spain that night. When they returned, she moved into his Chelsea flat.

Brian soon discovered Linda's feelings for Jimi and made a joke – or so it seemed – of treating him as a rival, which Jimi abetted with the shameless male chauvinism of the time. 'It turned into a silly competition between them,' she recalls. 'They'd sit in a club together, arguing about which one of them I'd be with by the next Christmas. Jimi sent me a present, pretending it was from Brian – an awful woollen hat with a bobble – and another one from him, a beautiful Thea Porter kaftan.'

Behind his seeming playfulness, Brian was crazed with jealousy of his former hero. One night at his flat, when Linda was going off alone to a Jimi gig, he fed her an overdose of sleeping-pills pretending they were amphetamines to keep her awake, then fled the premises. She was found, rushed to hospital and revived only with some difficulty. 'Then the Stones' office put it out that I'd tried to kill myself for love of Brian.'

In March 1969, Jimi was due to start another massive American tour, playing twenty-nine cities in ten weeks. Kathy, as usual, had no wish to go along but she agreed to join him in New York for a few days beforehand while he was working at the Record Plant.

She found him ensconced in the Pierre Hotel's luxurious Garden Suite – which up to then he'd been sharing with Devon Wilson – surrounded by 'the loudest, nastiest bunch I had ever come across. Many of the women were obviously whores,' she recalls in her autobiography, 'and the men all appeared to be pimps and drug dealers with their cool shades and little [cocaine] spoons hanging round their necks like badges of office.'

Being at the Record Plant while Jimi worked on tracks with his new obsessive perfectionism was 'as boring as hanging round backstage in Newcastle or Manchester. Only the food had improved.' And every attempt on her part to rid the suite of hangers-on and recreate some of the peace and seclusion of 23 Brook Street was coldly rebuffed. 'These people are my friends,' Jimi told her.

She put up with it until the day a man arrived carrying a sports bag and walking with a limp – because, as he explained, he'd recently been shot in the leg. He accidentally dropped the bag, which gaped open to reveal packets of white powder with a handgun lying on top of them.

Kathy fled to seek refuge with Angie Burdon, who was now divorced from Eric and staying in New York with a new man friend. The first flight home she could get went via Shannon in Ireland, involved two changes of plane and was packed with nuns and priests, who prayed aloud together when it hit turbulent weather. 'I was so relieved,' she recalls 'that I almost joined in with them.'

THIRTEEN
'I'M GOING TO DIE BEFORE I'M THIRTY'

These could be tricky times for someone who had done more than any musician of his race since Louis Armstrong to make audiences colour-blind. For as Jimi rose to international fame, it was inevitable that he should find himself in the sights of the Black Power movement.

Black Power rejected the pacifist doctrine of Dr Martin Luther King and the Civil Rights pioneers – all those heroic men and women who had stood up to tear gas, dogs and water cannon in the spirit of Mahatma Gandhi – and advocated vigorous, if necessary violent, resistance to white persecution and injustice. It called on its followers to cast off the stigma of their enslaved past by reconnecting with their original African roots, even repudiate the Christianity that had sustained their shackled forebears and become Muslims.

Above all, it urged them to awaken from generations of subservience and self-effacement and, in James Brown's words, to 'say it loud . . . I'm black and I'm proud'.

Its most visible manifestation was the Black Panther Party for Self-Defense, a paramilitary organisation, uniformed in black berets, leather jackets and dark glasses and claiming the same right to bear arms under the Second Amendment to the Constitution as every white citizen. (They also did social work like serving free breakfasts to underprivileged schoolkids.) Afro hair was obligatory, promulgating the movement's slogan 'Black is Beautiful'.

The US government's chief retaliatory weapon was a special unit of the FBI known as COINTELPRO (for Counter Intelligence Program), set up in the 1920s to combat any perceived threat to the nation's internal security and licensed to practise every kind of dirty trick to further its patriotic aims, assassination not excluded.

High on COINTELPRO's list in recent years had been rock musicians and their corrupting influence over young Americans through drugs and promiscuity. In 1967, working with British MI5, it had scored a notable coup by planting an informer in a weekend house party given by Keith Richard, thereby securing the drugs bust that landed both Richard and Mick Jagger in jail and so prevented the Rolling Stones from touring America in the foreseeable future.

In the gales of racial turmoil since then, the FBI's director, J. Edgar Hoover, had ordered the unit to focus on the Black Power movement – and in particular the Black Panthers – as 'the greatest threat to this country's safety'. All African Americans with high public profiles were expected to declare their solidarity with the cause, and many did; in Hoover's eyes, the very Stars and Stripes seemed sullied when, at the 1968 Olympic Games in Mexico City, sprinters Tommie Smith and John Carlos both gave clenched-fist Black Power salutes from the winners' podium.

The question had had little relevance for Jimi in London, where racial unrest was a rarity, always confined to its Brixton and Notting Hill districts, and the only 'revolutionaries' were the young white people toward whom the 1960s were not merely benign but bountiful. To be sure, they could find nothing to protest about nearer than the Vietnam War (the virulence of their protests in no way moderated by the fact that Harold Wilson's Labour government refused any direct involvement in it).

Opposed to the war though Jimi was, his time in the 101st Airborne made him still 'think like a soldier', as he told Eric Burdon when they heard the noise of demos outside the American Embassy in nearby Grosvenor Square. 'He'd parrot the Domino Theory he'd been taught in the army,' Burdon recalls. 'That America had to be in Vietnam to stop the world being taken over by the Communists.'

He did agree to a meeting with London's nearest to a black radical leader, Michael de Freitas, who called himself 'Michael X' after Black Power's charismatic young demagogue Malcolm X – the first of its figureheads to have been ssassinated. Kathy Etchingham went along too, and de Freitas, although born in Trinidad in the West Indies, received them in a room hung with Zulu spears and animal skins.

But no induction into British Black Power followed; instead, de Freitas berated Jimi for cohabiting with a white woman and the couple escaped as quickly as possible. (Despite the support of other celebrities including John Lennon, Michael X's London revolution fizzled out and he returned to Trinidad, where he was hanged for murder in 1975.)

After 1968, as Jimi began spending ever more time in America, he received regular invitations – which soon turned into exhortations – to commit himself to his Black Panther 'brothers'. But much as he sympathised with the movement – especially the 'Black is Beautiful' part – his long, languid body did not contain a militant corpuscle.

He grew adept at deflecting suggestions from hefty brothers in black berets and sunglasses that he should renounce his 'slave name' and embrace Islam, as the great heavyweight champion Muhammad Ali had famously done to huge professional cost, or else call himself something more suggestive of his African roots. In fact, he was rather proud of his lineage back to the Southern cottonfields and always said he was more conscious of his Native American roots than his African ones.

His friend Sharon Lawrence recalls how skilfully he handled

those prickly Panther emissaries, calling them 'Bro' and exchanging high and low fives with an enthusiasm that gave no hint of his yearning for the encounter to end.

He did his best to stay neutral in the race wars, refusing an invitation for a 'fireside chat' with President Nixon at the White House that would have made him the first black musician to be received there since James Brown after calming the race riots that followed Dr King's assassination.

Even so, he couldn't altogether resist the glamour of the Panthers, a fashion as well as a political phenomenon, and Black Power's infiltration of soul music through the likes of Brown, Aretha Franklin and the Chi-Lites. One day in Greenwich Village, he bought a copy of the Panthers' newspaper from a street vendor – a transaction that would have gone unnoticed had the vendor not shrieked 'That was Jimi Hendrix!' after him.

These minor racial thought-crimes were augmented by misunderstandings or by Jimi's unfortunate tendency to be flippant at the wrong moment. 'My brother was going through an airport security check and they asked if he had anything dangerous in his bag,' Leon Hendrix recalls. 'Jimi said, "Only my machine-gun." The cops beat him up for that.

'He was fooling around one time, hanging out of a window with an American flag in one hand, a rifle in the other, and someone took his picture. Then the Panthers asked him to go on a march and Jimi joked that if he did, he'd have to wear a football helmet for protection. That was twisted to make it sound like he was telling them to go out on the streets in body armour.'

All of which was more than enough to fall under suspicion as the 'black Messiah' that J. Edgar Hoover expected and had convinced the American government to expect to unleash bloody black revolution. Accordingly, COINTELPRO file number 163-25925 was opened on Jimi, describing him as 'a well-known Negro entertainer' and classifying him as 'of special interest',,. The file, in which Hoover took a personal interest, would eventually run to thirty-four pages, many of them subsequently 'redacted', that pious synonym for 'censored'.

However, the findings of COINTELPRO's sleuths proved disappointingly thin. It was the time of the Chicago Seven trial, when a group of white 'yippies' (i.e., militant hippies) led by Abbie Hoffman and Jerry Rubin stood in the dock for conspiracy and fomenting riot at the 1968 Democratic party convention. The file noted how the Seven's huge legal bill was being paid through benefit concerts by their many musician sympathisers: '*Word is*,' it added with wonderful smeary vagueness, 'Jimi Hendrix has consented to appear in one.'

On 3 May 1969, the Jimi Hendrix Experience crossed from America into Canada to appear at Toronto's Maple Leaf Gardens. In Detroit, their previous stop, they had been warned to expect a drugs search at Toronto International Airport, so the ever-practical Mitch Mitchell wore a leather suit he'd had specially made without pockets to advertise he had nothing incriminating on him.

Sure enough, they were met by a contingent of the Royal Canadian Mounted Police – the fabled 'Mounties' whose proud boast was that they 'always got their man' – and given an exhaustive going-over: not in private, as was usual, but in full view of the terminal crowds.

The Mounties got their man yet again: a flight bag carried by Jimi was found to contain what the official report described as 'six small packages inside a glass bottle'. A mobile laboratory was called to the airport to analyse the packages' contents and pronounced them to be hashish and heroin.

The hash was only to have been expected but the heroin seemed to astonish Jimi as it did everybody with him. It was common knowledge in his circle that he'd tried smack a couple of times but not been seduced by it; as he confided to Sharon Lawrence, he was terrified of needles and had met enough junkies to be aware of its ghastly consequences.

Now he protested that the stuff in his flight bag had been planted, though by whom and at what stage of that day's short journey were inexplicable. Taken to the Mounties' headquarters downtown, he was charged with two counts of possessing illegal narcotics then released on $10,000 bail pending a preliminary hearing on 19 June.

He was still allowed to do his show at the Maple Leaf Gardens that night – indeed, made his way there with a Mountie escort. Unwisely flippant yet again, he joked from onstage about the bust, even made up a little mock operatic aria about it.

The episode received almost no publicity in Canada or America and none whatsoever back in Britain. The tour's publicist, Michael Goldstein, afterwards claimed to have bribed an Associated Press editor with a case of liquor to stop the story going onto the wires.

However, it unleashed frenetic activity at the FBI through its Buffalo Bureau (Jimi having given his permanent domicile as New York) and brought an expotential growth in his COINTEL-PRO file. There it was alleged that the hashish had been found 'in his shaving kit', contradicting his claim that it had been slipped to him by a fan as 'a medication' without his knowledge. A lengthy teletype exchange with the Seattle bureau brought up his one previous conviction – for 'taking a motor vehicle without permission' as a nineteen-year-old in 1961 – and planted the totally false assertion that further action by the Seattle police might still be pending.

Six days earlier, backstage at the Oakland Coliseum, he had been handed a note that did not contain the usual female invitation to sex. It was from Diane Carpenter, with whom he had lived in

New York when he was nearly destitute, supported by her earnings as a teenage prostitute.

Instead of avoiding her, as he could easily have done – and most in his profession would have – he sent word to Diane to meet him at the airport before he left for his next gig There she produced a photograph of the child she claimed he'd fathered, a girl named Tamika now aged two. Jimi made no attempt to dodge the issue, commenting, 'She has my eyes,' chatting to Diane until his flight was called and taking Tamika's photo with him.

Any fear of paternity proceedings was now blotted out by his two drugs charges, the heroin one carrying a maximum prison sentence of twenty years. Sharon Lawrence knew about them thanks to her job with United Press International, and had resolved that if he really was on smack she would end their friendship

Jimi, however, vehemently denied it. Nor did Sharon see any telltale sign of junkie squalor and self-neglect in the still meticulous young man who sorted magazines into two piles, 'news' and 'music', moistened paper tissues to rub away the sticky rings of Coca-Cola bottles from tabletops and preferred to do his own ironing of the ruffled shirts that to professional pressers represented the ultimate challenge.

Likewise, she found him fully aware how many people were sponging off him, even though he could never be roused to do anything about it. He would recount with amusement how one fellow musician seeking a cash handout arrived by limo, then charged him for its hire.

There was nothing junkie-like, either, in his affection for Sharon's mother, who was still young and attractive but, more importantly, answered the yearning for domesticity that even his Brook Street roost with Kathy Etchingham had not satisfied. 'My mom was always one of the first people he went to see in

LA,' Sharon recalls. 'Basically, they were very alike – two lonely, emotional people. She'd drive him around and quite often take him to the airport when he left.

'Mom was a brilliant cook, and always made sure to fix his favourite dessert, strawberry shortcake. Jimi loved to watch her cook – and he always washed the dishes afterwards.'

His unease over the coming trial could not stop him using the drugs he habitually did, with LSD topping the list. On 23 May, he returned to Seattle, this time accompanied by one of his regular American women friends, Carmen Borrero. After openly tripping on the Center Coliseum stage, he felt an impulse to show Carmen around the scenes of his far-from-happy boyhood. A young male fan, waiting with an album to be autographed, found himself co-opted to chauffeur the pair in his beaten-up Volkswagen Beetle.

Jimi with the Experience could now claim to be the world's highest-paid rock performer – although he could also be seen across a range of small clubs, jamming for free. His show at New York's Madison Square Garden on 18 May earned $14,000 per minute; on 20 June, the Newport Pop Festival, in Northridge, California, paid him a record $100,000 for a notably lacklustre set (redeemed the next day by an onstage jam with assorted fellow artists including Eric Burdon and Buddy Miles).

As time went on it began to appear that the more lucrative the gig, the less Jimi's emotional involvement; the more spontaneous the jam and the smaller the stage, the brighter his brilliance. In a review of his Maple Leaf Gardens performance (in the issue that belatedly mentioned the drugs bust), *Rolling Stone* compared it to 'watching a bullfighter who's so good that no bull challenges him, and therefore there's no danger and therefore no suspense'.

The problem was that Jimi hadn't simply tired of going onstage to play the Same Old Shit; he'd also tired of doing it with the Same Old Sidemen.

The band that Chas Chandler had flung together around him had fulfilled its limited role perfectly well in Britain and Europe. But things were different in America, where so many great musicians clamoured to jam with him. In particular, playing with Jefferson Airplane's hugely inventive bass guitarist Jack Casady had shown up the limitations of Noel Redding.

Redding, of course, had been useful in other ways. His sense of humour had carried the Experience through many a sticky moment. He'd been the most insistent that they should find out exactly what Mike Jeffery was doing with those colossal earnings and invariably acted as group spokeman (albeit with little or no effect).

He had always felt a true regard for Jimi's 'open and loving mind' and now was appalled to see that mind progressively addled by drugs and the psychological pressure from all sides – management, audiences, courtiers, mistresses. 'He was being pulled so many ways, it's a wonder he held it together for long.'

Redding's autobiography, *Are You Experienced*, describes going into their dressing-room trailer at the Newport Pop Festival to find 'about eight black heavies who dwarfed Jimi He looked pet rified and I was chilled to the bone by his appearance . . . I really hated those people who . . . only worried that someone else was sucking his blood and they wouldn't get their cut.'

Signs of Jimi's restlessness were there to see during early 1969. In press interviews, he talked about taking a whole year off from performing and recording, writing songs for a different band, even returning to an idea he'd mentioned to his brother, Leon – perhaps sharpened by George Frideric Handel's ghost – and 'composing symphonies'. In his mind, however, the Jimi Hendrix Experience and the racial mix that had been imposed on it were already history.

Unknown to Redding or Mitch Mitchell, he had got back in touch with Billy Cox, his old buddy and protector in the 101st Airborne Division and bandmate in the King Kasuals. As pay-back for innumerable kindnesses, Jimi had wanted Cox to come with him to London in 1966 – before Chas Chandler decreed white sidemen only – but Cox at the time was too much on his uppers to accept the offer. 'I told Jimi, "I've only got three strings on my bass and the fourth is tied in a square knot,"' he recalls. 'Jimi said, "Well, I'll make it and I'll send for you."'

In the interim, Cox had moved house and changed phone numbers and Jimi knew only that he was living next door to a television repairman, who had to be bribed to deliver a message to him.

On 29 June, the Experience appeared at the Denver Pop Festival, headlining over the Mothers of Invention, Creedence Clearwater Revival, Three Dog Night and Joe Cocker. When Noel Redding arrived, several co-performers looked at him in surprise. 'Are you still in the band?' asked one. 'I heard that Hendrix had replaced you.'

The performances took place in Denver's Mile-High Stadium, aptly enough since Jimi took the stage almost levitating on his favourite acid, 'Owlsey Purple'. Angry that the festival wasn't free, its 17,000-strong audience ran amok and were met by police armed with tear gas. As it eddied towards the stage, Jimi said, 'I see some tear gas – that's the sign of the Third World War.'

A couple of numbers later, without forewarning Redding or Mitchell, he announced, 'This is the last gig we'll ever be playing together.'

Afterwards, in the continuing mayhem, the trio and their roadies fled the stadium in a two-ton metal truck. Their pursuers pounded on the sides and so many piled onto the roof that it started to cave in. Certain they were about to be crushed to death, they linked arms and shook hands and Noel Redding, ever the joker, vowed that if he survived, he was getting on a plane home and never coming back.

Actually, he was being serious for once. He did survive, and did get on a plane home and didn't come back. That seemed to be the finish of the Jimi Hendrix Experience.

From here on, Jimi's 'London period' was as good as over and his relationship with Kathy Etchingham definitely so.

He kept in touch with Kathy for a while after her exit from the Hotel Pierre, but his phone calls grew more infrequent and eventually ceased altogether. Kathy made no attempt at a reconciliation. She had been thoroughly frightened by the attaché case full of drugs and the handgun in Jimi's suite at the Pierre and her resolve to break away hardened as her best friend, Angie Burdon, descended into addiction that would prove fatal.

The Brook Street flat was in Kathy's name and she stayed on there alone for a while, diverted by her many musician friends like Dave Mason from Traffic and the dependably demented Keith Moon. 'My affair with Jimi was certainly the most important I had had . . . but there was no reason to be surprised that it was drawing to an end,' she recalls. 'After all, I was still only 22 years old.'

Meanwhile, big things were afoot for Jimi in New York. Mike Jeffery had taken over the lease of a basement club named Generation at 52 West 8th Street where Jimi had often played with friends like Junior Wells and Buddy Guy. Planning to relaunch it as a psychedelic grotto, Jeffery hired a young architect named John Storyk, only recently graduated from Princeton, who also happened to be an aspiring musician.

Storyk's blueprint for the new club included a small 'recording room' for the use of its performers. Then the engineer Eddier Kramer came up with a radical alternative. Rather than go on paying studio fees, which had reached an astronomical level with the *Electric Ladyland* album, he suggested it was more economic in the long run to build Jimi a full studio of his own.

Jeffery agreed: the club idea was scrapped and, in late 1968, Storyk had set to work on what would be the first recording facility ever tailor-made for a specific artist. In a nod to the album whose sky-high tab helped bring it into being – and Jimi's politer term for groupies – it was to be called Electric Lady Studios.

On 3 July 1969, Brian Jones, his great admirer and Kathy Etchingham's and Linda Keith's former lover, was found dead in a Sussex garden, aged 27. Now finally ejected from the Rolling Stones, Jones had bought the former home of A. A. Milne, author of the Winnie-the-Pooh stories, whose 1920s whimsy seemed at the furthest possible remove from rock-star depravity and excess.

Jones adored the Pooh books, and had introduced Jimi to them: when not talking Muddy Waters or Elmore James, they would discuss the adventures of that 'bear of very little brain' and his companions Christopher Robin, Piglet and the mournful donkey, Eeyore.

Jones had been surrounded by the same kind of spongers and con-artists that Jimi was, yet had died alone in his heated pool despite being an exceptionally strong swimmer. His demise would stand as rock music's greatest unsolved mystery for the next fourteen months.

Two days later, as a 'memorial' to the person who had founded and named them, the Stones played for free to an audience of around 250,000 in London's Hyde Park. Mick Jagger's performance, in a frilly white garment like a little girl's party dress, began with a reading from Percy Bysshe Shelley's poetic elegy *Adonais*, but ended with the simulated fellatio of a bulb-headed hand-mic that to some looked like yet another attempt to outdo Jimi.

He himself was currently trying to clean up his public image by appearances on America's two leading TV talk shows. On 7 July, his interlocutor was ABC's atypically young, hip and intelligent Dick Cavett. Clad in what resembled a sky-blue mini-kimono, he came across as both modest and witty.

'You're considered one of the best guitarists in the world,' Cavett began. 'Oh, no!' Jimi interrupted. 'How about one of the best sitting in this chair?' He then played a new song, 'Izabella', in which there was a brief glimpse of Mitch Mitchell back behind him on drums.

On 10 July came the turn of NBC's *Johnny Carson Show* but with a guest host, the black stand-up Flip Wilson. Also featuring Nina Simone, Wilson Pickett and Joe Tex, it was a major breakthrough in a medium that had always been queasy about showing African American musicians live. In sardonic reference to their victory, Wilson had positioned a large watermelon on his host's desk.

This time, Jimi spoke of his belief in music as 'a religious experience' of more value than 'politicians telling you hogwash about this and that' and 'all this violence . . . people running round the streets. I can see their point, but music is like a church, like going to a gospel church . . .' Afterwards, he introduced 'my new bass player, Billy Cox', and the old army buddies played 'Lover Man' in memory of Brian Jones.

He was moving upmarket in other ways, too. At the Scene, Devon Wilson introduced him to two exotically dressed young women named Colette Mimram and Stella Douglas who were about to open a boutique on nearby East 9th Street, in the new 'unisex' mode. Jimi, a unisex pioneer as a teenager in Seattle, was the first customer through their door.

Colette had been born in Casablanca and the boutique – which never did acquire a name – specialised in Moroccan fabrics as well as *outré* imports from London and Paris. 'Jimi loved our clothes, especially the Moroccan stuff, and he took the same size as me,' she remembers. 'He'd come into the shop every day to try things on or just hang out.'

Stella's husband, Alan Douglas, was a record producer in charge of the United Artists label's jazz division and famous for having teamed Duke Ellington with Max Roach and Charles Mingus on the *Money Jungle* album, regarded as one of the greatest piano trio works in jazz history. Douglas was someone else who saw the makings of a bebop genius in Jimi and would play a major part in his recording history, albeit, sadly, not in his lifetime.

Through Colette and Stella, he also become friendly with a wealthy young Manhattanite named Deering Howe whom he'd met when Howe's yacht was rented for a day trip for the Experience. Colette, Stella and Deering, in the old-fashioned phrase, 'took up' Jimi, introducing him to good restaurants in place of the endless tour 'greasy spoons', stimulating him to talk about subjects outside music that had always fascinated him, like art and politics. They were the first people he had met in years who weren't out to exploit or con him.

He became particularly close to Colette, but never in any uncomfortable or upsetting way for her. 'He was a perfect gentleman,' she says. 'A sweetie.'

Now that the 1960s were starting to ebb away, they had finally caught up with Mike Jeffery. The manager's former anonymous blue business suits and dark glasses were giving way to garish long-collared shirts and hipster flares; he had grown his sideburns, begun taking LSD and even – with the funds that were always at his immediate disposal if not his clients' – bought a house in Woodstock.

This traditional haven for artists and writers, 100 miles north of New York City, had become one for rock's super-elite also when Bob Dylan's manager, Albert Grossman, settled in the area. Dylan had soon followed, finding Woodstock offered the privacy he craved and a stimulus to his new country-tinged electric sound with the Band in the recording-sessions later known as the Basement Tapes. The Band, in their turn, had rented a communal pink-sided house-cum-studio in neighbouring West Saugerties that named their debut album in their own right, *Music from Big Pink*.

It was in the hope of Jimi benefiting from this potent creative atmosphere that Jeffery moved him to Woodstock – by now a generic name for a ring of hamlets as well as the town itself – for the process of forming a new band. Jimi made no objection, for he still revered Dylan; even more so since receiving a privileged preview of the Basement Tapes, which were to be witheld from the public until 1975.

Jeffery did not stint on accommodation, renting him an eight-bedroom stone house in the tiny village of Shokan, with ten acres of grounds, a pool, stabling and horses that were his to ride if he wanted. Dylan lived only a quarter of a mile away, but was still in seclusion after the motorcycle accident, three years earlier, that seemingly had ended his performing career.

Billy Cox was not the only trusty old friend Jimi called to Shokan for his new line-up. It also included Larry Lee, the big, amiable rhythm guitarist who'd worked with the two of them long ago in the King Kasuals. Lee had just completed his military service in Vietnam and was about to register at his local unemployment office when Billy's phone call came. The two other recruits reflected Jimi's feeling of liberation from the Experience's 'power trio' format for both were percussionists, drummer Juma Sultan and conga-player Gerardo Velez.

He seemed to have fully absorbed the Woodstock spirit, telling one visitor he wanted only to write music about 'tranquillity and beautiful things'. But after a few days, without a word to his fellow musicians – and much to Jeffery's fury – he vanished without trace.

Colette Mimran and Stella Douglas had gone to Morocco, Colette's birthplace, on a buying trip for their boutique and their wealthy friend Deering Howe was due to join them there. On the spur of the moment, Deering invited Jimi along. It took some covert arranging for, with his Canadian drug trial still pending, he had to get permission to travel abroad from the Royal Canadian Mounted Police.

His arrival came as an equal surprise to Colette and Stella. 'We were at the airport to meet Deering,' Colette recalls, 'and all the people who came off the plane first were asking us, "Are you anything to do with that weird guy who was on our flight?"'

With that, the buying trip was scrapped; they rented an old Chrysler sedan and devoted themselves to entertaining Jimi. The nine days that followed were the only holiday he'd ever had and unquestionably the most joyous time of his life.

Brian Jones had discovered Morocco ahead of him and been entranced by the teeming *souks*, or bazaars, displaying carpets, copper and brass of every description; by the brilliant textiles, tiles and ceramics especially in rich 'Berber blue'; by the lingering influence of its former French colonists; by the air of mystery and intrigue in its hurrying hooded figures, mingled with the sense of freedom and permissiveness long predating the Sixties; by its couscous and tagines and mint tea in little glasses; above all by the live music played spontaneously in streets and squares on all kinds of unrecognisable stringed instruments.

For Jimi, knowing he was in North Africa, and so connected to all this, however remotely, magnified its delights a thousandfold. He was especially charmed by the medieval town of Essaouira (formerly Mogador) on the Atlantic coast and the crumbling watchtower known as Borj El Baroud on a broad stretch of sand nearby. In years to come, a wishful legend would arise that he'd been inspired to write 'Castles Made of Sand' there.

Nor did his reluctant return alone to the States on 6 August quite end the adventure. Waiting for a connecting flight in Paris, he encountered Brigitte Bardot, the French film actress who

during his adolescence had indisputably been the world's sex-
iest woman. Their two-day off-the-radar affair added Jimi to a
roster of Bardot conquests that had included his first French fan,
Johnny Hallyday.

Only one thing marred the vacation. 'In Morocco, I took Jimi
to meet my grandfather,' Colette recalls. 'He was very old-school
French, and didn't approve at all of me being with Jimi. But he'd
recently remarried to a younger woman who was a clairvoyant
and who got Jimi immediately. "He's a genius," she said. "You
can tell by his forehead." And she told me, "A year from now,
you won't be friends with him any more." I assumed that meant
he would have found another woman, but Jimi seemed to see another meaning in it.' Then she read the Tarot cards to look into
his future – and the Death card turned up.

'After we got back to the States, he kept saying to me, "Only
eight months left" and "Only six months left". I asked what he
meant and he said, "I'm going to die before I'm thirty."'

FOURTEEN
'NOTHING BUT A BAND OF GYPSIES'

After the light and freedom of Morocco – to say nothing of being bedded by Brigitte Bardot – it felt like a chore for Jimi to return to rural upstate New York, make his apologies to the new band he'd left in limbo and go on trying to turn it into a successor to the Jimi Hendrix Experience.

He had brought its four members together without a thought of how they would function as a unit. Billy Cox and Larry Lee, his old friends, were downhome R&B men from Tennessee; Juma Sultan and Gerardo Velez were from sophisticated New York jazz-funk circles (and both of them percussionists). A hard-driving musical director, like his fellow Garfield High School alumnus Quincy Jones, might have welded the disparate elements together; easy-going, egalitarian Jimi couldn't, and never would.

Nor did the Woodstock area's beauty and seclusion promote any of the creativity it had for Bob Dylan and the Band. Seeing Essaouira and the Atlantic coast had made him even less inclined than before to country rambles and communing with Nature, though he did gamely try riding one of the horses that came with the rented house in Shokan, and managed to stay in the saddle. Jimi Hendrix on horseback in full costume is as treasurable a thought as him on the Queensway ice rink in London.

Mike Jeffery, whose house on Woodstock's Wiley Lane was only a couple of miles away, hovered constantly in the background, still fuming over Jimi's Moroccan escapade and fretting over the loss of his touring income, his choice of new sidemen and their all too obvious lack of progress.

The new sidemen were uncomfortably aware of the strained atmosphere between Jimi and Jeffery, on whom – with his cash payouts at live shows suspended – he was now completely reliant for money. 'The temperature used to drop by about ten degrees,' Gerardo Velez recalls, 'every time Mike came into the room.' Claire Morice, a cook who worked for Jimi and his retinue, later claimed he'd told her he was trying to get free of Jeffery's management.

Every musician in the district, hearing that Jimi was there, dropped by hoping for a jam with him and always got one. But the Shokan house was to produce no equivalent of Dylan and the Band's Basement Tapes. The nearest was a bootleg recording by local keyboard-player Mike Ephron, credited to 'Jimi Hendrix, Juma, Mike and Friends' and sold by mail order for $5.

Like Colette Mimram's clairvoyant step-grandmother in Morocco, Ephron's girlfriend had a premonition that Jimi would die before he was thirty. Feeling he needed rescuing from Jeffery, the couple even discussed 'kidnapping' him and taking him to a safe house in the district. Other people would soon have the same thought, although not with the same benign intent.

With Jimi still pondering over what to call the new band, Jeffery had already arranged their live debut at a conveniently accessible event. This was the Woodstock Music and Arts Fair, beginning on 15 August 1969, billed as 'an Aquarian Exposition' but actually a three-day pop festival, seemingly no different from others that had been taking place all over the country. It represented the most elastic use of Woodstock's name to date since the site was actually 43 miles to the south-west, a 600-acre dairy farm at White Lake near Bethel.

One of its co-promoters, the youthful Michael Lang, had been involved in the Miami Pop Festival, where Jimi had made a notable appearance the previous year. Finding him now so near at a hand seemed a lucky break to Lang who – swallowing hard – agreed to Jeffery's price of $32,000 for him to headline and close its final day.

To Jimi's great disappointment, Woodstock's most famous musical resident would not be among the cast. Bob Dylan had been pre-emptively booked to perform with the Band at a concurrent festival on Britain's Isle of Wight. But even without that logical headliner-of-headliners, Lang warned Bethel's local authority to expect a crowd of up to 50,000.

Early in August, with the Woodstock festival looming and the band still struggling, Jimi decided to send for Mitch Mitchell, who'd continued to back him after Noel Redding's departure but had since returned to Britain.

Checking into the already crowded Shokan house with his girlriend, Mitchell thought the new line-up 'a shambles', and that increasing its percussionists to three by adding his lone white face would not be much help. After he'd rehearsed with them for ten days, he recalls in his autobiography, they were 'probably the only band I've ever been involved with that did not improve over that time. I got the feeling that Jimi simply wanted to get through the [Woodstock] gig and start again.' At one point, he got so frustrated that he hurled his guitar across the room.

But at least the band now had a name. Referring back to his belief in music as 'a religious experience', and because the house stood atop a steep hill, Jimi first chose Electric Sky Church, but then, for no particular reason, changed it to Gypsy Sun and Rainbows.

The Woodstock festival's programme, meanwhile, had grown to thirty-two acts including Joan Baez, Arlo Guthrie, Richie Havens, Sly and the Family Stone, Tim Hardin, Canned Heat, Creedence Clearwater Revival, the Grateful Dead, Janis Joplin,

Jefferson Airplane, Santana, the Who, the Jeff Beck Group, Blood Sweat and Tears, Joe Cocker, Crosby Stills and Nash, Iron Butterfly, Ten Years After, John Sebastian, Ravi Shankar, the Paul Butterfield Blues Band and Johnny Winter. Tickets ($7 per day or $18 for the whole three days) were going at such a rate that the organisers now predicted a crowd of 100,000.

In the end, such hippy multitudes descended on farmer Max Yasgur's rolling cow pastures that the organisers soon gave up trying to sell tickets and declared it a free festival. The final total would be between 400,000 and 500,000, the largest crowd for a musical event ever recorded – arguably the largest convened for any purpose other than fighting battles. So inadequate were the boundary fences that the organisters soon had no option but to declare it a free festival.

Despite being held in late summer, normally a glorious season in those parts, there was heavy rain which caused lengthy delays in the running order and eventually turned the site to a quagmire reminiscent of the Great War's Battle of the Somme. In an age long before premium seating and 'glamping', most attendees lived in rudimentary tents, with only the most basic catering and toilet facilities. Yet the atmosphere was one of celebration and impermeable harmony; in the whole three days, there was not a single reported instance of violence. Farmer Max Yasgur himself took to the stage to admit having expected all kinds of problems from this use of his pasture, much to his shame in hindsight. 'You people have proven something to the world,' he said. 'That half a million young people can get together and have three days of fun and music and have nothing BUT fun and music, and I God bless you for it.'

Jimi's climactic performance introducing Gypsy Sun and Rainbows on Sunday, 17 August was scheduled to start at 11 p.m. By this third day, the roads for miles around had become choked by parked vehicles and performers were being ferried to the stage area by helicopter. No chopper had been provided for the night's headliners, however, so roadie Gerry Stickells had to be sent out to steal a pickup truck from the huge available choice for an hours-long journey through the (still miraculously good-tempered) chaos,,

Jimi and Co finally arrived backstage to discover the festival's running order had fallen so far behind, there was no hope of them finishing it as per the programme. Michael Lang offered an earlier slot but Mike Jeffery – as usual employing far more frigid aggression than was necessary – insisted on his group being the last to perform even though it meant waiting on site until the next morning. Since all the artistes' caravans were already taken, he and the new band were led to a small cottage 'about three muddy fields away', Mitch Mitchell would recall, and spent the rest of the night there 'freezing'.

They finally took the stage at 9 a.m. on the Monday morning, a time that the lowliest support band would have considered an insult. By then, the site was a sea of mud and the half-million crowd had dwindled to a mere 30,000 or so. Michael Wadleigh's Oscar-winning documentary *Woodstock* captures all the incongruity of that moment . . . Jimi wearing a white fringed jacket by Charlotte Mimram and a red headband, with the latest in his line of long-suffering white Strats . . . behind him six Marshall speakers in three giant stacks . . . in front, an audience whose colour seemed to have been rinsed away by the summer tempests until they resemble hippies no longer but the Victorian 'mudlarks' who used to scavenge the banks of the River Thames.

Things got off to a shaky start when the emcee introduced 'the Jimi Hendrix Experience' and Jimi delivered a lengthy correction which hardly stoked up excitement. 'Dig, we'd like to get something straight. We got tired of the Experience and every once in a while we was blowin' our minds too much, so we decided to change things around and call it Gypsy Sun and Rainbows for

232

short. It's nothing but a Band of Gypsies.'

Yet in the two-hour set that followed, almost half the eighteen songs were Experience numbers he used to call 'the Same Old Shit' – 'Purple Haze', 'Foxy Lady', 'Castles Made of Sand', 'Red House' and a fourteen-minute version of 'Voodoo Child', with no perceptible embellishment from Gipsy Sun and Rainbows beyond a double helping of conga drums. New compositions like 'Stepping Stone', 'Izabella', 'Message to Love' and 'Villanova Junction' could only sound like the Experience because the Experience had only ever sounded like Jimi.

To be sure, *Woodstock* virtually does away with the band, shooting him mainly in close-up and often from below – quivering white fringes on a tremolo-arm; an ecstatic red-bound face framed by a lowering Monday-morning sky that no one would ever want to kiss.

As much as a celebration and show of strength by the counterculture, the festival was a protest against the Vietnam War. Its organisers had announced that buying a ticket automatically enlisted the purchaser in the anti-war movement; several of its principal performers had delivered impassioned speeches on the subject, but thus far the most overt musical protest had been Country Joe McDonald's lampoon of the military draft, 'I-Feel-Like-I'm-Fixin'-to-Die Rag', with its delighted mass singalong.

Jimi's inclusion of 'The Star-Spangled Banner' towards the end of his set was, in itself, no surprise. He had played it several times before in shows and done an obvious rehearsal during a pre-festival jam at Woodstock's Tinker Street cinema that included two members of Santana.

But he had never played it quite as he did for those bleary, muddy hippies: slowed right down from its usual brassy bounce, punctuated by drawn-out vibrato, flights into double time and long dying falls erupting into a feedback cacophony that somehow mimicked the war's sounds – the whip of helicopter blades, the whistle of falling bombs, the whoomph of Napalm, the screams of its shredded victims. The former Airborne soldier also acknowledged the young conscripts being killed in their thousands by segueing into 'Taps', the mournful bugle-cry over a soldier's grave.

'You finally heard what that song was about,' the *New York Post* columnist Al Aronowitz would later write. 'That you can love your country but hate the government.'

At the time, in keeping with the moment, the applause was but desultory. For an encore, Jimi began another new song, 'Valley of Neptune', and forgot the words, apologised and fell back on that Same-iest of Old Shit, 'Hey Joe'.

His FBI file lists him accusingly among Woodstock's dramatis personae, expatiates on the amount of LSD consumed there, dwells with voyeuristic relish on the music's power to cause 'unrestrained and lewd behaviour' among its spectators yet makes no mention of 'The Star-Spangled Banner', possibly for fear of causing J. Edgar Hoover apoplexy.

He walked off stage, Mitch Mitchell recalled, 'cold, tired, hungry and unhappy with his performance'. He would never know he had just created the defining moment of Woodstock – and, many people believe, of the whole decade.

Jimi's two regular female companions, as opposed to the countless irregular ones, continued to be Devon Wilson and Carmen Borrero. Each had her appointed role and was perfectly content to share him with the other.

Devon was more like a personal assistant whose duties ranged from controlling the crowd around him (at which she was never very effective) to scoring his drugs. Latterly, she had persuaded him to try the heroin to which she was long addicted, even though he was awaiting trial for possession of the drug in Toronto with a plea of not guilty. However, with his phobia about needles, he did not inject it and never took enough in powder or pill form to become dependent .

Carmen was his 'public' girlfriend on occasions when he needed one, like the last trip back to Seattle. She was in every way different from the amiable Devon, with a fiery temper and a penchant for unlocking the darkness that lurked in Jimi, especially when he drank whisky, most especially if he suspected one of 'his' women of infidelity. A combination of both with Carmen led him to repeat the violence she'd suffered in Los Angeles: first, he tried to push her out of a window, then hit her with a bottle.

After his return from London, the *ménage à trois* increased to *quatre*. He had always kept in touch with Fayne Pridgon, his mistress-cum-mentor during his first, penniless days in New York. Now Fayne welcomed him back into her bed as indulgently as before, although surprised at the change in the kid with the processed hair who used to go at it so straightforwardly. 'Once, I remember waking and Jimi was . . . tying my foot to the bed-rail,' she would recall in her mesmerising 1982 interview with *Gallery* magazine. 'The other hand and foot had already been secured. Suddenly he was like a total stranger to me.'

Despite these ominous preliminaries, what followed had no S&M element, but afterwards 'I became terribly angry when it became clear he had no intention of letting me loose. He pulled the cover up around my neck, kissed me on the bridge of my nose and said he was going to a rehearsal.

To Fayne, Jimi had become 'like a speeding A-train, heading for a wall. He felt it, we all felt it. Something was leading to a boom, some big bang. He often said he didn't know if he would make it to thirty.'

Woodstock had increased Jimi's discomfort about staying on the fence where Black Power was concerned. Performing for such a huge, overwhelmingly white crowd inevitably brought cries of

'Uncle Tom' from the Black Panthers (just as it brought threats from redneck whites to beat him to a pulp if he ever defiled the National Anthem like that again).

The pressure was the greater because his new sideman, Juma Sultan, had links with the Panthers, as Gerardo Velez did with their Puerto Rican equivalent, the Young Lords. This pushed Jimi to an interview in which he seemed to make the commitment the Panthers had sought for so long. 'I naturally feel a part of them in certain respects, you know,' he said. 'But everybody has their own way of doing things.'

It bothered him, too, that his black audience was still nowhere near the size of his white one, especially not here in New York. That became painfully clear one broiling hot day just after Woodstock while he and Fayne were driving around Harlem in his Corvette with the top down. 'Some little kids were shooting water out of fire hydrants and filling every car that passed,' Fayne would recall. 'I told him to stop and turn around but he said, "No, they won't do it to me." I said, "They will, they don't know you." Well, they wet us all up and filled his little Corvette with water. It came as a big shock to him that kids in Harlem didn't know who Jimi Hendrix was.'

Nonetheless, a campaign was afoot to help Hendrix finally win over Harlem. Its driving force were musician twin brothers TaharQa and Tunde Ra Aleem (born Albert Raymond and Arthur Russell Allen), who had once shared an apartment with Jimi and to whom he'd given their stage name of the Ghetto Fighters.

How much clout the Aleems had in Harlem was demonstrated when some local hustlers began advertising a Jimi Hendrix concert that Jimi had never agreed to and knew nothing about. Walking along 125th Street with the twins one day, he saw a man in the act of putting up a poster for it. He angrily confronted the fly-poster, who immediately summoned backup, and he found himself looking down the barrel of a gun. When TaharQa and Tunde Ra mentioned their connections in the neighbourhood, the gangsters backed off and nothing more was heard of the supposed concert. One can only wish he could have gone on enjoying such protection.

The twins' first idea was for Gypsy Sun and Rainbows to play the Apollo theatre – where Jimi had once won the Friday-night talent contest – as a benefit for famine victims in the short-lived, tragic African state of Biafra. However, the Apollo refused to participate, fearing the event would be hijacked by white Hendrix fans from downtown.

It was therefore decided to make the benefit for Harlem's United Block Association, which had some 3,000 young African American and Puerto Rican members and epitomised the positive and community-minded side of Black Power. Mike Jeffery was aghast that no fee would be forthcoming, but the gig held such importance for Jimi that he had to agree. It was to be a one-day open-air event on 5 September, with undoubted Harlem favourites Sam and Dave, Big Maybelle and Maxine Brown in support.

A few days beforehand, Jimi gave a press conference at Smalls Paradise, the 135th Street nightclub where he'd once struggled to be heard. Rather than his usual gaudy gypsy threads, he wore a black djellabah he'd brought back from Morocco which made him look like a Benedictine monk. Inevitably, only one thing interested the press: would this be a 'black Woodstock'? 'I want to show that music is universal – that there's no white rock or black rock,' he told the *New York Times*.

On the afternoon of the show, he drove to Harlem in his Corvette with Carmen and Mitch Mitchell; they parked and set off for an exploratory stroll, leaving Jimi's guitar on the back seat. They had gone only a short way when a group of teenagers broke into the car and made off with the guitar. The Aleem twins' connections had to be called on again to trace the thieves and recover it before showtime.

The stage – strangely undersized and only about four feet high – had been sited on West 139th, facing down Lenox Avenue to create the largest frontal audience possible. About 5,000 people had turned up but the atmosphere was nothing like Woodstock's; as the Apollo management had predicted, they included many whites from downtown who did not realise on what sensitive turf they stood. Carmen, with her dyed blonde hair, was mistaken for one of the interlopers rather than a Puerto Rican kindred spirit. Jimi met with shouts of abuse for escorting 'a white bitch' and she had paper cups and other missiles thrown at her and her blouse ripped.

He was scheduled to go on at midnight, straight after Big Maybelle, who weighed 250 pounds and had a voice that could shatter a wineglass at twenty paces. Maybelle's '96 Tears' and 'Whole Lotta Shakin' Goin' On' set people a-bop all down Lenox and in the windows of surrounding buildings, but when she refused to come back for an encore, booing broke out.

Unfortunately, the first of Gypsy Sun and Rainbows on to the stage was Mitch Mitchell, the sight of whose white face redoubled the boos. When Jimi followed, even his white trousers brought jeers and catcalls as if he'd purposely chosen them to proclaim his primary allegiance, and eggs and a bottle were hurled at the stage, putting the Aleem twins in real fear that their getting-to-know-Jimi exercise was about to turn into a riot.

Jimi responded by working as hard as if this were an open-air Apollo Talent Night, with usually guaranteed crowd-pleasers like 'Foxy Lady', 'Red House' and 'Fire'. He included 'The Star-Spangled Banner' but deliberately eclipsed it by a version of 'Voodoo Child' that he introduced as 'Harlem's National Anthem'. Nonetheless, the crowd down Lenox Avenue kept melting away during his set until at the end only a couple of hundred were left. The best face that could be put on it was his percussionist Juma Sultan's comparison with a sporting fixture which had ended in a draw.

He would never have another chance to change that score.

September 1969 found Linda Keith making a concerted effort to overcome her drug addiction by undergoing both electric-shock and sleep therapy at St Thomas's Hospital in south London. But hearing that Jimi was to perform at the opening of a New York club named Salvation 2, she discharged herself from hospital and went over to see him. It was, as she describes it, another of their occasional 'little romantic flings', not in any way obstructed by Devon Wilson, with whom she remained 'great friends'.

Jimi, she recalls, seemed 'depressed and anxious', but did not tell her why. 'It was as if he wished he could go back in time to when things used to be simpler.'

Salvation 2 was a new uptown version of a place in Sheridan Square, Greenwich Village, where in former days Jimi had often played, then passed the hat around. Since then, like many clubs in the city, it had come under the control of the Mafia. That was not in itself a worry: many entertainers worked in places controlled by the Mob – indeed, it was almost impossible not to – and generally suffered no ill effects. What disquieted Jimi was a growing suspicion that they now also controlled his manager.

Ten days after Woodstock, Mike Jeffery had turned up at the Shokan house in a chauffeur-driven limo: an unusual departure for someone who took pride in doing everything on the cheap. He had informed Jimi that Gypsy Sun and Rainbows would be appearing at Salvation 2's opening and, to indicate that refusal was not an option, the chauffeur had produced a loaded revolver and began using a tree in the yard for target practice.

Despite this coercion – and Gypsy Sun and Rainbows' indifferent performance on opening night – Jimi was well-treated at

Salvation 2. The club soon became another venue for the late-night jam sessions he could not live without and its co-manager, Bobby Woods, was his main cocaine dealer, drawing on stock that the Mob imported into Manhattan by the ton.

He was therefore totally off-guard when he left the club on foot late one night to score something other than its in-house coke. During the short journey, he was accosted by four men and whisked away in a car.

His brother Leon maintains that the kidnap had been staged by Mike Jeffery with the assistance of his new Mafia buddies, to be followed by an equally bogus 'rescue' that would leave Jimi even more in thrall to him. Leon further believes that Jimi barely noticed what was going on. 'He just went on smoking grass, playing his guitar and hanging out.'

But Trixi Sullivan, still Jeffery's PA at the time, says it was completely genuine and Jeffery was as appalled as everyone else. 'Mike got a call one afternoon and I saw him go deathly pale. He said they'd got Jimi and a car was coming to pick him up and take him to where Jimi was being held.

'He told me later he'd been driven to this place in the middle of nowhere, then down a long drive. And behind every other tree, there was a man with a machine gun.' Negotiations took place and two days later, Jimi was returned to the house in Shokan, unharmed but, Trixi recalls, 'in shock'.

The episode never got into the papers and remained shrouded in mystery until 2011 and publication of a book entitled *American Desperado: My Life as a Cocaine Cowboy* by a convicted drug smuggler named Jon Roberts. In 1969, Roberts, then known as Riccobono, had been a young Mafia 'soldier', based at Salvation 2. Jimi, he claimed, had not been abducted by proper Mafiosi but 'wannabe wiseguys' desirous of getting into the music business, either by muscling in on his management or simply extracting a ransom for him.

According to *American Desperado*, Roberts and a colleague named Andy Benfante easily traced the kidnappers and told them, 'You let Jimi go or you're dead. Do not harm a hair of his Afro.' Once he was free, the wannabe wiseguys were given a beating that discouraged them from any further ventures into the music business.

Jimi's watchers in the FBI naturally had developed a strong interest in Salvation 2 and Roberts had been forced to flee to Miami, there becoming involved with the Medellín drugs cartel and ultimately facilitating its importation of $15 billion-worth of cocaine into New York. He changed his surname from Riccobono to confuse the feds when he fell under suspicion of 'whacking' Jimi's dealer, Bobby Woods, who was found shot five times in the head in 1971.

A surreal postscript to *American Desperado* claimed that in addition to the kidnap-rescue, Jimi owed its author a literal 'salvation two'. He had been wont to hang out at Roberts's beach house on Fire Island where – the old high-school athlete resurfacing – he liked to water ski, no matter how stoned he was. One day, evidently in that condition, he collapsed into the water and would have drowned but for Roberts's arrival in a speedboat with a rope.

However, as a junior player in the kidnap drama, Roberts would have been acting on orders from above. From what Jeffery told Trixi Sullivan, she deduced Jimi's release had been arranged through his record company, Warner/Reprise, whose most valuable property he was at that point. And the idea that a company founded by Frank Sinatra should still have had a helpline to senior figures in the Mafia cannot easily be discounted.

FIFTEEN
MILES AND MILES

Gypsy Sun and Rainbows lasted barely a month. Although Jimi worked on several tracks with them at the Record Plant, there was never enough finished material to make a debut album. Their only national exposure came with Jimi's second appearance on the *Dick Cavett Show* on 9 September when the burning topic was still Woodstock and his interpretation of 'The Star-Spangled Banner' which he described as 'beautful' with Cavett's smiling approval.

Afterwards, with the line-up minus Gerardo Velez and Larry Lee, he performed a new song called 'Machine Gun', another soundtrack of the Vietnam War, this time in the guise of a sleep-walking blues whose impact was mostly lost by having to be cut to two and a half minutes.

Mike Jeffery might have allowed the band to continue if they'd shown any sign of becoming good earners on the road. A nationwide tour had been arranged for them, starting in Boston on 18 September, but a few days beforehand Jimi cancelled it on the grounds that he 'did not feel physically or mentally capable of performing'; the promoters, Concert Ways, had to be paid $25,000 compensation and Jeffery decided enough was enough.

Velez and Juma Sultan were persuaded to sign individual con-tracts with a Jeffery offshoot company (aptly named Piranha Productions), the real object of which was to stop them working any further with Jimi. Rhythm guitarist Larry Lee independently

242

decided to leave, having always felt out of his depth, and Mitch Mitchell followed suit to spend more time at his new house back in Britain. Only Billy Cox stayed at his post like the old soldier he was, ready to play bass and provide Jimi with other reinforcement whenever needed..

The rented property in Shokan was vacated and given back to its owner in not quite the condition he'd last seen it. One of the bedrooms had been painted black, another acquired a mural of a flying saucer above a mountain and there were burn marks and spilt wax from candles everywhere.

Jimi accepted the end of the band philosphically, moving back into New York City and taking an apartment on his own on Greenwich Village's West 12th Street. After spending all those months in Woodstock without a sight of Bob Dylan, he spotted Dylan in the Village one day while walking along 8th Street with his Society friend, Deering Howe.

Equal star though he now was, he introduced himself like the humblest, fan: 'Uh, Mister Dylan . . . I'm a singer . . . my name's Jimi Hendrix . . .' Dylan, who could be such a curmudgeon, greeted him affably, belatedly praising his covers of 'Like a Rolling Stone' and 'All Along the Watchtower', even recalling their first brief encounter years before at the Village's Kettle of Fish café. Jimi, Deering Howe recalled, 'was on cloud nine'.

The word that Jimi Hendrix was seeking new sidemen quickly went around the top musicians, both American and British, who constantly passed through New York and, without exception, regarded an invitation to jam with him as the summit of their careers. In no time, he was rumoured to be planning a Cream-style supergroup with Jack Casady from Jefferson Airplane and Steve Winwood from Traffic.

Whatever new combination he settled on, the obvious favourite as drummer was Buddy Miles, the genial giant with the outsize Afro whom he used as an occasional session-player and sideman*e*. Though Miles now had a band of his own, the Buddy Miles Express, Jimi had maintained their connection, writing liner-notes for the Express's first debut album, *Expressway to Your Skull*, and producing one side of their second, *Electric Church*.

In the autumn of 1969, however, all this had to be put on hold when Jimi's career took a totally unexpected but irresistible detour with another man named Miles.

The latest British guitarist to offer a serious challenge to his crown was Yorkshire-born John McLaughlin, a pioneer of fusions between rock, blues, jazz and Indian classical music that would later come together in the Mahavishnu Orchestra. As it happened, McLaughlin had recently moved to New York to join drummer Tony Williams's jazz-fusion band, Lifetime.

Mitch Mitchell, an old friend of McLaughlin's, was back in town and came to see Lifetime at the Village Vanguard. Afterwards, Mitchell invited him to 'a monumental jam' with Jimi at the still-unfinished Electric Lady Studios that also included Buddy Miles. Jimi, McLaughlin recalls, 'was one of the humblest and nicest people I ever met'.

McLaughlin's eclectic brilliance had also given him an entrée into New York jazz circles, where he'd gone straight to the top by playing regularly with Miles Davis.

Since the late 1950s, Davis had been to modern jazz what Jimi now was to rock. A revolutionary stylist who refused to be put into any one category, he totally remade the form at regular intervals, with a spare, melancholy trumpet style which, like Jimi's guitar – or the plays of Harold Pinter or Samuel Beckett – was all about pauses and spaces. And nothing that rowdy rock could do had ever diminished his aura as the quintessence of cool.

Offstage, too, he broke the usual mould of the low-key, introverted jazzer with his wild un-Afro'd hair, his vast, gaudy wardrobe and expensive cars, his open contempt for white people, self-confessed misogyny and domestic violence and sometime career as a pimp to support his heroin habit.

By 1969, Davis was starting to experiment with rock and funk even as Jimi's solos were edging ever closer to Charlie Parker-style bebop. Realising what a brilliant fusion might be here, McLaughlin took him to a screening of *Monterey Pop*. In Jimi's guitar-burning scene, he could be heard softly exclaiming 'Damn! . . . *Damn!*', for him the highest form of praise, tinged with regret at never having thought of doing anything similar to his trumpet.

Jimi was thrilled to meet Davis, whose playing he had loved since Davis's seminal 1959 album *Kind of Blue* had been part of his father's jealously guarded record collection. As John McLaughlin had hoped, the two started jamming together, though only at their respective apartments, barely audible even in the next room.

Davis, who had been trained at the Juilliard School of Music, was astonished by Jimi's total ignorance of musical theory and in some of their initial meetings attempted to instruct him on the subject. But he soon gave up, acknowledging that Jimi's songs like 'that goddamned, motherfucking "Machine Gun"' (another high Miles Davis compliment) were beyond any theorising.

The relationship was not easy, for the arrantly racist Davis deplored Jimi's wide acquaintanceship among white musicians whom – with a few exceptions like John McLaughlin – Davis considered an inferior species. One day, when the British singer Terry Reid answered the door of Jimi's apartment, Davis refused to cross the threshold, growling, 'I want fucking Jimi Hendrix to open Jimi Hendrix's fucking door.'

The two would occasionally double-date, Jimi with Carmen Borrero, Davis with his long-suffering woman friend of the moment. In contrast with Jimi, Harlem accorded Davis the royal treatment it still denied Jimi. When they visited Smalls Paradise, he was shown to a special table in a curtained-off recess so that he and his guests could smoke a joint unobserved.

The Jimi–Miles fusion worked better than John McLaughlin had ever dared hope and they began making plans to record together with drummer Tony Williams. For Jimi, the only possible bass player was someone whose skill on the instrument tended to be obscured by his singing and songwriting and the sheer magnitude of his fame as one-quarter of the world's most beloved pop band.

On 21 October 1969, Davis, Williams and Jimi together sent a telegram to Paul McCartney in London, inviting him to join them in a recording session, to be produced by Alan Douglas. Their timing could not have been worse: the appointment of the Beatles' new manager, Allen Klein, had caused a rift between McCartney and the other Beatles which had driven him into self-imposed exile on his Scottish farm and to something close to a nervous breakdown. The polite refusal from the Beatles' aide, Peter Brown, said he was 'on vacation'.

Nor did the session ever take place without him, for Davis and Tony Williams, seized with visions of rock 'n' roll wealth, each demanded $50,000 upfront, and Douglas cancelled it. The only record of the Davis/Hendrix collaboration – the most sublime jazz-rock fusion conceivable – were the tapes made in Jimi's apartment, which have remained unreleased to this day.

Jimi spent the evening of his 27th birthday on 27 October watching the Rolling Stones perform at Madison Square Garden on the American tour – which Brian Jones's death had finally made possible and which now had a special urgency since dumping Allen Klein as their manager had left the Stones owing huge amounts of UK income tax.

As a privileged backstage visitor at the Garden, Jimi appears briefly in *Gimme Shelter*, the film documenting a journey that would end two months later with the infamous free concert on Altamont Raceway and the fatal stabbing of a black audience member by Hell's Angels in full view of the band as they played.

Amid the dressing-room melee, he can be seen chatting amiably to Keith Richard as Mick Taylor, Brian's absurdly young and innocent-looking successor on lead guitar, stares at him with undisguised adoration

For the show itself, he was given a seat onstage behind Richard's amp, from which he might have expected to be called to 'sit in' with the Stones, especially as this was his birthday. But Jagger was too wary of his special kind of sitting in to risk it.

The after-show party was given by Devon Wilson in a luxurious duplex apartment she'd borrowed for the purpose. Ostensibly a birthday celebration for Jimi, it was really to proclaim the success of a campaign to sleep with Jagger that had gone on all the time she'd been sleeping with Jimi. At the party, both men went off to an empty room together – it was presumed, for some kind of 'fight' over Devon.

In fact, Jagger was showing the thoughtfulness of which he was sometimes capable. Seven months after Jimi's drugs bust at Toronto International Airport, his trial was finally to begin on 8 December. Mick made some amends for annexing Devon by offering advice on the coming courtroom ordeal, based on his and Keith's experience in 1967. Jagger, however, still had no inkling of having been targeted by the FBI's COINTELPRO unit, in league with British MI5, which had triggered the bust that landed them both in jail and so kept the Stones out of America for three years.

In Jimi's case, despite his having been under COMINTELRPO surveillance for more than a year, the bust had been made by the Royal Canadian Mounted Police. Still, the FBI liaised closely with the Canadian authorities over his trial and made contingency plans with them in the event of an unsatisfactory verdict.

Jimi's file contains a memo dated 6 November and, as usual, circulated to J. Edgar Hoover, saying that 'if he is found innocent of the charges, the Canadian immigration [sic] would like to deport him if it can be proved he has criminal convictions in the U.S.'

He prepared for his court appearance by having his hair cut and, on the advice of one of his defence attorneys, Bob Levine, buying a conservative dark suit which, Levine recalled, made the effortlessly stylish gypsy 'look like a hick, fidgeting around and trying to loosen his tie'.

During the limo journey to LaGuardia airport for their flight to Toronto, Levine became uneasy about some items Jimi was slipping into his guitar case to take through the same customs hall where all the trouble had started. But he insisted there was nothing 'inappropriate', adding, with touching faith in his new 'respectable' look, 'Trust me, Bob. They'll never recognise me.'

They did, of course: the guitar case was searched, a 'capsule of unknown origin' was discovered and Jimi spent the night in detention while it was analysed.

His defence witnesses were to include the United Press International journalist Sharon Lawrence, who had come from Los Angeles despite a warning from someone close to Mike Jeffery that Jeffery wanted the trial to be 'a lesson' to Jimi and could turn very nasty with anyone seeking to obstruct that. As an example of someone who might help Jeffery turn nasty, she was given a name which, when she made enquiries through journalistic channels, turned out to be that of 'a major street-crime boss'.

She found Jimi released from custody – the suspect capsule in his guitar case having proved to be a legal medication – and fretting in a luxury suite at the Royal York Hotel. Before she could speak, he warned there were 'two guys [whom he named as Jeffery associates] listening on the other side of that door' and insisted they talk in the bathroom where no one could overhear them.

Happier times: Jimi and Kathy Etchingham, with whom he lived in an eighteenth-century pile in London's Mayfair once occupied by George Frideric Handel. Kathy learned to turn a blind eye to his incessant 'flirtations'.

Left: He wore blue velvet: Jimi in untypical relaxed mood.

Above: with Devon Wilson, the supergroupie he diverted from Mick Jagger – and whose own mysterious death came only a year after his.

Left: Jimi at the 1969 Woodstock festival: his solo rendition of 'The Star-Spangled Banner' was heard live by only a few hundred muddy hippies – but became the defining moment of 1960s rock culture.

Above: Jimi at his still-uncompleted Electric Lady studio, New York, in June 1970. Behind him, left, is his trusted engineer, Eddie Kramer.

Monika Dannemann, the former German ice-skating champion
who shared Jimi's last moments: her account of his death
would later change some fourteen times.

Jimi's younger brother, Leon, to whom he was a
surrogate father when they were children – but who
inherited only a single Gold Disc from his estate.

When the going was still good . . .

He told Sharon he was terrified the heroin charge would result in prison where, he said, he'd be 'dead in a week'. At the same time, he couldn't resist telling her excitedly about meeting Bob Dylan that day in the Village and what Dylan had said.

His backup during the three-day trial was impressive – although Sharon would never discover how much, if anything, the absent Jeffery had contributed towards its costs. Heading Jimi's courtoom team was one of Canada's leading attorneys, Henry Steingarten, and to handle the inevitable media storm, the veteran publicist Les Perrin – who'd done the same for Jagger and Richard after their trial – was brought over from London. Chas Chandler had also voluntered to be a defence witness, another demonstration of shaming generosity.

The defence did not dispute that hashish and heroin had been found in Jimi's bag but to make the 'possession' charge stick, the prosecution had to prove he'd *known* it was there. His explanation was that, a few days earlier in Beverly Hills, a female fan had put something into the bag that he'd taken to be the stomach remedy Bromo-Seltzer. Not until the results came back from the mobile lab at Toronto airport had he learned the truth. Sharon Lawrence and Chas Chandler both confirmed that fans were always slipping him gifts like teddy bears, scarves and jewellery that he barely looked at.

Under cross-examination, Jimi did not deny doing drugs but portrayed himself as a relative innocent who'd used cocaine only twice and acid only five times (to which the addition of 'per day' would have been closer to the truth).

He was shown the aluminium tube that had contained the hashish and asked if he knew what it was. 'A pea-shooter,' he suggested. On the heroin charge his counsel pointed out that he'd been carrying none of the paraphernalia needed for shooting up and his arms showed no trace of needle-tracks.

Having deliberated for eight hours, the all-male (and all-white) jury found him not guilty on both charges and he was acquitted amid loud cheers from the fans that had filled the courtroom. 'Canada,' he told waiting reporters, 'has given me the best Christmas present I ever had.'

Since the collapse of Gypsy Sun and Rainbows, he had been rehearsing and making demos with Billy Cox and Buddy Miles, a more comfortable fit in every way, not least because Miles was a singer as well as a drummer and could take some of the vocals with which Jimi still felt so very far from comfortable. But he planned no formal unveiling of the trio until one was imposed on him as a legal expedient.

After three years, his lawyers were still trying to reach a settlement with Ed Chalpin, the owner of the cut-price PPX label in New York who'd got him under contract just before his discovery by Chas Chandler and Swinging London. Though signed by Chalpin as Jimmy James, the contract seemed to have a watertight claim on a major share of Jimi Hendrix, but Chalpin had thus far rejected all offers while intermittently releasing substandard tracks that Jimi had made as Jimmy for PPX.

The latest attempt to be rid of this long-standing nuisance had been to offer Chalpin the entire proceeds of a live album by the still-unnamed trio, whether Jimi considered them ready or not. To add to the coercive feeling, the album was not to be for Warner/Reprise but for Capitol, Chalpin's outlet for his inferior PPX tracks.

An ideal venue for the concert to be live-recorded was within walking distance from Jimi's new Greenwich Village apartment. On Second Avenue at East 6th Street, in the shell of an old Yiddish theatre, was Fillmore East, opened the previous year as an outpost of Bill Graham's famous San Francisco Fillmore. There was no one in the promoting game Jimi respected and trusted more than Graham and he had no greater admirer.

It was arranged that, supported by a gospel ensemble, the Voices of East Harlem, he would do two shows on New Year's Eve 1969 – when the album would be taped – and another two on 1 January, which left just seven days for Miles, Cox and himself to rehearse. In a nod to Gypsy Sun and Rainbows, the album was to be entitled *A Band of Gypsys* and the trio took the same name.

Most of those who bought tickets didn't realise the Jimi Hendrix Experience had broken up and were confused to learn from the posters that they'd be seeing 'Jimi Hendrix: A Band of Gypsies'. At the opening show, names ceased to matter when Jimi delivered what *Rolling Stone* would describe as 'a rainbow barrage of fire-alarm feedback, knife-edge riffing, raw, soulful melodicism [sic] and sunlight harmonies that arced over Cox and Miles' roadhouse stomp with an almost classical grace'.

The greatest demand for tickets had naturally been for the second show on 31 December. The band took the stage just before midnight, Jimi in a beige leather suit with red stitching made for him by Colette Mimram. He counted down the seconds to the end of the Sixties – and the start of the last year of his life – then played an instrumental version of 'Auld Lang Syne' as a funky blues that would have got even Robert Burns grooving. That show lasted until 5.30 a.m.

He had never been more outspoken against the Vietnam War and in support of Black Power. A twelve-and-a-half-minute version of 'Machine Gun' was dedicated to 'the draggy scene that's going on [i.e., racial unrest], all the soldiers [i.e., black militant groups] who are fighting in Chicago and Milwaukee and New York. Oh yes, and the soldiers who are fighting in Vietnam.' 'Voodoo Child' he introduced as 'the Black Panthers' National Anthem'.

The Fillmore East shows revealed yet again how much more than a mere venue-provider and ticket-seller Bill Graham was.

Graham saw that a new Jimi Hendrix was developing – one who no longer had any need of onstage gimmickry yet still clung to them like a security blanket – and he made no bones about saying so: 'You humped your guitar. You played it with your teeth, you stuck it behind your back. You just forget to *play*.'

Jimi leapt back out there to do a storming set devoid of gimmicks, then returned and thrust a sweat-shiny face close to Graham's. 'All right, motherfucker?' he said. 'That good enough for you? You gonna let me go now? . . .'

Afer the final show, he gave an interview to the *New York Post*'s Al Aronowitz, summing up his hopes for 1970 in words that give one a chill to write: 'Earth, man, earth . . . I want to bring it down to earth. I want to get back to the blues, man, because that's what I am.'

SIXTEEN
'DAD, MY LOVE . . .'

On 28 January, Band of Gypsies played Madison Square Garden, headlining over Harry Belafonte, Blood, Sweat & Tears, Dave Brubeck, Richie Havens and the cast of the musical *Hair* in what was billed as a Winter Festival for Peace. The five-hour event served as a postscript to the previous year's Moratorium to End the War in Vietnam, in which half a million protesters had marched on President Richard Nixon's White House.

Jimi's FBI file showed his name topping a list of musicians 'scheduled' to join the march that also includes Peter, Paul and Mary, Arlo Guthrie and the *Hair* musical troupe. But he hadn't joined it nor, apparently, ever considered doing so.

Among those backstage at the Winter Festival for Peace was Johnny Winter, of all rock guitarists the most wintry-looking with his shoulder-length white hair. Although no stranger to rock 'n' roll excess, Winter was shocked by Jimi's ravaged appearance and by the crowd surrounding him. 'It was one of the most horrible things I'd ever seen. He came in with this entourage of people and it was like he was already dead.'

In a knot of genuine well-wishers, however, Jimi found Noel Redding, whom he hadn't seen since Redding's departure from the Jimi Hendrix Experience six months earlier. Their encounter was friendly and Redding was shown to a privileged seat on the stage beside Mitch Mitchell, both of them expecting an invitation to play sometime during the night.

As with most festivals, the running order fell far behind schedule and Band of Gypsys didn't go onstage until 3 a.m. Barely able to articulate, Jimi slurred vague obscenities about women's underwear and menstruation then, midway through his second song, 'Earth Blues', he mumbled, 'That's what happens when Earth fucks with space', stopped playing and sat down heavily in front of his amplifier stack. He had to be escorted offstage, at one point stumbling and falling off the apron.

Though he'd often performed high on LSD, it had never incapacitated him to this extent and evidence pointed to its having been fed to him without his knowledge. He himself suspected Devon Wilson of giving him a spiked pre-show drink in one of the control games she was always playing. But Buddy Miles later claimed to have seen Mike Jeffery slip him two tabs of 'Owsley Purple' on his way to the stage. Noel Redding's autobiography, *Are You Experienced*, would recall seeing the same, but with only one tab, from his vantage point in the wings.

In Miles's view, Jeffery had an obvious motive: sabotage of the new band, in which he saw little financial gain, despite its importance to Jimi at a moment when otherwise his life was beginning to fall apart. 'If there was anything that could have saved him, it was the Band of Gypsys,' Miles would reflect in the 1980s. 'Because it was putting him in a direction to bring him back to his roots and that's all the man wanted to do. But those people didn't want that. They wanted him to be a clown.'

During years of close collaboration, Miles said, he'd often seen Jimi suffer moments of despair; once even talked him out of jumping to his death from a high rooftop. 'And when you've got [Jimi's] kind of dedication and love for what you do, wouldn't you find it rather rude and rather ugly to see him throw his guitar out of a window and try to kill himself? I saw that, and I didn't like it. I didn't like pulling a man off a twenty-storey building and trying to save him because he was that sick. And that unloved.'

Whether or not Jeffery truly had engineered the Madison Square Garden debacle, it gave him ample excuse to terminate Band of Gypsys; Buddy Miles was fired and Billy Cox went home to Nashville of his own accord, believing his spell in the big time to be at an end.

For months, Jeffery had been pressuring Jimi to be sensible, forget about experimentation and agree to re-form the Jimi Hendrix Experience, for which a huge, hungry American public still remained.Now, such an instrumental security blanket suddenly seemed tempting, and was easily delivered: Mitch Mitchell had always stayed available while taking time out to back ex-Cream bassist Jack Bruce, and Noel Redding had never found much cash in his Fat Mattress.

Both signed contracts for an American tour to begin at the end of April; Redding then returned to Britain for the short time before rehearsals began, leaving Mitchell staying in the Village with Jimi and Devon Wilson.

During his absence, however, Jimi and Mitchell agreed that, this time around, the Jimi Hendrix Experience needed a bass-player of higher calibre. When Redding returned to New York, expecting to start rehearsals, he made repeated attempts to contact Jimi but was always blocked by Devon. Despite the long road they had shared, Jimi was incapable of telling him face-to-face that he'd been dropped. Instead, he discovered from a lawyer that the new Experience were already rehearsing with Billy Cox called back from Nashville to play bass.

Aside from Redding's huge hurt, the blow was a crippling financial one as he'd been relying on his tour earnings to solve his income tax problems and meet the demands of a pregnant wife who'd recently left him, alleging domestic violence and that he wasn't the baby's father.

On 25 March, Capitol released Band of Gypsys' eponymous

live album, the proceeds of which were to go to Ed Chalpin. For that reason, it had been kept to only six tracks, two of them written and sung by Buddy Miles. But 'Who Knows ', 'Message of Love' (later 'Message to Love') and, especially, the twelve-and-a-half-minute 'Machine Gun' were enough to reveal Jimi's radical change of style. After gatecrashing the previously all-white genre of hard rock, he was now pioneering the brand-new black one of funk.

Despite its poor sound quality, the album reached number 5 in the US. In the UK (where Track Records provided a strange cover showing doll-like figures of Jimi, Brian Jones, Bob Dylan and the disc jockey John Peel) it made number 8. Warner/Reprise tried to get a piece of the action by releasing studio versions of 'Stepping Stone' and 'Izabella' as a US single credited to Hendrix Band of Gypsys, but neither track managed to chart.

The reviews were cautiously approving. *Melody Maker*'s Chris Welch, one of Jimi's earliest British advocates, thought the music a little tame 'by today's freak-rate' but that his 'sense of drama and timing' was still unbeatable. In *Rolling Stone*, Loraine Alterman speculated that his 'supposed involvement with militant blacks' explained both the trio's unmixed racial make-up and his new gimmick-free performing style.

'It's as if Hendrix doesn't care about putting on a show for whitey,' she wrote. 'Rather, it is as if he is really into playing the guitar instead of shucking and jiving with fancy tricks . . . In the end, he is a musician, not a contortionist or juggler.' Nowhere in the media was there any inkling that Band of Gypsys were already history.

In London, meanwhile, Kathy Etchingham had long since given up hope of Jimi ever returning to pick up their old life again. Staying on at the Brook Street flat, she'd had no difficulty in finding someone else; not another musician from her wide acquaintanceship but an interior designer named Ray whom she took over from her friend Angie Burdon. Early in 1970, having seen more than her share of Swinging London – which no longer swung anything like it used to – she decided to marry Ray, put the clubs and discos behind her and buy a house in the suburbs.

Reports of her wedding somehow reached Jimi in New York and, shortly after his Madison Square Garden disaster, he phoned her to ask if they were true. When she admitted that they were, he announced he was coming to London the following weekend and asked her to book a limo to meet him at the airport.

She too was waiting when he arrived on an early morning flight, without an entourage and looking 'a complete wreck'. 'I was amazed to see him alone, because I'd never known him travel without some sort of company.'

On the limo-ride into town, he held her hand, 'clearly devastated' by the thought of her marriage and seeking ressurance that it was 'just a spur of the moment thing' and 'not serious'. 'He hadn't realised that we'd drifted apart. He still saw us as a couple and . . . couldn't believe I'd moved on.'

When he saw the wood-panelled flat at 23 Brook Street again, it had the marks of another man's occupancy and was already being cleared prior to Kathy's move to leafy Chiswick. Many of his possessions and decorative touches remained in evidence and she urged him to take whatever he liked. At this, she recalled, his eyes filled with tears. '"I don't want anything from the flat," he said. "I want *you*."'

She'd booked him into the Londonderry Hotel in Knightsbridge and he spent the next couple of days trying to persuade her to return to New York with him, assuring her he had rid himself of all the hangers-on and everything would be different from now on. Remembering the bags of cocaine and the handgun at the Hotel Pierre made that an easy one to fend off.

Fortunately, Stephen Stills and Graham Nash of Crosby, Stills and Nash also happened to be in town to record. A jam with them at Island Studios lightened Jimi's mood sufficiently for him to accept the situation with Kathy and the two were able to spend time together as friends. They went out shopping, as of old, and he bought her a pair of snakeskin boots.

He did take a few things away from the flat and Kathy took a few more to her new terrace house in Chiswick. But there was no room for the whole cupboard full of his paintings and poems, so she had to put them out for the dustmen.

The new Jimi Hendrix Experience's Cry of Love tour – one of the first to be named like a song or an album – opened at the Los Angeles Forum on 25 April 1970. It was to last far longer than these thirty-four American shows and have the worst of endings for Jimi, yet, ironically, he began it in the company of people who genuinely loved and wanted to protect him.

Firstly and most importantly, the Experience now included Billy Cox, watching his back as devotedly as in their days with the 101st Airborne. Despite Buddy Miles's unceremonious firing from Band of Gypsys, Miles and Jimi stayed friends and the re-convened Buddy Miles Express had been hired as a support act. Another support band, Ballin' Jack, contained two Seattle musicians, vocalist Luther Rabb and drummer Ronnie Hammon both of whom Jimi knew well, especially Rabb who'd been in his very first band, the Velvetones. Also along for several dates was Colette Mimram, the Moroccan couturier who'd shown Jimi her country a year earlier and by now had become something more than a friend. Colette had made him new clothes for the tour and they shopped for many more on the road.

Jimi had meant the tour to unveil his new funk-flavoured repertoire. However, audiences kept shouting for 'Purple Haze' and 'Voodoo Child' and he soon found himself doing the Same Old Shit with the same old help from the back of his neck and his teeth. To relieve his frustration, he would play the blues in private with Ballin' Jack, calling their sessions 'the Seattle Special'.

He could still rise to glorious new heights, almost always by way of cover versions. His set now featured Chuck Berry's 'Johnny B. Goode', in which even Berry's complex 'two guitar' lead was turned inside out. And jamming continued to produce his best moments, as in the impromptu seven-minute version of Carl Perkins's 'Blue Suede Shoes' just before a show to a completely empty theatre.

On 2 May, in Madison, Wisconsin, he came onstage drunk, but there was to be no repetition of his LSD collapse at Madison Square Garden. Still deeply ashamed of that night, he was making a conscious effort to cut down on drugs, although Devon Wilson still pushed them at him relentlessly. He had caught the flu – a particularly miserable malady if one is travelling – and also was showing his first signs of religion since going with his brother, Leon, to hear Little Richard preach. He'd taken to mentioning Jesus from the stage and a Bible became a fixture of his hotel or dressing rooms, always open at a particular page.

On 30 May, he reached Berkeley, California, where as a toddler he'd lived with a kind foster mother named Mrs Champ until torn away by a terrifying G.I. father he didn't know. Now its university's campus was in open revolt against the Vietnam War despite state Governor Ronald Reagan's zero-tolerance message to the National Guard: 'If it takes a bloodbath, let's get it over with.' In his show at the Community Center Theater, Jimi dedicated 'Machine Gun' to 'all the soldiers [i.e. students] fighting in Berkeley' and 'Voodoo Child' to the Black Panthers, who had been founded in nearby Oakland.

These days, he seemed to be regarded as the ally and sponsor of every radical group around: before he headlined the New York Pop Festival on 17 July, the Yippies, the Young Lords, the Black Panthers and their Caucasian offshoot the White Panthers all demanded his entire fee should be turned over to them.

His last-ever performance in the city where he'd all but starved and almost given up trying was marred by equipment malfunctions and some hostile elements in the audience; his farewell to the Big Apple was 'Fuck you and goodnight.'

When he returned to Seattle to play Sick's Stadium on 26 July, the welcoming family group lhad one conspicuous absentee. His brother Leon, no linger in the military, was doing time in Washington state's Monroe Penitentiary.

As a soldier, Leon had been infinitely more trouble-prone than Jimi, continually sent to the stockade for dealing weed or being 'a disruptive influence' (his superiors' hostility redoubling after what was seen as his brother's 'desecration' of the National Anthem at Woodstock). Like Jimi, he was spared Vietnam: his unit received orders to go, but at the last minute was stood down.

Denied leave to attend Jimi's 1969 Seattle show, Leon had gone AWOL, then failed to return to duty and spent several months dodging the Military Police and dealing drugs around the city. In the end, it was the regular police who finally caught him and handed him to the army, which instantly discharged him, then handed him back to the civilian authorities to face trial.

During all that time, Leon recalls, Jimi was supportive, albeit necessarily from a distance. 'He wanted to do a show at Monroe like Johnny Cash's at Folsom Prison, but Mike Jeffery wouldn't allow it.' Instead, Jimi tried to steer Leon and his fellow inmates to more elevated pursuits than smoking smuggled-in weed and brewing bootleg alcohol by sending $1,000 for them to start a film club.

Whatever the 'bodacious' Leon might get up to, Al Hendrix was never able to get too angry. Yet even as an international star, Jimi still found it difficult to impress their father – and the harder he tried, the less impressed Al seemed to be. 'When Jimi bought our dad a new house, he complained because his pick-up wouldn't fit into the garage,' Leon recalls. 'So Jimi got him another house.'

Jimi had long since given up trying to convey to Al everything that had happened to him across the Atlantic and how many of pop's household names were his fans. Leon recalls one of his trips home when the three of them were sitting around with his stepmother, June, and the best Al could come up with was 'So what's the weather like in London?'

'Jimi said, "It's rainy . . . same as here. That's why I like it."'

For the Sick's Stadium show, Jimi made his strongest gesture of support for the Black Panthers to date by asking them to provide security. The Panthers' Seattle chapter had grown particularly strong and was one of three receiving particular attention from the FBI at the personal order of President Nixon. The previous year, the head of the Chicago Panthers, Fred Hampton, had been assassinated and there'd been an eight-hour shoot-out around the Los Angeles chapter's premises. A similar offensive against Seattle's Panthers had been planned until the city's young Democrat mayor, Wes Uhlman, refused to give it it police backup.

The Panthers' small and low-key detail at Sick's was headed by Aaron Dixon, a former schoolfellow of Leon Hendrix who had marched with Dr Martin Luther King as a boy of eleven. Though his activities were mostly about providing free free medical and legal clinics, Dixon was on the President's personal list of one hundred sworn enemies and so, like Jimi, under constant surveillance. He says 'there's no doubt about it, no doubt at all' that the stadium that night swarmed with undercover FBI agents.

True to its reputation, Seattle helped forestall any trouble by flinging the rain down. By early evening, the worst had stopped but the puddly stage remained a perilous environment for giant Marshall stacks. Jimi still insisted on playing and, to begin with, did his best to invigorate the sea of umbrellas, raincoats and ponchos. 'You don't sound very happy, you don't look very happy,' he told them, 'but we'll see if we can paint some faces around here.'

Unfortunately, he'd been drinking whisky beforehand (as he tended to do with his father to show himself a 'real' man) and it had its usual bad effect. He became angry when someone threw a pillow onto the stage to be autographed – thinking it an insinuation that he'd once slept with the thrower – and his mood never recovered. At one point he gave the finger to an audience that included his own family and at another, left the stage altogether. He returned to finish the show, but refused to do an encore.

The night had been intended to prove himself once and for all to that hardest-to-please animal, a home-town audience, and make his father 'doubly proud' of him. And in his own eyes he had failed miserably on both counts; for Al still showed no comprehension of his music and back at the second expensive home he'd bought for him, they had a quarrel, aggravated as always by shots of Seagram's Seven.

To those who spent time with Jimi on that visit, it would later seem full of almost conscious goodbyes. For instance, he suddenly took it into his head to phone the former Betty-Jean Morgan, his first serious girlfriend, despite not having seen or contacted her since he left the army. Betty-Jean had married and divorced and was living in Seattle with her parents. She bore him no ill-will for her abrupt dumping in 1961 and they had a friendly talk about how he had named his first serious guitar after her and used to borrow her blouses to go onstage with the Rocking Kings.

Then a shy young woman who approached him for an autograph turned out to be his sister, Pamela, one of the four children in a row with physical problems born to his mother, Lucille, and subsequently taken into care.

Jimi had not seen Pamela for something like seventeen years

and he gave her the warmest of hugs, glad of that connection, at least, to his other three unlucky siblings, Joe, Kathy and Al junior.

After the post-show family party, despite the lateness of the hour, he insisted on a tour of all the places in Seattle that meant something to him, albeit seldom for happy reasons: James A. Garfield High School; Betty-Jean's house; streets where he'd lived with Al and Leon, virtually on the run from the city welfare authorities; even the detention centre where he'd been held after his arrest for 'joyriding'.

The most emotional stop was Harborview Hospital, where he had been born and where he'd last seen his dying mother in a wheelchair, in Leon's words, 'all glowing white like she was floating'. After missing Lucille's funeral, due to Al's drunkenness, he had never visited her grave, and decided he must do so now, despite recalling only that it was located in the semi-rural Renton Highlands. He searched for it until the early hours of the morning, but in vain.

When his father saw him off at Seattle airport – the last time they would ever be together – there was, as usual, no physical demonstrativeness, only a brusque paternal injunction to 'Keep your nose clean'. But, halfway down the ramp for his flight to Hawaii, Jimi suddenly halted, came back and stared into Al's face. He did the same thing twice more before being told he really must board now.

The new Jimi Hendrix Experience's only scheduled appearance in the Hawaiian islands was at Honolulu International Arena on 1 August. But Mike Jeffery had other ideas.

As a newly converted acid-head, Jeffery had been drawn to the island of Maui, which had a flourishing community of hippies and surfers from mainland America but little commercial exploitation as yet. Jeffery now planned to build a recording facility there, housed in geodesic domes designed by the architect/mystic Buckminster Fuller, which would turn the place into a kind of Woodstock with *leis* and grass skirts.

This in turn created a desire to get into movie production, as his fellow pop manager Robert Stigwood was doing with notable success. The previous year's box-office smash had been Dennis Hopper's *Easy Rider*, a blend of hippy sensibility and hard rock that had cost only pennies to make, and Hollywood was avid for more such tales from the counterculture. On the strength of Jimi's name, Jeffery raised a $450,000 advance from Warner/Reprise and hired a director named Chuck Wein, who had previously worked with Andy Warhol, to conjure a similar moneyspinner from Maui.

Jimi initially had no involvement in the film – to be entitled *Rainbow Bridge* – but he became friendly with Chuck Wein, a hippyish figure, thoroughly versed in all the cerebral subjects he was never able to explore with fellow musicians. Wein lent him crucial hippy texts like the Tibetan *Book of the Dead*, and they spent many hours discusing dreams, the occult, interplanetary travel and UFOs, of which Jimi claimed to have seen several, including one at Woodstock.

This immersion in hardcore counterculture made him realise for the first time how much he himself had unwittingly contributed to it. Through Wein, he met a woman known only as Terrain who carried around a book of his songs, said to decode the 'molecular structure' of each one. Terrain designed 'costumes' for horses and she and Jimi together bought a thoroughbred they named Axis Bold As Love – ordaining it was never to be ridden – which had 'a purple haze like a third eye' and was said to respond to colours rather than sounds.

The shooting of *Rainbow Bridge* was conducted according to hippy rules – or, rather, lack of them – and quickly became bogged down with little as yet to show for Warner/Reprise's money. To reinvigorate it, Jeffery pressured Jimi into filming an open-air performance with the Experience on Maui two days before their Honolulu show.

Billed as 'the Rainbow Bridge Vibratory Color/Sound Experience', this took place before an invited audience of 500 near the crater of the island's Olowahu volcano, 2,000 feet above sea level. The event, planned by Terrain, seated people according to their astrological signs and began with a lengthy chanting of 'Om' by a troupe of Hare Krishnas.

Wearing a turquoise and black-striped Hopi Native American 'medicine shirt', Jimi played a ten-song set for a crowd generally too spaced out to applaud or show any reaction. He then withdrew into a sacred Hopi teepee, where he spent forty-five minutes drinking beer, smoking pot and jamming, then emerged for a second set. This seemed to go over better, aided by the surprise appearance onstage of a dog dosed with LSD which bit him in the leg.

He also had a speaking part in *Rainbow Bridge* as one of the exemplars in various creative endeavours – music, art, surfing and yoga – whom its main character, played by fashion model Pat Hartley, encountered on her *Easy Rider*-esque 'journey'. For this, Jimi insisted on being filmed without his guitar, although whenever it was removed he would look anxiously around for it.

He grew friendly, too, with the set-decorator Melinda Merryweather and her boyfriend, the champion surfer Mike Hynson, who was also in the film. Devon Wilson had not come to Maui with him, meaning there was no heroin, and he resisted all suggestions to send for her. One night, Melinda got him to open up about that infinitely strange co-dependence in which, to her, Devon was 'the black widow' and Jimi 'the nectar'.

He so appreciated Melinda's sympathetic ear that, in his rented apartment, he composed a twenty-three-minute suite entitled 'Scorpio Woman', then put it on his tape recorder and gave it to her. 'I loved him,' she recalls now. 'You couldn't *not* love him.'

The filming mainly took place in a girls' private boarding school named Seabury Hall whose pupils were on their summer holidays. Jimi's conversations with Hartley and Chuck Wein, which far exceeded the film's requirements, contrasted strangely with an odour of school that the reek of grass could never quite obliterate.

In a series of gradually more relaxed and expansive monologues, he claimed to come from 'an asteroid off the coast of Mars' and described some of the vivid dreams he'd always had, but now called 'astral travelling'. In one, he'd found himself on a battlefield in Vietnam, tending to a wounded Vietcong soldier; in another, he'd had a sexual encounter with Queen Cleopatra of Egypt, who tried to turn him on to fetishes, and then he'd 'drowned in the wine'. Everyone present would later recall that last detail with a shiver.

There were other moments when he not only seemed aware of his approaching fate but calmly reconciled to it. In true hippy style, each day's filming concentrated on the cast member who was felt to radiate most energy. One morning, the art director, Steve Roby, told Jimi it was his turn and asked him what he wanted to shoot. 'I'm going to die and leave here,' was his reply. Another time, Roby offered help with the décor at Electric Lady Studios, although other work commitments meant it couldn't be until after September. 'Jimi said, "I won't be here,"' he would recall. 'Not "I won't be there" but "I won't be here."'

A casual inquiry from Wein about when he planned to return to Seattle brought the most chilling shaft of second sight. 'The next time I go to Seattle,' Jimi answered, 'it'll be in a pine box.'

He became so fond of Maui that after the Honolulu concert, when the road company dispersed back to America, he returned to the island to watch *Rainbow Bridge* wrap, even taking a room at Seabury Hall, which he called 'the Cosmic Sandbox'.

To Mike Jeffery's increasingly impatient summonses, he replied that he'd injured a foot in 'a surfing accident' and was unable to travel. In fact, the foot had been only slightly cut on some coral, but the film people made it look far worse by bandaging it dramatically and, to add verisimilitude, Jimi hopped around, supporting himself with a piece of driftwood like a psychedelic Long John Silver.

During these unprogrammed golden days on Maui before the inexorable machinery of the end his life ground into gear, he wrote to his father, apologising for the quarrel they'd had. Beginning 'Dad, my love . . .', he admitted he'd had to drink a lot before finding the courage to put pen to paper and begged Al, who normally barely had the patience to scan a newspaper sports page, to read every word of 'this instant but ageless wonderment of a letter'.

Rambling and full of hippy mumbo-jumbo, absorbed from his movie friends, it is nonetheless a veritable 'cry of love', full of reverence for Al and contrition for his own incurable unworthiness. 'I'm riff-raff, you know . . . You are what I happily accept as an angel, a gift from God . . .'

Most poignant is his plea, even at this late hour, for them to talk about the subject that has haunted him since the age of fifteen but always remained a guiltily closed book to Al.

Some day, he ventures, maybe he'll be allowed to ask 'questions of great importance and experience . . . of unanswered history and lifestyle of my mother that bore me – Mrs Lucille'.

SEVENTEEN
'HEY MAN, LEND ME YOUR COMB'

Hawaii was supposed to have been where the Cry of Love tour ended, giving Jimi a breathing space to get back into Electric Lady Studios, as he longed to do. But 7,000 miles away on a different island – this a diamond-shaped one off England's south coast – Ronnie and Ray Foulk had other ideas.

The Derbyshire-born brothers had moved with their widowed mother to the Isle of Wight during the 1950s when it was a sleepy place, living on its past as Queen Victoria's favourite holiday retreat. In those days, the only rock it offered were the British seaside's traditional sticks of hard pink sugar with A PRESENT FROM THE IOW in lick-proof letters all the way through. Come the 1960s, the Foulks were to create even longer-lasting souvenirs of their adopted home.

The pair staged their first Isle of Wight Pop Festival in 1968 without any previous experience (24-year-old Ronnie had been an estate agent, 23-year-old Ray an apprentice printer). Compared with what was to come, it was a modest affair featuring Jefferson Airplane, the Move and Fairport Convention, and passed off so peacefully that most of the island didn't even notice it. 'Our young brother, Bill [then a film student], told us we should book Jimi Hendrix, too,' Ronnie Foulk recalls. 'We tried, but he wasn't available.'

For their second festival the following summer, the Foulks pulled off the astounding coup of bringing Bob Dylan to the Isle of Wight – just when Jimi was longing to bump into him around Woodstock – with the lure that his favourite poet, Alfred Lord Tennyson had once lived near the island's Freshwater Bay.

The problem for their third (and, it would prove, final) festival in August 1970 was finding a headliner capable of delivering the same 150,000 people that Dylan had across the six miles of water from the Hampshire mainland. With the Beatles at the point of break-up and the Rolling Stones about to become tax exiles in France, Jimi was the obvious first choice, even though his British popularity had somewhat waned during his long absences in the US.

'The original idea was for the whole festival to be built around Jimi, the way the '69 festival was built around Bob Dylan,' says Ronnie Foulk. 'It would have brought him back to prominence in the same way that it did Dylan.'

This time, Jimi was said to be available and negotiations opened between Ronnie and Dick Katz of the Harold Davison booking agency with unofficial help from Chas Chandler (now riding high with his new discovery, Slade). Since the fee on offer of £10,000 was thought insufficient on its own to bring Jimi across the Atlantic and no other UK dates were in prospect, a series of further concerts were booked for him in Sweden, Denmark, West Germany, Holland, Austria and France. 'I'm still haunted by the thought that if we'd stuck to my original plan, Jimi might still be with us,' Ronnie Foulk says. In the days ahead, other people were to say 'if' with the same infinite regret.

Believing the deal as good as done, Foulk was suddenly called to London to meet Mike Jeffery. 'I was pretty apprehensive because Jeffery had a terrible reputation. But all he was concerned with was that Jimi would be getting paid more than any of the other artistes. Nothing else about the festival seemed to interest him.'

The plan was, as usual, presented to Jimi as a *fait accompli* and, as usual, he made no objection despite his exhaustion and generally poor physical state and his longing to get back to work at his Electric Studios

The two years-long construction of this first-ever customised recording facility had not been easy. Among the many problems for its architect, John Storyk, was that the basement premises on 8th Street lay directly above a subterranean river, the Minetta Creek, whose unstable water-table required a pump to operate twenty-four hours a day and be made completely soundproof so as not to disturb work in the studios.

When the spiralling costs had used up Jimi's and Mike Jeffery's joint investment, a further $30,000 had had to be borrowed from Warner/Reprise. It's since been alleged that a further, unspecified contribution came from Jeffery's Mafia contacts, which is impossible to substantiate but hardly implausible given the Mob's recent forays into rock culture with Manhattan clubs like Salvation 2.

Much of Electric Lady's expense stemmed from Jimi's wish for it to surpass his former recording home, the Record Plant, in musician-friendliness. With the love of interior decorating that so rarely found an outlet, he personally approved its soft pastel walls and furnishings and thick-pile carpet, ordained that the recording console be a haze-like purple and curated the various artworks that hung on the walls, among them a blow-up of the *Axis: Bold as Love* album cover and a Lance Jost mural that made the lobby feel like the bridge of a spaceship looking out. He was equally interested in the technical side, spending hours on the phone with Les Paul, the head of his profession and doyen of guitar multitracking, about the positioning of microphones.

He had taken Mitch Mitchell and Billy Cox into Electric Lady far ahead of the official opening, working in the completed Studio A while Studio B was still being finished. Though their immediate objective was a fourth Jimi Hendrix Experience studio album, provisionally titled *First Rays of the New Rising Sun*, they had already laid down enough tracks for about four albums, including 'Freedom', 'Drifting', 'Night Bird Flying', 'Straight Ahead' and 'Astro Man'.

Now there was no one standing over him with a stopwatch or insisting something was finished when he thought differently. So he could do nineteen takes of 'Dolly Dagger', a sour memory of the time when Devon Wilson had briefly deserted him for Mick Jagger and gone to new lengths in serving rock royalty. One day, Jagger had cut his hand and, rather than fetch a Band-Aid, Devon had licked away the blood. So Dolly Dagger was a witch-queen who 'suck[ed] the blood from the jagged edge . . . with a tongue that could scratch the soul out of the Devil's wife'.

Now Mick had moved on again, as he always did within minutes, and Devon was back in charge around Jimi, a role that had always involved a certain tolerance of his other amours. So it proved yet again when he announced that when he passed through London en route to the Isle of Wight Festival, he wanted to meet Linda Keith.

Since Linda's discovery of him in 1966, he had continued seeing her, their initial platonic friendship turning to covert bursts of passion that never went any further. But something had stuck with Jimi: in January 1970, not long after their most recent 'little romantic interlude', he'd written a song called 'Send My Love to Linda' whose lyric combined yearning and terrible prophecy: 'She made the sun shine in my eye/God, let me hold her once more before I die.'

In August 1970, Linda had just got engaged to the lawyer Lawrence Kershen and was with him when a phone call came from New York. 'It was Devon,' she recalls, 'saying that Jimi wanted to speak to me.' They made an arrangement to meet at London's newest 'in' club, Tramp, just before he played the Isle of Wight Festival.

To his real friends, like the Aleem twins and Sultan Juma, it seemed strange for Jimi to be disappearing overseas again when he was so immersed in recording at Electric Lady, spending four or five days a week there, recording his own material and nurturing other performers. 'He was made to feel he was always in debt,' Juma recalls. 'So he always had to keep moving.'

The Aleems were particularly dismayed because Jimi had proposed they should form a publishing company together. 'He said he was going to this place called the Isle of Wight,' Tahar-Qa Aleem recalls. 'But he said. "After I come back, I'll meet you on another island – in the South Pacific." 'We said, "What's it called?" '"Pago Pago", Jimi said, and gave us this big beautiful smile.'

Electric Lady's launch party on 26 August was attended by a celebrity crowd including Yoko Ono, Mick Fleetwood and Johnny Rivers. Among the lesser VIPs was the future punk star Patti Smith, not yet the fearless iconoclast she would become. Too shy to join the assembled VIPs, she was surprised to find Jimi sitting alone on the stairs. He told her he always felt that way at parties, too.

Next day, after working all night on a track called 'Slow Blues', he departed for London, never to see his beloved Electric Lady again.

He had asked his Moroccan couturier and friend Colette Mimram to go with him, but she hadn't renewed her resident's permit, the precious Green Card, and feared she might not be allowed back into the country.

Ever since, Colette has lived with another of those remorseful 'ifs': 'I often think that if I'd gone with him, what happened might not have happened.'

The Isle of Wight Festival would be Jimi's first live appearance in Britain for eighteen months and the London music press flocked to the Londonderry Hotel, where he was occupying the luxurious Park Suite.

None of his interviewers noticed anything amiss with him; on the contrary, he seemed in good spirits, full of creative confidence and, as *Melody Maker*'s Roy Hollingworth put it, 'six months pregnant with ideas'.

'I want a big band,' he told Hollingworth. 'I don't mean three harps and fourteen violins. I mean a big band full of competent musicians I can conduct and write for. And with the music we will paint pictures of Earth and Space so that the listener can be taken somewhere.

'I dig Strauss and Wagner – those cats are good and I think they are going to form the background of my new music. Floating in the sky above it will be blues – I've still got plenty of blues – and there will be western sky music and some opium music – you'll have to bring your own opium.'

The last in line to see him, because least important, was Stephen Clackson, a young freelance who'd been commissioned to write a brief gossip piece for the German magazine *M*. All the music press bigwigs had conducted their interviews under the watchful eye of a minder from publicist Les Perrin's office but when Clackson's turn finally came, the minder slipped away to meet a girlfriend and he had Jimi to himself.

Clackson tape-recorded about twenty minutes of the 'mundane fanzine stuff' his German editors required. When he was finished, Jimi seemed in no hurry to get rid of him and, after the recorder was switched off and a photographer had taken their picture together and departed, they fell into a conversation lasting several hours.

On the tape, Jimi had expressed a wish 'to have someone to pour myself out to' and that is what he did now, telling Clackson 'how he didn't recognise the person who was being written about, didn't know where it was all going, didn't trust the motives of people around him, not even his own father who . . . had bought or wanted to buy an estate in Hawaii with his money, and [Jimi] was staying well away, trying to sort his head out.'

Most surprisingly, Clackson recalls, 'He had nothing to do, nowhere to go.' As dinner time approached, 'all we ate were salted peanuts and we drank three or four bottles of Blue Nun that he ordered from room service. No drugs, no spliffs, no groupies, hardly the wild child of rock.'

The freelance had caught him in an unwontedly open and reflective mood but, thanks to the permanent high level of narcotics in his system, his mood-swings were becoming ever more sudden and extreme.

Kathy Etchingham had not realised he was back in London until she received an agitated early-morning phone call from Angie Burdon, the former wife of Eric. Angie was at the Londonderry where, she said mysteriously, Jimi had 'gone mad'.

Kathy arrived at the Park Suite to find the sitting room, where he had talked so thoughtfully to Stephen Clackson, totally wrecked and Angie and another young woman sitting there in only their underwear, clearly traumatised. Angie explained that they'd met Jimi at the Speakeasy the night before and agreed to accompany him back to the hotel for a threesome. But when they awoke this morning, he had 'gone berserk', banged their heads together and was now holed up in the bedroom, refusing to let them have their clothes.

In the bedroom, she found every window shut, a blow-heater going at full blast and Jimi lying on the bed, shivering uncontrollably. She would later recall how 'thin and grey' he looked, 'like he was suffering some kind of withdrawal symptoms' and how utterly different from 'the Jimi I had met and fallen in love with four years before. All the sweetness and gentleness had disappeared: the drugs and the stress had changed him beyond recognition.' An empty Jack Daniel's bottle testified to an additional spur to the vandalism next door.

All 'berserkness' now extinguished, he greeted Kathy quite normally, agreed to let her give the two women back their clothes and asked her to get rid of them. She sponged his feverish forehead with a damp cloth and left him sleeping, thankful all over again to have put that kind of life behind her.

When the Londonderry discovered the damage, he was forced to leave, and moved to the less particular Cumberland near Marble Arch, a popular haunt of rock musicians, said to be provided with 'running hot and cold hookers'.

No after-effects of the fracas were visible when he kept the date at Tramp he'd made from New York with Linda Keith. This time it was hardly a romantic tryst as Linda had her fiancé, Lawrence, with her and Jimi arrived with a newly acquired girl-friend, a 24-year-old Danish fashion model and actress named Kirsten Nefer.

Yet he made no secret of Linda's special place in his heart, reminding her how they'd sworn to be blood brothers by actually mingling their blood. He also gave her one of his guitars and, in a further chill moment of prophecy, told her he'd made a will in which she was to be remembered. 'He told me he was leaving his possessions to Kathy Etchingham, his royalties to Fayne Pridgon and his publishing to me.'

The next day, Linda left with Lawrence on a road trip to the South of France, little dreaming what news would be waiting for her in St Tropez.

The Isle of Wight's 'Bob Dylan festival' in 1969 had been held on the island's north coast, within earshot of the substantial village of Wootton, and brought storms of protest about its noise and supposed drugginess and immorality. So for 1970, the Foulk brothers chose a site in the sparsely populated West Wight, where rolling downs fall away into cliffs as sheer and white as the more celebrated ones of Dover.

Rather than the 'Jimi Hendrix festival' they originally planned, the Foulks had assembled a Woodstock-sized programme of Anglo-American talent for the five-day event. Co-headlining with the new Jimi Hendrix Experience (also for a fee of £10,000) would be the Doors, with Jimi's old rival in onstage outrage, Jim Morrison. There would also be the Who, Joni Mitchell, Chicago, Joan Baez, Mungo Jerry, Emerson Lake & Palmer, the Moody Blues, John Sebastian, Leonard Cohen, Jethro Tull, Donovan, Kris Kristofferson, Supertramp, Hawkwind and numerous smaller fry. The brothers' net had even scooped up Miles Davis in his new funk-rock incarnation.

Ronnie and Ray expected to improve on the previous year's attendance, but never bargained for the multitude that crossed the Solent to pitch camp on Afton Down. It was as if the world's hippies recognised this as the last hurrah for love and peace and guilt-free pot and making unprotected love in muddy tents and frolicking around in foam, and were determined to wring every last ounce of joy from it.

Their numbers soon became impossible to compute since the grassy slopes overlooking the stage allowed thousands to watch the performances without buying a ticket. The best estimate is around 400,000, nudging Woodstock very close; unlike at Woodstock, blissfully sunny weather persisted for the whole four days, but there was the same total lack of crime or violence.

A few years earlier, a north London wall had proclaimed CLAPTON IS GOD. Now on Afton Down, a corrugated iron perimeter fence – ultimately to fall flat as the Foulks gave in and declared it a free festival – read HENDRIX FOR POPE.

Jimi's performance on the Isle of Wight has passed into legend, but the truly extraordinary thing about it was that it was no problem. He arrived at the festival site on 30 August with the new Experience and their small retinue, on time and seemingly in full possession of his faculties. His one demand was his new Danish model girlfriend, Kirsten Nefer, who was arriving separately, should be allowed to watch his performance from the stage. The Foulks and their production team were amazed that Mike Jeffery hadn't bothered to put in an appearance.

Jimi had hoped to meet up with Miles Davis again, but Davis – looking even more rock star than jazzer – had performed on the previous day and departed. Still, there was a pleasant reunion with Richie Havens, who'd first steered Jimi to Greenwich Village. The two were observed in a huddle, Jimi complaining of the problems he was having with his management and Havens recommending his own lawyer to sort them out.

The visitors to Jimi's caravan dressing room included Noel Redding's mother, Margaret, who'd welcomed him into her home the first Christmas he was in England. Despite his peremptory dismissal of her son from the Experience, Margaret had travelled all the way from Kent to watch the show. 'Jimi jumped up and gave me a big kiss,' she would recall. 'He was the loveliest man, such a dear.'

With so many acts, and conflicting egos, the running order inevitably fell far into arrears and the recast Jimi Hendrix Experience didn't go on until the early hours of Sunday, 31 August. Beforehand there was a lengthy delay, during which a rumour circulated through the darkened masses that Jimi was in a nearby garden, 'out of it'.

In reality, a thoroughly domestic scene was taking place inside his caravan. The trailing sleeves of his 'butterfly' tunic were snagging his guitar strings. Margaret Redding and the festival emcee, Jeff Dexter, a former tailor, were busy with needles and threads, making them trail a little less.

When finally he walked up the ramp to the stage, Jim Morrison was sitting in the nearby artists' chill-out area. The Doors' self-styled 'erotic politican' – recently the first performer ever to be charged with public indecent exposure – would himself be dead inside eleven months. 'Hey, that's beautiful,' he shouted after Jimi. 'Like a priest going to the altar.'

A young woman journalist from France suddenly popped up to demand, 'Where do you get your inspiration?'

'From the people,' Jimi answered.

Under the lights, as the uncountable thousands waited, agog, there was a moment of seeming confusion. Jeff Dexter asked Jimi how to announce him and was told, 'The Wild Blue Angels.'

He had to ask Gerry Stickells to bring him a guitar pick, then said he'd forgotten the tune of 'God Save the Queen', which he'd decided to play in the same feedback-heavy style as 'The Star Spangled Banner'. But the British are less protective of their National Anthem, as evidenced in those days by the rush to get out of cinemas before it played at the end of the night's programme. Jimi's rendition brought little human feedback and he quickly moved on to his cover of 'Sgt. Pepper's Lonely Hearts Club Band'.

The set that followed was intermittently troubled by the noise of security men's walkie-talkies and extraneous music coming through the amps, but never enough to make Jimi's mood swing in the wrong direction. Although he gave maximum value in each song, Ray Foulk recalls that 'there was an undeniable fragility about him. He was clearly physically and mentally exhausted.'

Many fellow musicians were also present, not all at conventional vantage points. The virtuoso Scots guitarist Bert Jansch lay prone under the stage, letting the monster vibrations from above wash through him. David Gilmour, Pink Floyd's guitarist, who'd come merely as a spectator, ended up helping to mix the sound.

Tonight, as never before, Jimi wore his heart on his trailing sleeve, dedicating 'Foxy Lady' not only to his new Danish girl-friend Kirsten Nefer, there on the stage, but to Linda Keith wherever she was.

Something more than a name-check occurred in 'Red House', that memory of the scarlet-and-gold New York apartment where he and Linda had chastely stayed up all night after their first meeting. Now it had a new line with the same yearning clair-voyance as 'Send My Love to Linda': Think I gotta get out of here because my Linda don't live here no more.'

After two hours, he threw down his guitar and, with all his old humility and politeness, thanked the audience 'for being so patient . . . Maybe we'll do it again sometime,' he added. 'I do hope so.'

As the ovation rolled over the downs, someone threw what looked like a lighted firework at the stage. Actually a magne-sium flare used as a distress signal at sea, it lodged in the canopy, which promptly burst into flames. 'The band had already gone and the gear was being packed up,' Ray Foulk recalls. 'But there's been a legend ever since that Jimi played through fire.'

Among the festival's support team was John Pearse, co-founder of the Granny Takes A Trip boutique who now operated the charter company that flew in acts to Bembridge's tiny air-port. The fragile-looking Piper Aztec planes awoke misgivings in every musician who remembered what had happened to Buddy Holly and Patsy Cline; the one bringing in a member of Santana actually did crash-land in a nearby field.

Compared to what Pearse had seen in London clubs like the Speakeasy and the Bag O' Nails, Jimi's performance seemed 'plodding . . . like one long improvisation. The last time I saw him was on the airstrip at Bembridge.He was afraid he'd started losing his hair and I heard him say to one of the roadies, "Hey, man, lend me your comb."'

*

From the Isle of Wight he flew straight to Sweden, to go onstage at Stockholm's Grona Lund amusement park at nine o'clock that night. And from there everything went downhill, not steadily but at a gallop.

Swedish hotels were reluctant to take him after his behaviour at the Opalen in Gothenburg in January 1969. There were disputes with local promoters, with no significant management on hand to speak for him, and searching interviews with Scandinavian journalists that never let up. He went through them all uncomplainingly, although often slurring his words, rambling inconseqentially about the moon and stars and Winnie-the-Pooh and drinking whisky, as one interviewer noted, 'like water'.

In Stockholm, he was visited by the former student Eva Sundquist who claimed he was the father of her son, James Henrik Daniel, born exactly nine months after their brief tryst early in 1969. Although Jimi made no attempt to deny it, Eva would not get around to filing paternity proceedings until well after his death, when she'd have to take her place in line.

Chas Chandler happened to be in Gothenberg, the home of his wife Lotte's parents, and attended Jimi's show on 1 September, when he kept forgetting which song he was doing in the middle of his guitar solo and segueing into a different one. 'He looked wrecked . . . and was awful to watch,' recalled the man who knew best just how different it could be. When they met up afterwards, Chandler typically minced no words about what he'd seen; Jimi took it badly, despite knowing it was true, and the two parted in acrimony.

To round off the night's disaster, Billy Cox drank some punch which, unknown to him, had been spiked with LSD. In the throes of this involuntary first trip, all the impeturbability and common sense that Jimi so relied on completely deserted Cox; he became convinced somebody was tryng to kill him and refused to touch any food. Jimi was briefly recalled to normality in the general effort to calm his old friend's paranoia.

In Denmark, another of his chronic colds turned into a fever and the booker for his 2 September appearance at Aarhus's Vejlby-Risskov Hallen was alarmed to find him 'trembling and sweating a great deal'. Kirsten Nefer, arriving from London, found him seemingly unable to tune his guitar or decide what to wear and painfully self-conscious about the way he was looking. As she would later recall, his first words to her were, 'Oh God, Oh my God, no no I don't want you to see me like this.'

By showtime his condition was so bad that Kirsten had to help walk him onto the stage; he managed only 'Freedom' and 'Message to Love' before the performance was cut short and he was carried back to the dressing room. His minders requested cocaine to revive him, but none was available.

In Copenhagen, there was a noisy road-drill outside his hotel and, rather than face the hassle of pleading with another one to accept him, Kirsten took him home to stay with her parents. He was warmly welcomed by her mother, Birthe, as always happened with mothers, and enjoyed his first good night's sleep in months.

The Danish media were soon rife with rumours that one of their foremost celebrities and 'the greatest personality of beat' were engaged. In an interview with *Se og Hør* (See and Hear) magazine the two confirmed that they were 'seriously considering marriage . . . and afterwards will make their home in London.'

Expecting to continue the tour with him (and having already proved rather useful) Kirsten had taken time off specially from a film she was making in London. But then Jimi – for whom this was by no means the first such impulsive betrothal – suddenly seemed to cool on the whole plan, as he usually did; they had a row and Kirsten returned to London, though far from unwilling to forgive him.

Coincidentally, the United Press International reporter Sharon Lawrence, currently happened to be in Sweden covering the Rolling Stones tour that had kept them out of the Isle of Wight Festival. Sharon knew the Danish promoter of Jimi's disastrous Aarhus concert, who was also putting him on in Copenhagen. Having already had to give one audience their money back, the promoter feared going bankrupt if his attraction failed to deliver yet again.

Sharon reacted not as a wire-service reporter with a juicy lead but as a friend to whom Jimi had often turned in times of trouble. And her anxiety was shared by someone who had already shown uncharacteristic concern for Jimi's welfare. When she asked Mick Jagger for a brief leave of absence to go and check on Jimi in Copenhagen, Jagger readily agreed and the Stones paid her expenses.

After all the worrying reports, she found him thinner but sufficiently recovered from his flu and whatever else had ailed him to give a good account of himself at Copenhagen's KB Hallen. The next day, she felt reassured enough to fly back to the Stones, though Jimi wanted her to continue on to West Germany with him. Their farewell at the airport brought a very Jimi moment. He was depressed by the sight of his dingy, over-thumbed passport, so Sharon described how it could be freshened up with a soft cloth, a little facial soap and a hairdryer.

On 5 September, he was to headline a three-day 'Festival of Love and Peace' on an island off the Baltic coast named Fehmarn. Hoping to capitalise on the Foulk brothers' already famous offshore event, its promoters billed it as 'Isle of Wight des Kontinents'. A closer parallel was to be the notorious Altamont festival in California a year earlier.

On the evening of the fifth, gales and torrential rain lashed the island and Gerry Stickells refused to let Jimi go onstage despite heavy pressure from the promoters. All the festival's musicians, some 200-strong, were quartered in the same hotel and when they'd drunk all the bars dry, fighting broke out. It was an all too accurate forecast of the morrow.

In addition to armed riot police with dogs, German Hell's Angels were drafted in to provide 'security', as their American cousins had been supposed to do for the Rolling Stones at Altamont. And, faithfully emulating those American cousins, they ran amok, hurling wooden planks studded with six-inch nails – one of which hit Gerry Stickells – beating up hippies, burning down the press tent, even looting the box office. Their fascist regalia terrified Billy Cox, who remained in the grip of acid paranoia and was convinced he would never get off the island alive or else be 'captured by Nazis'.

When Jimi finally went onstage, at 1 p.m. on 6 September, he was booed for not having played through the previous evening's mini-hurricane. 'I don't care if you boo as long as you boo in key, you mothers,' he responded.

Despite further heavy rain and Hell's Angel thuggery, he managed to get through his whole set and turn the boos to damp cheers. However, a fresh eruption of violence close at hand forced him to end its finale, 'Voodoo Child', with the second verse, in unwitting valediction to millions who would soon mourn him: 'If I don't meet you no more in this world, well maybe I'll meet you in the next one.'

The trio then fled the stage in the nick of time before the Angels invaded and torched it, shooting a roadie named Rocky in the leg as he tried to dismantle the equipment.

EIGHTEEN
'JUST CALL ME HELIUM'

The wonder of it – the horror of it – was that Jimi should have died as he did with all those people milling around him . . .

After the debacle on Fehmarn island and Bill Cox's disastrous acid trip, the next show, at Rotterdam's De Doelen convention centre, had been cancelled. But Jimi still meant to honour the trio's remaining bookings, in Paris and Vienna and at a further pop festival in Essen. When they returned to London on 7 September, it was just to hire a substitute bass player since Cox was plainly in no state to continue.

Noel Redding was invited to take his old role again and magnanimously agreed, but somehow nothing came of it. When an approach to Blind Faith's Rick Grech also proved fruitless, the remaining European dates were cancelled. So the terrible irony is that *if* Jimi had stayed on the tour which seemed to be killing him, he probably would have lived.

He also got back together with Kirsten Nefer, following the tiff over their supposed engagement in Copenhagen. So *if* he'd stayed with that sensible, supportive young woman even just a week longer, he would assuredly have lived.

For now, a more immediate concern than Jimi's physical state was Billy Cox's ever-worsening acid-induced paranoia. The first night back in London, it got so bad that Jimi and Gerry Stickells had to take him to a doctor. The next day, while Jimi was at the Cumberland Hotel with Kirsten, they were called to Cox's hotel,

Church End Library
Tel 020 8359 3800
Email cnuichend library@barnet.gov uk

Customer ID: ********9411

Items that you have checked out

Title: Wild thing : the short, spellbinding life of
Jimi Hendrix
ID: 30131057570993
Due: 08 February 2022

Total items: 1
18/01/2022 14 24
Account balance: £0.00
Checked out: 1
Overdue: 0
Hold requests: 0
Ready for collection: 0

the Airways, where they found him in the throes of another extreme panic attack.

'Oh, Jimi,' he kept repeating, 'I'm gonna die.'

'No one's gonna die,' Jimi told him.

When medicine and human comfort proved equally ineffective, the only solution seemed to put him on a plane to Pittsburgh, to recuperate at the home of his respectable middle-class parents. *If* only, Billy had still been there in his full senses during the next few days, watching Jimi's back as of old . . .

While Kirsten was around, Jimi could do normal things – that, for him, were anything but normal – like going with her and her friend Karen Davis to a West End art-house cinema to see an 'intellectual' film, Michelangelo Antonioni's *The Red Desert*, then discussing how much he loved it with someone actually in 'the business', for Kirsten was currently taking a break from modelling to make a film in London.

On 10 September, to cheer himself up after Billy Cox's departure, he went to the Inn On The Park for the launch party of a solo album by the former Monkee Mike Nesmith. Ever since the ludicrous on-road teaming of the Monkees and the Jimi Hendrix Experience in 1967, Nesmith had felt grateful to Jimi for motivating him to break his bubblegum bonds and go solo as a country-rock singer-songwriter.

Now he was amazed by the humility with which 'one of the most important musical powers to come along in decades' talked about 'trying some new stuff with R&B' and 'working on' that supposed Achilles heel, his singing. 'It suddenly dawned on me that [Jimi] had no idea who he was or where he fit – that he could not see the hurricane because he was sitting in the centre of it.'

The following day, Jimi gave what would be his last-ever interview. Appropriately enough, it was with Keith Altham, whose advice Chas Chandler had sought about launching him in London four years earlier, who had first – jokingly – suggested the onstage torching of his guitar and had shared many moments with the offstage Jimi that would have astonished the fans of rock's 'wild man'. 'Like go-karting with him. And playing football on the beach in Majorca with him and Georgie Best. He was terrible at football, so we put him in goal because he had long arms.'

Altham had since left the *New Musical Express* to go freelance and the interview was to be for BBC Radio 2's *Scene and Heard* programme. It took place in Jimi's suite at the Cumberland, 'with a couple of girlfriends in the room and the TV on and lots of Mateus Rosé'.

He seemed in buoyant mood as he talked about the British tour he was planning for October with a new, expanded stage line-up including a second guitar and a keyboard player. By now quite comfortable with his radical stance, he mentioned that the Black Panthers had asked him to do a benefit.

Could his public expect more of the 'new, subdued' Jimi Hendrix, eschewing his old stage antics? Altham asked. Apparently not: 'Music has been getting too heavy . . . almost to the state of unbearable. I have this one little saying when things get too heavy, just call me helium, the lightest-known gas to man.'

While making no mention of his supposed engagement to Kirsten Nefer, he described the dream home he meant to have one day, very much as a dreamy little boy named Buster must have visualised it long ago in Seattle. 'I want to wake up in the morning and just roll over in my bed into an indoor swimming pool and then swim to the breakfast table . . . come up for air and get a drink of orange juice . . . then just flop over from the chair into the pool and swim into the bathroom . . .'

Although professing the lightness of helium, Jimi must have felt rather more like lead on the inside. For returning to London when he did meant facing up to two nagging problems that made the cancelled tour dates seem much preferable.

The first was Ed Chalpin, the New York record producer, whose 1965 contract with him effectively negated the management one he'd signed with Chas Chandler and Mike Jeffery a few months later and all his record deals in Britain and America since then.

After years of inconclusive litigation in America, Chalpin had launched a suit against Track Records and Polydor that was shortly to be heard in London's High Court. He was already here and requesting a pre-trial meeting, which Jimi – remembering how personal contacts with Chalpin always seemed to get him deeper into trouble – had so far managed to dodge. The lawsuit had had the effect of bringing the elusive Jeffery into town to talk to the Track people, but he'd soon disappeared off to Majorca again, strengthening Jimi's resolve to break away from him.

The second problem to be faced was the paternity suit from Jimi's one-time teenage girlfriend, Diane Carpenter, in respect of her daughter, Tamika, whom he'd already seemed to recognise. Now he was under pressure to take the blood test that would settle the matter one way or another, but was ducking it as assiduously as he was dodging Ed Chalpin. On 15 September, he was due to meet his American lawyer, Henry Steingarten, in London and Steingarten was sure to insist on his having the test.

If all that wasn't enough, Devon Wilson had heard of his 'engagement' to Kirsten Nefer and decided it was something to which she couldn't turn her practised blind eye. Kirsten had overheard Jimi on the phone to Devon in New York, telling her angrily to 'get off my back'. This had prompted Devon to fly over on 13 September, bringing two good friends of Jimi's with her. One was Stella Douglas, Colette Mimram's partner in his favourite Greenwich Village boutique; the other was Stella's record producer husband, Alan, whom Jimi revered as an intimate of jazz greats like Ellington and Mingus and was hoping to work with in this new phase of his music.

In the event, it wasn't to be Devon who parted Kirsten and Jimi. The film in which Kirsten had a role also featured George Lazenby, then celebrated for his one and only screen portrayal of James Bond. Lazenby was becoming annoyed by all the time off Kirsten was taking to be with Jimi and in the interests of her career she decided it would be foolish to antagonise him any further. Accordingly, she spent the night of Sunday, 13 September with Jimi at the Cumberland, then returned to the film set the next morning.

The following night was unusual for him in being without company in bed. Most of it he spent at the home of the pop impresario Tony Secunda, discussing with Secunda and Alan Douglas how to disentangle himself from Mike Jeffery even though he didn't yet have any successor to Jeffery in mind.

Jeffery's management contract ran out the following December but various deals with Warner/Reprise, notably over the *Rainbow Bridge* film, would tie Jimi to him for a further two years. Alan Douglas suggested that Jeffery might agree to bow out before December if Jimi continued paying him his 20 per cent on top of whatever his successor would demand. According to Stella Douglas, Jimi and her husband were discussing a possible partnership: 'Not on a business level but an artistic approach to a new kind of music with people like John McLaughlin and Miles Davis.'

Jimi subsequently phoned his younger brother, at the time still in prison in Washington state for drug dealing but due to be released soon. According to Leon Hendrix, he said his contract with Jeffery 'ran out in two weeks'. 'We were going to meet up in New York,' Leon recalls. 'Jimi said to me, "We'll have Electric Lady Studios. I want you to run the company and keep the crooks away. I'm no good at keeping the crooks away."'

When Kirsten had left his bed on Sunday, despite his protests, he'd made her promise to call him later. She did, but he was out and the Cumberland failed to pass on her message. The result was that from Tuesday, 15 September, for the last three days of his life, he was with Monika Dannemann.

The people around Jimi remembered Monika, if at all, as the rather sharp-faced German woman with long blonde hair and an ice-skating background with whom he'd had a one-night stand in Düsseldorf in January 1969, followed by a second in London a few months later. In other words, just one more Hendrix groupie among hundreds – by now, maybe thousands.

But it seemed everyone had been quite wrong. According to the 25-year-old Monika, she and Jimi had fallen in love on first meeting at Düsseldorf's Rheinhalle. As evidence, she would later produce colour photographs of the two of them in a bar with their heads together in seemingly intimate conversation. The photos had actually been of a largeish group, including Baron Reiner von der Osten-Sacken in his top hat and sidewhiskers, but it had been cropped so as to appear to be only of Monika and Jimi.

Her startling claim was that between their two brief trysts, in January and April of 1969, Jimi had asked her to marry him and they'd since become secretly engaged. But Monika's account featured none of the usual hasty backtracking on Jimi's part that had so annoyed Kirsten. She said he had spoken to her mother twice on the phone, suggesting the wedding should take place in October, when he'd next be touring Germany, and that he call a press conference to announce it. This idea was dropped because Monika's less liberal father, who knew nothing of the relationship, had chronic heart trouble and might suffer a relapse at the thought of his daughter marrying an African American.

Although no new wedding date had been mooted, they'd

discussed where they should live afterwards (Germany's Black Forest had been a possibility) and were already planning to have a child together. Jimi, she said, wanted a boy he could name Wasformi, a Native American word meaning thunder.

According to Monika, Jimi had asked her to meet him again in London; she'd been there since his return from the European tour and had tried to help during the Billy Cox crisis – meaning that, with Kirsten Nefer still very much around, he would have had two fiancées in the same city at once.

Monika was staying at the Samarkand Hotel, in Lansdowne Crescent, Notting Hill, an area still very far from chic with its shabby terraces and squares of bed sitting-rooms and hippy squats. The Samarkand was barely distinguishable from a not-very-grand private house and her basement room was more of a bedsit with a kitchenette and its own entrance reached by an iron spiral staircase down from the street. With what looks like canny foresight, she had also hired a car, a pale-blue Opel GT coupé.

Most of Jimi's circle at first paid her little attention – something that did not seem to bother him at all. The notable exception was a striking African American woman named Alvinia Bridges, part of the Stella Douglas–Colette Mimram fashion set, who would later work in music PR for major acts like the Rolling Stones. Alvinia took a liking to Monika and would later claim to have introduced Jimi to her.

For the three days Monika and Jimi were together, she would assert, he lived with her in her basement bedsit at the Samarkand, his whereabouts unknown to even his closest friends and musical colleagues. He spent a great deal of time there, not only in the activity that might have been expected, but also writing poetry and drawing. As well as an ice skater, Monika was an aspiring photographer and a painter. By her account, Jimi – that wistful would-be painter – was a huge admirer of her work and had persuaded her to give up ice-skating to concentrate on it.

However, he was still registered at the Cumberland, to which he would return periodically to make phone calls, leave new clothes he had bought or use room service – and where Kirsten Nefer was still leaving messages for him to call her. Monika's hired Opel sports car now proved to be of crucial importance; it made him dependent on her and its being only a two-seater enabled her to shut out Devon Wilson and any other potential competition.

Yet according to Stella Douglas, he stayed with Alan and her and continued sleeping with Devon, who was sharing their ac-commodation. As the sand in the hourglass ran out ever faster, he seemed to be everywhere at once, as if he really was capable of 'astral travel'.

Sharon Lawrence also happened to be in London, en route from the Rolling Stones tour back to Los Angeles. On the evening of 15 September, she was having a drink with the actress Judy Wong at Ronnie Scott's jazz club in Frith Street, Soho where Eric Burdon had just begun a week-long engagement with his new band, War.

As Sharon stood at the bar, Jimi arrived, accompanied by a blonde woman she didn't recognise and so drugged up that at first he didn't recognise even this closest of confidantes. When finally he did, he could only mumble: 'I'm almost gone.'

He'd brought his guitar with him, intending to jam with War, but the band's roadie refused to allow it. His friend Burdon had to agree that he was 'well out of it' and 'wobbling too much to play'.

When a worried Sharon phoned him the next morning at the Cumberland, he was coherent again but more agitated than she'd ever known him. He complained that he couldn't sleep or focus to write songs, mainly because of the Ed Chalpin court case. Mike Jeffery had promised to take care of it, he said, 'but now he's selling me out.' And it felt like everybody around him wanted something, from Devon to Alan Douglas . . . His speech was peppered with 'fucks', a novelty where Sharon was concerned, and down the line she heard crashes as if he was throwing furniture around.

That day, Wednesday, 16 September, was another when Jimi seemed to be everywhere, and of which dozens of people would later harbour indelible, though often conflicting, memories.

In the afternoon, he attended a birthday tea party for an actress named Judy Wong, who was borrowing a flat in South Kensington belonging to his *Rainbow Bridge* co-star, Pat Hartley. Alvinia Bridges and Stella Douglas were also present, Alan by now having returned to New York.

All his charm and calm now restored, Jimi kissed Judy on the cheek and sang 'Happy Birthday To You'. Then came what seems to have been his first public recognition of the unsmiling young German woman whom many took to be merely his driver. 'You know Monika and I are getting married,' Judy Wong would recall him saying.

As to the early evening, there would be three different accounts of his movements. According to Chas Chandler, he turned up unexpectedly at Chandler's flat and said he'd been listening to all the work they'd done together in the first heady days of the Jimi Hendrix Experience. 'He'd been in the studio for a year on and off and he wasn't happy with what he had in the can [and] asked would I produce him again? He wanted to record at Olympic Studios, where he'd done 90 per cent of his previous work . . . because he really felt that was the way to put it right.'

Chandler's memory seems to have been faulty, for he'd told a British music paper the same story some months earlier – but, considering the manager he'd been, who could deny him his percentage of Jimi's last hours?

At about the same time, according to Eric Clapton, he and

Jimi were both at the Lyceum Ballroom, off the Strand, to see a performance by Sly and the Family Stone. Clapton was clutching a left-handed white Fender Stratocaster he'd recently spotted in a West End guitar shop and bought as a gift for his 'darling Jimi'. He could see Jimi in an adjoining box, but the place was so crowded that they never managed to connect.

Monika's recollection of the same time period would not mention Chandler or Clapton; by her account, she and Jimi spent the whole day together and the early evening in quiet domesticity in her room at the Samarkand Hotel before going out later to Ronnie Scott's club. She took the opportunity to write her brother, Klaus Peter, a postcard to which Jimi added a message very like that of a prospective new family member: 'Hey! Remember me. Love and happiness to you . . . tell your mother and father to take care of themselves.'

What's certain is that he did finally get to jam with Eric Burdon and War at Ronnie Scott's. Just for two of their numbers, 'Mother Earth' and 'Tobacco Road', and without drawing attention to himself in any way: the inconspicuous sideman he'd always half-wanted to be, in this last performance of his life.

London at the time was enjoying the rare experience of a spectacular Indian summer. Thursday, 17 September brought another day of implausibly brilliant sunshine and cloudless royal blue above the deepening autumn tints of the parks.

At the Samarkand, Jimi and Monika didn't get out of bed until early afternoon. She then produced a camera and took him into the back garden the hotel shared with neigbouring private houses. As well as his fiancée, driver and minder, she had assumed the roles of his personal photographer and album cover designer.

There were twenty-nine colour shots, all taken in the garden and of undeniably professional quality. Their purpose, Monika later said, was to show the real Jimi Hendrix as opposed to the confected wild man of the PR handouts. Alas, they succeeded only too well for, in his pale blue Beau Brummel jacket and loosely knotted blue-and-white scarf, he looks gaunt and harassed although occasionally the sun in his eyes brings out one of his old quietly cocky half-smiles.

In some he is posed rather stiffly among the bushes with the favourite Fender Strat he called Black Beauty; in others he holds a wicker basket of plant cuttings as if he's back landscape gardening with his father; in others he sits at a fancy ironwork table, pouring tea from a china pot as if to symbolise the British culture he's embraced so wholeheartedly.

At around 3 p.m., Monika drove him to his bank, Martins in Edgware Road, to withdraw some cash, then on to Kensington Antique Market, a place selling clothes as well as antiquities in what he now knew to refer to as 'High Street Ken'.

There, while trying on yet more exotic new gear, he happened to spot Kathy Etchingham. She had not seen or heard from him since putting him to bed after the fracas at the Londonderry Hotel two weeks earlier, and was astonished when he came up behind her and gave her a hug.

Astonishment changed to shock at the way he looked. 'He seemed to have aged by about ten years,' she recalls. 'His hair was brittle and kept breaking off. All his humour and playfulness had gone.' He said he was staying at the Cumberland and, with a touch of his old insouciance, suggested Kathy should drop by and see him.

His craving for new clothes still being insatiable, Monika next drove him to Chelsea Antique Market. They also stopped off at the Chelsea Drug Store, a famous late-Sixties showplace, where he bought a newspaper and a writing pad. On the way along the King's Road, he sighted Devon Wilson and Stella Douglas, also out shopping. Monika pulled over for him to speak to them and they invited him to a party that night at the home of a mutual acquaintance, the music publisher Pete Kameron. In an Opel GT coupé there was, of course, no question of offering Devon and Stella a ride.

The Monika-driven tête-à-tête was to be interrupted nonetheless. Like everyone else who could that day, they were driving with the top down and on the way back to the Cumberland they got stuck in traffic in Park Lane next to an open-topped Ford Mustang, driven by a handsome young man with two attractive young women beside him.

The Mustang's driver was Philip Harvey, an underwriter with Lloyd's insurance company – for which extensive private means are required – and the son of a Conservative Member of Parliament, Sir Arthur Vere Harvey. His companions were a Canadian folk singer named Anne Day and a sixteen-year-old school student, Penny Ravenhill.

On seeing Jimi Hendrix in an open car a few feet away, other people would merely have smiled and waved but Harvey, with the assurance of his wealth and class, got Penny to call out an invitation to tea at his place. Jimi, who had already clocked the young women, replied that he'd be pleased to, but first would have to go to the Cumberland to pick up his messages. The Mustang followed him there and stood by to lead the way.

At the Cumberland, he parked the clothes he'd bought and made two phone calls. The first was to producer Eddie Kramer about their next recording session in New York; the second was to his lawyer, Henry Steingarten, although still not about his blood test in the Diane Carpenter paternity case. He'd asked Steingarten to investigate ways of disentangling himself from Mike Jeffery sooner than December.

Philip Harvey turned out to live in the poshest part of Marylebone in a mews flat full of antique furniture and costly fabrics that the design-conscious Jimi beheld with unabashed envy. Tea was followed by wine and joints and, as evening drew on, Anne Day and Penny Ravenhill cooked a meal of vegetables and rice.

Both women had assumed that Monika was simply Jimi's driver and for much of the time she gave no impression of being otherwise. 'She was very cold and aloof,' Penny recalls. 'There didn't seem to be any relationship between them.'

However, as his two hostesses became more and more overtly flirtatious, and he more responsive, everything suddenly changed. When Jimi left the room to use the toilet, Monika went after him and began shouting abuse through the door, including that he was 'a fucking pig'.

'Jimi followed her outside and [she] was screaming at him in the road for several minutes . . . and [he] was not answering,' Penny recalls. 'Philip asked me to go out and calm things down because he didn't want the neighbours to be upset . . . but she turned on me, so I went back inside.

'Eventually, Jimi came back inside to apologise and say goodbye . . . very embarrassed about Monika's behaviour. And then he was gone.'

Sharon Lawrence hadn't spoken to him since their phone conversation on Wednesday morning when she'd heard him cursing and throwing furniture about. By Thursday evening she'd become so concerned about him that she phoned the Cumberland, fearing he might have done himself some mischief far worse than he'd inflicted on any wastepaper basket or stool.

The hotel switchboard operator proved not to be the usual automaton but a motherly-sounding woman whom Jimi had clearly charmed to bits. She told Sharon that she'd been worried about him, too; for instance, when he'd booked a call to America, then refused to take it. The concierge went up and checked his suite, but found it in perfect order – and empty.

To round off the seeming cast of thousands, Mitch Mitchell was also in London on the night of 17 September. Mitchell had recently become a father and had taken a few hours off from parenting to drive up from his home in Sussex and pay a call on Gerry Stickells. The roadie lived in Elgin Crescent, only a couple of streets away from the Samarkand, but had no idea that Jimi was so close. That very day, they had discussed some business on the telephone, Stickells under the impression that Jimi was at the Cumberland. He would afterwards recall that Jimi seemed 'in a great mood'.

Later that evening, Mitchell had arranged with former Cream drummer Ginger Baker to pick up Sly Stone and take him to the Speakeasy. Mitchell knew that Jimi would want to see Stone, his chief pacemaker into the realm of funk, and take part in the jam that was sure to follow. He therefore used Stickells's phone to call the Cumberland and, getting no reply from Jimi's suite, left a message, hoping to see him later onstage with Sly.

Mitchell was to wait for him at the Speak until 4 a.m., in vain.

Monika's various accounts of what happened that night and the next morning were to differ from and often contradict each other. But they would be consistent in not recording the slightest friction between Jimi and her, at Philip Harvey's flat or anywhere else, and portraying an intensely private romantic idyll to the end.

According to Monika, they returned from Harvey's to her room at the Samarkand at about 8.30 and she cooked them a meal of spaghetti (sometimes to be recollected by her as fish fingers and chips) in its kitchenette. Jimi had bought a bottle of red wine and one of white; he tried some of the red but then switched to the white, again drinking only a little.

Afterwards, he had a bath and washed his hair. While Monika took her turn to wash hers, he used a notebook they shared to write a poem entitled 'The Story of Life', which he dedicated to her. 'The story of life is quicker than the wink of an eye,' it ended. 'The story of love is hello and goodbye until we meet again.'

She would remember phone calls during the evening from Chas Chandler and Mitch Mitchell (although Mitchell later attested he didn't have the Samarkand's number and had phoned the Cumberland to suggest he meet Jimi at the Speakeasy). But Jimi hadn't wanted to talk to either of them and tried to make her laugh by pulling faces as she was fobbing them off.

At about 1.45 a.m., with her hair still wet, Monika drove him to the party at Pete Kameron's to which Devon Wilson and Stella Douglas had invited him that afternoon. She had wanted to go with him but he dissuaded her by saying the other likely guests were 'not nice people' and he would only drop in for half an hour. In fact, he intended to confront Devon there and tell her once and for all to stop trying to run his life.

Monika therefore dropped him outside Pete Kameron's flat – which happened to be in Great Cumberland Place, a few metres from the Cumberland Hotel – then returned to the Samarkand to finish drying her hair.

Kameron was a 49-year-old American music publisher and artistes manager who'd been closely involved in setting up the Track record label. As well as Devon and Stella, his party guests included many other people Jimi knew, like Mike Nesmith and Angie Burdon, ex-wife of the former Animals vocalist who was to enter the story so dramatically a few hours later.

Angie would later recall that when Jimi arrived at the party, he seemed 'uptight and jumpy'. He ate some Chinese food, but drank little or nothing. Kameron always had plenty of drugs – indeed, Devon proved already too far gone to be talked to seriously – but Jimi himself took only a single Durophet amphetamine or 'black bomber'.

When Monika returned to collect him half an hour later, as arranged, he seemed reluctant to leave or even for her to come in. He asked Stella Douglas to stall her over the entryphone and, according to Angie, other people leaned out of the window and shouted down, 'Why don't you fuck off and leave him alone?' Shortly before 3 a.m., he left abruptly without saying goodbye – for him, an unheard-of lapse in politeness.

To revert to Monika's narrative (or narratives): when they returned to the Samarkand, despite the two meals Jimi had had that night, he was hungry again, so she made him two tuna fish sandwiches. He took only a nibble at one, then stretched on the bed, fully dressed. Certain that he'd be unable to sleep, as he so often could not, but with no roadies on hand to slip him a 'downer', he asked Monika if she had 'something' he could take.

She had. It was a powerful German-made sleeping tablet named Vesparax, of which she kept a supply due to residual pain from the injury that had ended her skating career. Each tablet was a double dose that had to be broken in half. Half a tablet was reckoned more than sufficient for a man of Jimi's size, inducing up to eight hours' sleep.

Monika would claim that she first tried to persuade him to drift off naturally and they lay and talked, with Jimi pledging his eternal devotion, until around 7.15. She herself then took a whole Vesparax, a double dose, and fell asleep at once.

When she awoke – at around nine according to one later statement, just before eleven according to another – Jimi was beside her, apparently sleeping peacefully, and she decided to go and buy some cigarettes in nearby Portobello Road. She took particular care not to wake him, she said, for he didn't like her going out alone 'because of Mike Jeffery and all that stuff'. The implication was that he was afraid of Jeffery, and believed his manager might be looking to harm anyone close to him.

Lansdowne Crescent is not in a commercial area and the nearest source of cigarettes would have been a Finch's bar and wine store about a ten-minute walk away. When Monika returned,

Jimi still seemed to be sleeping, but had changed position on the bed. Approaching nearer, she saw 'a trickle of something' come from his mouth, then realised she'd stepped on a ten-tablet 'blister pack' of Vesparax with nine of its blisters broken. One of the tablets turned up later under the bed; he had apparently taken the other nine, or eighteen times the normal dose.

Monika's immediate instinct, she would say, was to phone his doctor, but she knew only that it was a man named Robertson with a practice in Harley Street. She then thought of contacting Alvinia Bridges, the one member of Jimi's circle with whom she was friendly, in the hope that Alvinia might have the doctor's number.

Alvinia was staying with Judy Wong in South Kensington but, as Judy informed Monika, was not there at present. She had been out at Ronnie Scott's, watching Eric Burdon perform with War, and was spending the night with Burdon at the Hotel Russell in Bloomsbury.

Burdon's 1986 autobiography, *I Used to Be an Animal but I'm All Right Now*, recalls the the moment in the hotel bedroom when he became woozily aware of Monika on the phone to Alvinia, saying, 'Jimi's so stoned that he can't wake up.' To Burdon it was a far from unfamiliar or dangerous situation and he chipped in impatiently with the usual remedy: 'black coffee and a slap in the face'.

As he settled down to sleep, however, alarm bells started ringing: he phoned Monika back and told her to call an ambulance without delay. She protested she couldn't 'have people round . . . there's all kinds of stuff [i.e., drugs] in the house.' Flush it down the toilet, Burdon said, but get the ambulance.

Alvinia herself recalls that for her alarm bells took no time to start ringing. 'Monika was hysterical, she said [Jimi] was throwing up, regurgitatating all over the place. And I screamed and I was pulling shoes on . . . I said, "Turn him over, turn him over."

But obviously she was panicking and she didn't turn him over.'

Alvinia went in a black taxi to the Samarkand, leaving Burdon to follow. By her account, when she arrived the ambulance had already taken Jimi away and Monika, too, had gone, leaving the basement front door open. 'I was blessed that I'd told the cabbie to wait. I asked him, "Where's the nearest hospital?" and he said, "St Mary Abbot's."' She asked him to take her straight there.

Burdon's autobiography tells a different story of coming into Lansdowne Crescent by mini-cab 'in time to see the flashing blue lights of the ambulance turning the corner' at the other end. Nor, in his memory, was the room deserted; Alvinia was there, trying to comfort a distraught Monika and 'on the bed I could see the impression of where Jimi had lain.'

Monika – she would initially maintain – had followed the ambulance in her hired car to St Mary Abbot's hospital in Marloes Road, Kensington, arriving at around 11.45 a.m. In the A&E department, she was able to catch only a brief glimpse of Jimi, 'sitting in a chair like you have at the dentist' while doctors tried to resuscitate him, but was then hustled out of the room.

She would later allege that no one at the hospital recognised him or 'seemed to give a hoot' when she tried to explain who he was and that he should have VIP treatment. She was also conscious of 'some racial feeling' when staff realised the two of them were in a relationship.

Soon afterwards, Alvinia arrived, as did Gerry Stickells with fellow roadie Eric Barrett. Stickells had initially been told only that there was 'a problem with Jimi at the hotel' and, assuming it was a drug bust, had naturally rushed to the Cumberland.

Monika tried again, twice, to see Jimi but in vain. At one point, she would claim, a nurse came into the waiting room and told her his heart had stopped but the resuscitation team were working on him and he'd be all right. Then another nurse came and told her he wasn't.

He was officially pronounced dead at 12.45 p.m., with formal identification provided by Gerry Stickells. Monika could not face the grim ceremony after her last look at Jimi, lying there with a smile on his face, she said, 'as if he was just asleep and having this beautiful dream.'

That was one part of her story, at least, that no one would question.

NINETEEN
GOODNIGHT SWEET BLACK PRINCE

'The Jimi Hendrix Experience is over,' America's ABC news announced in its early evening bulletin of 18 September 1970. 'The acid rock musician died today in a London hospital, apparently from an overdose of drugs. During his short career, Hendrix flailed his electric guitar into some of the most unusual sounds of an unusual music.'

Over film footage of Jimi on- and offstage, reporter Gregory Jackson called him 'one of the best-known, highest-paid performers in recording history whose onstage gyrations could make Elvis Presley look like a PE teacher. At rock festivals, Hendrix was paid $50,000 for a single performance, his albums sold in the millions.

'He should have been a millionaire,' Jackson added on a prescient note of scepticism. 'It's not known if he saved his money. But it is known that today Jimi Hendrix is dead . . . He was 28 [sic].'

Britain's music press unanimously mourned the paradox summed up in *Disc and Music Echo*'s headline GENTLEMAN JIM – INVENTOR OF PSYCHEDELIC POP. Michael Lydon in the *New York Times* was one of the few obituarists to look beyond the 'wild man' cliché, calling Jimi 'a genius black musician, a guitarist, singer and composer of brilliantly dramatic power [who] spoke in gestures as big as he could imagine and create.'

But for most of the world's media, the story was simply of a

303

rock star destroying himself in what was becoming a familiar way, this one further outside normal society than ever. Several news reports made the false assertion that he'd died from a heroin overdose , creating a widespread feeling he'd got no more than he deserved.

In London, the trusty Les Perrin was mobilised to deal with a clamorous press pack. The announcement of the drug overdose had come directly from the hospital but Perrin refused to confirm it until after the post-mortem and inquest that would inevitably follow. The hard-bitten old PR was deeply affected by Jimi's death, telling reporters that in four years he'd never given a moment's trouble and how, despite his 'exotic and extrovert' appearance, 'he was a very warm and nice man with a rather delightful sense of humour and I loved him tremendously.'

Leon Hendrix was in his cell at Monroe penitentiary, waiting ts start his shift in the kitchens, when a fellow inmate shouted to him that his brother was dead. Then came a loudspeaker call to prisoner number 156724 to report to the chaplain's office.

There his father broke the news to him on the telephone, having just heard it from Jimi's lawyer, Henry Steingarten. 'But don't worry,' the tearful Al – never good with emotion at the best of times – added confusingly, 'He's gonna be all right.' Rather than the counselling he would have recieved today, Leon was put on lockdown in his cell for the next seventy-two hours lest his anguish should disrupt the prison routine.

Mike Jeffery was staying at the Majorca home of his former PA, Trixi Sullivan, who now lived on the island. According to Trixi, Jeffery had invited Jimi out there for a break 'because things seemed to be turning bad for him in London'. The day before his death, he'd tried to phone Jeffery at Sgt. Pepper's (the club he'd once flown back specially from the US to open) but had been unable to reach him. Jeffery's attempt to return the call had been thwarted by an electrical storm that temporarily blotted out telephonic communication with the UK.

'When Mike heard what had happened, he flew straight back to London to deal with the situation,' Trixi recalls. 'I offered to go with him, but he said no, he'd better be on his own because there was going to be so much shit flying around.'

Kathy Etchingham was at home in Chiswick in the early afternoon when her friend Madeline Bell phoned to tell her that she'd heard about Jimi's death on the radio. She rushed out to buy a copy, but found no mention of it. Then the newsvendor told her there was one more edition to come, at 3 p.m. In that, it was the front-page splash.

Fayne Pridgon had by now moved uptown from Harlem up to Brooklyn. She had friends among the police and a squad car stopped outside her house to relay what its crew had just heard over their radio. One of the cops threw her a package of drugs, saying she was going to need them. She felt numb, but not really surprised, remembering how 'Jimi had always thought that one day he was just going to lay down and die.'

After Jimi failed to show at the Speakeasy, Mitch Mitchell had driven back to his home in East Sussex and hadn't yet gone to bed when the roadie Eric Barrett phoned him. The feeling, Mitchell would say, was 'a bit like when Jimi crashed his car in Benedict Canyon and came in and told me about it. "Did I dream that?"'

Noel Redding received the phone call lying in bed in a New York hotel after a heavy night's drinking. Thinking it was a prank, Redding banged the receiver down. He realised his mistake when a succession of grief-stricken young women came knocking at his door, asking if they could commit suicide by jumping from his window.

It was an especially heavy blow for someone whose rock stardom had seemed as incongruous as his top-heavy Afro and for whom Jimi had been 'the first person I was close to'. Redding would write in his autobiography how he found comfort in the last quarter he expected – a church.

Eric Clapton was at his country house in Surrey when he learned he no longer had a rival who could blast him off any stage and a friend who never ceased to admire and defer to him. As it happened, Jimi had been due to visit him with some other people a few days later. The usually chilly Clapton would later confess he 'went out into the garden and cried all day'. Often on the edge of suicide himself, he kept asking rhetorically how Jimi could have gone 'and not taken me with him'.

Among Jimi's musical peers, other famously flinty hearts were to be similarly touched. Bob Dylan burst into tears. The headline on an interview with Mick Jagger was I AM SHATTERED.

Keith Altham had conducted the last-ever formal interview with Jimi; their conversation on BBC Radio 2, reproduced in *Record Mirror*, now became a retrospective scoop. The freelance Stephen Clackson also found he had a hot property in the off-the-record chat, three weeks earlier, when Jimi had talked so unguardedly and had seemed so very oppressed, unhappy and alone.

Clackson took the story to the *Sunday Mirror*, which rewarded him lavishly and provided him with a car and driver to keep him under wraps while Jimi's confidences were tabloidised. But unfortunately, a Saturday-night printers' strike kept the paper off the streets.

The next issue of *Billboard* contained two black-bordered pages with a valediction from the organisers of the Monterey International Pop Festival, on which Jimi's name would always be written in fire. The first page said:

> *To a black gypsy* **cat**
> *who rocked the* **world**

when it needed to be **rocked**.
Sleep well.

The other simply said:

Goodnight Sweet Black Prince

Knowing that a media storm would soon erupt, Gerry Stickells had lost no time in spiriting Monika Dannemann away from St Mary Abbot's hospital. Monika was reluctant to go, saying that Jimi had always feared being mistaken for dead while merely 'astral travelling' and had made her promise that if a situation like this ever arose, she would sit with him for three days and nights to ensure he wasn't buried alive.

That afternoon, two police officers went to the Samarkand Hotel to take a statement from Monika. Nowadays, the scene of any death in unusual circumstances would be cordoned off with official blue and white tape but in 1970 the basement room was left just as it had been the previous night, with the street door unlocked and visitors free to come and go as they pleased.

During a cursory examination of the room, one policeman picked up the notebook containing Jimi's poem 'The Story of Life' which, as he'd wished, Monika had not yet read. She feared it might be taken away as evidence but the officer merely glanced at the drawings she'd done on the preceding pages, then put it back.

She would say that Stickells and Eric Barrett also came to the room that afternoon and 'took away some of Jimi's stuff', seemingly less interested in things like clothes than in 'messages [he] had received', which in those days before mobile phones or answering machines, would all have been on paper. When his 'Black Beauty' Strat was added to the pile, Monika pleaded that he'd always promised it to her, so Stickells left it.

Later, she was photographed being escorted from the flat by both roadies. Since she clearly couldn't spend the night there, a room had been booked for her at the hotel where Eric Burdon was staying, the Lincoln House in Marylebone. That night, she, Alvinia and Judy Wong – who'd answered her first panic-stricken phone call about Jimi – went to Ronnie Scott's again to see Burdon perform with War. It was, Judy recalled, 'more like a wake'.

In the flurry of leaving the Samarkand, Monica had forgotten the notebook containing 'The Story of Life'. The roadies told her not to go back for it but the next morning, before anyone else was awake, she did so.

Sharon Lawrence had learned of Jimi's death from a newsbill in Bond Street. For now, though, the duty of a showbusiness reporter for United Press International had to come before her personal feelings. On Saturday, 19 September, she talked to Eric Burdon in his room at the Lincoln House and Burdon introduced her to Monika as 'an old and special friend of Jimi's'.

The canny Sharon was unimpressed by the 'waxen blonde, dressed from head to toe in black' and, strangely, not weeping or showing any sign of grief. 'At the back of my mind it registered that here was someone who craved attention.' Questioning her about Thursday night and Friday morning proved uphill work, for Monika kept changing the subject to that of her art; how she now felt a mission to 'paint everything life-size for Jimi and exhibit it all over the world'.

'She was befuddled and her mind seemed to be focused more on her fledgling career . . . and what Jimi had said about her work.' By the end, Sharon's professional detachment was starting to wear thin. 'I didn't care about her damn paintings. He was dead and I wanted to know how and why.'

When Monika checked out of the Lincoln House later, there was an uncomfortable scene: she had brought no money with

her, Eric Burdon refused to pay for her night's stay and an un-
sympathetic receptionist threatened to impound her luggage.
A German journalist hovering nearby came to her aid with
seeming chivalry and offered to find her a taxi. Relieved to be
speaking her native tongue, she did not demur when he hopped
into the back beside her.

The journalist was from the huge-circulation, sensationalist
Bild-Zeitung. During the taxi ride, Monika talked at length about
Jimi but, since he took no notes, was unaware he was treating it
as an interview. *Bild* duly published a front-page splash, headed
I GAVE JIMI THE TABLETS and quoting her saying: 'the
intrigues of the people he worked with finished him off.'

If Eric Burdon baulked at putting his hand in his pocket, he
still felt a responsibility towards Monika and the woman friend
who'd been caught up in Jimi's death, Alvinia Bridges. To spare
them press harassment for the rest of the weekend, he suggested
they accompany him to his native Newcastle upon Tyne where
his band was to play its next gig.

The press got wind of their departure and there were fist-fights
among photographers on the platform at King's Cross station as
Monika (with a blanket over her head) and Alvinia entrained for
their 200-mile journey north and the cost-free hospitality of Burdon's mother.

The following Monday, 21 September, a post-mortem on Jimi
was carried out by Professor Robert Teare, consultant pathologist and Professor of Forensic Medicine at Charing Cross
Hospital's medical school.

That evening, BBC-TV's flagship news programme, *24 Hours*,
included an item about pop stars and drugs in which Eric Burdon
– now back from Newcastle – agreed to take part. To the show's
toughest interviewer, Kenneth Allsop, he spoke mainly about his
own attitudes, but Jimi's death inevitably came up and Burdon,

clearly in a highly emotional state, implied it had been suicide. 'He was happy dying. He died happily and he used the drug to phase himself out of existence and go someplace else.'

Burdon later admitted he was stoned and Allsop 'took me apart, fried me'. As he left the studio, he met an executive from Polydor, Jimi's original UK record label, who hissed that after what he'd just said he'd never work in Britain again.

Two days later, the Inner West London Coroner, Gavin Thurston, opened the inquest on Jimi at Westminster Coroner's Court. Thurston was no stranger to celebrity sudden death, having also conducted the inquest into that of the Beatles' manager, Brian Epstein, from an alcohol and barbiturates overdose in 1967.

Before the court there was already a statement by Monika and one by Gerry Stickells as the identifier of Jimi's body. Monika's – which described herself as 'artist' and made no mention of having been Jimi's fiancée – said that at the time of his death he'd been 'very happy' and had 'never talked of killing himself'. This first official account of realising something was wrong with Jimi said nothing about having gone out to buy cigarettes immediately beforehand.

Stickells's statement was a piece of pure fiction, claiming that Jimi 'sometimes took sleeping-pills and amphetamines' but that he'd never seen him do hard drugs or even smoke cannabis. The roadie further fantasised that in the previous three weeks he'd been 'perfectly able to work when he should have done except for one day when he was tired and had a cold'.

After routine evidence from one police witness, the proceedings were adjourned for seven days until 28 September pending the results of further forensic tests. The next day, Monika flew home to Düsseldorf where she posed for press photographs with a selection of her paintings, once more looking strangely un-grief-stricken.

When the court reconvened, Professor Robert Teare delivered his post-mortem findings that Jimi had died from 'inhalation of vomit due to barbiturate intoxication'. In his stomach had been a half-digested meal including whole grains of rice – presumed to have been the Chinese food he'd eaten at Pete Kameron's party. Teare had found only a low level of alcohol in his blood and no visible signs of drug addiction such as needle marks in the arm.

The only others to give evidence were Stickells, who simply repeated his pre-hearing statement, and Monika, who departed from hers, as she would continue to do something like fourteen times. Now in the witness box she claimed to have awoken next to Jimi at 10.20 a.m. rather than around eleven, as she'd previously said, and added the detail of going out to buy cigarettes.

Strangely, neither Eric Burdon not Alvinia Bridges were called to give their crucial respective accounts of what followed. Had they done so, it would have revealed a major inconsistency between their version of the night's events and Monika's.

She was to claim to have found Jimi insensible at various hours of the morning but none earlier than 9 a.m. Burdon, on the other hand, would recollect her SOS call to Alvinia in 'the first light of dawn', and his and Alvinia's separate taxi journeys to the Samarkand Hotel taking place only minutes afterwards. Yet the ambulance had been called to the Samarkand, as its dispatcher's log confirmed, at 11.18. That suggested several hours had passed when Jimi desperately needed help but received none.

The coroner, Gavin Thurston, seemed solely concerned with the suicide angle that had obsessed the newspapers since Burdon's appearance on *24 Hours*. Indeed, the inquest had an air of being little more than a formality. Thurston ruled there was insufficient evidence of Jimi's 'deliberate intent' to kill himself and so recorded an open verdict – i.e., that his death was suspicious but no firm conclusion could be reached.

The next morning's *Daily Mirror* carried a double-page spread headed JIMI'S LAST MESSAGE TO MONIKA and, below, a quotation from his poem 'The Story of Life': 'hello and goodbye until we meet again'.

In accord with the inquest verdict, the *Mirror* said it had not been a suicide note but expressive of a living relationship, revealing the 'wild man of pop' and 'frenzied entertainer' as 'gentle, quiet and strictly private'. His 'German girlfriend [not fiancée]' had consented to share only those words of the poem – although, of course, they were the most poignant, and saleable.

The accompanying interview quoted Monika as saying Jimi had had 'no worries' nor communicated any sense of feeling his life was no longer worth living. She thought he must have taken the fatal dose of Vesparax while she was drifting off to sleep, for they weren't at the bedside but in a cupboard and he'd have had to get up to reach them.

As for the cigarettes, she now said she'd meant to go out and buy them but hadn't yet done so when she noticed he was 'ill'.

Mike Jeffery had never been more inconspicuous than he became immediately after Jimi's death. Normally, a manager who lost a major client with such suddenness would put out an impassioned personal tribute to the client, both as an artiste and a friend, and give interviews all over the place, perhaps adding a consoling word for his bereft fans. But nothing of that kind came from Jeffery.

His professional associates – the record company executives and tour-promoters whose meal ticket had just gone up in smoke like a Jimi Strat – sought urgent meetings and conference calls with Jeffery in vain. Ronnie Foulk, who still had unfinished business with him over the Isle of Wight Pop Festival, recalls that 'for about four days, he simply vanished.' Dick Katz from the Harold Davison booking agency, another crusty old-timer who'd grown personally fond of Jimi, was infuriated by this behaviour and told people Jeffery was using the the time to 'manipulate Jimi's money'. 'The word "Mafia" was mentioned, too,' Foulk recalls.

No trace was ever found of the will in which Jimi had told Linda Keith he had left his publishing to her, his possessions to Kathy Etchingham and his royalties to Fayne Pridgon. He was held to have died intestate which meant that under the laws of New York state, his official domicile, everything went to the father who'd never shown his music an ounce of understanding or respect.

Linda Keith didn't learn of his death until she and her fiancé, Lawrence, arrived in St Tropez on their road trip through France during which they'd seen no British newspapers or television. There, to her amazement, Linda ran into her New York friends Roberta Goldstein and Mark Hoffman, whom she'd been with four years earlier when she first saw Jimi onstage at the Cheetah Club. And Hoffman had owned the scarlet apartment – the Red House, as Jimi named it – where he and Linda later spent the night, just talking. Now, in glamorous 'St Trop', Roberta told her what had been headline news on both sides of the Atlantic ten days earlier.

'Roberta and Mark were staying with some friends in the hills behind the town and Lawrence and I spent a very subdued evening with them there,' Linda recalls. Although she was with the man who would become her first husband, she could not repress 'a feeling of huge disappointment. I'd never stopped thinking that Jimi and I would get together someday, when his life settled down – perhaps even in our old age. That was never going to happen now.'

Al Hendrix decreed that the funeral should take place in Seattle, much to the dismay of friends like Sharon Lawrence and Eric Burdon, who'd often heard Jimi say he'd like to be buried in

London. Sharon telephoned Al to plead for a quiet ceremony in some city parish church, but got nowhere. 'Would you be knowing,' he broke in, 'how much money there is?'

The job of bringing Jimi's body home was entrusted to Pat O'Day, the Seattle deejay and promoter who'd organised his disastrous return visit to James A. Garfield High School two years before. The soiled clothes in which he'd died had had to be disposed of and he still wore the makeshift outfit provided by the undertaker, a lumberjack-style shirt and plain blue jeans. After all the gorgeous threads he'd so delighted in, this was the final indignity.

Organising the funeral was so daunting to Al that he gave over most of the arrangements to a female family friend named Freddie Mae Gautier who had known Jimi since he was a baby. Numerous celebrities had expressed a wish to attend, among them Jimi's one-time employer, Little Richard, whose offer to stage-manage the whole show had to be firmly declined.

The service, on 1 October at Dunlap Baptist chapel, was attended by Seattle's dynamic mayor, Wes Ulhman, and 200 mourners, with several hundred uninvited ones massed outside to honour Jimi as the city never had in his lifetime.

For many interested parties, it was also the moment when Mike Jeffery publicly resurfaced although he contributed nothing to the obsequies but an enormous floral tribute in the shape of an acoustic guitar. A more attentive manager would, of course, have made it a Strat.

Leon Hendrix had been given a day's leave from Monroe penitentiary to attend on condition his father paid for three US Marshals to guard him. He arrived in handcuffs, which his escort removed for the service. Among the congregation were a generous sprinkling of Jimi's former women friends, like Melinda Merriweather from Hawaii and Devon Wilson, whom Al had never met before but who informed him to his bewilderment that she and Jimi had been planning to marry.

The large musician contingent included Mitch Mitchell, Noel Redding, Johnny Winter, Buddy Miles, John Hammond Jr. and Miles Davis (who normally was so flinty, he hadn't attended his own mother's funeral). Eric Burdon, however, stayed away in protest. To Mitchell and Redding, waiting for Gerry Stickells to call them out before the crowd, it felt strangely like a gig in the old days with the Jimi Hendrix Experience.

The pallbearers were led by James Thomas, former manager of Jimi's first grown-up band the Rocking Kings. It was an open-casket service and he now wore the formal black suit he'd bought for his drugs trial in Toronto. His father showed him the love that had been witheld all his life, stroking his forehead and moaning 'My son!'

The eulogy was given not by his manager, as might have been expected, nor by one of the world's great guitarists, but by the family friend, Freddie Mae. In it, she quoted from his song 'Angel', another seeming reference to his mother, Lucille: 'Fly away my sweet angel/Tomorrow I'll be by your side.' Leon read a poem he'd written, saying that Jimi and Lucille were together now.

The cortège of twenty-four limos then drove to Greenwood Memorial Cemetery, where Jimi was interred next to his grandmother, Zenora. Lucille was in the same cemetery, but Al couldn't remember where. (Actually, she was just a few feet away, so Leon's poem had got it right.)

The mourners filed past the open grave, throwing in notes and guitar picks – all but Mike Jeffery, who stayed in his limo, whatever emotion he felt. blotted out by its darkened windows Devon Wilson collapsed in hysterics and tried to throw herself onto the casket as the first clods of earth struck it. Leon had intended to use this moment when his three US Marshals would be off guard to make a break for freedom, and had accomplices standing by with a getaway car. Instead, he waved them away: saying a proper goodbye to his brother became more important.

'When I die,' Jimi had once said, 'I'm not going to have a funeral, I'm going to have a jam-session. And knowing me, I'll probably get busted at my own funeral.' So later that day, Mitchell, Redding, Johnny Winter and the Buddy Miles Express got together for a 'musical wake' that should have been spectacular. But somehow it didn't feel like a proper jam without Jimi.

TWENTY
'A TALL BLACK GUARDIAN ANGEL IN A HAT'

He was not to be allowed to rest in peace. In the decades that followed, Jimi's death would be replayed over and over, with as many variations, and improvisations, as one of his guitar solos.

But at the time it soon faded from the headlines as the 27 Club claimed two more members in quick succession. A month later in Los Angeles, Janis Joplin overdosed on heroin and in July 1971, Jim Morrison, no longer the Doors' angelic satyr but an overweight, bearded American in Paris, suffered a fatal heart attack in his bath.

By then, the Club had also silenced a crucial witness to Jimi's last days when Devon Wilson died in a mysterious fall from a ninth-floor bedroom at New York's fatality-prone Hotel Chelsea. The only clue was a recent surge in Devon's smack habit, seemingly brought on by grieving for him. Not long previously, she had told Sharon Lawrence how much she regretted all the ways in which she'd exploited and tormented him.

Sharon never had any doubt that he had taken the overdose of Vesparax deliberately and that 'The Story of Life' (which Monika Dannemann had shown her) was more than just the poem or song lyric so many others believed. 'Those pages were . . . nothing that Hendrix would have put on record,' she would recall. 'They were the words of a tired and troubled man. He took his own life – I'm convinced of that.'

Chas Chandler, who understood his temperament as well as anyone, was equally convinced to the contrary. 'I don't believe for one minute that he killed himself,' Chandler said, and kept repeating to his own premature dying day. 'That was out of the question.'

But for the present nothing came from those who'd shared Jimi's final hours, and minutes, to reinforce either viewpoint. Monika, after her time in the tabloid spotlight, was presumed to have returned to Düsseldorf and her ice-skating pupils; Eric Burdon, who'd first floated the suicide idea with such adverse consequences for himself, kept his head well down thereafter; Gerry Stickells maintained a roadie's absolute discretion, comparable with that of a butler in a Victorian stately home.

One substantial and revealing portion of Jimi's last day was never even known about: his chance encounter with the young Lloyd's underwriter Philip Harvey and the tea-and-joints party with Harvey, Penny Ravenhill and Anne Day that had shed such a different light on his relationship with Monika.

Soon afterwards, Harvey's MP father was elevated to the House of Lords as Lord Harvey of Prestbury. Fearful that his connection with a druggy, dead rock star might embarrass his newly ennobled parent, Harvey swore both women to secrecy about the whole episode.

From the beginning, there was suspicion that Mike Jeffery might somehow have had a hand in Jimi's death but it sprang from the general dislike and mistrust of Jeffery rather than any solid evidence. No one in the media then had an inkling of his past as a British intelligence agent, licensed to kill, nor of the Mafia connections he'd already employed when those two 'wannabe wiseguys' had kidnapped Jimi a year earlier.

Evidently aware of what people were saying and thinking, Jeffery broke his invisibility rule and gave *Rolling Stone* an interview refuting the idea that 'The Story of Life' had been a pointer to suicide. 'I've been going through a whole stack of papers, poems and songs that Jimi had written,' he said, 'and I can show you 20 of them that could be interpreted as a suicide note.'

Jimi, he added, had never said anything to him about wanting to change management. What might have seemed like conflict between them had mainly sprung from Jimi's 'incredible genius'. 'The common thing with artists of that calibre is that they're constantly artistically frustrated.' He sounded like a manager of wisdom and understanding, equal to the best of them.

The benefits of Jimi's death to Jeffery were immediate. *Rainbow Bridge*, the film he had co-produced, was mocked on its 1971 release for its hippy self-indulgence and incoherence, yet people still went to see it for the seventeen minutes of Jimi performing live on the edge of Maui's Olowahu volcano.

Jeffery also controlled the rights to *Jimi Plays Berkeley*, a documentary about his appearance at Berkeley Community Center in May 1970. This was now sent on a cinema tour that also featured stage performances by two recent Jeffery signings, Cat Mother and Jimmie & Vella.

In real estate terms, the benefits were even greater. Jeffery bought Jimi's half-share of Electric Lady Studios for $240,000 and repaid the $30,000 he'd borrowed from Warner Brothers to complete them, so gaining total control of what had been Jimi's greatest dream-come-true. In future years, Electric Lady would become a huge success, used by David Bowie, the Rolling Stones and Pattie Smith among others – although Jeffery wouldn't be around to see it.

A few weeks after Jimi's funeral, finding herself in New York on assignment for United Press International, Sharon Lawrence made a pilgrimage to Greenwich Village to look at his former apartment building on West 12th Street. When a friendly

319

doorman let her into the apartment, she found it stripped of his guitars, stereo equipment, records, even his treasured Moroccan rugs and cushions. The doorman told her everything had been taken by 'people from the office'.

Al Hendrix would later recall that few of Jimi's effects ever reached him, and those only of the cheaper sort. According to his brother Leon, they all fitted comfortably under the family's ping-pong table.

From 12th Street Sharon walked the few blocks to Electric Lady where she bumped into Mike Jeffery outside. To her surprise, Jeffery hugged her in tears that seemed completely genuine and asked, 'Why did he do it? He had everything to live for.'

Long gone by now was Jeffery's *Get Carter* look of navy blue suits, turned-down moustaches and dark glasses, worn both outdoors and in. Photographs of him remained as scarce as ever, but one he gave to Trixi Sullivan early in 1973 – the last that would ever be taken – shows a beachcomber-like figure in a flowered shirt, wide-brimmed straw hat and faded Levis.

His main business sphere was still Majorca, where, in addition to his nightclubs, he wanted to open a recording studio like the one he'd intended for Maui but never got past the design stage. His plan was to buy a *finca* (estate) on an unspoiled stretch of coast where musicians could work without distraction and also stay instead of wasting money in the island's tourist hotels. 'I'd just been on my travels around Europe,' Trixi recalls, 'collecting sums of money that Mike was owed to help finance it.'

In February 1973, the Ed Chalpin lawsuit, which had been postponed by Jimi's death, finally received judgment at the High Court in London. At issue was whether the one-dollar contract he'd signed with Chalpin's PPX company in 1965, then breached by signing with Chas Chandler and Jeffery, entitled Chalpin to a cut of his earnings in perpetuity. During the years of litigation, a large proportion of his record royalties had been withheld pending its settlement, from which Jeffery alone was now owed the management percentage.

The High Court threw out Chalpin's claim, ordering him to pay the costs of the action but, as some slight compensation, allowing him to keep the albums of Jimi material that PPX had already released. Before the verdict came a touch of drama: Jeffery was arrested by the police on a warrant for failing to appear in a lower court to answer a drugs charge for which he was on bail.

Bail was granted again on condition that he surrender his passport. However, his lawyer successfully argued that he needed it to return to Majorca the next weekend.

On 5 March, Jeffery boarded a scheduled Iberia flight from Palma back to London for the end of the Chalpin hearing. The journey involved crossing French airspace and that day the country's air-traffic controllers were out on one of their frequent strikes, with their counterparts in the military standing in for them.

As the Iberia DC9 flew through thick cloud over north-west France, it collided with a charter flight from Madrid also en route to London. The charter plane was only clipped but the DC9 broke in two and all its sixty-eight passengers and crew were killed, some falling as already-frozen corpses onto the small town of La Planche.

Jeffery's body was beyond recognition but Gerry Stickells – reprising a recent role at St Mary Abbot's hospital, Kensington – was able to identify some of his personal jewellery.

The adminstration of his estate went to his long-estranged wife, Gillian; subsequently, an affadavit to the British tax authorities stated that, after settlement of outstanding loans and liabilities, its value would be 'nil'. Many of the young musicians who'd passed through his hands, Noel Redding among them,

believed he'd faked his death and melted away to some unknown tropical paradise with all the money that should have
been theirs.

Nor was that quite the end of the Mike Jeffery mystery. In
1981, his remains were exhumed from Hither Green cemetery
in south-east London by a special order from the Home Office,
for reasons never to be explained. Afterwards, at his father's re-
quest, they were cremated.

Obsessed with covering his tracks all his life, he even took
his secrets to the grave twice over as if to make sure they stayed
there.

After four years of incessant touring and mega-hitmaking, Jimi
had died virtually broke. He owned no home of his own, had
made no investments and, after the surreptitious clearance of
his apartment, did not even leave that many guitars. The newspapers estimated him to have been worth a mere $400,000; in
fact, it was only around $23,000, most of which would go in US
taxes.

His affairs, moreover, were now in the hands of a father whose
sole experience of business derived from twenty years as a self-
employed landscape gardener and who had not the first idea how
to manage his legacy, if there was to be such a thing. But, as
soon became clear, all kinds of people were more than happy to
help.

Soon after Jimi's death, Al Hendrix was approached by consortium of Seattle lawyers and businessmen to sanction a Jimi
Hendrix Memorial Foundation, a non-profit body dedicated to
giving the city's young African American population the facilities and opportunities Jimi himself had so lacked in boyhood.

The consortium claimed to have acquired a 146-acre site
outsde Seattle, which was to be turned into a combined music
venue and camping ground and, after three years, named the

Jimi Hendrix Memorial Park and donated to the city. In return for authorising the use of Jimi's name and likeness on fundraising merchandise, Al would be a vice-president of the foundation and receive a salary.

He willingly consented, and at first everything seemed to go swimmingly. The foundation rented an impressive suite of offices in downtown Seattle, with fifteen phone lines to handle the expected flood of subscribers at $20 or $10 each. Jimi's unofficial aunt, Freddie Mae Gautier, became a director and a role was found for his brother, Leon, newly released from Monroe penitentiary and in need of an alternative to drug dealing.

The first two memorial concerts were great successes, although neither took place on the 146-acre site the consortium claimed to own but at different city venues. Al was brought onstage and introduced to the audience, fulfilling a longing for stardom that he'd buried long ago among his bulbs and seedlings.

Then an article in the *Seattle Post-Intelligencer* by investigative reporter Walter Wright revealed some devastating facts about the foundation. Rather than working for free, as required by its non-profit status, staff were selling Jimi merchandise on commission and one of its senior executives had a criminal conviction for dealing in stolen airline tickets.

Al withdrew his support, causing the city to cancel the foundation's licence. When he next visited the office, he found it deserted and every bit of merchandise gone, down to the miniature rubber stamps for inking Jimi's face onto the backs of concertgoers' hands.

No trace was ever found of the thousands of dollars that had passed through the foundation – nor of the 146-acre site that was supposed to have become the Jimi Hendrix Memorial Park. One of the 'businessmen' in the consortium was subsequently indicted in connection with eight armed robberies and committed suicide; another was shot dead by his wife.

Clearly, somebody was needed to protect the naive Al from similar situations, but it was not to be Jimi's lawyer, Henry Steingarten, since Steingarten belonged to the same firm as Mike Jeffery's attorney, Mike Weiss. This hadn't been problematic in Jimi's and Jeffery's lifetimes when their interests basically coincided but was unacceptable now that they did not.

In Steingarten's place, Al hired Los Angeles-based Leo Branton, a fellow African American – though so light-skinned that most people took him for white – and Second World War army veteran. To these impeccable credentials in Al's eyes, Branton added seeming total empathy with Jimi: not only did he represent black music stars like Nat King Cole and Dorothy Dandridge but also Black Panthers and other dissidents under attack from the US government. At the time Al met him, he defended the radical feminist Angela Davis at her trial for complicity in the kidnap and murder of a judge, and secured her acquittal.

Branton's first task was to determine just how much of Jimi's earnings had been misappropriated by Mike Jeffery and where the money had gone. The numbers were soon revealed to be considerable. Yameta, the Bahamas-based tax shelter set up by Jeffery for his pop protégés and himself, had received around $1 million generated by Jimi, including $250,000 when he signed with Warner/Reprise.

Pragmatically, Branton decided that unravelling Yameta would be too time-consuming even for a possible million-dollar outcome. And anyway, in a never-published interview before his death, Jeffery had claimed *he* realised the company was serving him badly and had not used it since 1968.

With Branton came a vigorous, at times ruthless, tidying-up of Jimi's affairs. Mitch Mitchell and Noel Redding – neither of whom had gone on to greater things since the Jimi Hendrix Experience – were persuaded to waive all their rights to the trio's future royalties for lump sums of £325,000 and £175,000 respectively (Mitchell's the larger for having been Jimi's sideman in the two bands that followed). But there was nothing for the Experience's second bass player, Billy Cox, despite the breakdown he suffered after the last European tour, nor for Buddy Miles, who'd always understood he and Jimi to have been partners in Band of Gypsys.

Meanwhile, the two paternity suits that might have given Jimi heirs superseding his father, tidied themselves up. Diane Carpenter's claim in respect of her daughter Tamika failed in 1972 because he'd died before he could give the crucial blood test. In 1975, a Swedish court ruled him to have been the father of Eva Sundquist's six-year-old son, James Daniel, as a result of 'two intercourses', but the decision had no validity in the US where it mattered.

What finally sparked serious interest in the circumstances of Jimi's death was America's Watergate scandal, beginning in 1971, which unmasked some of the highest officials in the land as vengeful petty criminals and ultimately brought the resignation of President Richard Nixon just in time to avoid impeachment.

In Watergate's climactic year, 1974, it emerged that presidential paranoia had by no means been exclusive to Nixon. An article by Seymour M. Hersh in the *New York Times* exposed a CIA domestic surveillance programme, codename MHCHAOS, set up by Nixon's predecessor, Lyndon Johnson – but greatly expanded under him – whose scale far exceeded that of the FBI's COINTELPRO.

Operating totally outside the law, MHCHAOS had spied on 7,200 organisations and individuals deemed to be a national security threat, and compiled an index of 30,000 more as potentially subversive. Among the obvious targets, such as the Black Panthers and anti-war protesters, were surprising choices like the Women's Liberation movement and the Jewish educational organisation, B'nai B'rith. The agency went so far as to purchase a garbage-disposal company so that it could retrieve material from suspects' waste-bins without arousing suspicion.

In 1979, the student newspaper at California's Santa Barbara University – a former stop-off for the Jimi Hendrix Experience – used the Freedom of Information Act to gain access to whatever MHCHAOS had on Jimi. Back from the CIA came six typewritten pages, heavily redacted in the continuing, unspecified interests of national security. When the student journalists requested more, they received a further seven with similarly blanked-out sections. They were nonetheless able to find Jimi's name still on the index of those who, if the government ever saw fit to declare a national emergency, would be rounded up and placed in 'detainment camps'. According to his brother Leon, he was listed as a public menace at the same level as Osama Bin Laden after 9/11.

Hence the enduring belief that what happened in the Samarkand Hotel's basement bedsit was a political assassination. Nor can it be dismissed as mere conspiracy-theorising. When America's intelligence service ran amok, a young black man to whom millions of young white people listened might easily have put himself in extreme jeopardy by playing 'The Star-Spangled Banner' with feedback. But from all the CIA whistleblowers who have since emerged there has never been the slightest hint of such a plot.

'It's funny the way most people love the dead,' Jimi had mused to a *Melody Maker* interviewer in 1969. 'Once you're dead you're made for life. You have to die before they think you are worth anything.'

Although nobody had ever needed convincing he was worth something, the two albums of his released in 1971 enjoyed the sales surge that always follows the death of a major recording-artiste. In April came *The Cry of Love*, containing ten of the songs Jimi had intended to put onto a double album, among them 'Angel' and 'Astro Man', and featuring guest musicians like Stephen Stills, Steve Winwood and Buddy Miles. His long-time engineer, Eddie Kramer, and Mitch Mitchell made the selection, with input from Mike Jeffery as 'executive producer'. It went to number 2 in the UK and 3 in the US, selling half a million copies in a month and eventually going platinum with a million-plus.

Then in October came *Rainbow Bridge*, billed as 'the original motion-picture soundtrack' but consisting of further Electric Lady tracks that Jimi would have regarded as unfinished, among them a first studio version of 'The Star-Spangled Banner'. When this reached only number 15 in the UK and 16 in the US, Warner/ Reprise's president Mo Ostin declared Jimi's life on record to be 'essentially . . . all over'.

There remained, however, a cache of studio tapes with dozens of Jimi songs that he'd left at various stages of development. His new lawyer, Leo Branton, took possession of these on Al Hendrix's behalf and turned them over to Alan Douglas, the jazz producer with whom Jimi had hoped to collaborate, to see what could be salvaged and brought up to releasable standard.

This resulted in two more albums in 1975, *Midnight Lightning* and *Crash Landing*, the first of which reached number 5 in the US and went gold. Douglas attracted heavy criticism for wiping much of the original instrumentation behind Jimi and bringing in new session musicians and backup singers, but Mitch Mitchell testified that the tapes as they stood would have been unusable. Less defensible was Douglas's appropriation of a 50 per cent songwriting credit and the royalties that went with it on five *Midnight Lightning* tracks.

For a later album, *The Jimi Hendrix Concerts* in 1982, Douglas subcontracted the job of mixing to a young British musician/

producer named John Porter who, by a strange coincidence, had once been the deejay at Mike Jeffery's Club A Go Go in Newcastle. Indeed, Porter had been in the job when Chas Chandler brought Jimi up to the north-east, newly arrived from New York and longing to meet Eric Clapton.

He remembers the cloak-and-dagger atmosphere that surrounded his work on *The Jimi Hendrix Concerts*. 'The tapes were sent to me in plain brown envelopes, with nothing written on the spools. Where Jimi was concerned, no one seemed to be straight with anyone else. There was such a lot of shit obviously going down.'

By an even stranger coincidence the following year, Porter married Linda Keith, who had some claim on being the love of Jimi's life and was now to feel he'd never quite left her.

Linda's desire to become a mother spurred her to give up drugs once and for all and in the process she consulted a faith-healer named E. G. Fricker who was also a clairvoyant. 'He told me that a tall black guardian angel in a hat was watching over me and that I'd have two children.'

After the birth of her daughter, Chloe, Jimi appeared to her in a dream, although only fleetingly and with a single, puzzling statement: 'This is not it.' His meaning became clear when she became pregnant with her second daughter, Fleur.

TWENTY-ONE
"SCUSE ME WHILE I KISS THE PIE'

Life after Jimi had taken some time to settle down for Kathy Etchingham. Following his death, she'd accepted an offer to sell her story of their two-and-a half years together to the *News of the World*, innocently supposing that what she told a sympathetic-seeming ghostwriter would be what appeared in the paper. Instead, she found herself portrayed to its six-million Sunday readership, in her words, as 'as a stupid, oversexed and drug-soaked groupie'.

Then her first marriage had been a throwback to a world she thought she'd escaped by leaving Jimi. Her husband, Ray, an interior decorator when they met, went on to work for the celebrated British drug-smuggler Howard Marks, shipping the stuff all over the world hidden inside rock bands' amplifiers. Kathy found herself under suspicion by Britain's Customs authorities until a timely four-year jail sentence for Ray facilitated a divorce.

Eventually, she'd found normality in a junior hospital doctor with an impressive public school and Cambridge background. After their marriage in 1977, he had become a general practitioner and Kathy an estate agent; they'd had two sons and settled in suburban Ealing, west London.

Her one remaining close friend from the 1960s was a sad testament to her own good fortune in getting out of them unscathed. She remained close to Angie Burdon, Eric's ex-wife and her one-time room-mate at Zoot Money's house, despite Angie's irreversible slide into alcoholism and heroin addiction.

In 1981, Kathy was alerted to the imminent British publication of *Scuse Me While I Kiss the Sky*, a biography of Jimi by the African American poet David Henderson that had appeared in the US under a different title three years earlier. The book suggested that during her time with Jimi, Kathy had introduced Jimi to alcohol and had been permanently spaced out on LSD. '"Acid and alcohol," Henderson said, "took Jimi to another place,"' her autobiography recalls, 'by which I assumed he meant "killed him".'

Henderson further alleged that in the days of the Jimi Hendrix Experience, that supposed beacon of non-discrimination, Noel Redding and Mitch Mitchell were sometimes guilty of 'racial slurs' in front of him. They would use "nigger" and "coon" in banter, but it must have had an effect on Jimi.'

Kathy had stayed in contact with both Redding and Mitchell, both of whom were outraged by the allegations about them and agreed to some concerted action against Henderson's book. She also decided to involve Monika Dannemann, of whose existence she'd been unaware until Jimi's death. Having no knowledge of Monika's present whereabouts, Kathy could only put an advertisement into the London *Evening Standard*, asking her to get in touch. Within hours, a firm of London solicitors responded on her behalf.

After the ghoulish limelight of September 1970 was switched off, Monika had not returned home to Düsseldorf but settled in Britain, bringing over her widowed mother to join her. Little had been heard of her since then apart from an interview with the American writer Caesar Glebbeek on the fifth anniversary of Jimi's death in 1975, when she announced that he'd been murdered by the Mafia, but she'd been too frightened to say so at the time.

Monika readily agreed to join forces with Kathy, Redding and Mitchell against the David Henderson biography and a meeting was convened at Kathy's Ealing home. She was, Kathy recalls, 'the thinnest person I had ever seen . . . dressed in an extraordinary pastiche of Jimi's style, crushed velvet bell-bottoms, a big hipster belt and a frilly shirt'.

Aside from her Mafia bombshell, Monika's account of Jimi's death had undergone several further, and very crucial, changes. Rather than trying to keep her Vesparax sleeping pills from him, as she'd previously claimed, she now admitted having given him some which failed to work, so she'd given him more 'because they were very weak'.

And, rather than following the ambulance to St Mary Abbot's hospital by car, as per her previous account, she had ridden in it with Jimi and so witnessed a serious error on the part of its crew, who had sat him in a chair 'with his head lolling forward' – the worst possible posture for anyone in a respirational crisis. When she tried to protest that he should lie flat, she had been assured he'd be all right and they would both be 'laughing about it' by that afternoon. Then, when they'd reached the hospital, Jimi had received inadequate and uncaring treatment because of the colour of his skin.

Following Kathy's initiative in 1981, the UK publication of *Scuse Me While I Kiss the Sky* was cancelled. When it finally appeared several years later, the references to her in relation to LSD and alcohol had been removed – but not those about Noel Redding's and Mitch Mitchell's alleged racial slurs. Although Monika had not been a complainant, Kathy recalls, she claimed credit for the legal victory.

Friendly relations between Jimi's two exes continued, for Monika was living at Seaford in Sussex, not far from the home of Kathy's in-laws, and one weekend invited her over with her husband. They found every wall in Monika's small house covered with her paintings of Jimi. When they left, she asked them to stay in contact but not to telephone at the time of a full moon 'because that's when Jimi and I are in communciation. We go travelling together on the astral plane.'

In 1990, Redding and Mitchell (neither of whom had ended up notably affluent) both published autobiographies. One night, Kathy was telephoned by Redding from Ireland, where he now lived, 'in a terrible state and in tears'. Monika, he said, was suing him over a passage in his book, *Are You Experienced*, about her exit from the Samarkand Hotel to buy cigarettes just before realising something was wrong with Jimi. Although she'd recounted this herself, at the inquest and elsewhere, she claimed Redding was accusing her of negligence.

Monika's libel action against Redding went ahead, only to be thrown out by a judge who described her as 'paranoid' and 'vexatious'. The episode led Kathy to reflect on how heavily the official record of Jimi's death leaned on Monika's testimony and to wonder, as few seemed to have done before, just how reliable it was. With her inside knowledge of him, she felt he was being misrepresented in his grave as much as he had been in his life.

She therefore decided to investigate the events of 18 September 1970 for herself and speak to the several eyewitnesses who, inexplicably, had not been called to give evidence at the inquest.

On her own, she had no idea how or where to begin. But it chanced that at the recent launch party for Mitch Mitchell's book, *The Hendrix Experience*, she'd discovered that Mitchell's girlfriend, Dee, shared her doubts about Monika. Dee had formerly worked for the BBC as a researcher, and agreed to join Kathy on her mission.

Dee soon traced the two-man ambulance crew who'd answered the call to the Samarkand Hotel, and whose memories of it remained equally vivid eleven years later.

The first, Reg Jones, recalled that when they arrived, they hadn't needed to ring or knock as the door to the basement room

had been wide open and 'there wasn't another soul in sight.' Jimi
– whom neither Jones nor his colleague, John Saua, recognised
– had been lying on the bed 'with vomit all over him and the
pillow . . . dried, like he'd been lying there a long time' and was
clearly beyond help.

They had called the police on the ambulance's radio and
two young 'beat' bobbies had quickly arrived, neither of them
recognising Jimi. Normally when a body was found in such
circumstances, the plainclothes CID would be called in. But
the policemen, thinking this merely another of the black drug
addicts for which Notting Hill was notorious and keen to shift
the resulting paperwork onto someone else, ordered that he be
taken straight to hospital.

Jones was insistent that he'd found no one else in the basement flat, that no one had gone with Jimi in the ambulance to
St Mary Abbot's and that he'd clearly been dead by the time he
arrived there. When Kathy and Dee talked to John Saua, Jones's
partner that night, Saua corroborated everything he had said.

The pathologist who carried out the post-mortem on Jimi,
Professor Robert Teare, had since died, but his successor at Charing Cross Hospital's medical school, Rufus Crompton, who'd
worked under Teare, agreed to review his report. Crompton
concluded that the Vesparax Jimi took had been enough to kill
him, whether he vomited or not. A toxicologist colleague confirmed that as few as four tablets, each carrying its double dose,
could have been fatal for someone in Jimi's physical condition.

Crompton underlined another detail that had been overlooked
in 1970: that Jimi couldn't have been breathing by the time he
reached St Mary Abbot's because 'his lungs were full of fluid,
half a pint in one of them'.

Jimi's friendship with Eric Burdon gave Kathy easy access to one
of the most crucial but reticent witnesses to the affair. According
to Burdon's 1986 autobiography, he hadn't reached the flat until

after the ambulance's departure and seen only Jimi's 'impression' on the bedclothes. Since his subsequent damaging television appearance, hinting at suicide, he had avoided further public comment.

Now, in a taped telephone conversation with Kathy, he admitted that when he had arrived, half-stoned after a night at Ronnie Scott's, he thought Jimi had still been in the flat but he hadn't liked to look directly at the bed 'because of the mess [i.e., vomit]'. A further character entered the story with Burdon's revelation that before the ambulance arrived, he and his personal manager, Terry Slater – aka 'Terry the Pill' – had cleansed the place of drugs. It was then that he'd seen Jimi's poem, 'The Story of Life', which he'd taken to be a suicide note.

After months of digging that would have done credit to an investigative journalist, Kathy had compiled a dossier that contradicted Monika's version – or, rather versions – of events at almost every turn. Its central point was the weird discrepancy in the timetable of Jimi's death. Monika claimed to have found she couldn't awaken him at around 11 a.m. and the ambulance, its dispatcher's log showed, had been called at 11.18. Yet Burdon and Alvinia Bridges were both adamant that they'd gone to the Samarkand Hotel in answer to her SOS so early in the morning that the cars parked around Lansdowne Crescent were still covered with dew. What had happened during those uncharted hours? Was it possible Jimi had lain there, capable of being resuscitated, as people around him panicked and argued and futilely flushed drugs down toilets?

Kathy sent her file to the Attorney General, who took it seriously enough to instruct the Crown Prosecution Service to reopen the Jimi Hendrix case. The job was given to Scotland Yard's special investigation unit, then designated SO1, headed by a senior officer, Detective Superintendent Douglas Campbell.

Campbell, a fatherly-looking man with whom Kathy developed

a strong rapport, seemed genuinely committed to uncovering the truth about Jimi. Nonetheless, he and his all-male squad, backed by all the technological resources of 'the Yard', did not take the inquiry much further than she had by herself.

A key source was to have been Angie Burdon, who was at Pete Kameron's party when Jimi turned up there a few hours before his death, and recalled other guests shouting through the window at Monika to 'fuck off and leave him alone'. Despite the fog of heroin and alcohol in which Angie now lived, that memory remained clear. But before her testimony could be recorded, she pulled a knife on her man friend of the moment; he pulled one back and stabbed her fatally in the chest.

Other eyewitnesses of Jimi's last night were under no legal compulsion to answer questions and not under oath when they did so. Eric Burdon and Alvinia Bridges were both in America and DS Campbell passed the job of interviewing them over to the FBI. The Bureau's zeal in probing the death of such a prominent figure in its files can well be imagined.

Gerry Stickells said he had nothing to add to his previous statements and it was left at that. Only Terry 'the Pill' Slater cooperated to any extent, saying he had arrived at the flat just as the ambulance was leaving (though he'd previously told Kathy he'd seen Jimi, lying on the bed, looking 'knackered').

Terry the Pill admitted clearing the flat of drugs and burying some in Lansdowne Crescent's communal garden across the road (without mentioning he had gone back the next day to retrieve them but found they had vanished). To his amazement, his interrogators showed him a photograph of himself burying the stash. The regular police had been lying in wait, apparently expecting the whole affair to end with Jimi being busted.

The investigation ended any friendly relations between Kathy and Monika, who at some moments said she welcomed it and at others protested furiously that she was being accused of lying and Kathy was trying to 'reinvent' Jimie's death. Indeed, Campbell's team seemed to have demolished Monika's version of Jimi's ambulance journey to St Mary Abbot's hospital with herself supposedly in attendance, and what had followed. They established that he hadn't been transported sitting in a chair, only brought out of the flat in one because using a stretcher was impossible on the iron spiral staircase up to the street. The hospital's staff had all behaved correctly and, anyway, he'd been dead before they saw him, probably even before he was put into the ambulance.

'[DS Campbell's team] told me they thought Monika was barking mad,' Kathy later wrote, 'but she had her story so well worked out after 20 years, they couldn't do much about it . . . One of them said he thought all the witnesses were f-ing lying for different reasons of their own.'

At the end of a year, Scotland Yard decided there was insufficient new evidence to justify reopening the inquest and terminated the inquiry. A private investigation by a former police superintendent named Dennis Care, initiated by Jimi's father, came to the same dead end not long afterwards.

The London Ambulance Service had conducted its own internal inquiry and in January 1992 issued a statement further undermining Monika's credibility: the ambulance crew had acted 'in a proper and professional manner . . . There was no one but the deceased at the flat when they arrived nor did anyone accompany them in the ambulance to St Mary Abbot's Hospital.'

Nonetheless, there remained an odour of the discrimination Jimi had so seldom suffered in London. He clearly would have been dealt with differently if he'd been in his £112 per-day suite at the Cumberland Hotel, rather than in a bedsit in shabby, racially tense Notting Hill, where he could be tagged as 'just another black junkie'.

'I was told he'd been lucky to get an autopsy,' Kathy recalls.

★

In 1992, the Jimi Hendrix Experience were somewhat tardily inducted into the Rock & Roll Hall of Fame. Neil Young's citation speech, in his usual head-scratching, aw-shucks country-boy mode, told the invariable guitarist's tale of being simultaneously mesmerised, mystified and motivated by Jimi while recognising that he himself could never be more than a humble follower.

'There was no technique that you could take note of . . . no chords I could recognise . . . I didn't know what any of it was . . . I just looked at it and I heard it and I felt it and I wanted to do it and I said to myself that maybe someday I could go to that neighbourhood.'

Mitch Mitchell and Noel Redding, two ageing elves in wingpoke collars, duly received two-thirds credit for the earthquake in which they'd played bit-parts. Al Hendrix was brought onstage, encased in a tuxedo, and received a huge ovation as the man who, it was assumed, had first spotted his son's genius and set him on the road to fame.

Al seemed close to tears. 'I'm just too emotional over these deals,' he muttered, dabbing his eyes with a handkerchief. 'I'm just thankful you all remember Jimi and that's the best I can say.'

A stage full of top rock guitarists past and present – Jimmy Page, Carlos Santana, Keith Richards, Steve Cropper and the Edge from U2 – supported by Redding, Mitchell and a dozen more premier instrumentalists, then played 'All Along the Watchtower' to Neil Young's vocal. It was the kind of jam Jimi would have loved. Yet on that particular song, even those massed maestri couldn't match him on his own.

By the early 1990s, his estate, largely consisting of song-copyright and record royalties, was estimated to be worth around $80 million and to be earning $3 million a year. Yet his sole heir, still lived modestly in Seattle and continued working as a landscape gardener. When, in 1993, Al filed suit against his lawyer and de facto business manager, Leo Branton, many people wondered what had taken him so long.

In 1974, having retrieved Jimi's song copyrights from diverse places on Al's behalf, Branton had assigned the worldwide rights to a Panamanian company named Presentaciones Musicales SA, a tax shelter set up for another of his clients, Nat King Cole. Since PMSA could not do business on American soil, a company named Japage handled domestic matters like negotiating with Warner/Reprise and employing Alan Douglas to produce Jimi's posthumous albums. Al was guaranteed an income of $50,000 per year (subsequently raised to $100,000) which at the time seemed to him munificent.

In 1993, it was announced that Jimi's song catalogue was to be sold on to America's giant MCA corporation by the two other offshore companies who now controlled them in the US and Europe respectively. Al's consent was not needed as he'd signed away his rights to the songs rather than merely renting them out, as he'd supposed. His lawsuit against Branton claimed that in the past twenty years, as Jimi's estate had ballooned in value to $80 million, he'd received only around $2 million. Also named in the suit were Alan Douglas and various other companies that had profited from Jimi since 1974.

Al accused Branton of fraud, not only in grossly underpaying him but negotiating agreements on the exploitation of Jimi in which he'd represented both sides. Branton vehemently denied any wrongdoing and countersued for defamation. Since the Hendrix family could not afford the huge legal costs, they were loaned around $4 million by Paul Allen, the co-founder of Microsoft and a fanatical Jimi fan.

After two years, the case was settled out of court with no outright victory for either side. Al got back Jimi's copyrights together with around $1 million but Branton and his co-defendants were awarded compensatory payments over time, undisclosed to the media but thought to be between $5 million and $10 million.

In Britain, the *Independent* headlined its report on the settlement with a paraphrase of 'Purple Haze', SCUSE ME WHILE I KISS THE PIE.

The 27 Club continued to enrol new members like there was no tomorrow – which, for them, there wouldn't be.

Pete Ham, vocalist and songwriter with Badfinger, once regarded as natural successors to the Beatles, hanged himself in 1975; the artist and musician Jean-Michel Basquiat overdosed on heroin in 1988; Kurt Cobain, lead singer with Nirvana, the second-biggest rock act to come out of Washington state, turned a shotgun on himself in Seattle in 1994; Richey James Edwards, rhythm guitarist and lyricist of the Manic Street Preachers, disappeared without trace in 1995; Amy Winehouse, the most exciting female vocalist since Aretha Franklin, succumbed to 'accidental alcohol poisoning' in 2011.

Yet, rather like fellow guitarists in his lifetime, none of these varied symbols of cruelly curtailed talent could ever compete with Jimi.

In the mid 1990s, a British Hendrix buff named Tony Brown began piecing together what remains the most detailed chronology of his final days. A plumber by trade, Brown approached the task in much the same spirit as clearing a long-silted-up drain.

Like Kathy Etchingham before him, he spoke to the ambulance crew who'd gone to the Samarkand Hotel, Reg Jones and John Saua. Each reiterated that the door to the basement flat had been open when they arrived, that they hadn't recognised the person they were to collect, that no one else had been there to greet them and one else had accompanied them and their charge to St Mary Abbot's Hospital.

As quoted by Brown, their testimony recreated the full grimness of the scene – the curtains drawn; the gas fire full on, sucking every bit of oxygen from the air; the fully dressed figure lying on the double bed on his back. 'If he'd been lying on his side, he'd probably have pulled through,' John Saua said.

Brown also interviewed the two doctors on duty in St Mary Abbot's casualty department that morning, Surgical Registrar John Bannister and Medical Registrar Martin Siefert – neither of whom had known who Jimi was when he arrived. An Australian long working in London, Bannister recalled how they'd had to go through the motions of resuscitating him, even though he was dead and evidently had been for some time, 'hours rather than minutes'.

One part of Bannister's interview gave the story a startling new twist. He said that the effort to revive Jimi had been hampered by 'the large amount of red wine that oozed from his stomach' – this although the post-mortem had found very little alcohol in his bloodstream and, according to Monika Dannemann, he'd had only a sip of red wine that night 'In my opinion,' Bannister told Tony Brown, 'there was no question that [he] had drowned, if not at home, then certainly on the way to the hospital.'

In a subsequent interview with *The Times* of London, Bannister again described the 'masses of red wine oozing out of [Jimi's] nose and mouth' and matting his hair. The two doctors had used a suction device to try to clear his airway but it kept filling up again. 'It was horrific. The whole scene is very vivid because you don't often see people who have drowned in their own red wine.'

Brown talked at length to Monika, for whom he felt great sympathy despite the many holes in her account of Jimi's death and the number of times she had revised it. She'd lately done so yet again in an interview with his old New York mentor Curtis Knight, who was writing a book about their time together in the Squires. Hitherto, she'd claimed to have initially talked Jimi out of taking the Vesparax to get himself to sleep; now she described seeing him with several tablets on his open palm, and knocking them onto the floor.

In the 1980s, she had married the German hard rock guitarist Uli Jon Roth, who cared for her enough to accept there would always be a third, Afro-haired person in their relationship. They'd stayed together for seventeen years, Monika art-directing Roth's album covers as she'd intended to do for Jimi's, and collaborating in writing some of his songs.

She still had the 'Black Beauty' Fender Stratcaster of Jimi's that his roadies turned over to her on the day of his death. Roth would sometimes play it in appearances with his band, the Scorpions, but was intimidated by its still having Jimi's original strings. Monika would never consider selling it, despite the vast offers she received. One, Roth recalls, was $1 million from Microsoft's Paul Allen, another 'seven-eight-nine million from some kind of Arab art dealer'.

Since the Scotland Yard investigation, she had become fiercely hostile towards Kathy Etchingham, viewing her as an ally no longer but a rival. In 1994, Kathy was shown the manuscript of a book Monika was hawking around British publishers that amounted to a declaration of war. It alleged Jimi had warned her to beware of Kathy because she was a liar and a cheat and had stolen all his possessions.

Kathy sued for defamation and the case went to the High Court in London. It was settled, however, when Monika agreed to apologise, undertook not repeat her false allegations and paid token damages of £1,000.

In 1995, she brought out a different book, entitled *The Inner World of Jimi Hendrix*, with the stated aim of revealing 'his personal and spiritual essence'. Published by the respected house of Bloomsbury, it was a glossy production, containing the colour photographs she'd taken of Jimi in the Samarkand Hotel's garden on his last day alive and the portraits of him she had painted since. It carried warm endorsements from Al Hendrix, Al's wife June, and adopted daughter Janie, whom she'd visited in Seattle and who accepted that she'd been Jimi's fiancée.

There was huge sadness in her pictures of him with just a few hours left, looking exhausted and a little lost as he posed with Black Beauty, half-hidden by foliage, or poured tea from the china pot. And the portraits were remarkable likenesses, good enough for any album cover. Mostly they showed a Jimi in various states of performing rapture, but the blue one of him standing with arms wrapped protectively around Monika, her flaxen head pillowed on his chest, finally won her some of the sympathy she'd hitherto been denied.

The evidently ghostwritten text was divided between a commentary on the paintings, with asides on Jimi's powers as 'a traveller in time and space', and a catalogue of the victimisation Monika claimed to have suffered, culminating in Scotland Yard's inquiry into his death. Kathy was not named but her mocking characterisation as 'a Miss Marple-type fan' – after Agatha Christie's spinsterly amateur sleuth – was instantly recognisable and the dossier with which she'd triggered the inquiry was dismissed as 'fantasy'.

It was clearly a breach of Monika's court-imposed undertaking to make no further damaging allegations against Kathy. But, rather than crank up the legal process again, Kathy gave an interview to America's *Musician* magazine which spurred its editor, Bob Doerschuck, to make his own investigation of Monika.

The magazine's cover story concluded that her relationship with Jimi had been little more than that of star and groupie and certainly not the idyll she claimed. Doerschuck had even managed to track down Philip Harvey, the young Lloyd's underwriter who had witnessed her berating a mortified Jimi just hours before his death.

When the article appeared, Kathy heard nothing from

Monika. Then she discovered someone was spreading a malicious story involving not only herself but her doctor husband: that he'd married her after saving her life when she was found on the street suffering from a heroin overdose. There was no doubt that Monika was the perpetrator and no alternative for Kathy but to take her back to the High Court.

In those days, the UK media could gleefully bill the case as a 'catfight' between two of Jimi's old girlfriends. Before the hearing, Monika seemed to exude confidence, posing for a photo spread in *Hello!* magazine with no less a supporter than his father, Al.

But in court, it was a different story. 'The contrast between the two women could not have been more stark,' noted the *Independent*. 'Dannemann with her Marianne Faithfull fringe, a superannuated rock chick, and Etchingham in the sleek nineties bob and the executive suit. While Dannemann's life had frozen on the day Jimi died, Kathy, a mother of two, had had the sense to let the sixties go.'

Monika's efforts to ingratitate herself with the judge, including giving him a copy of her book, were in vain. She was found guilty of contempt and left the High Court with her last shreds of credibility blown away.

The next day, 1 May 1996, she went into her garage, connected two pieces of hose to the twin exhausts of her new Mercedes, fed them through its front windows, then got in, switched on the engine and waited for the carbon monoxide fumes to kill her, perhaps comforted by those images of Jimi as a space-traveller and an angel and of his arms around her and her head pillowed on his sky-blue chest.

She was fifty.

EPILOGUE
THANKS, JIMI

I n 2002, Al Hendrix died from heart failure, aged eighty-six, after years of declining health. His second wife, June, having predeceased him, the bulk of the estate he'd inherited from Jimi, by now worth well in excess of $80 million, went to June's daughter, Janie, whom Al had adopted and who'd effectively taken over its management.

Eleven other family members, including Janie's four siblings, received minor bequests. But Jimi's closest surviving blood relation, his younger brother, Leon, got nothing. Well, not quite nothing; he received one of Jimi's Gold Discs, picked out for him so not one of the most significant. It rankled all the more because of Jimi's cavalier way with such awards. 'He'd just throw his Gold Discs in the bottom of a closet,' Leon recalls. 'Or use them to chop up weed.'

According to Leon, Al had always promised he would inherit a quarter of the estate in a trust fund, known as 'Bodacious' – his father's indulgent word for his rebellious nature – to benefit his six children. Now it transpired that in 1998, Al had made a new will with no such provision.

The effect was to plunge the whole Hendrix extended family into turmoil. Leon sued Janie and his cousin Bobby Hendrix, who helped run the estate, for exerting 'undue influence' over his ailing father to disinherit him. The lawsuit also bore the names of seven other family members, including Janie's sister,

Linda, who were dissatisfied with their bequests.

Janie and Bobby replied that the will came as much a surprise to them as to Leon, but that Al had been in in full possession of his senses when he'd altered it and that prior to his death he and Leon had been 'estranged' owing to the latter's drug use and constant demands for money.

By the time the case came before Washington State's supreme court in 2004 there was an additional claimant to a share of Jimi's posthumous wealth. This was Joseph Hendrix, the first of four children in a row with serious birth defects to whom Al's first wife, Lucille, had given birth after Jimi and Leon. Joe had been the only one of the four to spend any time at home rather than being institutionalised in babyhood and Jimi had never forgotten the anguish of seeing him taken away when his care became too great a burden to Al.

Despite Joe's obvious physical resemblance to Al, the judge ordered a DNA test to establish his parentage beyond any doubt. With Al deceased, the only way of comparing his DNA with Joe's was to use a sample he'd given some years earlier while fighting a paternity suit (suggesting he and Jimi hadn't entirely lacked common ground). Against that, Joe tested negative and his claim was dismissed to the audible outrage of his family members in the courtroom.

In the matter of the will, the star witness for the plaintiff was the redoubtable Aunt Delores, who had been such an ally to Jimi and Leon when they were small and who had herself benefited so little from her famous nephew that now, aged 84, she was living on social security. She testified Al had told her directly that Leon would be taken care of and, like all his blood relatives, reiterated how much Jimi would have wanted it.

The judge accepted that Janie had exercised a degree of influence over Al and said that his decision might also have been prompted by Leon's drug history and financial demands.

However, all that concerned the court was the validity of the will – i.e. whether Al had fully understood what he was doing, and undoing, when he signed it. The verdict was that he had and Leon's claim was dismissed.

The advent of DNA testing was unable to help a party whose potential claim on Jimi's estate superseded Al's – the boy born to Swedish student Eva Sundquist in 1969 as James Henrik Daniel Sundquist and subsequently pronounced by a Swedish court to be Jimi's only son. Indeed, he had grown up with a startling re-semblance to Jimi around the mouth and eyes, but no discernible talent on the guitar or any other instrument.

Although the Swedish court's 1975 ruling carried no weight in America, Al Hendrix met James as a seven-year-old and, through his then lawyer Leo Branton, agreed to settle four million Swed-ish kronor, around $1 million, on the boy. But in 1994, now aged 24 and renamed Jimi Hendrix Junior, he filed suit against Al in Los Angeles, accusing his putative grandfather of concealing the full extent of Jimi's estate from him. To convince the American courts of his legitimacy, he told *Rolling Stone*, he would seek a DNA test, even if meant exhuming Jimi's remains.

The lawsuit was not pursued, however, and he now report-edly lives quietly in Stockholm as Sasha James Henrik Daniel Hendrix.

The new century continued to throw up TV documentaries and articles about Jimi's death, all boasting 'revelations' that seldom withstood serious scrutiny and invariably casting Mike Jeffery as the arch-villain, since he was dead and thus unable to sue for libel.

In 2004 came an American TV doc, *Jimi Hendrix: The Last 24 Hours*, directed by Mike Parkinson, with contributions from Steve Roby, Chuck Wein and Melinda Merryweather who had worked with Jimi on the *Rainbow Bridge* documentary. This

'revealed' that Jeffery had a background in British military intelligence and had been robbing Jimi blind, but added the new
wrinkle that he'd deliberately sabotaged Jimi's career – including
planting the heroin found on him in Toronto – to thwart his new
experimental music and get him back to playing what the fans
wanted.

The film was full of suggestions that Jimi's death had been
'a political assassination' by the FBI for his support of the Black
Panthers or as part of the CIA's MHCHAOS programme or else
Jeffery's revenge for his defection. What it *wasn't* full of were
Jimi's actual last twenty-four hours, which were depicted mostly
in blurry 'reconstructions' with actors not only playing Jimi and
a Monika Dannemann without a trace of German accent, but
also the ambulance-men collecting him from the Samarkand
Hotel and doctors trying to resuscitate him at St Mary Abbot's
hospital.

In 2009, the memoirs of the Animals' former roadie and fellow
Tynesider James 'Tappy' Wright levelled more specific charges against Mike Jeffery. At the time of Jimi's death, according
to Wright, Jeffery was desperate for money, having borrowed
$30,000 from the Mafia to pay his taxes 'and then [the Mob]
wanted $45,000 back'. Jimi had recently signed a life-insurance
policy for $2 million, 'which meant he was worth more to Mike
dead than alive'.

Jimi Hendrix: The Last 24 Hours had also seized on this idea,
but it was a fallacy. Insurance companies routinely provided pol-
icies on major rock stars – like the one for $1 million covering
Jimi's hands – but the beneficiaries were record companies not
managers.

In an interview with the American author Harry Shapiro for
Classic Rock magazine, Tappy Wright claimed to have received
Mike Jeffery's drunken confession, not long before Jeffery's own
violent death, that he'd had Jimi murdered. 'I had no bloody

choice,' he supposedly confided. 'It was either that or I'd be broke or dead.'

As at so many other points in Jeffery's career, there was an echo of the cult film about Newcastle's gangland that ends with Michael Caine as Jack Carter pouring a bottle of whisky down his victim's throat before clubbing him to death. 'It was like that scene in *Get Carter*,' Wright told Shapiro. 'Some villains from up north . . . and booze down the windpipe.' He hadn't spoken up before, he said, for fear that something equally unpleasant might happen to him.

You might think there could be no more credible insider but for two things. Firstly, Tappy had a book to promote and secondly, he also retailed the myth that Jeffery had 'staged' Jimi's kidnapping in New York in 1969 when it had been all too dangerously genuine.

Noel Redding died in 2003 from complications arising from cirrhosis of the liver, aged 57. His mother, Margaret, who so adored Jimi, had predeceased him by only three weeks. He is commemorated by a plaque in the Irish village of Ardfield near his last home, a square named after him in his native Folkestone and a special edition of the Fender jazz bass. At the time of his death he was preparing to sue Jimi's estate for £3.26 million in alleged 'lost earnings' from his time in the Jimi Hendrix Experience.

Mitch Mitchell kept playing drums for Jimi to the last, in the 'tribute' shows constructed around him in the same way as for Frank Sinatra, Michael Jackson and the Freddie Mercury-less Queen.

Mitchell's latter years were dogged by financial anxiety. In 1994 he had sued the British publishers of a new edition of David Henderson's biography *Scuse Me While I Kiss the Sky* for alleging that Redding and he had used racial slurs in front of Jimi. In a decision one cannot imagine being handed down today, the court ruled that back in the 1960s, it had been acceptable banter; Mitchell lost his libel action and subsequent appeal and had to pay costs of around £100,000.

In 2008, he died in his sleep in Portland Oregon after the final show of an eighteen-city Jimi tribute tour also featuring Billy Cox and Buddy Guy. Aged 61, he was one of a rare breed of rock musician whose deaths have been attributed to natural causes.

Many other key figures in the story are no longer around to enlarge further on it: Chas Chandler and Gerry Stickells and Devon Wilson and Buddy Miles and Angie Burdon and Bill Graham and Mike Nesmith and Philip Harvey and Curtis Knight and Gavin Thurston, the coroner whose inquest into Jimi's death was so laughably inadequate as to suggest some plot.

One of the two hospital doctors who tried to resuscitate Jimi, Martin Siefert, has since died but the other, John Bannister, has gone on to merit a biography in his own right. Returning to his native Australia in 1972, Bannister left medicine to become a property developer in Sydney and Perth, then, aged 67, started a company named Macquarie Medico Legal, offering finance for medical reports in personal injury cases, which he sold in 2016 for $Aus20 million.

Bannister vividly recalled the late morning when a young black male whom neither he nor Martin Siefert recognised was brought into St Mary Abbot's A&E department, 'very blue and very cold, with his whole upper part covered in vomit,' having been dead, at Bannister's rough estimate, 'for two or three hours . . . certainly before he was put into the ambulance'.

Bannister also reiterated his statement of four decades earlier that 'about a bottle of red wine' seemed to have been poured over Jimi, since his hair was matted with it, and that, rather than choking on the copious vomit, he had 'drowned in wine'.

Ironically, the young doctor who had to ask colleagues 'Who's Jimi Hendrix?' became a passionate devotee of his music in later life. 'All these years afterwards, I still get phone calls from his fans who've somehow tracked me down and want to hear the story first-hand.'

Leon Hendrix is now in his early seventies but could pass for fifty, a small, trim figure with an (admittedly grey) ponytail, dark glasses and a straggly rock 'n' roll beard. His utter dissimilarity to Jimi is heightened by his brother's Afro-aureoled face on the T-shirt under his black satin blouson.

He recalls how, as a thirteen-year-old who'd previously emulated eighteen-year-old Jimi in everything, he asked their father to buy him a guitar, too. Al refused, 'because he said he didn't want to have two idiots in the family.'

Then when he was twenty, Jimi gave him one of his own guitars and offered to teach him to play. But Leon had lost interest in the idea ('I found I could get girls without playing music') so he slung the gift into a corner and forgot about it during his subsequent careers as a draughtsman at the Boeing plant, landscape gardener, band-booker and crack cocaine-dealer.

It wasn't until he was fifty and at rock bottom that, by his account, he received a fraternal wake-up call from the Hereafter. One night, lying in bed in a drugged stupor, he saw the guitar Jimi had given him suddenly start to vibrate in its corner as if physically shaking off the years of neglect. A purple flame lit the room ('purple is the colour of royalty in the spirit world') and he seemed to hear Jimi's voice inside his head say, 'What do you want to do, Leon? It's been long enough and it's time for you to pick up that guitar. It's all you have left.'

He began learning to play and with that came the motivation to kick his long-ingrained cocaine habit. 'I got off of drugs completely . . . went to Eric Clapton's Crossroads centre in Antigua. Noel Redding was there at the same time.'

Nothing approaching Jimi's genius fell on him at that late

stage, but he has since earned a livelihood from songwriting, re-cording and performing. He makes regular British tours, albeit at rather small venues in out-of-the way places like Hunstanton, Norfolk, and Eastleigh, Hampshire, where the Hendrix name never fails to draw its measure of grey-haired, stooping men in pastel polo-shirts who were once frantic, kaftaned hippies.

During these years, he has seen Experience Hendrix, the corporation headed by his adoptive sister Janie, encompassing record-royalties, publishing, merchandising and the numerous other income-streams generated by Jimi's 'name and likeness', grow into the fifth-highest-grossing deceased-superstar estate after Elvis Presley's, John Lennon's, George Harrison's and Bob Marley's.

Leon's share of all this is zilch. 'But, hey, I'm cool with that,' he insists, rather too frequently. 'Life's too short to bear malice. I'm a happy camper.'

He has always been certain that Jimi's death was foul play. 'Music in the Sixties was like the wild west – guns, briefcases full of cash, the Mob. I've no doubt that my brother was murdered. I just want to know who did it.'

The usual suspects line up for their identity parade: Mike Jef-fery, in revenge for Jimi's defection . . . the Mafia, because he belonged to them and was getting out of line . . . the FBI or CIA, for playing 'The Star-Spangled Banner' at Woodstock. Although no shred of evidence against any of them has ever emerged, Leon accepts the roadie Tappy Wright's scenario of a contract killing, bolstered by John Bannister's testimony that 'Jimi drowned in wine' and the revelation of the American military's 'enhanced interrogation' techniques during the Iraq War. 'I believe he didn't choke on his vomit, man, like has been said all these years. He was *waterboarded*.'

By Leon's account, Jimi's spirit did not confine itself to that single purple-lit visitation, but has watched over him ever since, just as when they were children. The visions have not been confined to him, nor purely supervisory. 'Now I've given up drinking, my only pleasure is women. But I still can't compete with my brother. Some of my girlfriends tell me Jimi has come to them in a dream and made love to them.

'I'm Bluetooth to Jimi's wi-fi. Sometimes when I'm onstage performing and get stuck on a chord, I'll ask him, "What do I do now?" And he always tells me, "Reach for it."'

There remains, of course, one person who could furnish a definitive account of what went on in a stifling Notting Hill basement around the lonely silhouette stretched on the double bed. But he hasn't yet done so, even to Jimi's closest relative. 'I've never had any straight answers from Eric Burdon,' Leon Hendrix says.

Burdon declined to be interviewed on the subject for this book because he was working on 'his own Jimi Hendrix story'. That may finally illuminate the 'lost' hours between Monika Dannemann's realisation that something was wrong with Jimi and his removal to St Mary Abbot's hospital.

The former Kathy Etchingham has settled in Australia with her husband. Recently, when her teenage grandchildren discovered Jimi's music, Kathy didn't reveal she had once lived with him, and changed the subject by suggesting they listen to the Beatles instead.

Yet the memory still burns bright of the shy, funny, fastidious, chaotic, considerate, shameless guy with whom she spent two and a half stormy years and, less happily, of the sad shadow he'd become when she bumped into him at Kensington Antique Market on the last afternoon of his life. 'I felt bad because I didn't accept his invitation to drop by and see him at the Cumberland,' she recalls. 'But if I had done, I wouldn't have found him there.'

She remains convinced that Jimi never intended to spend the night of 17/18 February with Monika in her room.

'I think he'd only called in there to pick up his guitar and then he was going to go back to the party he'd just left. But she must have begged him to stay and Jimi never could say "no".'

'The fact is that they got together on the Tuesday and by the Friday he was dead. I don't know whether Monika fed him the Vesparax tablets or he took too many by accident [possibly in his fuddled state thinking they were relatively harmless Mandrax]. But it would never have happened if he hadn't been in the clutches of a crazy fan and his physical resistance hadn't been so low that just a few were enough to kill him.'

'In 1970, we didn't know anything about stalkers who went after celebrities and that they could be women as well as men, who fantasised that the person they were stalking was madly in love with them.'

She recalled how, when the two were still on friendly terms, Monika had taken her aside and pumped her for personal information about Jimi, as it later seemed, to add credence to her portrayal of his fiancée. But one detail that remained constant through all her versions of his last hours convinced Kathy that she'd never really known him.

'That was when she talked about making Jimi two tuna fish sandwiches – one of the few things he'd never have asked for or eaten. He hated tuna. We both did.'

Over the years, Jimi has invested rainy, hilly Seattle with some of the same glamour that Presley gave to Memphis and the Beatles to Liverpool, and made it a similar place of pilgrimage. Its monorail-girt city centre now boasts a museum financed by his greatest corporate fan, Microsoft's Paul Allen, dedicated jointly to his music and the sci-fi he loved, and housed in a Frank Gehry-designed building representing a smashed-up guitar. There is also a Hendrix Music Academy, run by his niece, Tina, and offering free tuition, instruments, mentoring and even food to young talent that might otherwise go to waste, as his own very nearly did.

In 1970, he had been interred in Greenwood Memorial Park beneath a modest headstone, inscribed 'Forever In Our Hearts'. But as his posthumous value grew, his remains were moved to a more prominent position – beneath a domed gazebo thirty feet high, supported by three columns of 'rainbow' marble etched with images of his face and quotations from his songs, which now attracts around 60,000 visitors a year.

A row of tablets commemorate his father, his Japanese-American stepmother, June, and his grandmother, Zenora. His mother, Lucille, however, was left in her pauper's grave under her second husband's surname of Mitchell. For that reason alone, one can surmise that Jimi may never rest entirely in peace.

Other monuments are scattered at random throughout the city and its environs: a life-size bronze statue, playing guitar down on one knee in the Capitol Hill district; an Afro-headed bust in the library of James A. Garfield High School; a 'memorial rock' at Woodland Park Zoo; a Jimi Hendrix Post Office Building in the suburb of Renton.

A local entrepreneur named Pete Sukov claimed to have identified the very house in the old Central District where Jimi lived between the ages of ten and thirteen and first strummed on a one-string ukulele salvaged from a heap of gardening refuse. When the house was marked for demolition to make way for a new apartment block, Sukov bought it and had it transported whole to a trailer park he'd acquired for the purpose, near Greenwood cemetery.

There it mouldered until the local authority pronounced it 'an eyesore' and ordered its demolition. But Sukov salvaged a few hopefully appreciating fragments – kitchen cabinets, a claw-footed bathtub and the back door.

So with the wider world: there is a Jimi Hendrix Hotel in

Essaouira, Morocco, where he spent the only real vacation of his life. Just off Grafton Street in Dublin stands an Afro-haired, guitar-playing statue generally believed to be of Jimi, though it's actually of Phil Lynott from Thin Lizzy.

Each May Day in the city square of Wrocław, Poland – the self-appointed 'Guitar Heart of Europe' – an event known as the Thanks Jimi Festival attempts to break its previous year's record for how many players, both professional and amateur, plus special guests like his brother Leon, can get together and perform 'Hey Joe'. Since the first such 'guitar forest' in 2003, the number has risen from 588 to 7,411.

For London, the city that first glorified then destroyed Jimi, he has become a tourist attraction like Big Ben, Royal Horse Guards in plumed helmets and breastplates or the Yeoman Warders of the Tower. In 1997, Kathy Etchingham persuaded the English Heritage organisation to award a blue plaque to number 23 Brook Street as the former home of James Marshall Hendrix, 'guitarist and songwriter,1942–1970', joining the one to George Frideric Handel, 'Composer 1685–1759' outside number 25 next door.

Thenceforward, the two houses and musical émigrés were amalgamated in a joint museum with collections of eighteenth-century instruments on the lower floors and a recreation of the flat Jimi and Kathy used to share at the top. It is known as Handel and Hendrix in London, evoking a double-act of Afro hair and shoulder-length periwig, knee-breeches and crushed velvet flares, a combustible guitar and *Water Music*.

At Marble Arch, the Cumberland Hotel has been rebranded the Hard Rock Hotel following its acquisition by the American restaurant-chain in 2018. With its drenching neon and memorabilia-hung walls, it is an alternative Hall of Fame for past musician guests from Buddy Holly and the Crickets to Bob Dylan, Stevie Wonder and Diana Ross. But by far the greatest cachet bequeathed by the old Cumberland is to have been Jimi's favourite hotel, even given as 'usual address' on his death-certificate.

Sadly, though, the most poignant of his later London haunts wants nothing to do with him. In now madly chic Notting Hill, the Samarkand still operates as an hotel, but in the American style of self-contained apartments, catering mostly to overseas student and conference groups and bookable only online. Its leafy double frontage in Lansdowne Crescent shows no name nor any sign of being in the hospitality business. Beside its locked main door, a small brass plaque reads PRIVATE HOTEL NOT OPEN TO THE PUBLIC. NO INQUIRIES PLEASE.

Access to the basement flat is unchanged from when Jimi and Monika used to come and go – the same iron spiral staircase down to a white front door with a pastiche Victorian look. A padlocked gate at the stairhead prevents any closer inspection.

The hotel has the same private owner it did in 1970, Henry Danvers Hall, better known as 'Danny'. And it soon becomes clear what kind of 'inquiries' he doesn't want. According to the female caretaker of the next-door house, Jimi's death on his premises remains a taboo subject with Danny Hall; fifty years on, he still refuses to talk about it – sometimes even admit to it – apparently viewing it as a curse rather than a major commercial opportunity. (Think what some people would pay to spend a night in the room where Jimi Hendrix died.)

For a long time, the next-door's caretaker was mystified by the tour buses that regularly stopped outside the Samarkand and the bouquets of flowers left at the impassable threshold down to the its basement. Finally, one of Mr Hall's hotel workers let slip the reason, but she has never dared to raise the matter with him.

My phone call to the Samarkand is answered by Mr Hall himself. Perhaps mistaking me for a potential booking, he is initially polite, even rather playful. But at the mention of Jimi's name, he shouts 'I'm not interested!', threatens to call the police if I don't stop bothering him and bangs the receiver down.

The most surprising – and charming – Jimi monument is to be found on the Isle of Wight, a place he visited only once for a few hours to co-headline the Foulk brothers' mighty 1970 pop festival eighteen days before his death.

It is a life-size bronze statue recognisable in every detail from its Fender Strat to its trailing sleeves. The statue was commissioned from the sculptor John Swindells by John Giddings, whose modern festivals have continued to bring top music names to the island, although not on the Foulks' epic scale.

Originally, Giddings hoped it would be erected on Afton Down, the site of the 1970 festival. Jimi, he argued, had as much cultural significance as the island's most famous resident poet, Alfred Lord Tennyson, whose own monument stands at the summit of Tennyson Down just south of Totland. But the National Trust, which owns this whole tract of wind-furrowed grassland, baulked at creating a coastal counterpart to Handel and Hendrix in London . . . Tennyson and Hendrix in Wight?

Instead, the statue found a home in the garden of Dimbola Lodge in Freshwater Bay, a house once owned by the great Victorian portrait photographer Julia Margaret Cameron. Some local residents thought it inappropriate – but what a subject for Cameron Jimi would have made. And his braided hussar jacket would have been quite familiar to her.

From his plinth there's a magnificent view of Afton, its white cliffs and the rocky shore below that inspired Tennyson's miniature masterpiece, *The Eagle*:

> *. . . Close to the sun in lonely lands*
> *Ring'd with the azure world he stands.*

357

WILD THING

The wrinkled sea beneath him crawls.
He watches from his mountain walls . . .

The perfect setting for a sea-air guitar rendering of 'All Along the Watchtower'.

SOURCE NOTES

Chapter 1: 'He was hearing music but he didn't have an instrument . . .'
Interviews with Leon Hendrix. *Voodoo Child* documentary, dir. Bob Smeaton, 2010. *Jimi Hendrix: Starting At Zero, His Own Story*, edited by Alan Douglas and Peter Neal, Bloomsbury, 2013. *Room Full of Mirrors: A Biography of Jimi Hendrix* by Charles R. Cross, Sceptre, 2006. *My Son Jimi* by James A. Hendrix, Aljas Enterprises, 1999.

Chapter 2: 'Jimmy was a hippy before anyone knew what a hippy was'
Paul McCartney: the Life by Philip Norman, Weidenfeld & Nicolson, 2016. *Slowhand: The Life and Music of Eric Clapton* by Philip Norman, Weidenfeld & Nicolson, 2018. Jimmy's statement to Seattle police, 1961. *Voodoo Child* documentary. *Starting At Zero*, ed. Alan Douglas and Peter Teare. Extract from Jimmy's service record, 1961. Interviews with Leon Hendrix and Billy Cox.

Chapter 3: 'I still have my guitar and amp . . .'
Conversation with Billy Cox. *Room Full of Mirrors* by Charles R. Cross. YouTube clip of Larry Lee. 'Black Gold: the Secret of the Motown Millions' by Philip Norman, *Sunday Times Magazine*, 1970. Conversation with Wilson Pickett, 1973. 'Harlem's Cool Side: the Apollo theatre' by Philip Norman, *Sunday Times*

Magazine, 1968. *Showman, the Life of David O. Selznick* (Hattie McDaniel episode), Andre Deutsch, 1993. Interview with Fayne Pridgon in *Gallery* magazine, 1981. YouTube clip of Isley Brothers.

Chapter 4: 'Everything's so-so in this big raggedy city of New York'

Interview with Leon Hendrix. *My Son Jimi* by James A. Hendrix. Article on Stax Records by Philip Norman, *Sunday Times Magazine*, 1973. Interviews with Little Richard, 1985 and 1996. *Room Full of Mirrors* by Charles R. Cross. YouTube clip of Joey Dee.

Chapter 5: 'I've got just the person for you'

The Stones by Philip Norman. Interviews with Linda Porter, formerly Keith. *No Direction Home: The Life and Music of Bob Dylan* by Robert Shelton, Omnibus Press, 1986. *Stoned* by Andrew Loog Oldham, Vintage, 2003. Online interview with Robbie Robertson. Interview with Trixi Sullivan. *I Used to Be an Animal but I'm All Right Now* by Eric Burdon, Faber & Faber, 1986. *The Life and Times of Little Richard: the Quasar of Rock* by Charles White, Harmony, 1984.

Chapter 6: 'Quite honestly, Chas . . . he's almost too good'

Interviews with Linda Porter, Trixi Sullivan, Rod Harrod, Zoot Money, Kathy Etchingham, Keith Altham. E-mail to Peter Trollope from Vic Briggs. Cutting from *Newcastle Journal*. *The Profession of Violence* by John Pearson, 1972. *Slowhand* by Philip Norman. *Stone Free: Jimi Hendrix in London September 1966-June 1967* by Jas Obrecht , University of North Carolina Press, 2018. YouTube clip of Brian Auger. Online memoir by Terry Reid.

Chapter 7: 'Oh my God, I'm not God any more'

Through Gypsy Eyes: My Life, the Sixties and Jimi Hendrix by

Kathy Etchingham., Gollancz, 1998. *Eric Clapton: the Auobiography*, Arrow 2008. *Are You Experienced: The Inside Story of the Jimi Hendrix Experience* by Noel Redding and Carol Appleby, Fourth Estate, 1990. *The Hendrix Experience* by Mitch Mitchell, Mitchell Beazley, 1990. *My Son Jimi* by James A. Hendrix. Interviews with Trixi Sullivan. YouTube interview with Chris Squire.

Chapter 8: 'Go out and buy us a tin of lighter fuel'
Interviews with Keith Altham, Kathy Etchingham. *Through Gypsy Eyes* by Kathy Etchingham. *Slowhand* by Philip Norman. YouTube clips of Eddie Kramer, Roger Mayer. *Are You Experienced* by Noel Redding and Carol Appleby. *The Hendrix Experience* by Mitch Mitchell. *On Ilkley Moor: The Story of an English Town* by Tim Binding, Picador 2001. *Stone Free: Jimi Hendrix in London* by Jas Obrecht, University of North Carolina Press, 2018. *Jimi Hendrix: The Final Days* by Tony Brown, Omnibus Press, 1997.

Chapter 9: 'Not on my network'
Slowhand by Philip Norman. *Eric Clapton: Life in 12 Bars*, documentary dir. Lili Fini Zanuck, 2017. *Sunday Mirror*, August 1967. *Who I Am: The Autobiography of Pete Townshend*, HarperCollins, 2012. *Rhytmi* magazine (Finland), July 1967. *The Stones* by Philip Norman. *Monterey Pop* documentary, dir. D. A. Pennebaker, 1967. *Are You Experienced* by Noel Redding and Carol Appleby. *Paul McCartney: the biography* by Philip Norman.

Chapter 10: 'From rumor to legend'
Interviews with Linda Porter, Trixi Sullivan, Keith Altham, Zoot Money, Kathy Etchingham. *Gallery* magazine, 1981 interview with Fayne Pridgon. *Through Gypsy Eyes* by Kathy Etchingham. *Los Angeles Times* and *Esquire* magazine June–July 1967. YouTube clip of Mickey Dolenz. *Bill Graham Presents: My Life Inside Rock*

and Out by Bill Graham with Robert Greenfield, Da Capo Press, 2004.

Chapter 11: 'He was a life-saver'
Interviews with Trixi Sullivan, Neville Chesters, Robert Wyatt, Sharon Lawrence, Leon Hendrix. *Jimi Hendrix: A Brother's Story* by Leon Hendrix with Adam Mitchell, Thomas Dunne Books, 2012. *Seattle Post-Intelligencer* story on Pat O'Day. 'Cynthia Plaster Caster' interview on BraveWords website. *Room Full of Mirrors* by Charles R. Cross. *Jimi Hendrix: The Man, the Magic, the Truth* by Sharon Lawrence, Sidgwick & Jackson, 2005. *Are You Experienced* by Noel Redding and Carol Appleby.

Chapter 12: Electric Ladies
Interviews with Trixi Sullivan, Kathy Etchingham, Neville Chesters, Linda Porter. BBC-TV clip *A Happening for Lulu*, Jan. 1969. *John Lennon: The Life*, *The Stones* and *Slowhand* by Philip Norman. *Through Gypsy Eyes* by Kathy Etchingham. *The Hendrix Experience* by Mitch Mitchell. *Are You Experienced* by Noel Redding and Carol Appleby. *Handel in London* by Jane Glover, Macmillan, 2018.

Chapter 13: 'I'm going to die before I'm thirty'
Interviews with Leon Hendrix, Kathy Etchingham, Colette Harron, formerly Mimram, Sharon Lawrence. *The Stones* by Philip Norman. *Small Town Talk: Bob Dylan, The Band, Van Morrison, Janis Joplin, Jimi Hendrix & Friends in the Wild Years of Woodstock* by Barney Hoskyns, Faber & Faber, 2016.

Chapter 14: 'Nothing but a Band of Gypsies'
Interviews with Linda Porter, Trixi Sullivan. *Woodstock* documentary, dir. Michael Wadleigh, 1970. *Small Town Talk* by Barney Hoskyns. *New York Post* articles by Al Aronowitz passim.

The Hendrix Experience by Mitch Mitchell. *Gallery* magazine interview with Fayne Pridgon. *American Desperado: My Life as a Cocaine Cowboy* by John Roberts and Evan Wright, Crown, 2011.

Chapter 15: Miles and Miles
Interviews with John McLaughlin, Sharon Lawrence. *Dick Cavett Show*, ABC-TV, 9 September 1969. *Paul McCartney: the Biography* and *Mick Jagger* by Philip Norman. *The Hendrix Experience* by Mitch Mitchell. *Miles: the Autobiography by Miles Davis*, Picador 1987. *Bill Graham Presents* by Bill Graham and Robert Greenfield. *Small Town Talk* by Barney Hoskyns. Al Aronowitz article, Rock's Backpages website.

Chapter 16: 'Dad, my love . . .'
Interview with Aaron Dixon. Jimi's FBI file. *Jimi Hendrix: A Brother's Story* by Leon Hendrix. *Through Gypsy Eyes* by Kathy Etchingham. *Are You Experienced* by Noel Redding and Carol Appleby. *The Hendrix Experience* by Mitch Mitchell. *Room Full of Mirrors* by Charles R. Cross. *Rainbow Bridge* film, dir. Chuck Wein, 1971. Interview clips with Wein and Melinda Merryweather. Online article by Steve Roby.

Chapter 17: 'Hey, man, lend me your comb'
Interviews with Linda Porter, Kathy Etchingham, Colette Mimram, Stephen Clackson, Keith Altham, Ronnie and Ray Foulk, Sharon Lawrence. *Message to Love* documentary of IOW Festival, dir. Murray Lerner, 1997. *The Final Days of Jimi Hendrix* by Tony Brown, Omnibus Press, 1997.

Chapter 18: 'Just call me helium'
Interviews with Stephen Clackson, Keith Altham, Sharon Lawrence, Kathy Etchingham, Leon Hendrix, John Pearse, Eve

Slater (widow of 'Terry the Pill'). YouTube clip of Alvinia Bridges. *The Hendrix Experience* by Mitch Mitchell. *Slowhand* by Philip Norman. *The Final Days of Jimi Hendrix* by Tony Brown. *Until We Meet Again: The Last Weeks of Jimi Hendrix* by Caesar Glebbeek, UniVibes, 2011.

Chapter 19: 'Goodnight Sweet Black Prince'

ABC news bulletin announcing Jimi's death. Interviews with Leon Hendrix, Kathy Etchingham, Trixi Sullivan, Ronnie Foulk, Keith Altham, Sharon Lawrence, Linda Porter. *Jimi Hendrix, the Man, the Magic, the Truth* by Sharon Lawrence. *Scene and Heard* programme on BBC Radio 2. *Wonderful Tonight; George Harrison, Eric Clapton and Me* by Pattie Boyd with Penny Junor, Three Rivers Press, 2007. *The Final Days of Jimi Hendrix* by Tony Brown. Alvinia Bridges clip on YouTube. *I Used to Be an Animal but I'm All Right Now* by Eric Burdon. *The Hendrix Experience* by Mitch Mitchell. *Are You Experienced* by Noel Redding and Carol Appleby. *Seattle Post-Intelligencer* funeral coverage. *Jimi Hendrix: A Brother's Story* by Leon Hendrix.

Chapter 20: 'A tall black guardian angel in a hat'

Interviews with Linda Porter, John Porter, Trixi Sullivan. *Jimi Hendrix: the Music, the Magic, the Truth* by Sharon Lawrence. Articles by Seymour M. Hersh on MHCHAOS, *New York Times*, December 1974. Article on difficulties over Jimi's estate 'A Piece of Jimi Hendrix's Rainbow' by Jerry Hopkins, *Rolling Stone*, December 1976.

Chapter 21: 'Scuse Me While I Kiss the Pie'

Interview with Kathy Etchingham, Leon Hendrix. *Through Gypsy's Eyes* by Kathy Etchingham. Interview with Monika Dannemann by Caesar Glebbeek, 1975. Settlement of lawsuit against Leo Branton, *Washington Post*, July 1995. *The Inner World of Jimi Hendrix* by Monika Dannemann, Bloomsbury, 1995. Interview with Dr John Bannister re Jimi's time of death.

Epilogue: Thanks, Jimi

Interviews with Leon Hendrix. 'Jimi's Swedish-born son, Jimi Hendrix Junior fails to win share of his estate', *Rolling Stone*, 1994. *Jimi Hendrix: The Last 24 Hours* documentary, dir. Mike Parkinson, 2004. 'Leon Hendrix claim on brother's esate is rejected', *New Musical Express*, September 2004,. Tappy Wright interview with Caesar Glebeek, *Classic Rock*, 2009.

ACKNOWLEDGEMENTS

This book enormously benefited from the lengthy and detailed interviews which Jimi's brother, Leon, gave me during his British tour in June 2018. I owe a similar debt of gratitude to the two most important women in Jimi's life, the former Kathy Etchingham and Linda Keith, and to the former Trixi Sullivan for her unique observations of Jimi's manager, Mike Jeffery.

Special thanks to my research associate Peter Trollope, who first alerted me to the fiftieth anniversary of Jimi's death and showed his customary brilliance in tracing sources. I'm also grateful to the UK's two foremost Hendrix experts, David Stubbs and Roger Smith, for fact-checking the manuscript, and to Diana Donovan for allowing the late Terence Donovan's sumptuous portrait of Jimi to appear on the cover of the UK edition.

Thanks also to Alan Samson, who commissioned the book; Peter Matson, my long-time agent and friend in New York; Lucinda McNeile, my ever-supportive editor; Fiona Petheram, Jonathan Sissons and Tim Binding at Peters, Fraser & Dunlop; Felicity Price for her empathetic legal reading, Cathy Dunn for her dedicated picture research far beyond the norm, and Susan Howe, Rights Director at Orion.

My heartfelt gratitude for their invaluable help to Keith Altham, Dr John Bannister, Carole Bedford, Pattie Boyd, Vic Briggs aka Antion Vikram Singh, Alexandra Burkholder, Chris Charlesworth, Neville Chesters, Stephen Clackson, Billy Cox,

ACKNOWLEDGEMENTS

Brenda Cox, Aaron Dixon, Magdalena Fijalkowska, Ray Foulk, Ronald Foulk, Brian Fraser, Natasha Fraser-Cavassoni, Rod Harrod, Nicky Hayward, Sharon Lawrence,Tom McGuinness, Zoot Money, John Pearse, Ron Pluckrose, John Porter, Gail Rebuck, Karl Simpson, the late Chris Stamp, Chris Welch and Robert Wyatt.

Dedicated to Sue and Jessica, as always, and to the memory of Michael Sissons.

Philip Norman,
London 2020.

PICTURE CREDITS

The author and publisher are grateful to the following for permission to reproduce photographs:

p.1 (above) Getty/Hulton Archive; (below) Getty/Estate of David Gahr; p.2 (above) Getty/Gilles Petard; (below) Getty/Estate of David Gahr; p.3 (above) Getty/Michael Ochs Archives; (below) Shutterstock/Barry Peake; p.4 Getty/Jan Olofsson; p.5 (above) Alamy/Trinity Mirror/Mirrorpix; (below) Shutterstock/Polak; p.6 Getty/Ed Caraeff/Morgan Media; p.7 Getty/GAB Archive; p.8 Getty/Rolls Press/Popperfoto; p.9 Alamy/Trinity Mirror/Mirrorpix; p.10 Getty/Hulton Archive; p.11 Getty/Fred W. McDarrah; p.12 Getty/Corbis Premium Historical; p.13 Getty/Fred W. McDarrah; p.14 Getty/William Vanderson; p.15 Shutterstock/Jon Freeman; p.16 Getty/Michael Ochs Archives.

ABOUT THE AUTHOR

Philip Norman was born and brought up on the Isle of Wight. He joined the London *Sunday Times* at the age of twenty-two, after winning a nationwide contest for young writers, and became a renowned interviewer for its iconic colour magazine with subjects ranging from Elizabeth Taylor and Little Richard to P.G. Wodehouse and Libyan dictator Colonel Muammar Gaddafi. In 1981, he published *Shout!*, a ground-breaking biography of the Beatles which has remained in print ever since, and is still regarded as the definitive history of the band. This was followed by internationally bestselling biographies of the Rolling Stones, Elton John, Buddy Holly, John Lennon, Mick Jagger and Paul McCartney.

INDEX

A Happening For Lulu (BBC) 200, 201
Acklen, 'Uncle' Teddy 44
Adler, Lou 150, 154
Albritton, Cynthia 180–1
Aleem, TaharQa and Tunde Ra
    236–7, 238, 272
Alfred, Lord Tennyson 1
Ali, Muhammad 213
Allen, Hoss 46
Allen, Paul 338, 341, 353–4
Allsop, Kenneth 309–10
Altamont Raceway, California 247,
    282, 283
Alterman, Lorraine 256
Altham, Keith
  and Chandler 133
  hears of Jimi's death 306
  interviews Jimi 163, 285–6
  on Jimi 122
  journalist 9, 101, 125
*American Desperado: My Life as a Co-
    caine Cowboy* (Roberts) 240–1
American music 8
Animals, The 83–5, 91, 92, 121, 125
  'The House of the Rising Sun'
    84–5
Apollo Theater, Harlem 52, 237–8
Arden, Don 92, 125
Aronowitz, Al 80, 234, 252

Atkins, Chet 45
Atlantic Records 70
Auger, Brian 101, 102
'Auld Lang Syne' 251

Badfinger 339
Bag O'Nails club, London 98, 104,
    122, 132, 141
Bahamas 92–4
Baker, Ginger 103–4, 297
Ballard, Hank 33
Ballin' Jack 258
Band of Gypsys
  album covers 256
  appearances 253
  end of 255
  Miles and 325
  songs 254
    'Auld Lang Syne' 251
  US success 256
  live album
    A Band of Gypsys 251, 251–2,
    256
Band, The
  albums
    Music from Big Pink 225
Bannister, John 340, 349–50, 351
Bardot, Brigitte 227
Barrett, Eric 300, 307–8

Barry, Jack 109–10

Basquiat, Jean-Michel 339

Baxter, Jeff 'Skunk' 78–9

BBC 72

BBC radio 124, 286, 306

Beach Boys, The 43, 61

Beatles, The
  cover versions 148
  end of 269
  and Klein 246
  in New York 55–6, 66
  see Jimi play live 7, 126, 149
  style 72
  unknown 29
  albums
    Rubber Soul 121
    Sgt.Pepper's Lonely Hearts
      Club Band 1, 148, 149, 168
  songs
    'Robert' 182
    'Got to Get You into My Life'
      109
    'Sgt. Pepper's Lonely Hearts
      Club Band'. 278

Beck, Jeff 132

Bel, Madeline 305

Belafonte, Harry 253

Benfante, Andy 241

Benson, Ernestine Jeter (Aunt) 24,
  30, 177, 178

Berry, Chuck 24, 133–4, 185
  'Johnny B. Goode' 30, 59, 259

Best, George 286

Big Apple club, Munich 114

Big Brother and the Holding Company 151

Big Maybelle 237, 238

Bild-Zeitung (newspaper) 309

Bill Graham Presents (Graham) 156

Billboard 306–7

Black and White Minstrel Show (BBC)
  113–14

black musicians 23, 72

Black Panther Party for Self-
  Defense 211–12, 213, 236,
  259–62, 286

Black Power movement 211–15, 236,
  251

Blackwell, Robert 'Bumps' 26, 59

Bland, Bobby 'Blue' 45

Blind Faith 284

Blood, Sweat & Tears 253

Bloomfield, Mike 87, 190

Blue Mink 305

blue plaques 355

Bob Dylan and The Band
  albums
    The Basement Tapes 225

Bob Fisher and the Bonnevilles 49

Bobby Taylor and the Vancouvers
  47

Booker T. and the M.G.'s
  'Green Onions' 58

Borrero, Carmen 189–90, 218,
  234–5, 237–8, 245

Bowie, David 319

Boyle, Mark 184

Branton, Leo 324, 338

Breakaways, The 112

Brian Auger Trinity 108, 112

Bridges, Alvinia
  Jimi's death 309, 311, 334, 335
  and Judy Wong 308
  and Monika 290, 300–1, 307
  at party 292

Briggs, Vic 101–2, 108, 112

Brook Street, Mayfair 9

Brooks, Rosa Lee 60–2

Brown, James 51, 179, 211, 214
Brown, Maxine 237
Brown, Peter 246
Brown, Tony 339–40
Brubeck, Dave 253
Bruce, Jack 103–4, 126, 149, 201, 255
Buddy and Stacey 63–4
Buddy Miles Express 244, 258, 316
Burdon, Angie (née King)
    and Jimi 298–9
    and Kathy 135, 142, 165, 210, 274
    slide into addiction 221, 330, 335
Burdon, Eric
    and The Animals 84–5
    background 142
    BBC interview about Jimi's death
        309–10
    and Bridges 300
    divorce 210
    on Jimi 114, 118, 189–90
    and Jimi 333–4
    and Jimi's death 311, 318, 335
    and Jimi's funeral 314, 315
    and Monika 308–9
    new Animals line-up 106–7
    in New York 151
    refuses interview 352
    solo career 94
    War 291, 293, 308
    I Used to Be an Animal but I'm All
        Right Now 300–1, 334
Burke, Solomon 50, 51
Burns, Tito 134
Burroughs,, William S. 121

Café Au Go Go 83, 87, 159–60
Café Wha?, New York 78, 79, 85
Cameron, Julia Margaret 357
Campbell, Douglas 334–5, 336

Campbell, Glen 61
Capitol Records 256
Care, Dennis 336
Carlos, John 212
Carpenter, Diane 68–9, 216–17,
    287
Casady, Jack 198, 219, 243
Cat Mother 319
Cavett, Dick 223, 242
CBS Records 130
Chalpin, Ed
    contract with Jimi 120
    Jimi records with 160
    lawsuit against 168–9, 205, 250,
        287, 292, 320–1
    record boss 65–6, 256
Chandler, Chas
    Animals' bass-player 6, 93–101
    background 116
    control and 168
    and Cream 103
    funds album 130
    health 195
    and Jeffery 158
    and Jimi 115
    on Jimi and acid 133
    Jimi visits 292–3
    and Jimi's death 318
    and Jimi's drugs trial 249
    Jimi's manager 9, 85, 86–7, 106–8
    manager 181, 269
    money at airport 120
    producer 112
    rejected by Jimi 195–7
    returns 202
    rings Jimi 298
    sees Jimi live 280
    34 Montagu Square 121, 134,
        135–6

Upper Berkeley Street 162
Chapman, Thomas 129
Charles, Ray 14, 34, *35*, 55
Checker, Chubby 70
Cheetah Club, New York 71, 75
Chelsea Pensioners 118
Chesters, Neville 172–3, 174, 181,
    183, 186
Chicago Seven trial (1969) 215
Chiffons, The 149
'Chitlin' Circuit'
    Apollo Theater 52
    drugs and 55
    hard times on 115
    James Brown and 79
    Little Richard and 59
    segregation 6, 186
    style 63
    travelling on the 48
Chong, Tommy 47
Christgau, Robert 155, 199
CIA 325, 347, 351
Civil Rights Act (1964) 186
Civil Rights movement 7, 62–3, 65,
    211
Clackson, Stephen 273–4, 306
Clapton, Eric
    background 102–4
    biography 8
    childhood 29
    'darling Jimi' 141, 293
    drugs-bust 203
    hears of Jimi's death 306
    on Jimi 140–1
    Jimi's idol 86
    learning guitar 25
    sees Jimi live 110, 142, 149
Clarke, Jenny 90, 91
Classic Rock (magazine) 347

Cliff Bennett and the Rebel Rousers
    109
Cline, Patsy 279
Club A' Go Go, Newcastle 90–2, 327
Club Baron, Nashville 45, 49
club-owners 43
Cobain, Kurt 339
Cocker, Joe 148
COINTELPRO (FBI Counter Intel-
    ligence Program) 212, 214–15,
    216, 247
Cole, Nat King 338
Collins, Bootsy 17
Columbia Records 79, 87
Cooke, Sam 50, 52, 53, 54, 63
Coronation Street (ITV) 127
corruption 124–5
Cox, Billy 48–50
    Band of Gypsys 223, 228, 255
    drink spiked 280–1
    guitar guarantor 46
    and Jimi 220, 250
    Jimi Hendrix Experience 243, 255,
        258, 270
    Jimi tribute tour (2008) 349
    on Jimi's guitar 43
    King Kasuals 44, 45
    military service 38–9, 40, 42
    no lump sum 324
    paranoia 283, 284–5, 290
    supportive 51
Cox, Brenda 39, 51
Crabbe, Buster 16
Cream
    and Chandler 103
    headliners 148
    power trio 108, 146, 200–1, 202
    roadies 174
    see Jimi live 126

Cream—*contd*
  albums
    Disraeli Gears 140
  songs
    'Sunshine of Your Love' 126,
      201
credit cards 206
Creedence Clearwater Revival 220
Crompton, Rufus 333
Cromwellian Club, London 97, 108
Cropper, Steve 58, 337
Crosby, Bing 12
Crosby, Stills and Nash 258
Crying Shame 40
Cumberland Hotel, London 294–8
  Jimi stays at 284, 286, 288, 291,
    292
  Jimi's overdose at 301, 336
  link with Jimi 355–6
  passing messages on 289
  reputation of 275
Curtis Knight and the Squires 65,
    71, 75, 160, 169

Daily Mirror (newspaper) 312
Daley, Richard 187
Daltrey, Heather (née Taylor) 138
Daltrey, Roger 138, 152
Danelectro Silvertone guitar 33, 174
Dannemann, Klaus Peter 293
Dannemann, Monika 289–302,
    307–12, 330–2
  argument with Jimi 335
  and Brown 340–3
  death 343
  and Jimi 207, 318
  and Kathy 335–6
  marriage 341
  meets Jimi 201–2

The Inner World of Jimi Hendrix
    341–2
Daughters of the American Revolu-
    tion 159
Davis, Angela 324
Davis/Hendrix collaboration 245–6
Davis, Jr., Sammy 150
Davis, Miles 244–6, 276, 277, 288,
    315
  Kind of Blue 245
Day, Anne 295, 296, 318
de Freitas, Michael (Michael X) 213
Decca Records 121
Dee, Joey 66–8
Del Morocco club, Nashville 44
Denny Laine's Electric String Band
    149
Denver Pop Festival (1969) 220
Dexter, Jeff 278
Dick Cavett Show (US TV) 242
Dixon, Aaron 261
Doerschuck, Bob 342
Doggett, Bill
  'Honky Tonk' 32
Dolenz, Micky 159
Don Covay & the Goodtimers
  'Mercy Mercy' 57, 58
Doors, The 9, 156, 276, 278
Douglas, Alan 287–8
  and Jimi 291
  record producer 224, 246
  and studio tapes 327, 338
Douglas, Stella 223–4
  on Jimi 288, 291
  Kameron's party 298–9
  and Monika 295
  in Morocco 226
  at party 292
  and Wilson 287

Driscoll, Julie 101
drug scene 74–5
Dunbar, Aynsley 107, 108, 147
Dylan, Bob
  on album cover 256
  appearance 76
  goes 'electric' 84
  hears of Jimi's death 306
  Isle of Wight festival 230, 268–9
  Jimi's idol 79–80, 243, 249
  moves to Woodstock 224–5
  albums
    Blonde On Blonde 76–7
    Highway 61 Revisited 65–6
    John Wesley Harding 1
  songs
    'All Along the Watchtower'
      1–4, 193–4
    'Like a Rolling Stone' 65, 79
    'Rainy Day Women numbers
      12 & 35' 76–7

Easy Rider (film) 264
Edge, The (U2) 337
Edwards, Richey James 339
Eire Apparent 172, 182
  albums
    Sunrise 195
Electric Flag, The 190
Electric Lady Studios, New York
  270–1
  beginnings 222, 244, 266
  Jeffery and 319
  launch party 272
  Lawrence visits 320
  Leon and 288
Ellington, Duke 48, 224
Elliott, Cass 153, 157
EMI label 121

Ephron, Mike 229
Epiphone Wilshire guitar 46
Epstein, Brian 75, 83, 126, 310
Eric Burdon and the New Animals
  106
Esquire (magazine) 155
Etchingham, Kathy
  affair with Jimi ends 221
  and Angie Burdon 135, 142, 165,
    210, 274
  arguments with Jimi 134–6
  background 97
  and Coronation Street 127
  first marriage 257, 329
  hears of Jimi's death 305
  and Jimi 114–18, 162
  on Jimi 294
  Jimi 'goes mad' 274–5
  and Jimi's death 329–36, 352–3
  Jimi's possessions 275
  and Jimi's promiscuity 165, 209
  and Keith Moon 141
  later life 352
  life after Jimi's death 339
  and Linda Keith 99–100
  meets Jimi again 257–8
  and Michael X 213
  on Mitchell 147
  and Monika 335–6, 341–3
  on Monika 353
  on Noel 107
  second marriage 329, 343
  sells story 329
  23 Brook Street 203–5
  Through Gypsy Eyes: My Life, The
    60s, and Jimi Hendrix 111, 257
Evening Standard (newspaper) 305,
  330
Experience Hendrix 351

Expressen (newspaper) 145
Eye (magazine) 173

Fabulous (magazine) 125, 126
Factory, The (Warhol studio) 198
Fairport Convention 268
Faithfull, Marianne 73, 143, 144
Fame, Georgie 97, 107
Farmer, Philip Jose 130
'Fat Jack' Taylor 54–5
Fat Mattress 197, 255
Fats Domino 148
FBI
    COINTELPRO program 212,
        214–15, 216, 247
    file on Jimi 216, 234, 248, 253
    and Jimi's death 335, 347, 351
    and The Panthers 261
    rock musician list 212
    and Salvation 2 241
Fender Jazzmaster guitar 69, 70, 78,
    307–8
Fender Stratocaster 55, 57, 83, 86, 96,
    174, 293, 294
Festival of Love and Peace, Feh-
    marn (1970) 282–3
festivals 7, 9, 150–5, 185, 218–20,
    229–34, 260, 268–9, 273–9
Fillmore auditorium, San Francisco
    156, 174
Fillmore East, New York 250–2
Findlay, Dave 92
Findlay, Tommy 90, 92
Fitzgerald, Ella 52
Fitzgerald, F. Scott 185
Flack, Roberta 12
Fleetwood, Mick 272
folk music 77
Foulk, Bill 268, 276

Foulk brothers 276–7
Foulk, Ray 9, 276, 278, 279
Foulk, Ronnie 268, 269, 276, 312–13
Fowley, Kim 130
Franklin, Aretha 179
Free Press (newspaper) 191
Freedland, Nat 190–1
Freedom of Information Act, US
    325–6
Freeman, Bobby
    'C'mon and Swim' 57
Fricker, E. G. 328
Fritsch, Johannes 145
Fugs, The 80
Fuller, Buckminster 264

Gallery (magazine) 161, 235
Garcia, Jerry 189
Garfield High School, Seattle 30–1,
    35, 178–9
Garland, Tony 95, 101
Gautier, Freddie Mae (aunt) 314, 315,
    323
Gehry, Frank 353–4
Generation Club, New York 221
Georgie Fame and the Blue Flames
    107
Get Carter (film) 89, 90
Ghetto Fighters 236
Giddings, John 357
Gilmour, Dave 278–9
Gimme Shelter (film) 246–7
Glebbeek, Caesar 330
Golden Triangle label 64
Goldstein, Michael 173, 216
Goldstein, Roberta 75, 82, 87–8, 166,
    313
Gorgeous George 58
Got That Feeling; Jimi Hendrix Plays,

Curtis Knight Sings (Chalpin) 169

Graham, Bill 156, 174, 251–2

Granny Takes A Trip (London boutique) 117, 279

Grateful Dead, The 63, 80, 152

Great Dixieland Spectacle 12–13

Grech, Rick 284

Green, Richard 122

Greenwich Village, NY 77

Greenwood Memorial Park, Washington 354

Grehan, Ray 90

Grossman, Albert 77, 224

groupies 157–8, 191, 192, 209

Guthrie, Arlo 253

Guy, Buddy 221, 349

Gypsy Sun and Rainbows 230–4, 242–3
   Harlem concert 237–8
   Salvation 2 club 239–40
   Woodstock set 233–4
   songs
      'Machine Gun' 242, 245

Hair (musical) 253

Hall, Danny 356–7

Hall, Delores Jeter (Aunt) 28, 345

Hallyday, Johnny 108–9, 111–12, 227

Ham, Pete 339

Hammon, Ronnie 258

Hammond Jr., John 79, 87, 143, 183, 315

Hampton, Fred 261

Handel and Hendrix in London (museum) 355

Handel, George Frideric 204, 205, 355

Harborview Hospital, Seattle 263

Harlem, New York 52

Harold Davison booking agency 269, 313

Harrison, George 200

Harrod, Rod 96, 98–9

Hart, Lorenz 137

Hartley, Pat 265, 266, 292

Harvey, Arthur Vere, Baron Harvey of Prestbury 295, 318

Harvey, Philip 295, 296, 318, 342

Havens, Richie 77–8, 87, 253, 277

Heath, Junior 34

Hello! (magazine) 343

Hell's Angels 247, 283

Henderson, David 330–1, 348

Hendricks, Bertran (paternal grandfather) 13

Hendricks family 22

Hendricks, Zenora (paternal grandmother) 13, 21–2, 46–7, 188–9, 315, 354

Hendrix, Al (James Allen) (father) 13–28
   birth defects 13
   boxer 14
   childhood 13–14
   death 344
   divorce 18–19
   gambler 19
   hears first album 176
   and Jimi 29, 37, 51, 187–8
   Jimi's death and funeral 304, 313, 314–16
   and Jimi's estate 320, 337–8
   and Jimi's financial affairs 322–3
   and Leon 261
   meets and marries Lucille 14–15
   military service 15
   and Monika 342, 343

Hendrix, Al—*contd*
  patches up marriage 17–18
  remarries 111
  reunited with Jimi 16, 177–8
  Rock & Roll Hall of Fame induction 337
  and saxophone 30
  work 19, 22, 32
  My Son Jimi 111
Hendrix, Al junior (brother) 19, 263
Hendrix Band of Gypsys 256
Hendrix, Bobby (cousin) 344–5
Hendrix, Janie (step sister) 177, 188, 342, 344–5, 351
Hendrix, Jimi ('Buster'/James Marshall)
  amp misuse 108
  appearance 5, 75
  arrives in London 94–5
  bank account 206, 294
  'Black Beauty' Fender 294, 307, 341, 342
  blue plaque 355
  brought to London 6–7
  busking 81
  causes criminal damage 170
  Chalpin lawsuit 168–9, 320–1
  change of name 16
  childhood 11, 15–28
  children and paternity suits 69, 217, 280, 287, 325, 346
  CIA file 326
  contracts 65, 120, 139, 150, 160, 250, 287, 320–1
  death 4, 7, 8, 301, 330–6
  announced 303–4
  case reopened 334–6
  diary 206
  disappears 225

  drug-use 141, 165, 219
  amphetamine use 49
  cocaine 202
  LSD 77, 80, 148, 152, 218
  marijuana 67, 137
  drugs charges and trial 215–17, 247–50
  education 30–1, 35
  electric guitars 26, 30, 41, 53, 55, 78
  fashion icon 173–4
  FBI file 216, 234, 248, 253
  first audition 31
  first guitar 24–5
  'flirtatiousness 136
  foster mother 16
  on gigging 51
  'goes mad'. 274–5
  goes to New York 51–2
  Gold Discs 344
  guitar abuse 83, 86, 97, 114, 122, 127, 148, 153, 174
  guitar-burning 134, 153
  guitar-playing style 5, 60, 159
  hair 43, 54, 81, 88, 178
  has hands insured 185
  homes
    Benedict Canyon 191
    Greenwich Village property 243, 319
    Shokan home 225, 228, 230, 243
    34 Montagu Square 121, 162
    23 Brook Street 9–10, 203–5, 257, 355
    Upper Berkeley Street 162–3
  illness 281
  interviews 126, 136, 144–5, 181, 219, 252, 273, 280, 285–6, 326
  jamming sessions 83, 95, 183, 218,

245, 259

joyriding 36

Kameron's party 299

kidnapped in NY 240, 348

left-handed 16–17, 25

love-letters 54

memorial concerts 323

military service 7, 35–8, 39, 40–1, 212–13

monuments to 354–5, 357

mood-swings 82

music in childhood 22, 25

music press 113, 122, 155, 168, 256, 303

name changes 61, 65

'Octavio' foot pedal 132

outfits 32, 34, 57–8, 60, 62, 115–16, 161, 175, 232, 251, 265

on parents 17–18

perfectionist 167–8

pets 21, 162–3

photo-shoots 6, 125, 294

post-mortem and inquest 309, 311–12

press 145, 163–4, 237

promiscuity 6, 44, 60, 67, 81, 147, 161, 189, 209, 275, 286

record collection 116–17, 205

relationship with father 16, 68, 110–11, 113, 261, 263, 267

relationships 33, 36, 38, 41, 60–2, 68–9, 186–7. See also Borrero, Carmen; Dannemann, Monika; Etchingham, Kathy; Morgan, Betty-Jean; Nefer, Kirsten; Pridgon, Lithofayne 'Fayne'; Sundquist, Eva; Wilson, Devon (Ida Mae)

and religion 259

returns home 161

science fiction passion 117, 130, 264

session musician 50–1

song catalogue 338

song-copyrights 338

spiked drink 254

Stingray car 183, 191

'The Story of Life' (poem) 298, 307, 308, 312, 317, 318–19

studio musician 57, 64

takes overdose 300

Tarot reading 227

tv appearances 63–4, 222–3, 242

violence towards women 189–90, 235, 274

and whisky 28, 137, 170, 189, 235, 262, 275, 280

'will' and estate 275, 313, 322, 337–8

Hendrix, Joseph (brother) 18, 263, 345

Hendrix, June (Ayako Jinka) (stepmother) 111, 177, 187–8, 261, 342, 354

death 344

Hendrix, Kathy (sister) 18, 263

Hendrix, Leon (brother)

behaviour 193

on Burdon 352

childhood 18–22

criminal 176

drug rehab 350

drug-use 178

and father 261

and father's estate 344–5

gang member 187

hears first album 176

jailed 260, 288

Hendrix, Leon (brother)—*contd*
  and Jimi 26, 214, 350
  Jimi Hendrix Memorial Foundation 323
  on Jimi's CIA file 326
  Jimi's death and funeral 304, 314–15, 316, 351–2
  and Jimi's effects 320
  on Jimi's kidnap 240–1
  on Jimi's songs 167
  later years 350–1
  on Little Richard 27
  and Little Richard 60, 259
  musician 350–1
  on Jimi 23, 24, 50, 57, 192
  and Ray Charles 35
  reunited with Jimi 177–8
  spends time with Jimi 189
  A Brother's Story 176
Hendrix, Lucille (née Jeter) (mother) (*later* Mitchell)
  background 15
  and children 18–20
  divorce 18–19
  and Jimi 31, 115, 315
  marriage 14–15, 17–18
  pauper's grave 354
  remarriage and death 27, 167, 263
Hendrix Music Academy, Washington 354
Hendrix, Pamela (sister) 19, 262–3
Hendrix, Pearl (aunt) 188, 189
Hendrix, Tamika Laurice James (daughter) 69, 217, 287, 325
Hendrix, Tina (niece) 354
Henry, Clarence 'Frogman' 46, 57
Hersh, Seymour M. 325
Hillman, John 120
Hoffman, Abbie 215

Hoffman, Mark 75, 76, 81, 82, 313
Hollies, The 167
Hollingworth, Roy 273
Holly, Buddy 48, 279
Hollywood Bowl, Los Angeles 161–2, 190
Honey (magazine) 125, 126
Hooker, John Lee 185
Hoover, J. Edgar 212, 214–15, 253
Hopper, Dennis 264
Hotel Opalen, Gothenburg 169–70, 280
Howe, Deering 224, 226, 243
Howlin' Wolf 25, 73
'Killing Floor' 104
Humperdinick, Engelbert 133, 134
Hyde Park Towers, London 95–6, 114, 121
Hynson, Mike 265

Ilkley, Yorkshire 128–9
Imperials, The 45
Impressions, The 49–50
Independent, The (newspaper) 339, 343
interracial relationships 13
Island Studios, London 258
Isle of Wight Festival (1969) 230
Isle of Wight Pop Festival (1968) 268
Isle of Wight Pop Festival (1969) 275–6
Isle of Wight Pop Festival (1970) 9, 268–9, 273–9, 357
Isley Brothers 57–8, 64
  'Testify' 57
  'Twist and Shout' 55–6

Jackie (magazine) 125
Jackson 5 8

Jackson, Gregory 303
Jagger, Mick 142–4
    advice for Jimi 247
    and Devon Wilson 157, 271
    and drugs 189
    drugs-bust 212
    Epstein and 83
    hears of Jimi's death 306
    on Jimi 150
    and Marianne Faithfull 73
    performances 222
    and Sharon Lawrence 282
James, Elmore 25, 61
James, Etta 53
James, Thomas 34
Jansch, Bert 278
Japage (company) 338
Jefferson Airplane 63, 80, 156, 268
Jeffery, Gillian 116, 321
Jeffery, Mike 89–95, 108
    appearance 320
    background 346–7
    bribes 125
    Chalpin lawsuit 287, 292
    club owner 221
    The Cry of Love album 327
    Foulk brothers and 269
    and guns 119
    Jimi's death and funeral 304–5,
        314, 315–16
    interviews 318–19
    and Jimi's death 312, 319, 347
    and Jimi's drugs trial 248
    Jimi's fear of 300
    and Lawrence 320
    manager 7, 84, 99, 101–2, 116, 172,
        181, 185, 201, 202, 237–43, 288
    and Maui island 263–4
    plane death 321–2

on record 167
resentment 177, 188, 190
'spikes' Jimi's drink 254–5
strained atmosphere with Jimi
    228–9, 267
and Trixi 119–20
and USA 149–54, 155
in Woodstock 224
'Jimi Hendrix Chord' 130
Jimi Hendrix Experience, The
    album covers 137–8, 163, 168, 199,
        270
    board games 128
    contracts 166
    cover versions 259, 278
    Cry of Love tour 258–63
    demise of 197–9
    drug-use 182, 200
    European tour 164–6, 201, 269,
        283
    European tours 7
    experience racism 186
    first live recording 185, 202
    and gonorrhea 147
    Hallyday tour 108–12
    Hawaii 263
    highest-paid performers 218
    Isle of Wight Pop Festival 277–9
    and Jeffery 146
    last gig 220–1
    and Martin Luther King's death
        185
    play 'Sgt. Pepper's Lonely Hearts
        Club Band' (song) 149
    'Purple Haze' 339
    Rainbow Bridge 264–7, 319
    reform 255
    Rock & Roll Hall of Fame induc-
        tion 337

Jimi Hendrix Experience, The—*contd*
    Scandinavian tours 166, 169,
        280–1
    supports The Monkees 158–9
    Top 10 hits 125, 133
    touring 126–8, 133, 146–8, 164–5
    tv appearances 122, 123, 149, 162,
        200, 202
    US success 164, 194, 200, 327
    US tours 156–62, 172–94, 209
    albums
        Are You Experienced 131, 137–9,
            148, 163–4, 176
        Axis: Bold as Love 166–8, 190,
            270
        Crash Landing 327
        The Cry of Love 326–7
        Electric Ladyland 2, 183, 190,
            198, 199–200, 205
        First Rays of the New Rising Sun
            271
        The Jimi Hendrix Concerts 327–8
        Midnight Lightning 327
        Rainbow Bridge 327
    songs
        'All Along the Watchtower'
            1–4, 193–4, 198, 199, 337
        'Angel' 326
        'Astro Man' 271, 326
        'Blue Suede Shoes' 259
        'Burning of the Midnight
            Lamp' 163
        'Castles Made of Sand' 28, 50,
            167, 226
        'Dolly Dagger' 271
        'Drifting' 50, 271
        'EXP' 166
        'Fire' 132, 138–9
        'Foxy Lady' 138, 188, 279

'Freedom' 271
'God Save the Queen' 278
'Gypsy Eyes' 205
'Hey Joe' 110, 112, 121, 125, 130,
    137, 153, 193, 200, 201
'I Don't Live Today' 138
'If 6 Was 9' 167
'Izabella' 223
'Killing Floor' 110
'Land of 1,000 Dances' 110
'Little Wing' 50, 166
'Lover Man' 223
'Machine Gun' 259
'May This Be Love' 138
'Night Bird Flying' 271
'Purple Haze' 129–30, 132–3,
    137, 149, 150, 153, 155, 179,
    193, 259
'Red House' 138, 279
'Scorpio Woman' 266
'Send My Love to Linda' 271
'She's So Fine' 167
'Slow Blues' 272
'Spanish Castle Magic' 166–7
'The Star-Spangled Banner' 7,
    190, 233, 238, 242, 326, 327
'Stone Free' 113
'Straight Ahead' 271
'Third Stone From The Sun'
    138
'Up From the Skies' 166
'Voodoo Child' 259, 283
'Voodoo Child (Slight Return)'
    199, 200, 201
'Wait Until Tomorrow' 166
'Wild Thing' 104–5, 110, 153, 174
'The Wind Cries Mary' 135–6,
    137, 138, 149, 155
'Johnny B. Goode' 259

'Jimi Hendrix, Juma, Mike and Friends' (bootleg recording) 229

Jimi Hendrix Memorial Foundation 322–3

Jimi Hendrix Memorial Park 322, 323

Jimi Hendrix: The Last 24 Hours (tv documentary) 346–7

Jimi Plays Berkeley (documentary) 319

Jimi tribute tour (2008) 349

Jimmie & Vella 319

Jimmy James and the Blue Flames 79, 85, 137

Jinka, Donna (step sister) 178

Jinka, Linda (step sister) 178, 344

Jinka, Marsha (step sister) 178

Joe Cocker 220

Joey Dee and the Starliters 66–8

John, Elton 9, 148

John Mayall's Bluesbreakers 102

Johnny Carson Show (NBC) 223

Johnny Guitar (film) 24

Johnson, Lyndon 325

Johnson, Pete 155

Johnson, Robert 103, 104, 131

Jones, Brian
  on album cover 256
  background 143
  death 222, 223
  drug-use 97, 144
  drugs-bust 203
  girlfriends 73, 115
  and Jimi 151, 152, 193–4, 208–9
  lead guitarist 83
  and Morocco 226

Jones, Davy 158

Jones, Johnny 45, 46

Jones, Nick 122, 168

Jones, Peter 122

Jones, Quincy 31, 66, 228

Jones, Reg 332–3, 339

Joplin, Janis 151, 156, 183, 317

Kameron, Pete 295, 298, 311, 335

Katz, Dick 269, 313

Kay guitars 25, 30

Kearney, Pete 80

Keith, Alan 73, 74, 87–8

Keith, Linda 73–83
  arguments with Jimi 138
  and Brian Jones 85–7
  daughters 328
  on Devon Wilson 157–8
  drug treatment 239
  drug-use 208
  hears of Jimi's death 313
  and Jimi 96, 117–18, 165–6, 208–9, 239, 275
  Jimi dedicates songs to her 279
  Jimi visits 271–2
  and Jimi's publishing 275
  and Kathy Etchingham 99–100
  and Keith Richard(s) 142
  marries Porter 328

Kellgren, Gary 198

Kennedy, John F. 185–6

Kennedy, Robert 185

Kershen, Lawrence 271, 275, 313

King, Albert 45

King, Angie *see* Burdon, Angie (née King)

King, B. B. 3, 45, 46, 183

King Kasuals 39–41, 43–4, 46, 48–9, 220, 225

King, Dr Martin Luther 63, 184–5, 211, 261

Kingsway Studios, London 112, 130, 137
Klein, Allen 52, 197, 246
Klein, Sheila 74
Klubb Karl club, Sweden 169–70
Knight, Curtis 65, 71, 75, 160, 340
Kooper, Al 183
Korner, Alexis 100
Kramer, Eddie
 engineer 131, 132, 137, 138, 166, 198
 and first live recording 185
 on Jimi 168
 Jimi calls 295
 posthumous album 326
Kray Twins 91

Lambert, Kit 99, 121–2
Lang, Michael 229–30, 232
Lawrence, Margaret 175, 217–18
Lawrence, Sharon
 background 8–9
 interviews Jimi 175, 192–3, 213–14, 216
 on Jimi 187–8
 and Jimi 217, 248–9, 282, 291–2
 Jimi's death and funeral 308, 314, 317–18
 meets Jimi 175–6
 and Monika 308
 phones Jimi's hotel 296–7
 visits Jimi's apartment 319–20
Lazenby, George 288
Lee, Arthur
 'My Diary' 61
Lee, Harper
 To Kill a Mockingbird 1
Lee, Larry 45–6, 49, 50, 225, 228, 242–3

Lee, Peggy 53
Leeds, Gary 167
Lennon, John 29, 98, 162, 203
Levine, Bob 248
Lewis, Jerry Lee 133–4
Lifetime 244
limbo-dancing 69–70
Lincoln House Hotel, London 308
Little Richard
 arrested 48
 character 5. 60
 fires Jimi 64
 Jimi visits 118
 and Jimi's funeral 314
 musician 59–60, 63
 preacher 26–7, 259
 and Rosa Lee Brooks 61
 songs
  'Good Golly Miss Molly' 60
  'Tutti Frutti' 60
 The Quasar of Rock 59
Little Willie John 54
 'Fever' 53
London Polytechnic 103–4, 140
Londonderry Hotel, London 257, 273, 275, 294
Los Angeles Forum 258
Los Angeles Times (newspaper) 155
LSD (lysergic acid diethylamide) 63, 133, 152, 234, 254, 280
Lulu 200, 201
Lydon, Michael 303
Lynott, Phil 355

M (magazine) 273
McCartney, Linda (née Eastman) 173, 199
McCartney, Paul
 childhood 29

and Jimi 1, 246
left-handed 25
Monterey festival 150
sees Jimi live 98
Sgt. Pepper album 121, 148–9
McCoys, The
'Hang On Sloopy' 79
McDaniel, Hattie 47
McKenzie, Scott 152
McLaughlin, John 244–5, 288
McVay, Terry 94
Madison Square Garden, New York
218, 253–4
Mafia
and Jeffery 270, 313, 347
and Jimi's death 7, 330, 351
Jimi's kidnap 240–1
and Salvation 2 239
magazines, teenage 125, 126
Majorca 92
Malcolm X 62–3
Mamas and the Papas 152, 161–2
Mankowitz, Gered 125
Manny's Music, NY 78, 174
Mansfield, Jayne 66
Maple Leaf Gardens, Toronto 215,
216
Mark Boyle's Sense Laboratory 181
Marks, Howard 329
Marquee Club, London 109
Marshall amplifiers 102, 108, 127,
131, 148
Marshall, Jim 102, 107
Martin, Charlotte 141
Martin, Dean 150
Marvelettes, The 49
Mason, Dave 193, 221
Maui, Hawaii 264–7
Mayer, Roger 132

Mayfield, Curtis 49–50, 50, 61, 67
MCA Records 338
McDonald, Country Joe 233
Melody Maker (magazine) 138, 141,
155, 199, 326
Memphis, Tennessee 58
Merryweather, Melinda 265–6, 315,
346
MHCHAOS (CIA programme)
325–6, 347
MI5 212, 247
Miami Pop Festival (1968) 230
Michael X 213
Mighty Hannibal 51
Miles, Buddy 254–6
The Cry of Love album 326
demos with Jimi 250
fired 258
and Jimi's funeral 315
no lump sum 324–5
own band 243–4
sees Jimi live 190
Milne, A. A. 222
Mimram, Colette 223–4, 226, 227,
232, 258, 272
Mingus, Charles 224
Mitchell, Dee 332, 333
Mitchell, John 'Mitch'
arrested 162
background 107–8
contracts 255
death 349
and drugs 137
drummer for Jimi 223
hair 125
in Harlem 237–8
Jimi's death and funeral 305, 315
and hotel rooms 182
and Jimi 199, 244

Mitchell, John 'Mitch'—*contd*
  Jimi Hendrix Experience 2, 7, 110,
    111–12, 146–7, 270
  Jimi tribute tour (2008) 349
  last gig 220–1
  later years 348–9
  leaves band 243
  in London 297
  loss of Chandler 197
  'musical wake' 316
  paid lump sum 324
  and 'racial slurs' 330, 331, 348–9
  returns to play 230
  rings Jimi 298
  Rock & Roll Hall of Fame induc-
    tion 337
  sees Jimi again 254
  on studio tapes 327
  at Woodstock 232, 234
  The Cry of Love album 326
  The Hendrix Experience 332
Mitchell, William 27, 28
Model T Fords ('Tin Lizzies') 11–12
Money Jungle (Ellington, Roach and
    Mingus album) 224
Money, Ronni 96, 97, 99, 113
Money, Zoot 96, 97, 113–14, 156
Monkees, The 158–9
Monterey International Pop Festival
    306
Monterey Pop (documentary) 151,
    152, 245
Monterey Pop Festival (1967) 7,
    150–4, 155
Moon, Keith 97, 115, 141, 152, 221
Moore, Thomas W. 154
Morgan, Betty-Jean 33, 36, 38, 41,
    262
Morice, Claire 229

Morrison, Jim 9, 156, 183, 276, 278,
    317
Most, Mickie 85
Mothers of Invention, The 185, 220
Move, The 268
Museum of Pop Culture, Seattle
    353–4
music, black 47–8
Musician (magazine) 342–3

Naked Lunch (Burroughs) 121
Nash, Graham 167, 258
Nashville 44–6
National Trust 357
Nefer, Birthe 281
Nefer, Kirsten 275, 277, 279, 281–2,
    284–91
Nesmith, Mike 159, 285, 298
New Musical Express (NME maga-
    zine)) 101, 106, 122, 163
New York Pop Festival (1970) 260
New York Post (newspaper) 234, 252
New York Times (newspaper) 163
Newport Pop Festival, California
    (1969) 218, 219
News of the World (newspaper) 329
Night of Light (Farmer) 130
Nightingale, Anne 144–5
Nilsson, Harry 148
Nirvana 339
Nixon, Richard 204, 214, 253, 261,
    325
Norman family 11
Null, Lotte (*later* Chandler) 121,
    134, 135–6, 162, 280

Obermaier, Uschi 202
'Octavio' foot pedal 132
O'Day, Pat 178–9, 314

Ofarim, Esther 148
Oldham, Andrew Loog 74–5, 82–3, 143, 197
    Stoned 83
Olympic Studios, London 130–2, 163, 292
100 Club, London 116
Ono, Yoko 98, 162, 203, 272
Osten-Sacken, Baron Reiner von der 201, 289
Ostin, Mo 150, 327
Otis, Charles 160

Page, Jimmy 132, 337
Page, John 16
Pallenberg, Anita 73, 143
Pappalardi, Felix 140
Parkinson, Mike 346
Paul Butterfield Blues Band 183
Paul, Les 270
Pearse, John 117, 279–80
Peel, John 256
Pennebaker, D. A. 151, 152
Penniman, Robert 64
Peppermint Lounge, New York 66
Perkins, Carl
    'Blue Suede Shoes' 259
Perrin, Les 175, 249, 304
Peter Jay and the Jaywalkers 104
Peter, Paul and Mary 253
Phillips, John 150, 151
Phillips, Sam 197
Pickett, Wilson 48, 223
    'In the Midnight Hour' 79
    'Mustang Sally' 70
Pilcher, Norman ('Nobby') 203
Pink Floyd 148
Pink Poodle, Clarksville 39–40
Piranha Productions 242

pirate radio stations 124
plane crashes 279
'The Plaster Casters' 180–1
Pluckrose, Ron 9
Poitier, Sidney 200
Polydor Records 121, 130, 287, 310
Porter, John 327–8
PPX label 65–6, 120, 160, 169, 250, 320–1
Presentaciones Musicales SA 338
Presidents, the 44
Presley, Elvis 23, 25, 58, 101, 197
Price, Alan 84, 94
Pridgon, Lithofayne 'Fayne' 52–5
    hears of Jimi's death 305
    Jimi visits 64, 81, 138, 161, 235–6
    and royalties 275
Procol Harum 149
psychedelic clubs 133

Quashie, Mike 69–70

Rabb, Luther 258
race wars 211–15
racism 47–9
    black musicians and 6, 159
    British 113–14
    M. Davis and 245
    Presley and 23
    riots 7
    segregation 63
    in Utah 185–6
Rainbow Bridge (film) 264–7, 288, 319
Rainbow Bridge Vibratory Color/ Sound Experience (1970) 265
Ratpack, The 149–50
Ravenhill, Penny 295, 296, 318
RCA label 52
Ready Steady Go! (ITV) 122

Reagan, Ronald 259

record industry 124–5

Record Mirror (music paper) 113, 122, 306

Record Plant studios 183, 198, 209, 242, 270

Red Desert, The (film) 285

Redding, Margaret 123, 147, 277, 348

Redding, Noel 106–8
  contracts 255
  death 348
  diary 206
  dropped 255
  drug rehab 350
  drug-use 137, 165, 182
  Fat Mattress 197
  Jimi's death and funeral 305–6, 315, 316
  on Jeffery 321–2
  on Jimi 153
  and Jimi 157, 183, 199, 219
  Jimi Hendrix Experience 2, 7, 110–12, 123, 146–7, 284
  Jimi makes a 'move' on 170
  last gig 220–1
  loss of Chandler 197
  paid lump sum 324
  personal problems 255–6
  and 'The Plaster Casters' 180
  and 'racial slurs' 330, 331
  'replaced' 220
  Rock & Roll Hall of Fame induction 337
  sees Jimi again 253–4
  songwriting 167
  on touring 173
  Are You Experienced 219, 254, 332

Redding, Otis 50, 51, 151, 156

Reid, Terry 104, 245

Rhytmi (magazine) 145

Richard(s), Keith 142–4
  drugs-bust 212
  girlfriends 73, 82, 157
  and guitars 78, 80, 87
  Jimi and 247
  and Jimi's death 337
  sees Jimi live 110

Rivers, Johnny 272

Roach, Max 224

Roberts, Jon 240–1

Robertson, Robbie 79–80

Roby, Steve 266, 346

Rock & Roll Hall of Fame 4, 337

rock bands 145–6

Rocking Chair nightclub, Seattle 14, 34

Rocking Kings 32–4, 174, 177, 262, 315

Rolling Stone (music paper) 155, 218, 251, 256, 318–19

Rolling Stones, The 73–6, 82–3
  and The Animals 85
  death of Jones 222
  discovered 122
  drugs-bust 212
  and groupies 157
  influence of 63
  and Jimi 142–4
  see Jimi live 7
  and Sharon Lawrence 282
  tax exiles in France 269
  US ban 208, 247
  US tour 246–7
  songs
    'Wild Thing' 131
    'Mother's Little Helper' 75
    'Ruby Tuesday' 75

Ronnie Scott's, London 291, 293, 308

Rose, Tim
  'Hey Joe' 85–6
Roth, Manny 78
Roth, Uli Jon 341
Royal Albert Hall, London 202
Royal Canadian Mounted Police
  215, 226, 247
Rubin, Jerry 215

Salvation 2 club, New York 239
Sam and Dave 237
Samarkand Hotel, London 290, 297,
  334, 356–7
Santa Barbara University, California
  325–6
Santana, Carlos 337
Saua, John 333, 339–40
Saville Theatre, London 126, 149
Scene and Heard (BBC Radio) 286,
  306
Scene club, New York 183, 198–9
Scotch of St James club, London 96,
  97, 98
Scuse Me While I Kiss the Sky (Hen-
  derson) 330–1, 348
Se og Hør (magazine) 281
Seabury Hall, Maui 266, 267
Seattle Post-Intelligencer (newspaper)
  323
Seattle, USA 11–12
Secunda, Tony 288
Segovia, Andrés 145
Sgt. Pepper's (club), Majorca 185,
  304
Shaar, Charles 72
Shapiro, Harry 347
Shindig (TV show) 73
Shiroky, Carol 69, 70
Shokan, Woodstock 225

Sick's Stadium, Seattle 260, 261–2
Siefert, Martin 340, 349
Simone, Nina 223
Sinatra, Frank 149–50, 241
Slade 196, 269
Slater, Terry 334, 335
Sledge, Percy
  'When a Man Loves a Woman' 70
Sly and the Family Stone 293
Smalls Paradise, New York 245–6
Smith, Patti 272, 319
Smith, Tommie 212
Soft Machine 172, 181, 184
soul music 214
Spanish Castle ballroom, Seattle 33,
  166, 178
Speakeasy Club, London 207, 274,
  297, 305
Squire, Chris 109–10
Stamp, Chris 99, 121–2, 199
Stanley III, Owsley 152, 165
Stan's Hillside Club, Folkestone 123
Starr, Ringo 121, 162, 189, 203
Stax label 58
Steel, John 85
Stein, Seymour 83
Steingarten, Henry 249, 287, 295–6,
  323
Stevens, Cat 133
Stickells, Gerry
  and Jeffery 321
  and Jimi 278, 283
  Jimi's death and funeral 301–2,
    307–8, 310, 315, 318, 335
  and Mitchell 297
  roadie 127, 131, 174, 181, 206, 232
Stigwood, Robert 264
Stills, Stephen 258, 326
Stone, Sly 297

Storyk, John 221–2, 270
Sukov, Pete 354
Sullivan, Trixi
    and Albert Hall gig 202
    background 119–20
    and Chandler 195–6
    drug-use 166
    and groupies 147, 191
    hears of Jimi's death 304–5
    and Jeffery 91, 320
    on Jeffery 92, 93, 94
    on Jimi's kidnap 240, 241
    on money 206
    touring 181, 185, 187
Sultan, Juma 225, 228, 236, 239, 272
Summers, Andy 96
Sunday Mirror (newspaper) 144, 306
Sunday Times Magazine (newspaper) 8
Sundquist, Eva 170–1, 280
Sundquist, James Daniel (son) 280, 325, 346
Supro Ozark guitar 30, 33
Swindells, John 357
Swinging London 7–8, 86, 97, 115–16, 122, 257
Syn (band) 109–10

T-Neck label 57
Taylor, Derek 150
Taylor, Mick 247
Teare, Prof Robert 309, 311, 333
Tennyson, Alfred Lord 1, 230, 269, 357–8
Terrain (Maui hippy) 264–5
Tex, Joe 223
Thanks Jimi Festival, Poland 355
'The Star-Spangled Banner' 351
Thee Experience club, Los Angeles 174
34 Montagu Square, London 121, 135–6, 162, 203
Thomas and the Tomcats 34
Thomas, James 315
Three Dog Night 220
Thurston, Gavin 310, 311–12
Time (magazine) 70
Times, The (newspaper) 340
To Sir With Love (film) 200
Top of the Pops (BBC) 122
Tork, Peter 159
Townshend, Pete 110, 114, 141–2, 152, 153
Track Records 99, 121, 130, 166, 256, 287
Tramp nightclub, London 272, 275
Travers, Mary 78
Troggs, The
    'Wild Thing' 70, 79, 131
Trollope, Peter 8
Troutbeck Hotel, Ilkley 128–9
Turner, Ike 60
    'Rocket 88' 62
Turner, Tina 60, 62
24 Hours (BBC) 309–10
'27 Club' 4–5, 156, 317, 339
23 Brook Street, London 203–5, 257, 355

Uhlman, Wes 261, 314
United Artists Records 224
United Block Association, Harlem 237
Upper Berkeley Street, London 162–3
Upsetters, The 59, 60, 62

Van Ronk, Dave 2

INDEX

Vejlby-Risskov Hallen, Aarhus, Denmark 281
Velez, Gerardo 225, 228, 229, 236, 242
Velvetones 32, 258
Vietnam War 182–3, 212–13
  America and 37
  black Americans and 66
  demonstrations against 233, 253, 259
  Jimi and 7, 40, 251
VIPs, The 98
Voodoo Child (Netflix docu 2010) 17, 25, 29, 37

Wadleigh, Michael 232
Walker Brothers 9, 133, 134, 167
Walker, Junior
'Shotgun' 63–4
Walker, T-Bone 44, 79
War (band) 291, 293, 308, 309
Warhol, Andy 198, 264
Warner/Reprise Records 149–50, 264–5
  Chalpin lawsuit 169
  deals with 288, 338
  Jimi signs 160, 324
  Jimi's kidnapping 241
  money borrowed from 270
  release Are You Experienced 163
  release studio versions 256
  singles on 155
Watergate scandal 325
Waters, Muddy 25, 82
Watts, Charlie 75
Wein, Chuck 264, 266, 346
Weiss, Mike 323
Welch, Chris 256
Wells, Junior 221

Wenner, Jann 155
Whisky A Go Go club, Los Angeles 156, 174, 189
White Panther Party 260
Who, The 126, 141–2, 152, 153, 174
Wiggles, Mr
'Homeboy' 64
Wild Ones
'Wild Thing' 70
Williams, Tony 244, 246
Wilson, Devon (Ida Mae)
  death 317
  and 'Dolly Dagger' 271
  and drugs 259, 299
  gives party 247
  influence of 234–5, 255, 265, 287, 291, 298
  and Jimi 209, 223
  Jimi's funeral 315, 316
  Linda Keith on 157–8, 239
  meets Jimi 189, 207
  and Monika 295
  and S. Douglas 287
  'spikes' Jimi's drink 254
Wilson, Flip 223
Wilson, Jackie 50
Winehouse, Amy 339
Winter Festival for Peace (1970) 253
Winter, Johnny 183, 253, 315, 316
Winwood, Steve 110, 149, 198, 243, 326
Wolfe, Randy 78
Womack, Bobby 50–1
Wong, Judy 292, 300, 308
Woods, Bobby 240, 241
Woodstock (1969) 7
Woodstock (festival 1969) 229–34
Woodstock (film) 232, 233
Wright, James 'Tappy' 347–8, 351

Wright, Walter 323
Wyatt, Robert 6, 181, 187, 191
  'Slow Walkin' Talk' 191
Wyman, Bill 75

Yameta Ltd 92, 120, 139, 150, 206, 324
Yasgur, Max 231
Yes (band) 109
Yippies (Youth International Party) 260

Young, Alphonso 44, 46, 49
Young Lords (civil right group) 236, 260
Young, Neil 337
Youngblood, Lonnie 65, 77

Zoot Money 9
Zoot Money's Big Roll Band 96